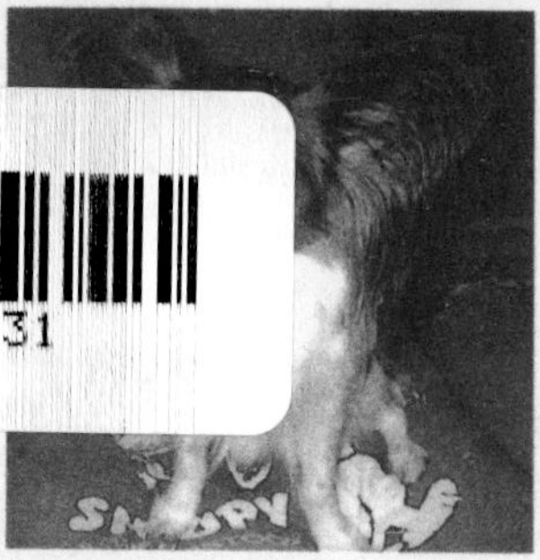

空知英秋(の犬)

Hideaki Sorachi('s Dog)

He never comes, no matter how long you wait for the guy.
'Cause he's shy.
And I don't mean just shy–it's worse.
He's shy, but he'd be embarrassed if that got out, so he acts like a tough customer, but he'd be even more embarrassed if it got out that he's trying to hide being shy, so on top of that he pretends to be shy too...
He's a pathetic shy guy, see?

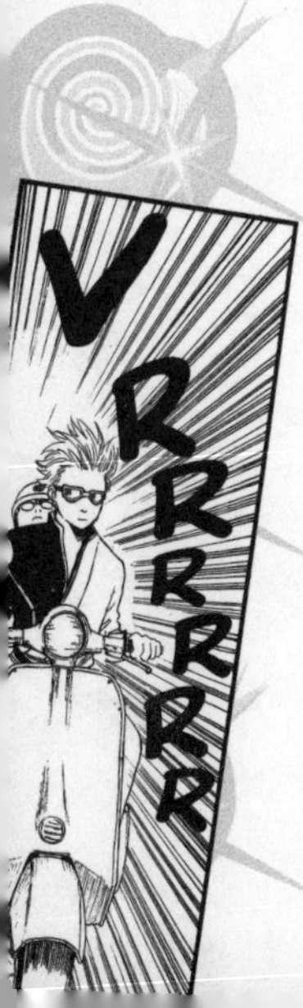
VRRRRRR

Hideaki Sorachi was born on May 25, 1979, and grew up in Hokkaido, Japan. His ongoing series, ***GIN TAMA***, became a huge hit when it began running in the pages of Japan's ***Weekly Shonen Jump*** in 2004. A ***GIN TAMA*** animated series followed soon after, premiering on Japanese TV in April 2006. Sorachi made his manga debut with the one-shot story *DANDELION*!

GIN TAMA VOL. 2
SHONEN JUMP ADVANCED Manga Edition

STORY & ART BY HIDEAKI SORACHI

Translation/Matthew Rosin, Honyaku Center Inc.
English Adaptation/Drew Williams
Touch-up Art & Lettering/Steve Dutro
Cover & Interior Design/Sean Lee
Editor/Annette Roman

Printed in the U.S.A.

Published by VIZ Media, LLC
P.O. Box 77010
San Francisco, CA 94107

10 9 8 7
First printing, September 2007
Seventh printing, June 2017

RATED T+ FOR OLDER TEEN

PARENTAL ADVISORY
GIN TAMA is rated T+ for Older Teen and is recommended for ages 16 and up. It contains suggestive situations.

ratings.viz.com

viz media
www.viz.com

THE WORLD'S MOST CUTTING-EDGE MANGA
SHONEN JUMP ADVANCED
www.shonenjump.com

Vol. 2

Fighting Should Be Done With Fists

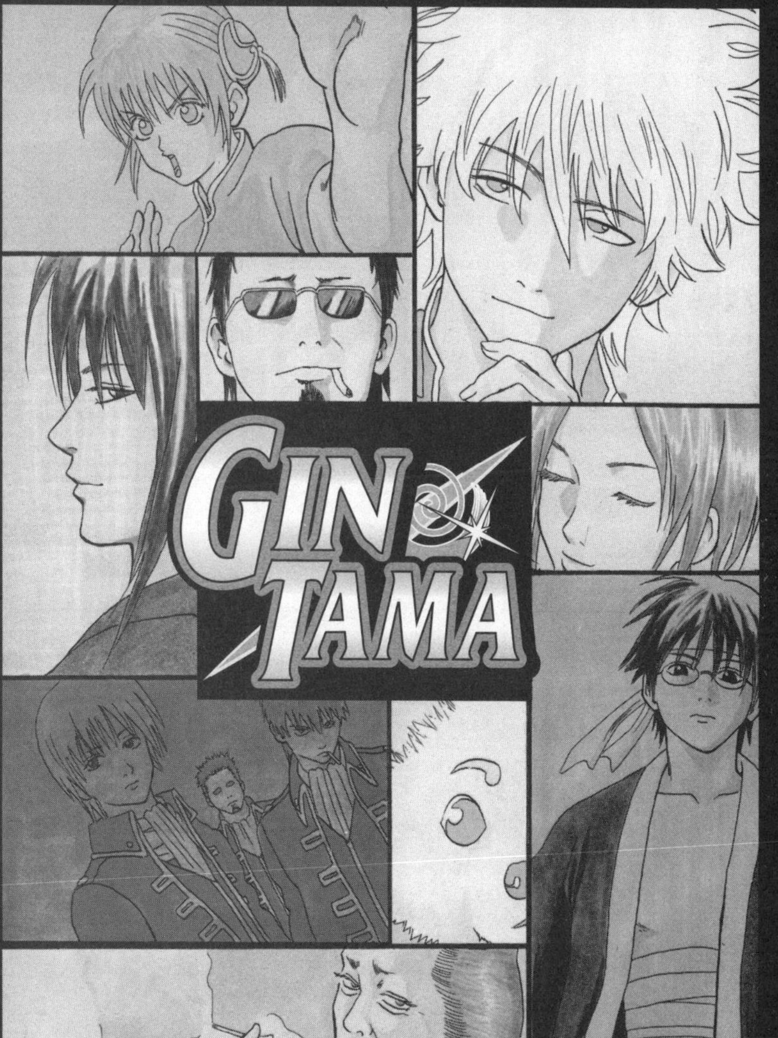
GIN TAMA

STORY & ART BY **HIDEAKI SORACHI**

Cast of Characters

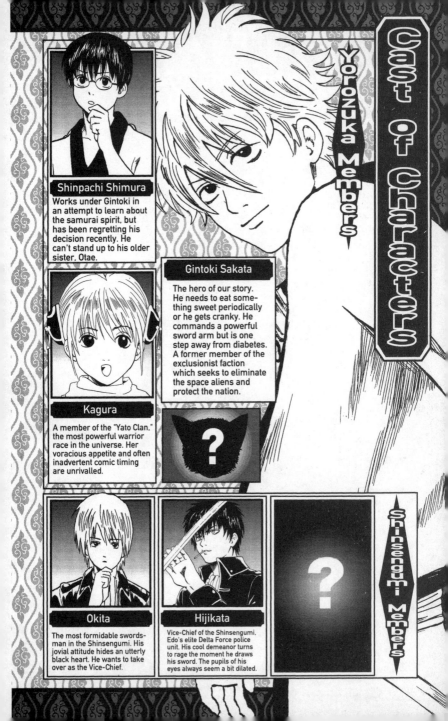

Yorozuka Members

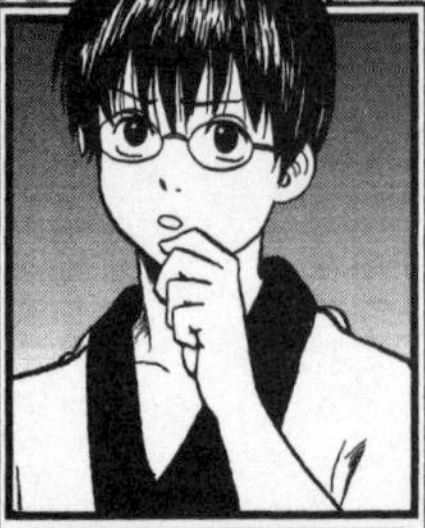

Shinpachi Shimura

Works under Gintoki in an attempt to learn about the samurai spirit, but has been regretting his decision recently. He can't stand up to his older sister, Otae.

Gintoki Sakata

The hero of our story. He needs to eat something sweet periodically or he gets cranky. He commands a powerful sword arm but is one step away from diabetes. A former member of the exclusionist faction which seeks to eliminate the space aliens and protect the nation.

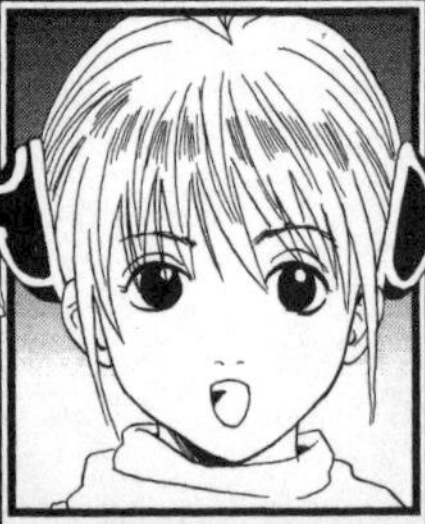

Kagura

A member of the "Yato Clan," the most powerful warrior race in the universe. Her voracious appetite and often inadvertent comic timing are unrivalled.

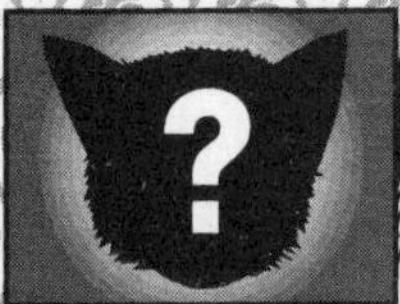

Shinsengumi Members

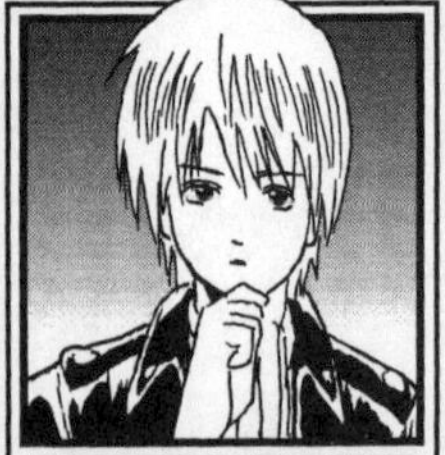

Okita

The most formidable swordsman in the Shinsengumi. His jovial attitude hides an utterly black heart. He wants to take over as the Vice-Chief.

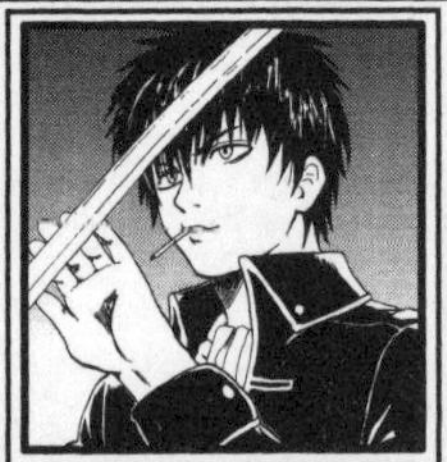

Hijikata

Vice-Chief of the Shinsengumi, Edo's elite Delta Force police unit. His cool demeanor turns to rage the moment he draws his sword. The pupils of his eyes always seem a bit dilated.

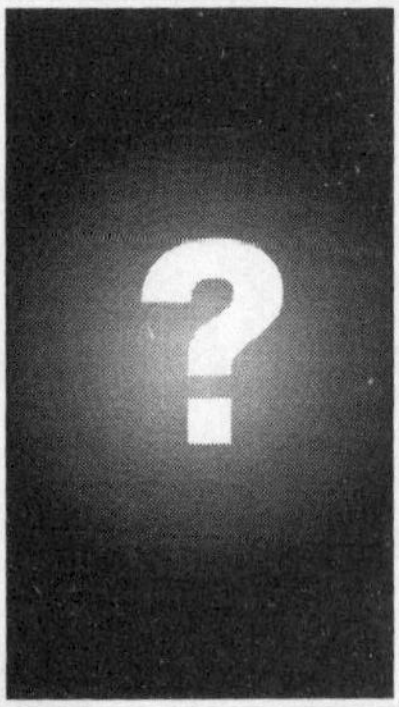

Other Characters

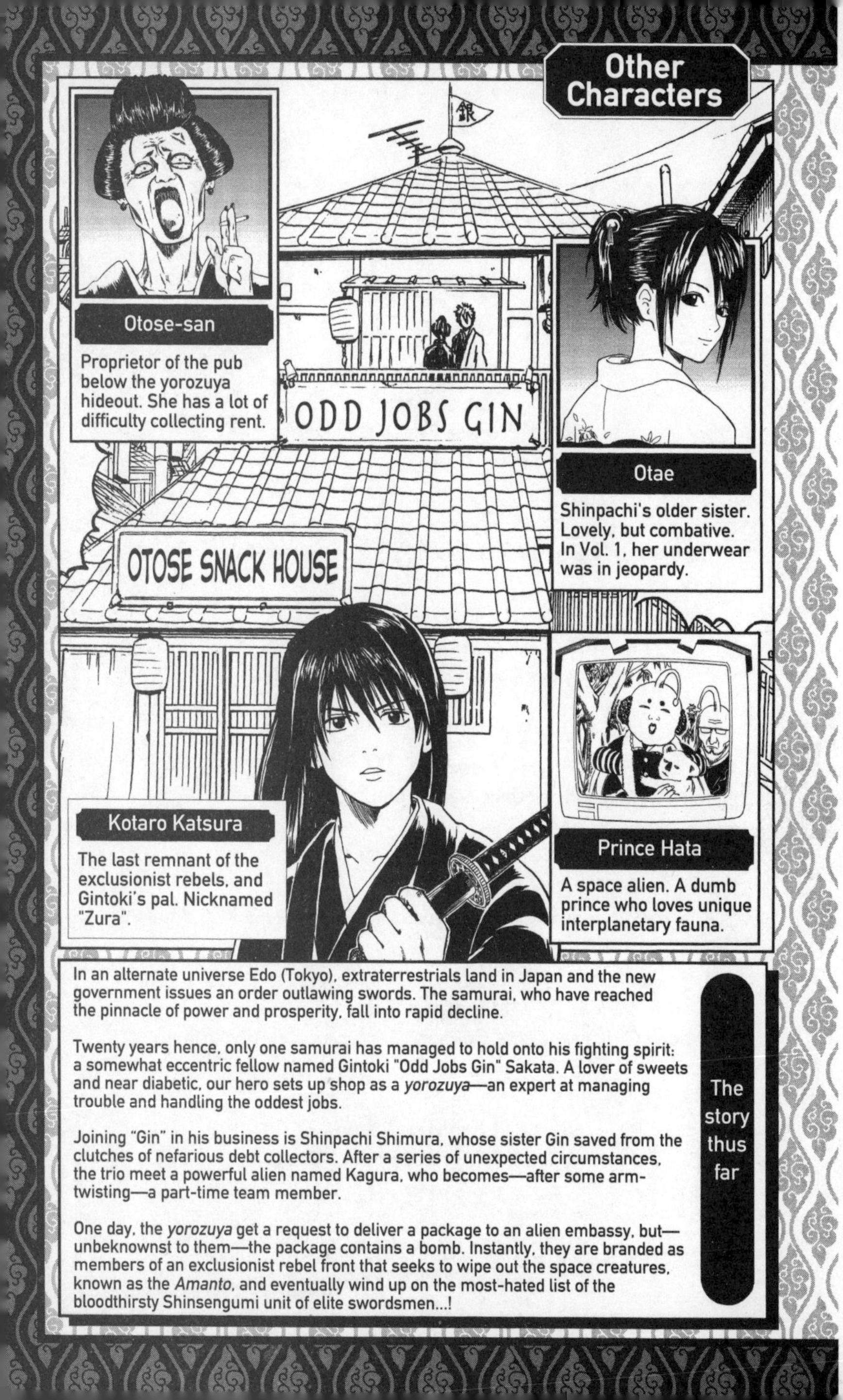
ODD JOBS GIN
OTOSE SNACK HOUSE

Otose-san

Proprietor of the pub below the yorozuya hideout. She has a lot of difficulty collecting rent.

Otae

Shinpachi's older sister. Lovely, but combative. In Vol. 1, her underwear was in jeopardy.

Kotaro Katsura

The last remnant of the exclusionist rebels, and Gintoki's pal. Nicknamed "Zura".

Prince Hata

A space alien. A dumb prince who loves unique interplanetary fauna.

The story thus far

In an alternate universe Edo (Tokyo), extraterrestrials land in Japan and the new government issues an order outlawing swords. The samurai, who have reached the pinnacle of power and prosperity, fall into rapid decline.

Twenty years hence, only one samurai has managed to hold onto his fighting spirit: a somewhat eccentric fellow named Gintoki "Odd Jobs Gin" Sakata. A lover of sweets and near diabetic, our hero sets up shop as a *yorozuya*—an expert at managing trouble and handling the oddest jobs.

Joining "Gin" in his business is Shinpachi Shimura, whose sister Gin saved from the clutches of nefarious debt collectors. After a series of unexpected circumstances, the trio meet a powerful alien named Kagura, who becomes—after some arm-twisting—a part-time team member.

One day, the *yorozuya* get a request to deliver a package to an alien embassy, but—unbeknownst to them—the package contains a bomb. Instantly, they are branded as members of an exclusionist rebel front that seeks to wipe out the space creatures, known as the *Amanto*, and eventually wind up on the most-hated list of the bloodthirsty Shinsengumi unit of elite swordsmen...!

WHAT THIS MANGA'S FULL OF
vol. 2

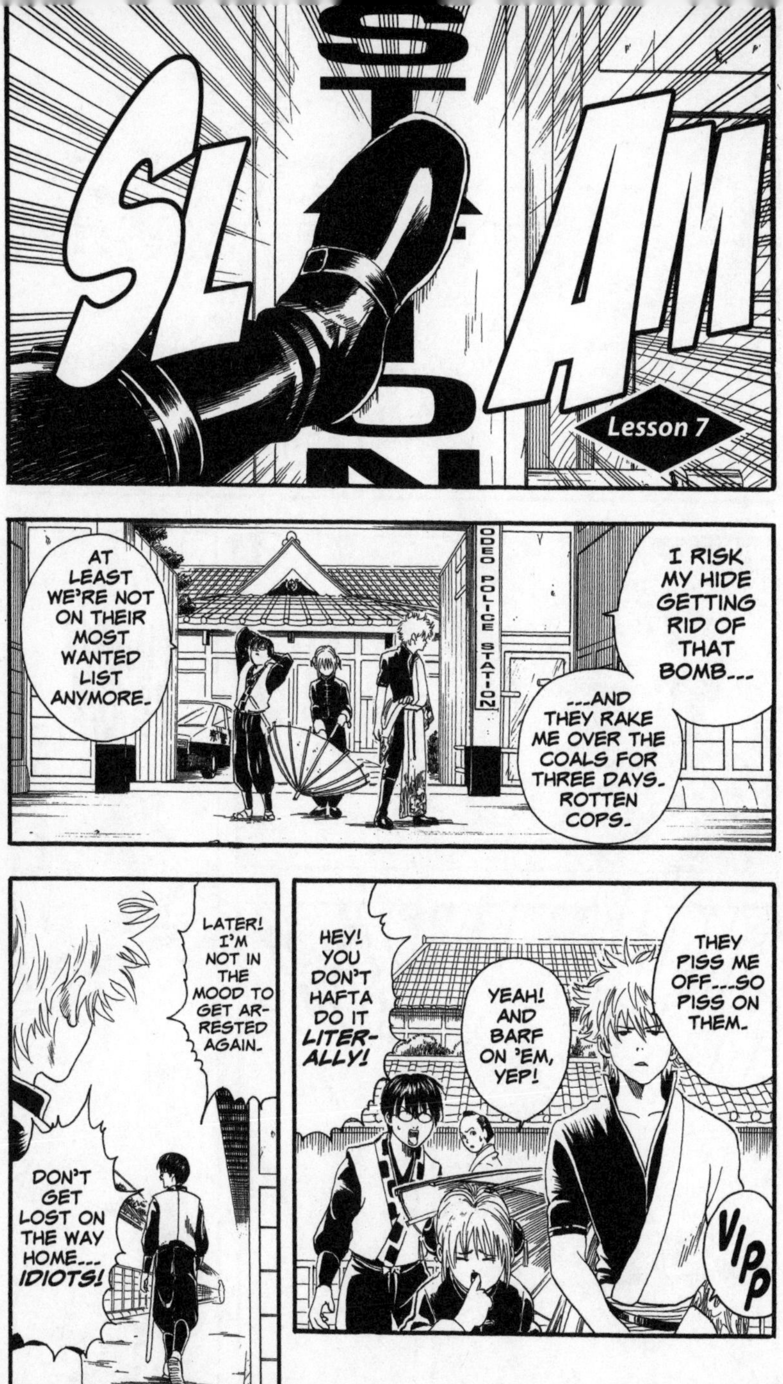
SLAM
Lesson 7
I RISK MY HIDE GETTING RID OF THAT BOMB...
...AND THEY RAKE ME OVER THE COALS FOR THREE DAYS. ROTTEN COPS.
ODEO POLICE STATION
AT LEAST WE'RE NOT ON THEIR MOST WANTED LIST ANYMORE.
THEY PISS ME OFF...SO PISS ON THEM.
YEAH! AND BARF ON 'EM, YEP!
HEY! YOU DON'T HAFTA DO IT LITERALLY!
VIPP
LATER! I'M NOT IN THE MOOD TO GET ARRESTED AGAIN.
DON'T GET LOST ON THE WAY HOME... IDIOTS!

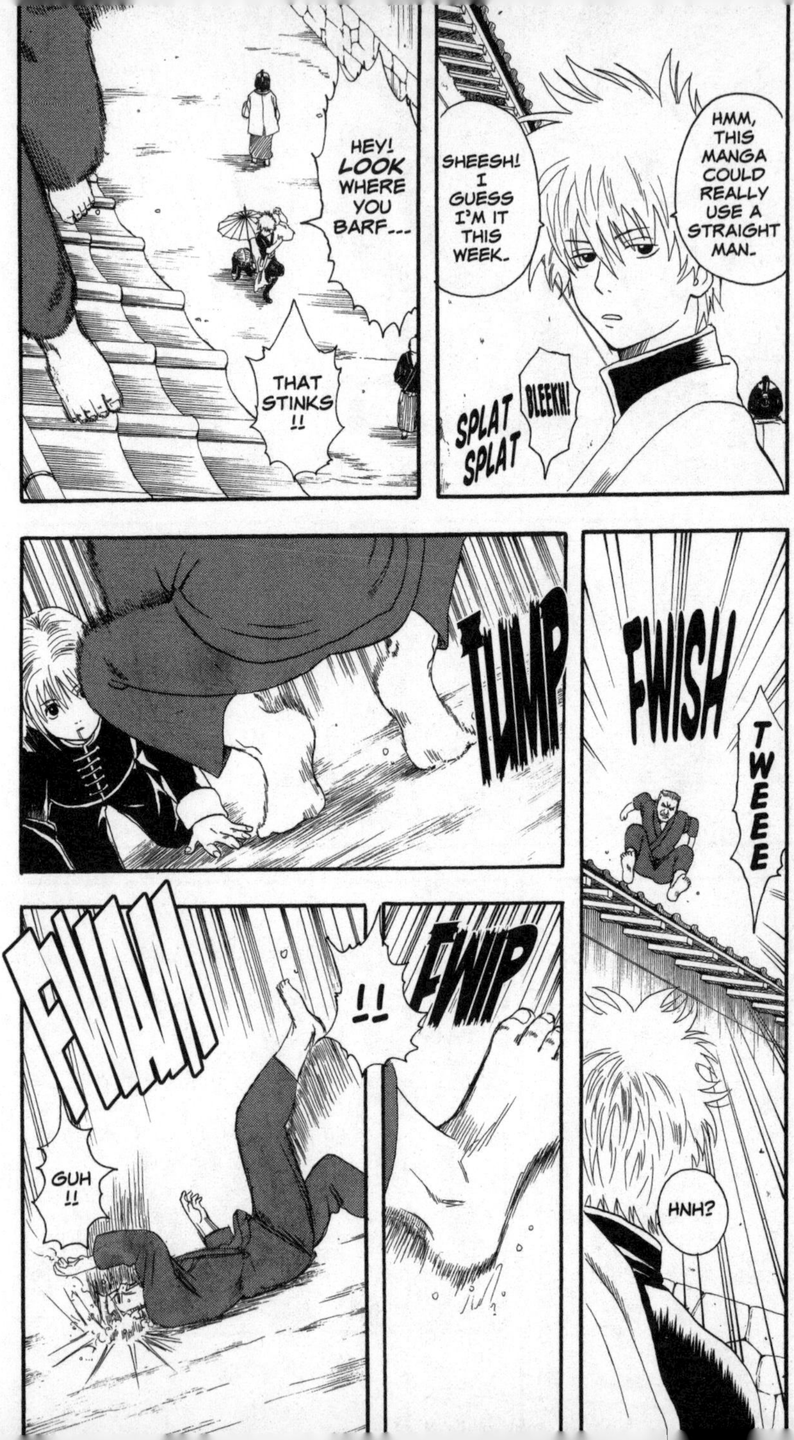
HMM, THIS MANGA COULD REALLY USE A STRAIGHT MAN.
SHEESH! I GUESS I'M IT THIS WEEK.
BLEEKH!
SPLAT SPLAT
HEY! LOOK WHERE YOU BARF...
THAT STINKS !!
FWISH
TWEEE
HNH?
TUMP
FWIP
!!
GUH !!

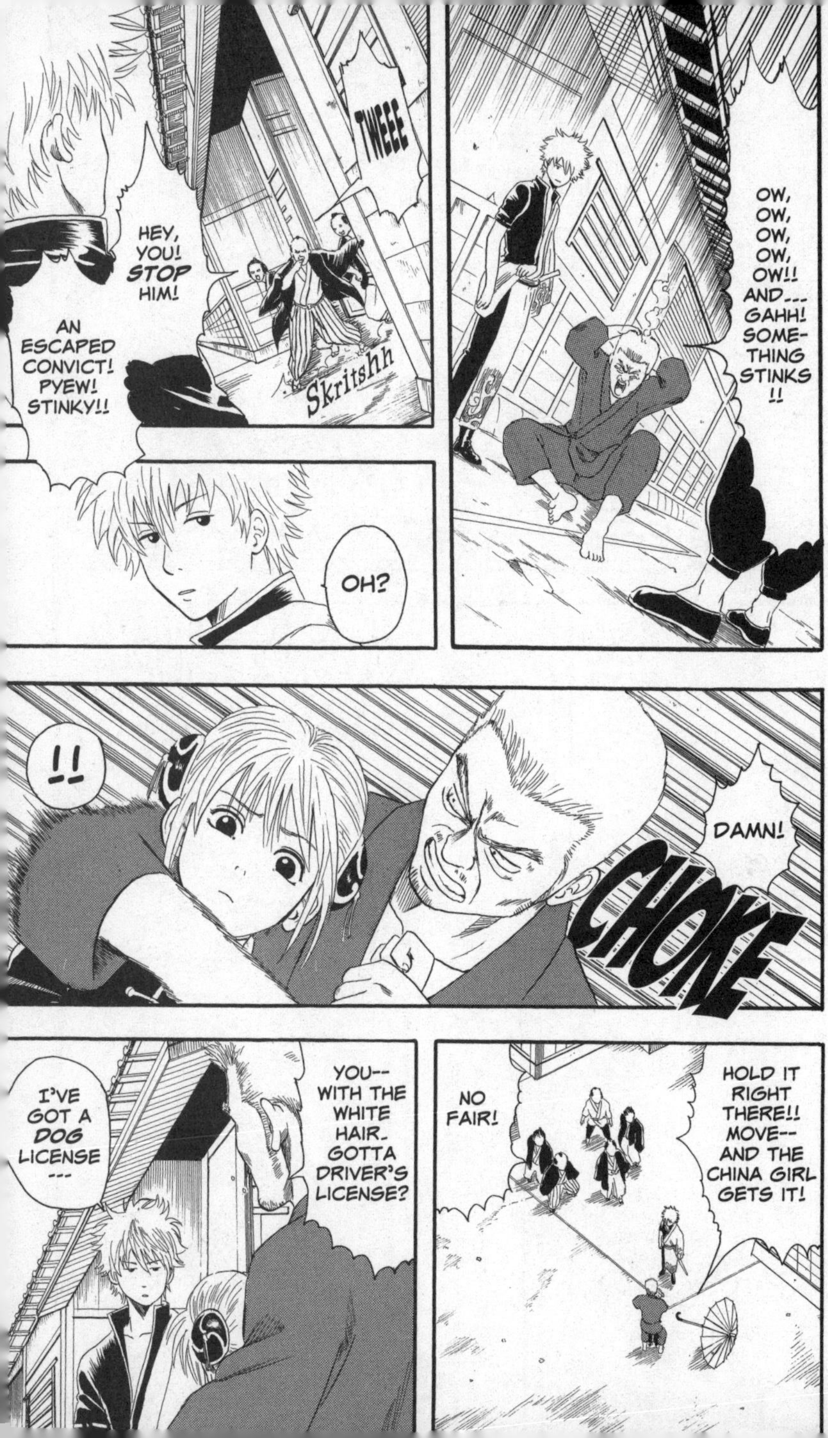
OW, OW, OW, OW, OW!! AND... GAHH! SOMETHING STINKS!!
TWEEE
HEY, YOU! STOP HIM!
AN ESCAPED CONVICT! PYEW! STINKY!!
Skritshh
OH?
DAMN!
CHOKE
!!
HOLD IT RIGHT THERE!! MOVE-- AND THE CHINA GIRL GETS IT!
NO FAIR!
YOU-- WITH THE WHITE HAIR. GOTTA DRIVER'S LICENSE?
I'VE GOT A DOG LICENSE ---

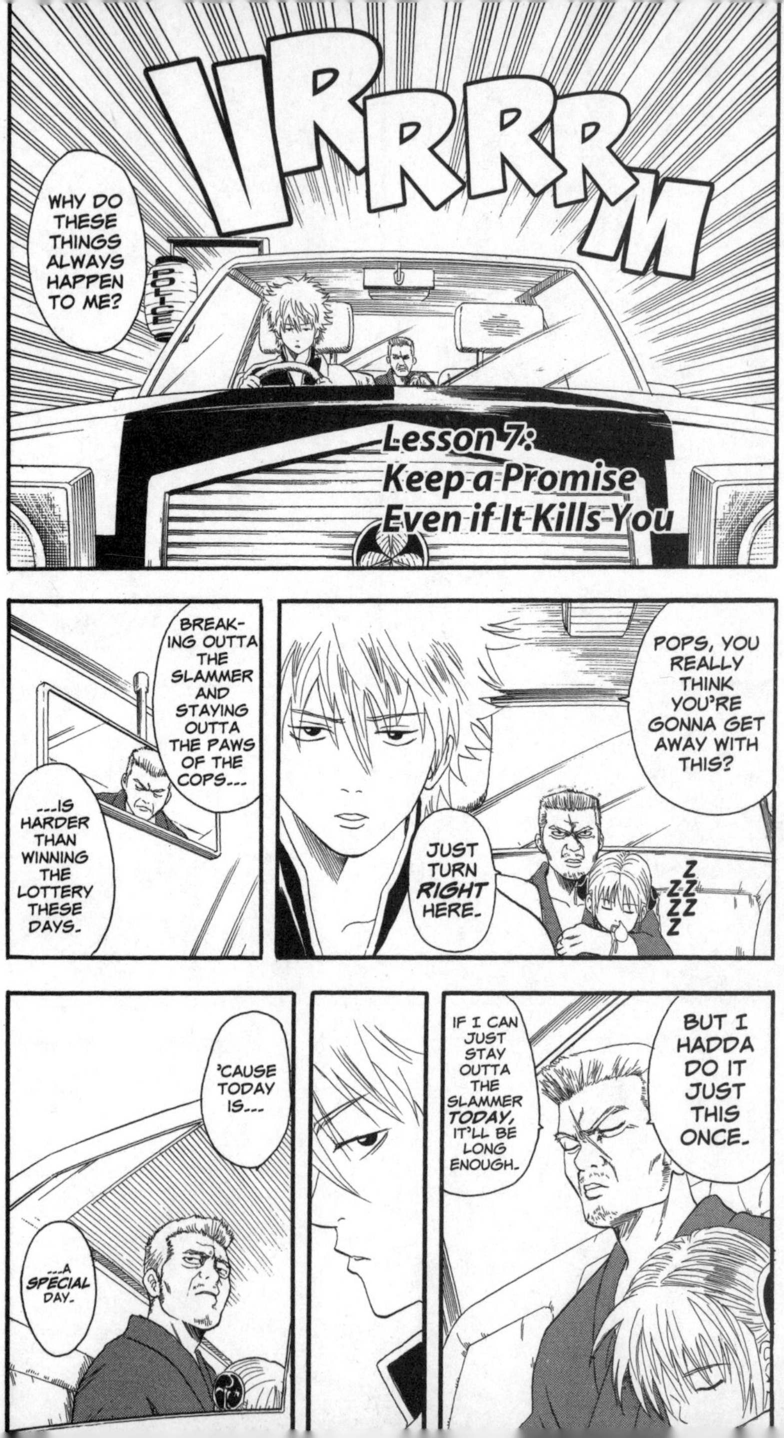
VRRRM
WHY DO THESE THINGS ALWAYS HAPPEN TO ME?
POLICE
Lesson 7: Keep a Promise Even if It Kills You
POPS, YOU REALLY THINK YOU'RE GONNA GET AWAY WITH THIS?
JUST TURN *RIGHT* HERE.
Z Z Z Z Z Z Z
BREAK-ING OUTTA THE SLAMMER AND STAYING OUTTA THE PAWS OF THE COPS...
...IS HARDER THAN WINNING THE LOTTERY THESE DAYS.
BUT I HADDA DO IT JUST THIS ONCE.
IF I CAN JUST STAY OUTTA THE SLAMMER *TODAY,* IT'LL BE LONG ENOUGH.
'CAUSE TODAY IS...
...A *SPECIAL* DAY.

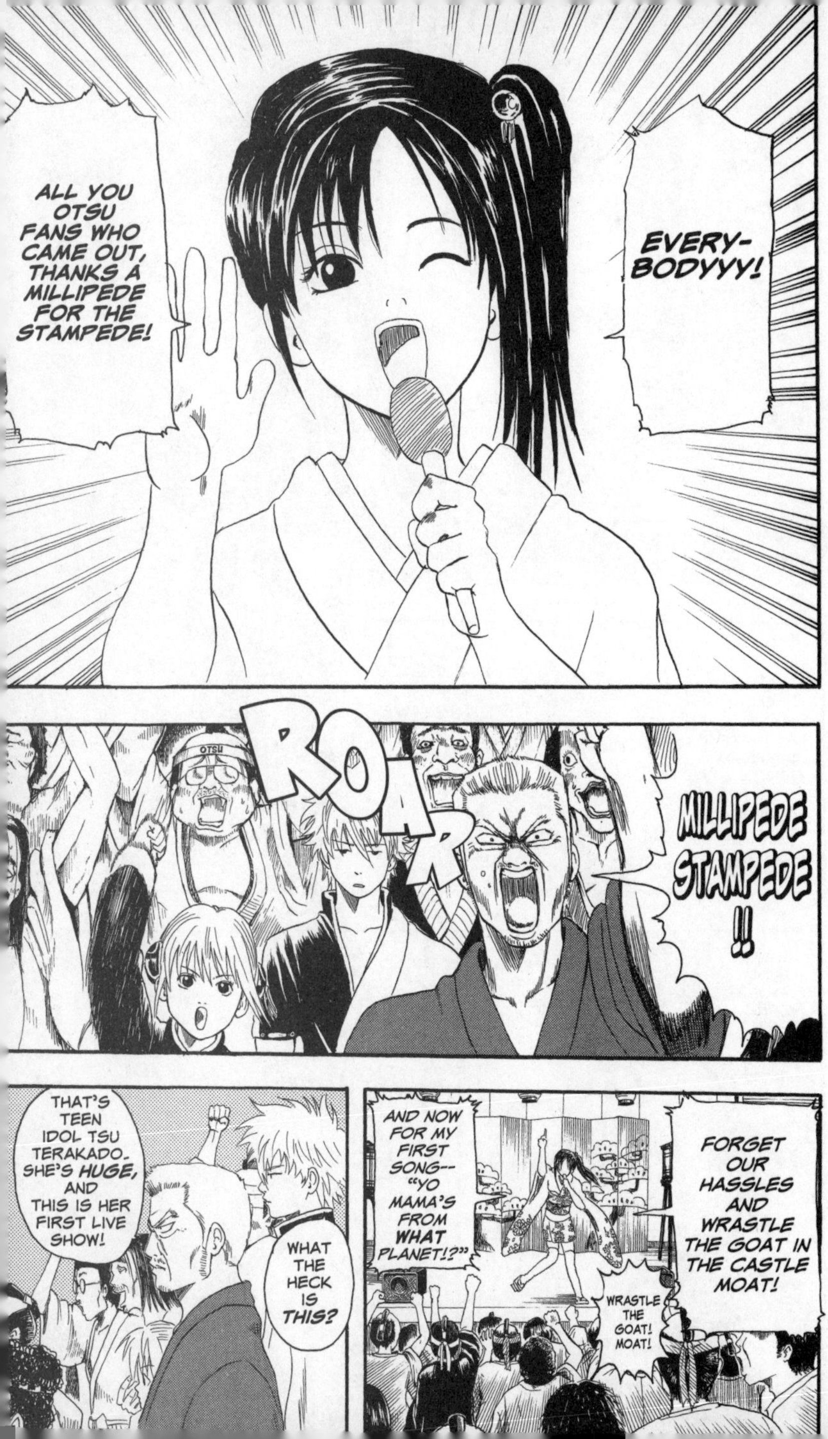
EVERY-BODYYY!
ALL YOU OTSU FANS WHO CAME OUT, THANKS A MILLIPEDE FOR THE STAMPEDE!
MILLIPEDE STAMPEDE!!
ROAR
OTSU
AND NOW FOR MY FIRST SONG-- "YO MAMA'S FROM WHAT PLANET!?"
FORGET OUR HASSLES AND WRASTLE THE GOAT IN THE CASTLE MOAT!
WRASTLE THE GOAT! MOAT!
WHAT THE HECK IS THIS?
THAT'S TEEN IDOL TSU TERAKADO. SHE'S HUGE, AND THIS IS HER FIRST LIVE SHOW!

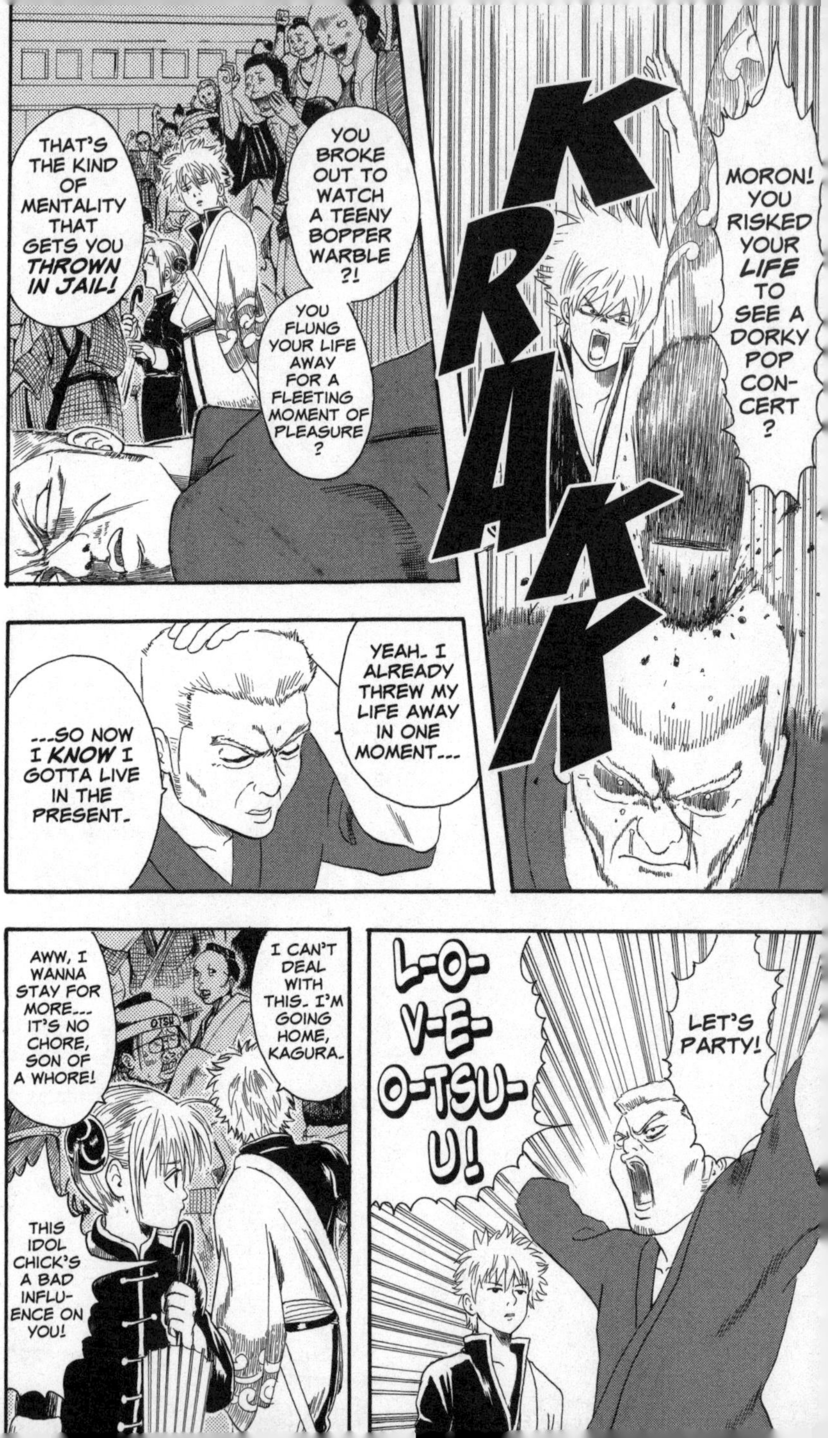
KRAKK
MORON! YOU RISKED YOUR LIFE TO SEE A DORKY POP CONCERT?
YOU BROKE OUT TO WATCH A TEENY BOPPER WARBLE?!
YOU FLUNG YOUR LIFE AWAY FOR A FLEETING MOMENT OF PLEASURE?
THAT'S THE KIND OF MENTALITY THAT GETS YOU THROWN IN JAIL!
YEAH. I ALREADY THREW MY LIFE AWAY IN ONE MOMENT...
...SO NOW I KNOW I GOTTA LIVE IN THE PRESENT.
LET'S PARTY!
L-O-V-E-O-TSU-U!
I CAN'T DEAL WITH THIS. I'M GOING HOME, KAGURA.
AWW, I WANNA STAY FOR MORE... IT'S NO CHORE, SON OF A WHORE!
THIS IDOL CHICK'S A BAD INFLUENCE ON YOU!

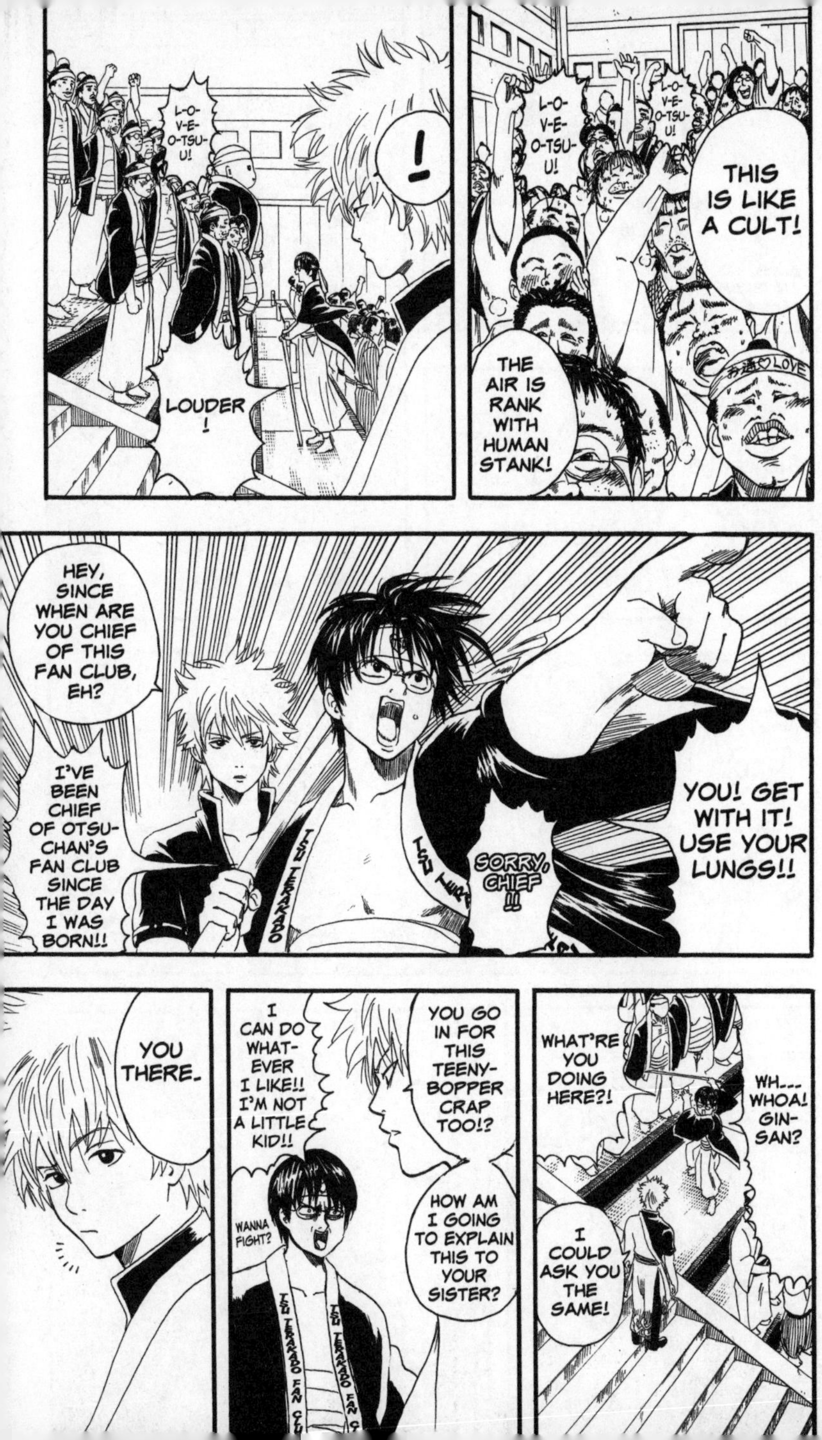
L-O-V-E-O-TSU-U!
L-O-V-E-O-TSU-U!
THIS IS LIKE A CULT!
お通♡LOVE
THE AIR IS RANK WITH HUMAN STANK!
L-O-V-E-O-TSU-U!
!
LOUDER!
YOU! GET WITH IT! USE YOUR LUNGS!!
SORRY, CHIEF!!
TSU TERAKADO
HEY, SINCE WHEN ARE YOU CHIEF OF THIS FAN CLUB, EH?
I'VE BEEN CHIEF OF OTSU-CHAN'S FAN CLUB SINCE THE DAY I WAS BORN!!
WH... WHOA! GIN-SAN?
WHAT'RE YOU DOING HERE?!
I COULD ASK YOU THE SAME!
YOU GO IN FOR THIS TEENY-BOPPER CRAP TOO!?
I CAN DO WHATEVER I LIKE!! I'M NOT A LITTLE KID!!
HOW AM I GOING TO EXPLAIN THIS TO YOUR SISTER?
WANNA FIGHT?
TSU TERAKADO FAN CL
YOU THERE.

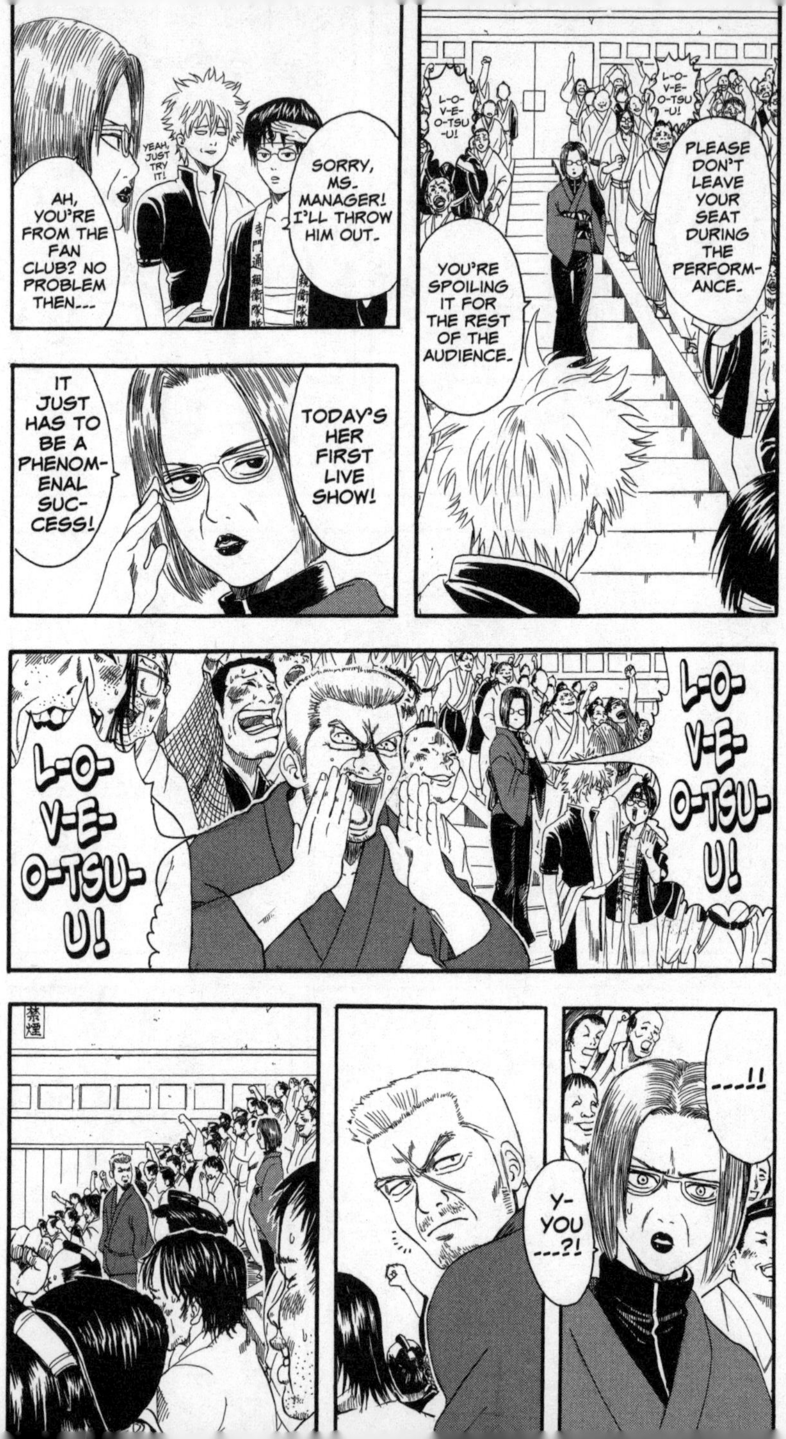
L-O-V-E-O-TSU-U!
L-O-V-E-O-TSU-U!
PLEASE DON'T LEAVE YOUR SEAT DURING THE PERFORMANCE.
YOU'RE SPOILING IT FOR THE REST OF THE AUDIENCE.
SORRY, MS. MANAGER! I'LL THROW HIM OUT.
YEAH, JUST TRY IT!
AH, YOU'RE FROM THE FAN CLUB? NO PROBLEM THEN...
TODAY'S HER FIRST LIVE SHOW!
IT JUST HAS TO BE A PHENOMENAL SUCCESS!
L-O-V-E-O-TSU-U!
L-O-V-E-O-TSU-U!
...!!
Y-YOU...?!
禁煙

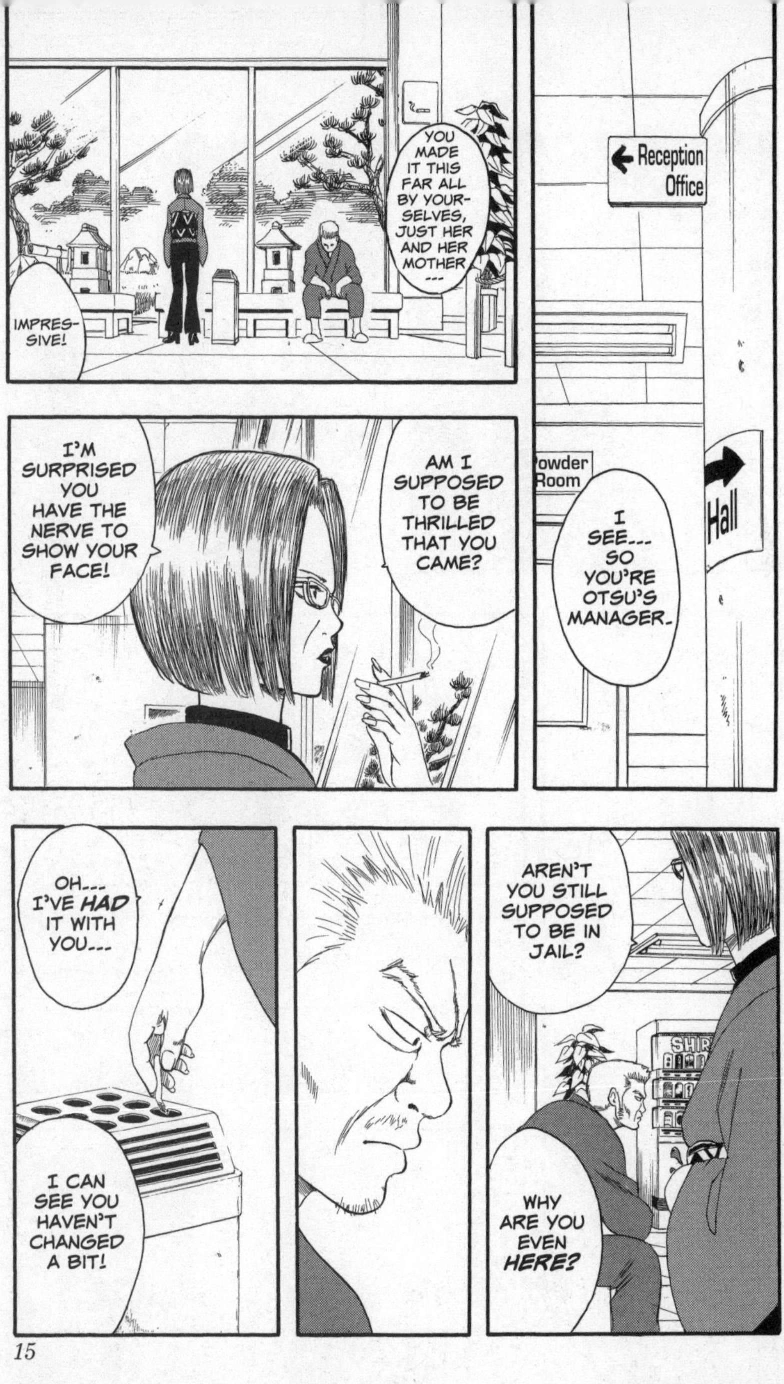
Reception Office
Powder Room
Hall
I SEE... SO YOU'RE OTSU'S MANAGER...
YOU MADE IT THIS FAR ALL BY YOURSELVES, JUST HER AND HER MOTHER...
IMPRESSIVE!
AM I SUPPOSED TO BE THRILLED THAT YOU CAME?
I'M SURPRISED YOU HAVE THE NERVE TO SHOW YOUR FACE!
AREN'T YOU STILL SUPPOSED TO BE IN JAIL?
WHY ARE YOU EVEN *HERE?*
OH... I'VE *HAD* IT WITH YOU...
I CAN SEE YOU HAVEN'T CHANGED A BIT!

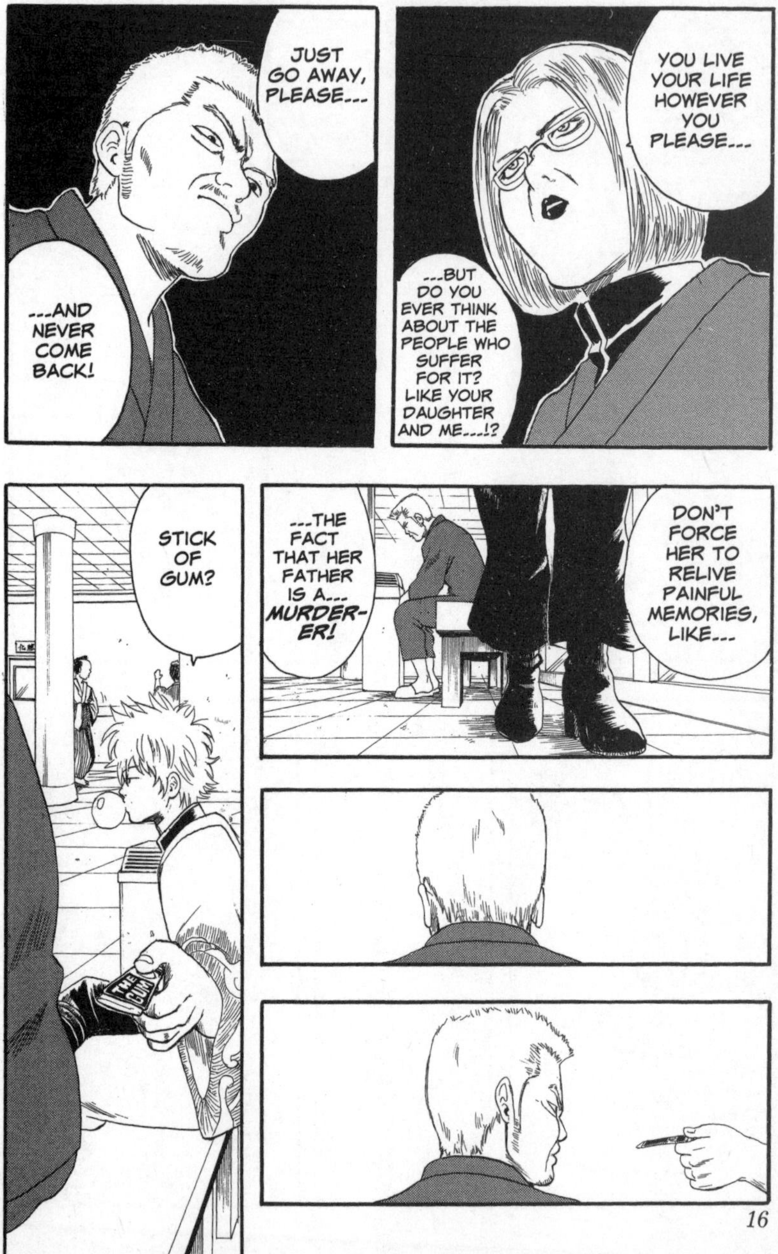
YOU LIVE YOUR LIFE HOWEVER YOU PLEASE...
...BUT DO YOU EVER THINK ABOUT THE PEOPLE WHO SUFFER FOR IT? LIKE YOUR DAUGHTER AND ME...!?
JUST GO AWAY, PLEASE...
...AND NEVER COME BACK!
DON'T FORCE HER TO RELIVE PAINFUL MEMORIES, LIKE...
...THE FACT THAT HER FATHER IS A... MURDERER!
STICK OF GUM?
THE GUM

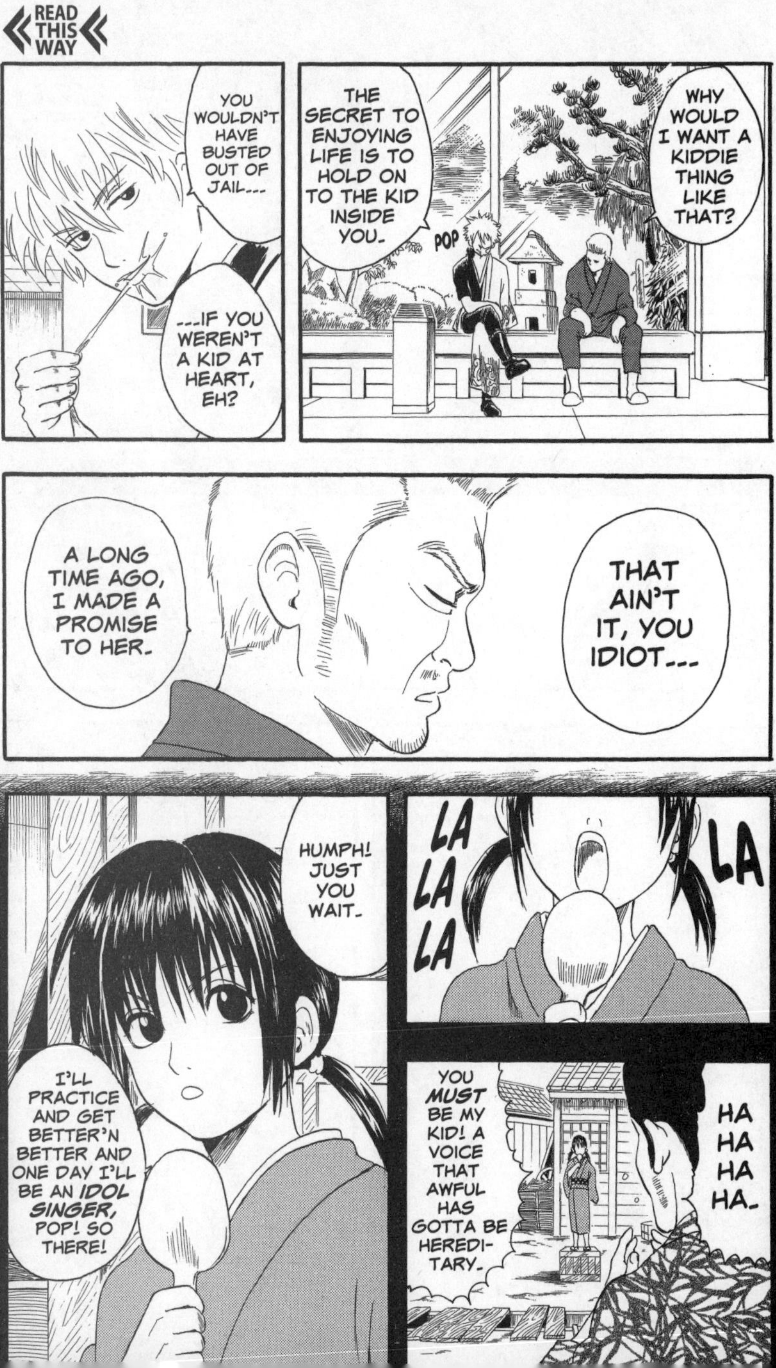
READ THIS WAY
WHY WOULD I WANT A KIDDIE THING LIKE THAT?
POP
THE SECRET TO ENJOYING LIFE IS TO HOLD ON TO THE KID INSIDE YOU.
YOU WOULDN'T HAVE BUSTED OUT OF JAIL...
...IF YOU WEREN'T A KID AT HEART, EH?
THAT AIN'T IT, YOU IDIOT...
A LONG TIME AGO, I MADE A PROMISE TO HER.
LA
LA LA LA LA
HA HA HA HA.
YOU *MUST* BE MY KID! A VOICE THAT AWFUL HAS GOTTA BE HEREDITARY.
HUMPH! JUST YOU WAIT.
I'LL PRACTICE AND GET BETTER'N BETTER AND ONE DAY I'LL BE AN *IDOL SINGER*, POP! SO THERE!

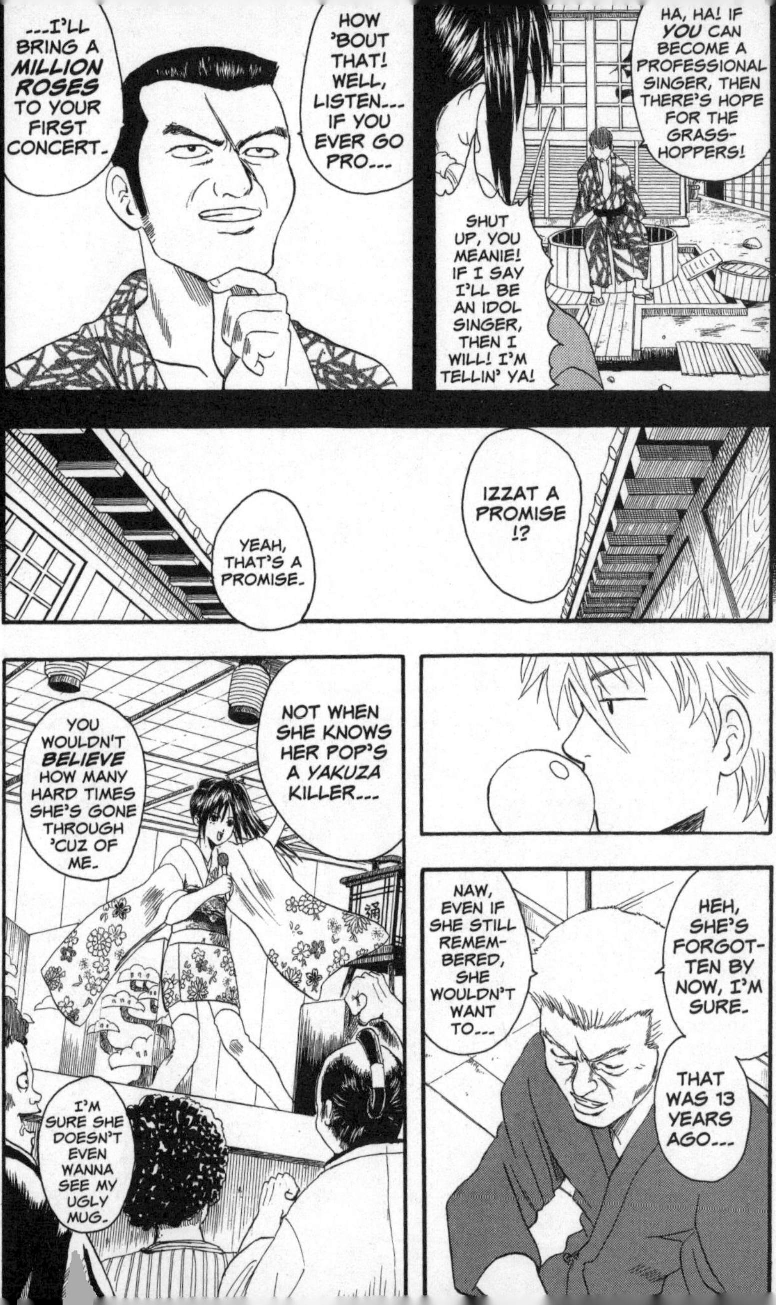
HA, HA! IF YOU CAN BECOME A PROFESSIONAL SINGER, THEN THERE'S HOPE FOR THE GRASS-HOPPERS!
SHUT UP, YOU MEANIE! IF I SAY I'LL BE AN IDOL SINGER, THEN I WILL! I'M TELLIN' YA!
HOW 'BOUT THAT! WELL, LISTEN... IF YOU EVER GO PRO...
...I'LL BRING A MILLION ROSES TO YOUR FIRST CONCERT.
IZZAT A PROMISE !?
YEAH, THAT'S A PROMISE.
HEH, SHE'S FORGOT-TEN BY NOW, I'M SURE.
THAT WAS 13 YEARS AGO...
NAW, EVEN IF SHE STILL REMEM-BERED, SHE WOULDN'T WANT TO...
YOU WOULDN'T BELIEVE HOW MANY HARD TIMES SHE'S GONE THROUGH 'CUZ OF ME.
I'M SURE SHE DOESN'T EVEN WANNA SEE MY UGLY MUG.
NOT WHEN SHE KNOWS HER POP'S A YAKUZA KILLER...

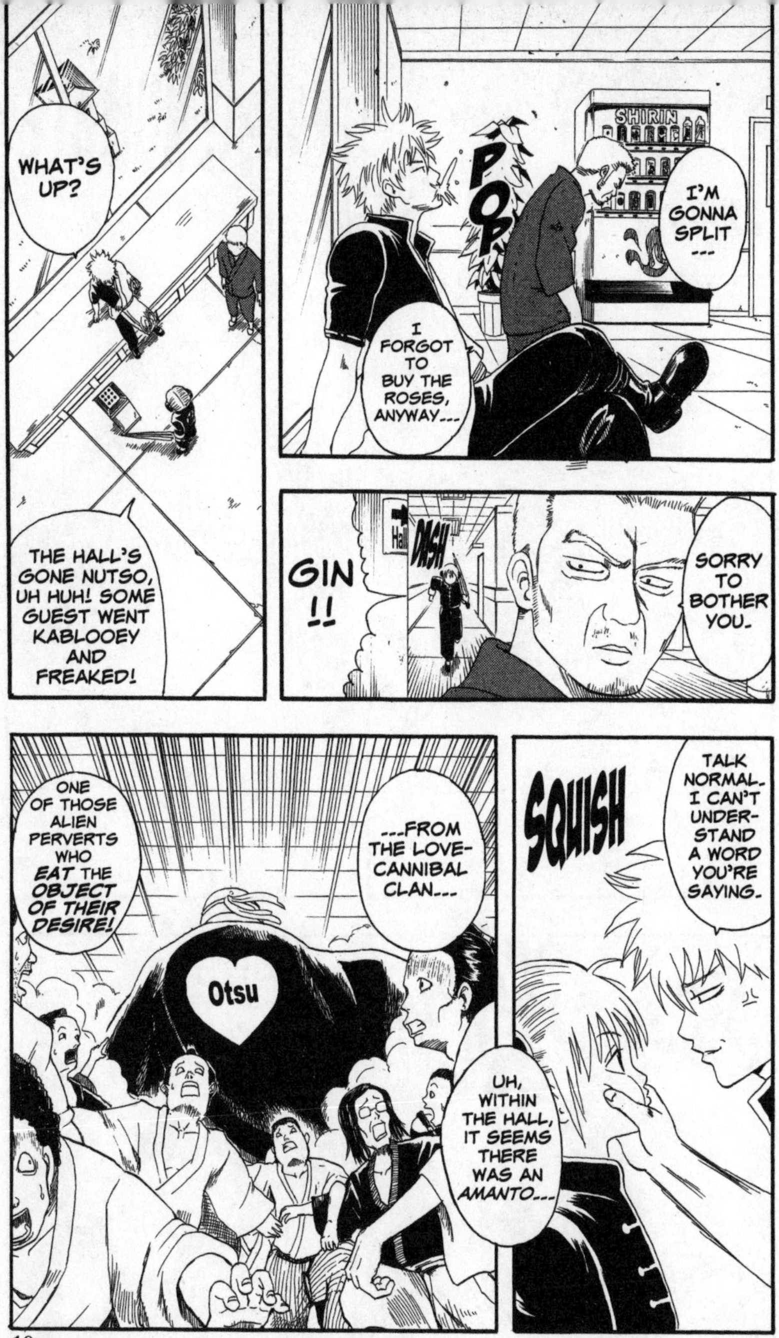
SHIRIN
I'M GONNA SPLIT ---
POP
I FORGOT TO BUY THE ROSES, ANYWAY---
SORRY TO BOTHER YOU.
Hall
DASH
GIN !!
WHAT'S UP?
THE HALL'S GONE NUTSO, UH HUH! SOME GUEST WENT KABLOOEY AND FREAKED!
TALK NORMAL. I CAN'T UNDER-STAND A WORD YOU'RE SAYING.
SQUISH
UH, WITHIN THE HALL, IT SEEMS THERE WAS AN *AMANTO*---
---FROM THE LOVE-CANNIBAL CLAN---
ONE OF THOSE ALIEN PERVERTS WHO *EAT* THE *OBJECT OF THEIR DESIRE!*
Otsu

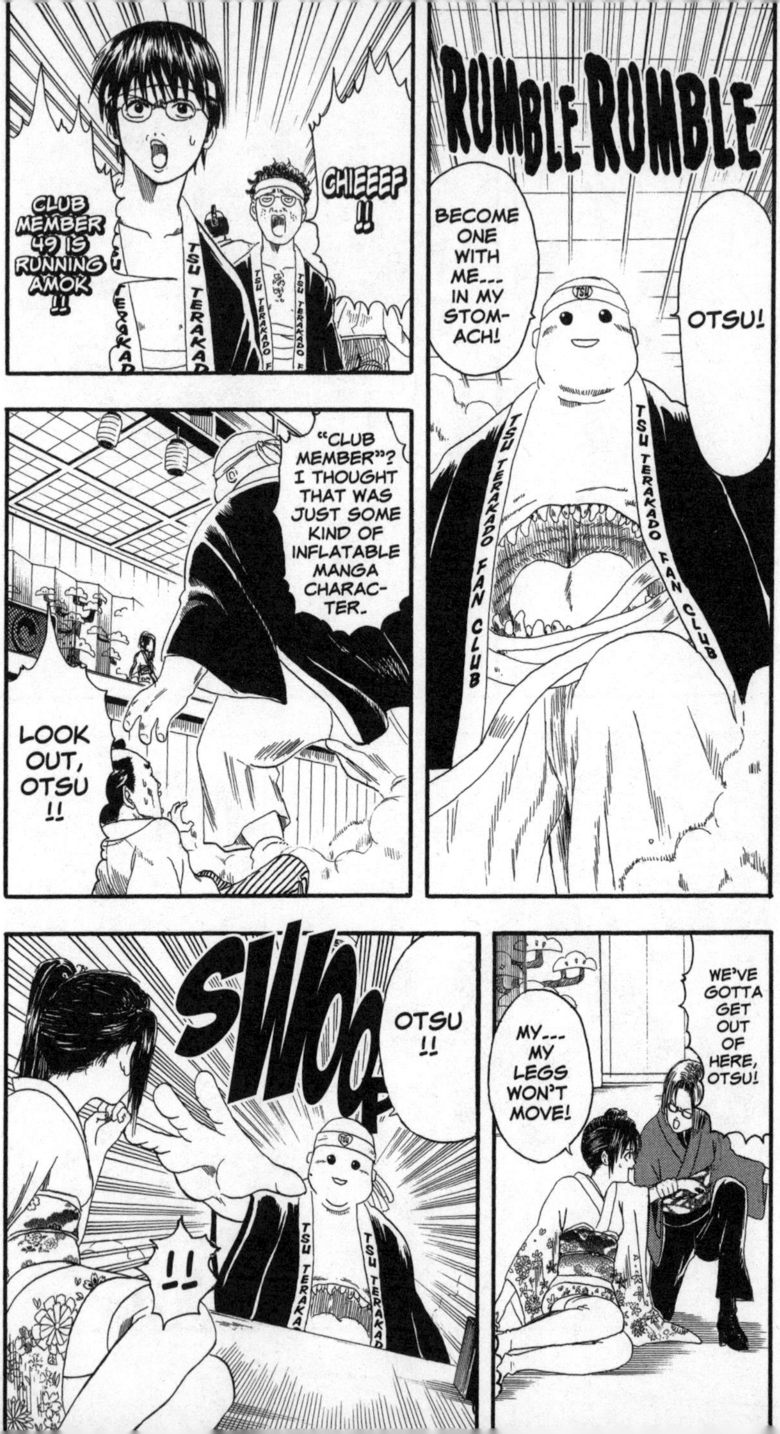
RUMBLE RUMBLE
OTSU!
BECOME ONE WITH ME... IN MY STOMACH!
TSU TERAKADO FAN CLUB
TSU TERAKADO FAN CLUB
CHIEEEF!!
CLUB MEMBER 49 IS RUNNING AMOK!!
"CLUB MEMBER"? I THOUGHT THAT WAS JUST SOME KIND OF INFLATABLE MANGA CHARACTER.
LOOK OUT, OTSU!!
WE'VE GOTTA GET OUT OF HERE, OTSU!
MY... MY LEGS WON'T MOVE!
OTSU!!
SWOO
!!

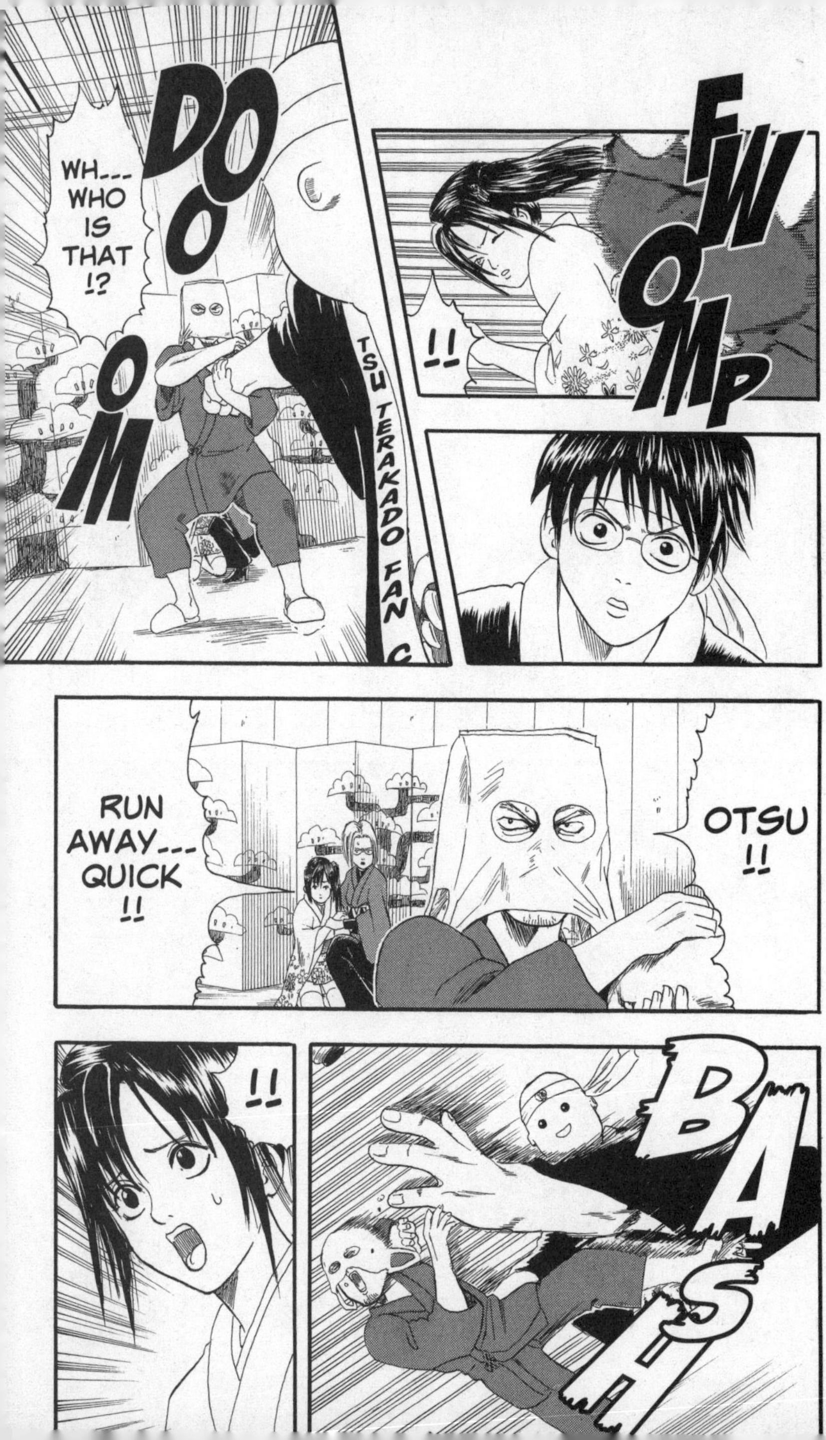
FWOMP
!!
DOOOM
WH--- WHO IS THAT !?
TSU TERAKADO FAN C
OTSU !!
RUN AWAY--- QUICK !!
BASH
!!

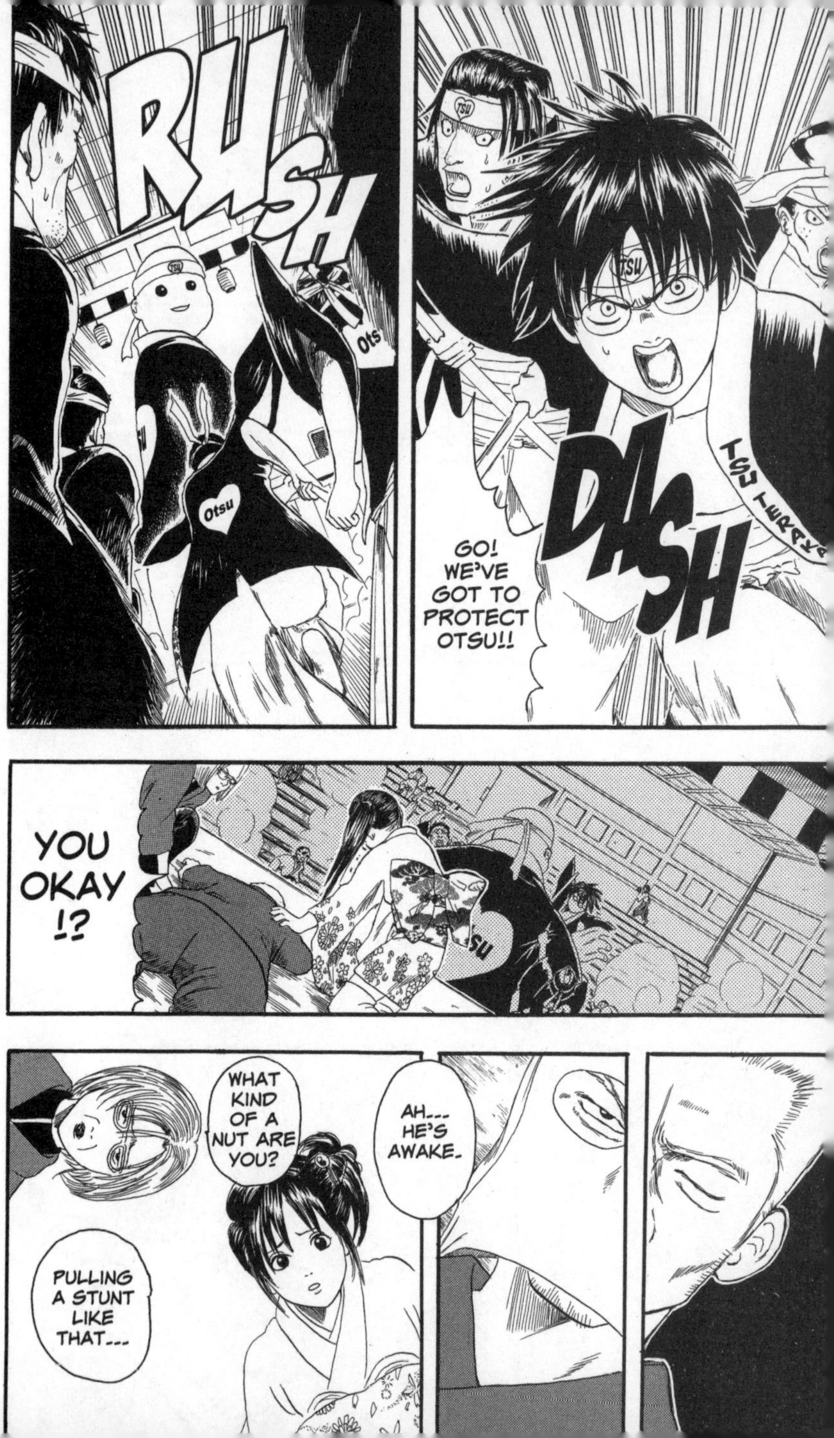
TSU
TSU
GO! WE'VE GOT TO PROTECT OTSU!!
DASH
RUSH
TSU
Ots
Otsu
YOU OKAY!?
AH... HE'S AWAKE.
WHAT KIND OF A NUT ARE YOU?
PULLING A STUNT LIKE THAT...

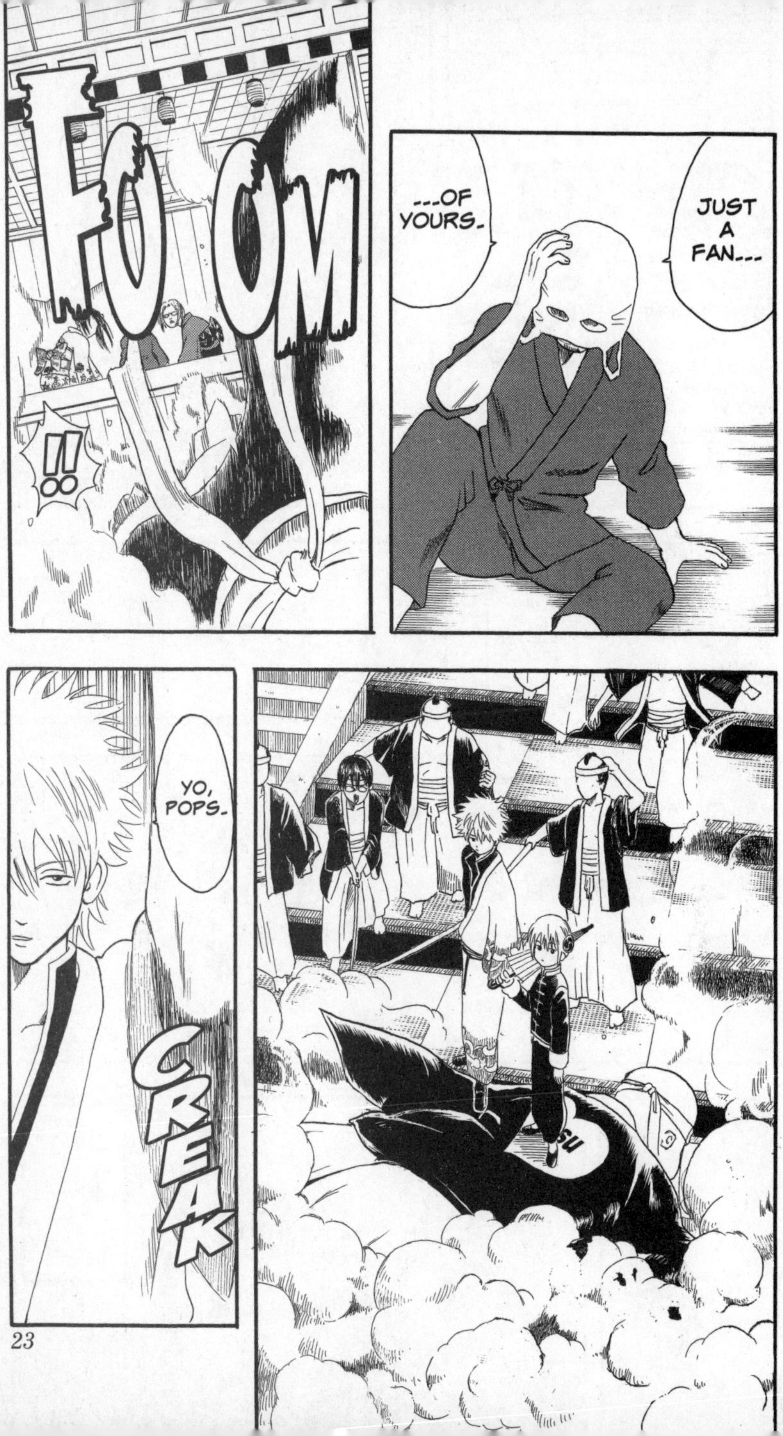
JUST A FAN...
...OF YOURS.
FOOM
!!
YO, POPS.
CREAK

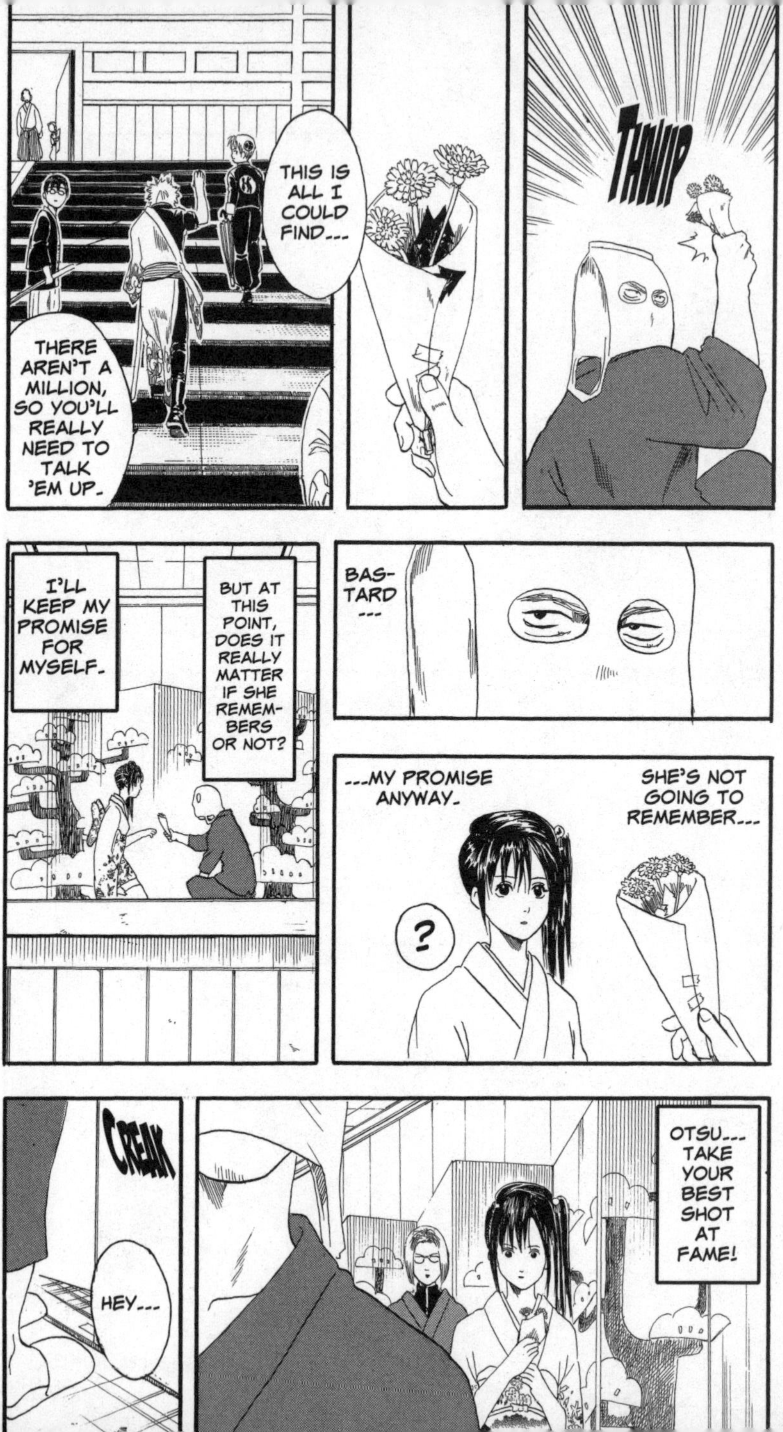
THWIP
THIS IS ALL I COULD FIND...
THERE AREN'T A MILLION, SO YOU'LL REALLY NEED TO TALK 'EM UP.
BASTARD...
SHE'S NOT GOING TO REMEMBER...
...MY PROMISE ANYWAY.
?
BUT AT THIS POINT, DOES IT REALLY MATTER IF SHE REMEMBERS OR NOT?
I'LL KEEP MY PROMISE FOR MYSELF.
OTSU... TAKE YOUR BEST SHOT AT FAME!
CREAK
HEY...

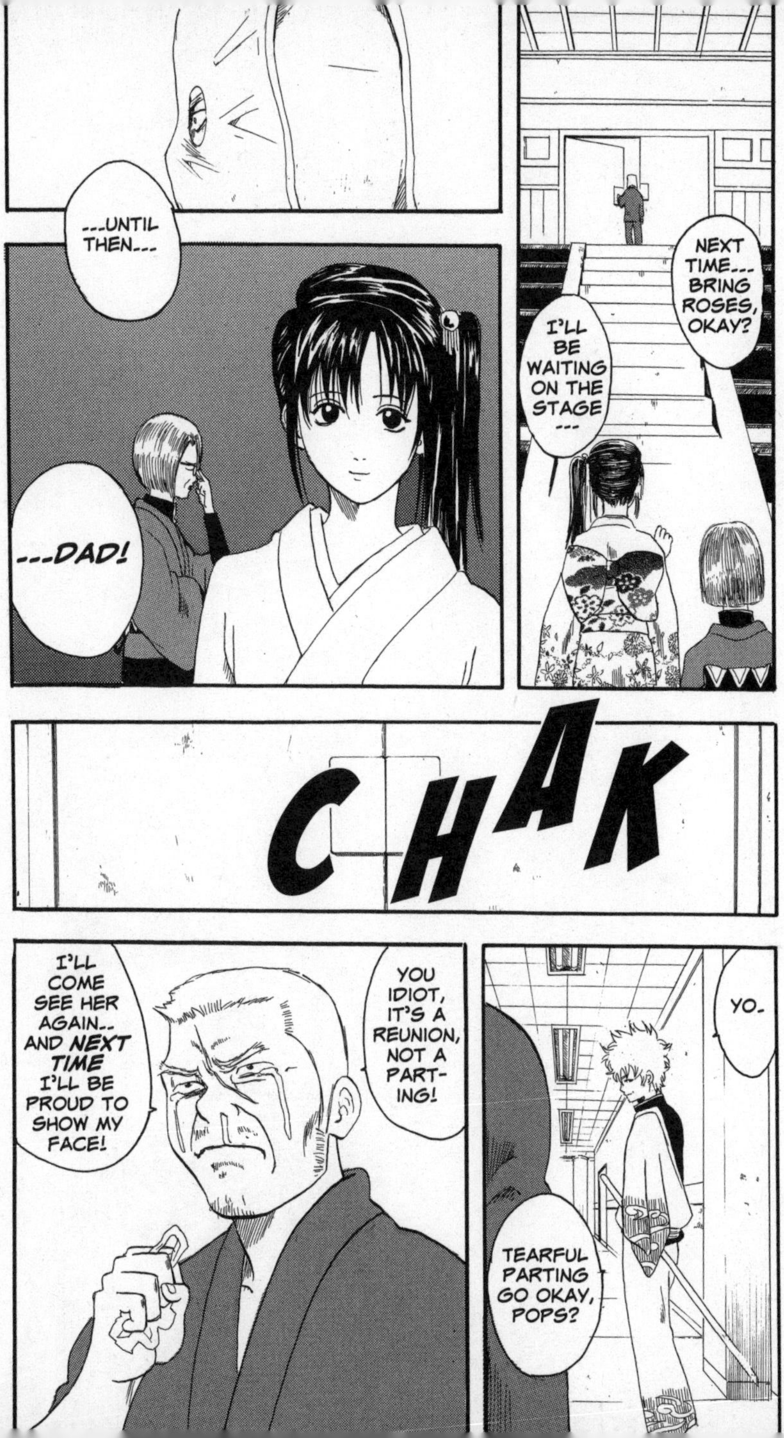
NEXT TIME... BRING ROSES, OKAY?
I'LL BE WAITING ON THE STAGE ---
---UNTIL THEN---
---DAD!
CHAK
YO-
TEARFUL PARTING GO OKAY, POPS?
YOU IDIOT, IT'S A REUNION, NOT A PARTING!
I'LL COME SEE HER AGAIN.. AND NEXT TIME I'LL BE PROUD TO SHOW MY FACE!

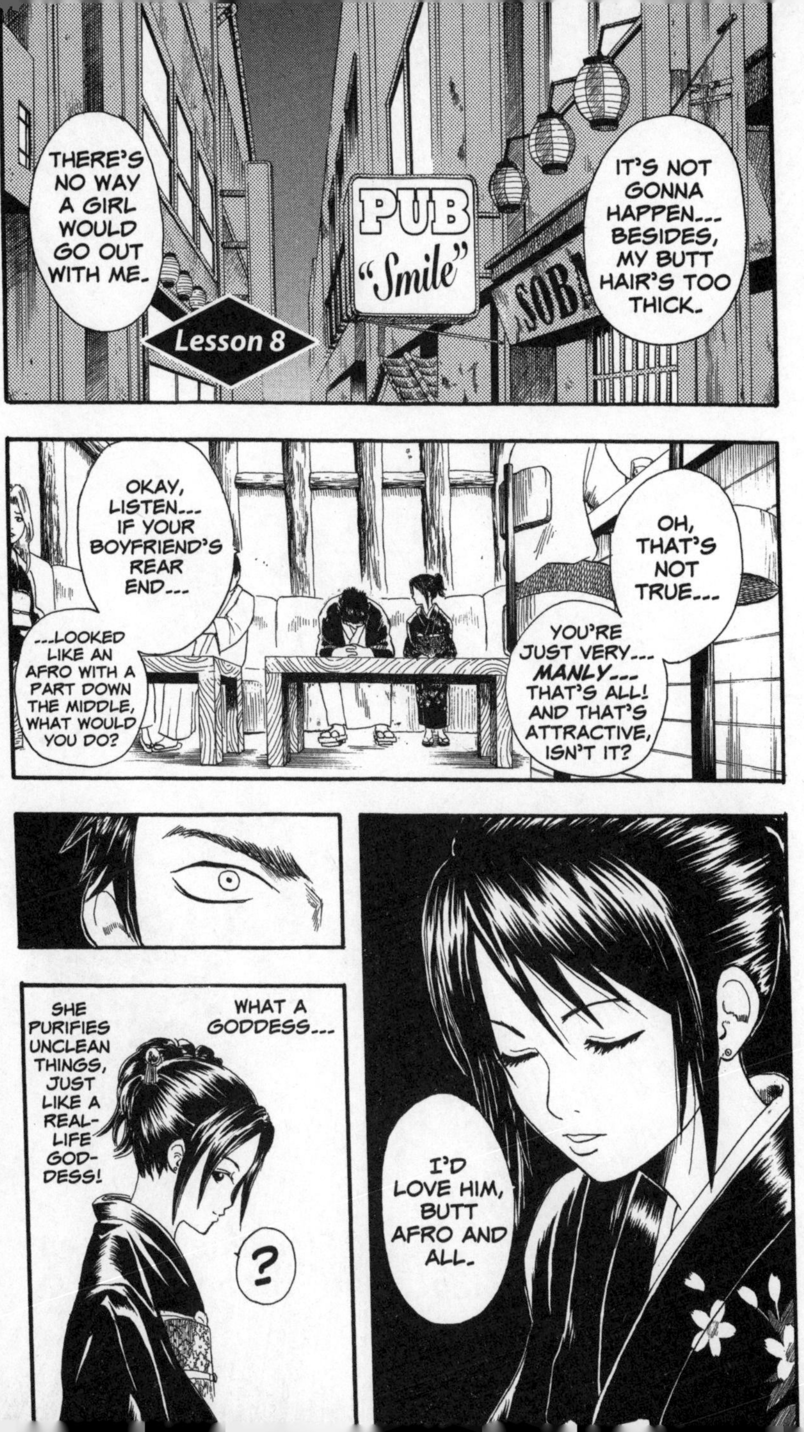
IT'S NOT GONNA HAPPEN... BESIDES, MY BUTT HAIR'S TOO THICK.
SOBA
PUB
"Smile"
THERE'S NO WAY A GIRL WOULD GO OUT WITH ME.
Lesson 8
OH, THAT'S NOT TRUE...
YOU'RE JUST VERY... MANLY... THAT'S ALL! AND THAT'S ATTRACTIVE, ISN'T IT?
OKAY, LISTEN... IF YOUR BOYFRIEND'S REAR END...
...LOOKED LIKE AN AFRO WITH A PART DOWN THE MIDDLE, WHAT WOULD YOU DO?
I'D LOVE HIM, BUTT AFRO AND ALL.
?
WHAT A GODDESS...
SHE PURIFIES UNCLEAN THINGS, JUST LIKE A REAL-LIFE GOD-DESS!

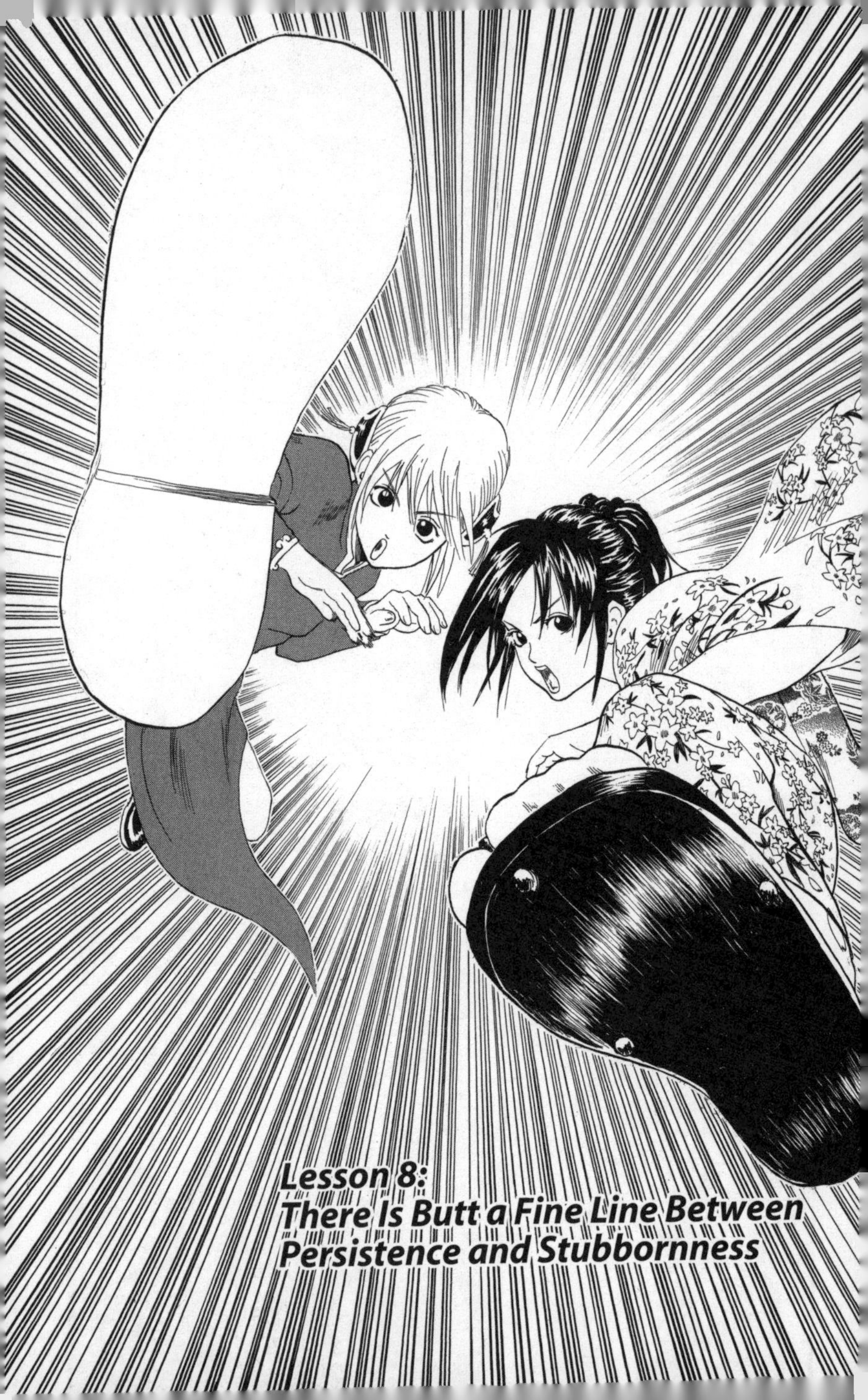
Lesson 8:
There Is Butt a Fine Line Between
Persistence and Stubbornness

READ THIS WAY

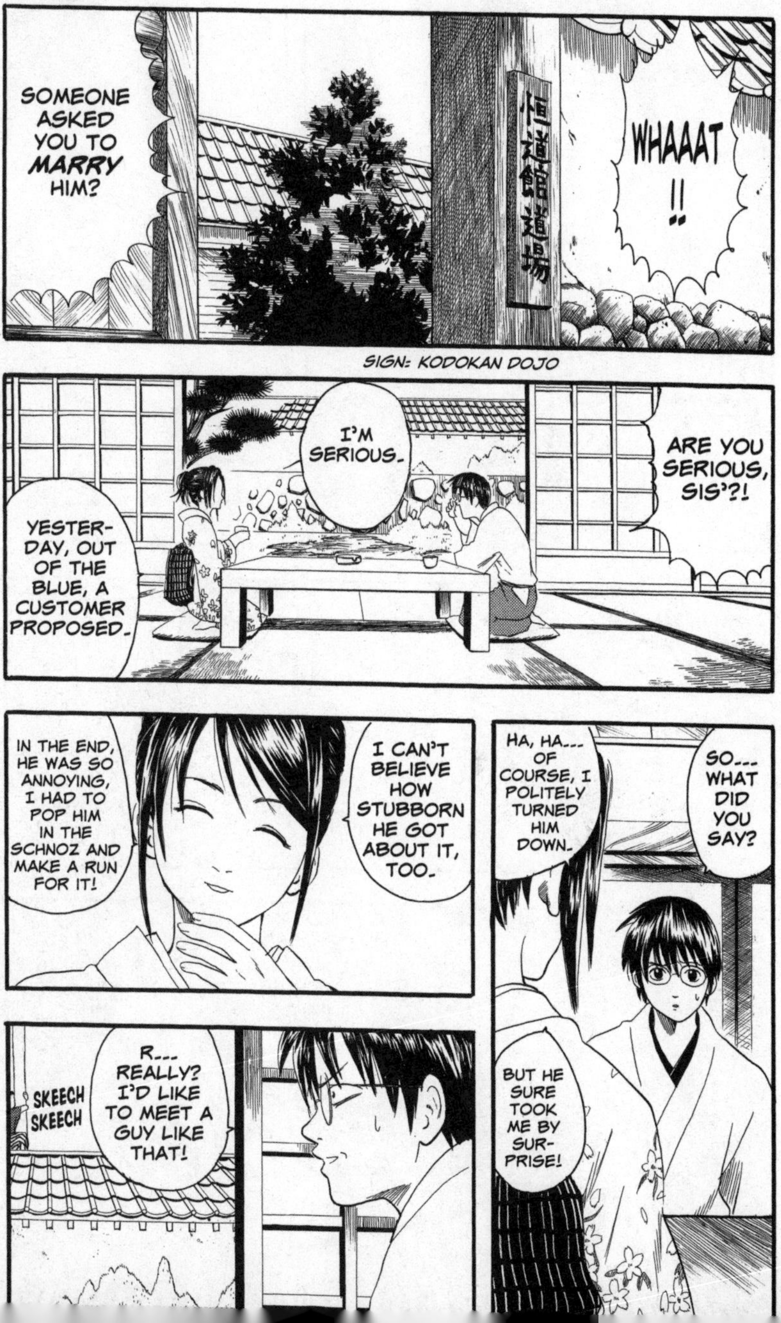
WHAAAT !!
SOMEONE ASKED YOU TO *MARRY* HIM?
恒道館道場
SIGN: KODOKAN DOJO
ARE YOU SERIOUS, SIS'?!
I'M SERIOUS.
YESTER-DAY, OUT OF THE BLUE, A CUSTOMER PROPOSED.
SO... WHAT DID YOU SAY?
HA, HA... OF COURSE, I POLITELY TURNED HIM DOWN.
BUT HE SURE TOOK ME BY SUR-PRISE!
I CAN'T BELIEVE HOW STUBBORN HE GOT ABOUT IT, TOO.
IN THE END, HE WAS SO ANNOYING, I HAD TO POP HIM IN THE SCHNOZ AND MAKE A RUN FOR IT!
R... REALLY? I'D LIKE TO MEET A GUY LIKE THAT!
SKEECH SKEECH

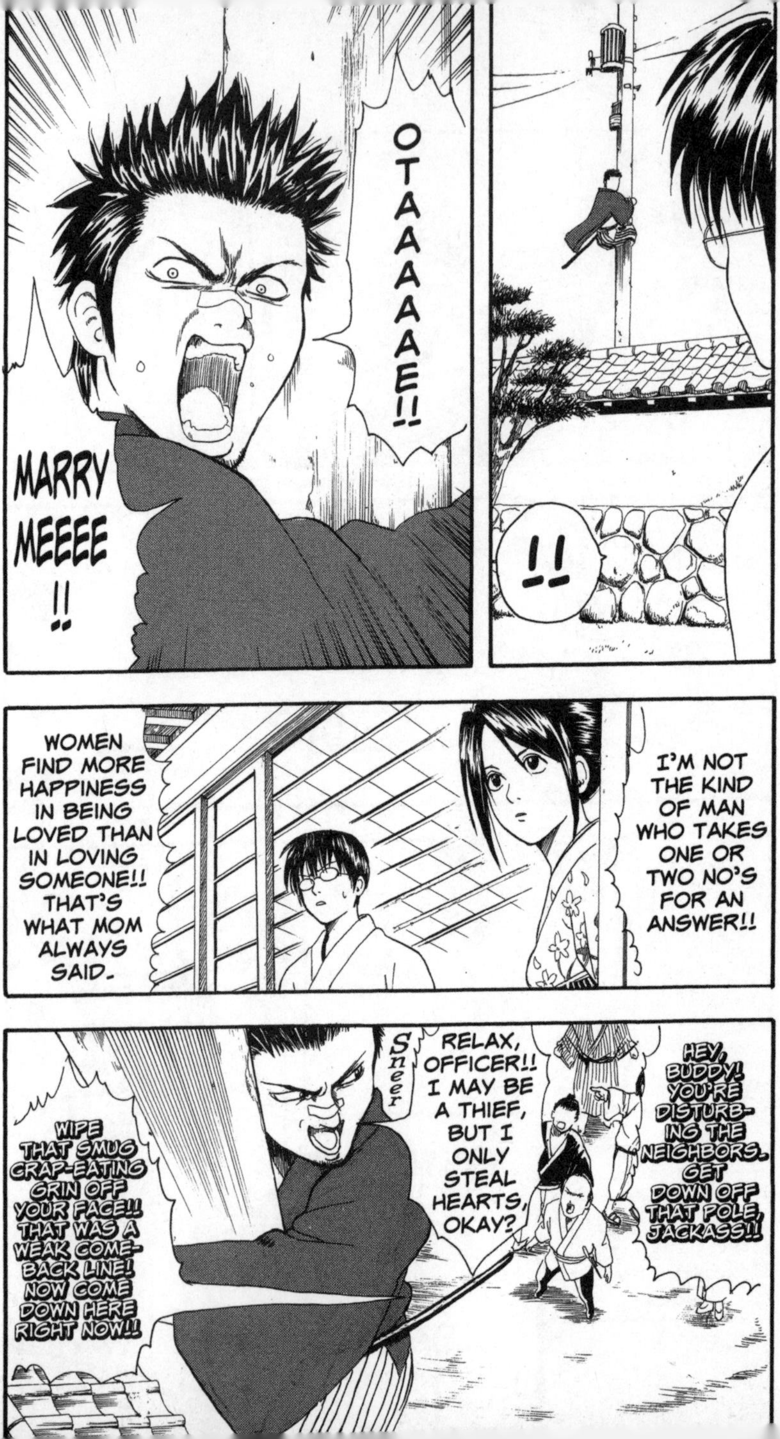
!!
OTAAAAAE!!
MARRY MEEEE!!
I'M NOT THE KIND OF MAN WHO TAKES ONE OR TWO NO'S FOR AN ANSWER!!
WOMEN FIND MORE HAPPINESS IN BEING LOVED THAN IN LOVING SOMEONE!! THAT'S WHAT MOM ALWAYS SAID.
HEY, BUDDY! YOU'RE DISTURBING THE NEIGHBORS. GET DOWN OFF THAT POLE, JACKASS!!
RELAX, OFFICER!! I MAY BE A THIEF, BUT I ONLY STEAL HEARTS, OKAY?
Sneer
WIPE THAT SMUG CRAP-EATING GRIN OFF YOUR FACE!! THAT WAS A WEAK COMEBACK LINE! NOW COME DOWN HERE RIGHT NOW!!

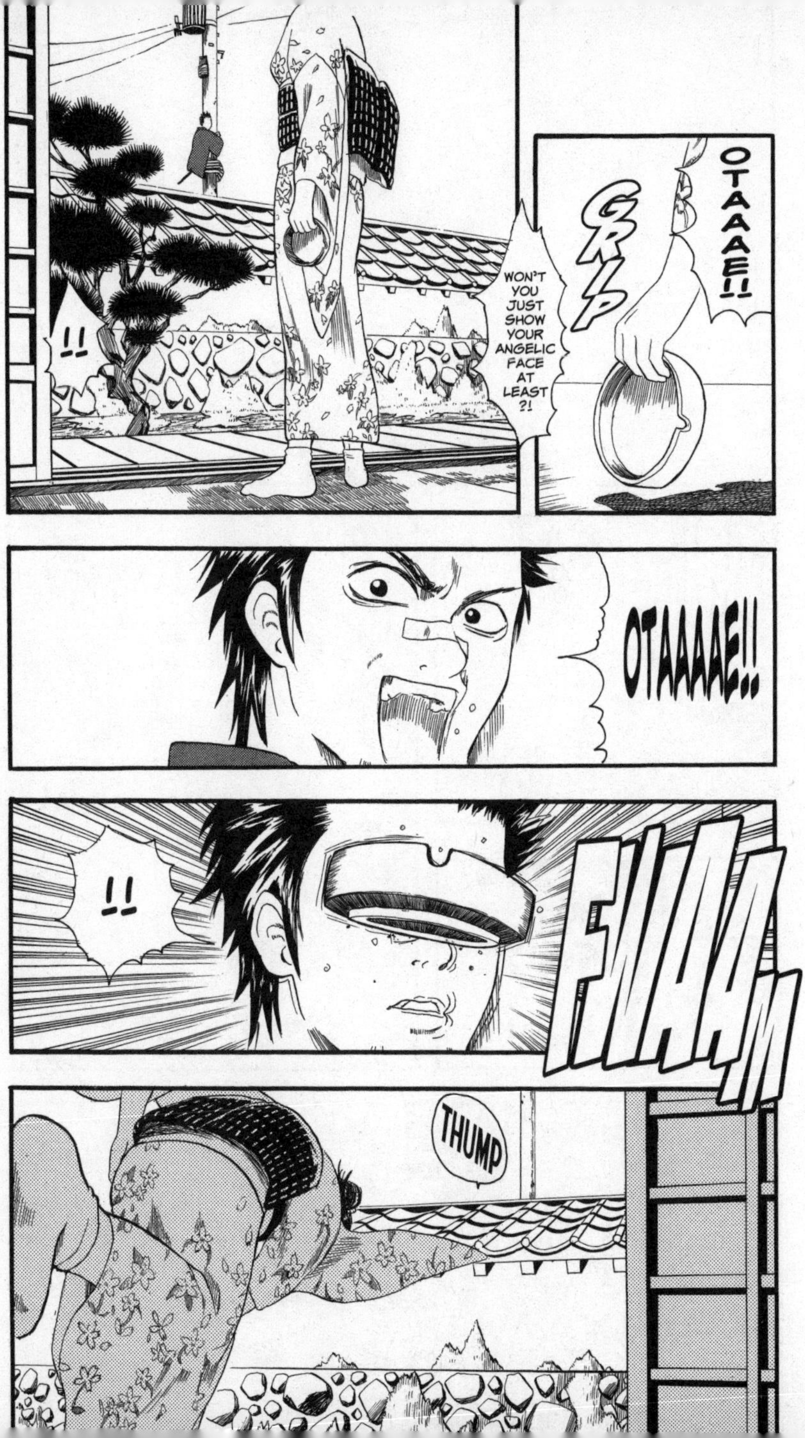
OTAAAE!!
GRIP
WON'T YOU JUST SHOW YOUR ANGELIC FACE AT LEAST?!
!!
OTAAAE!!
FWHAM
!!
THUMP

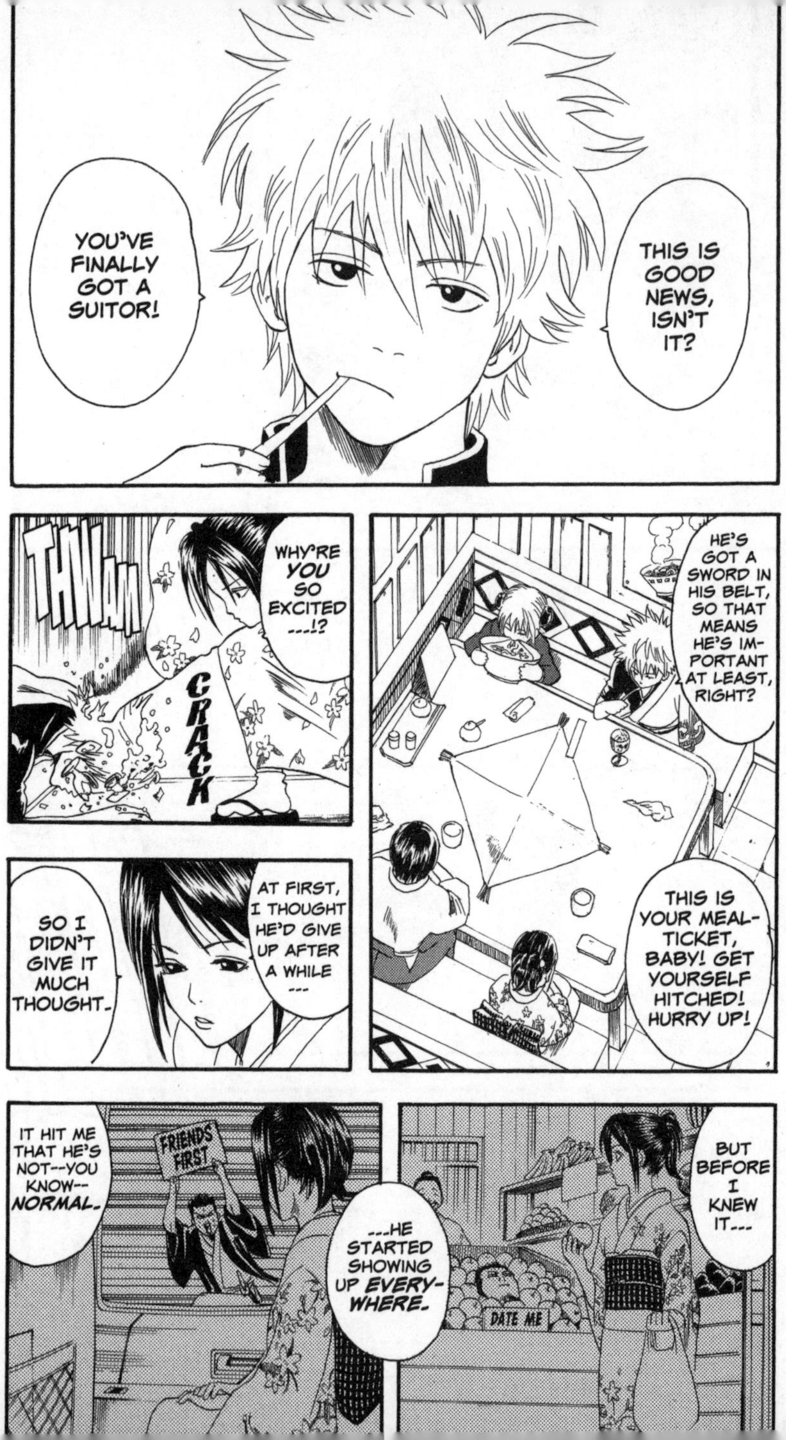
THIS IS GOOD NEWS, ISN'T IT?
YOU'VE FINALLY GOT A SUITOR!
HE'S GOT A SWORD IN HIS BELT, SO THAT MEANS HE'S IMPORTANT AT LEAST, RIGHT?
THIS IS YOUR MEAL-TICKET, BABY! GET YOURSELF HITCHED! HURRY UP!
THWAM
WHY'RE YOU SO EXCITED ---!?
CRACK
AT FIRST, I THOUGHT HE'D GIVE UP AFTER A WHILE ---
SO I DIDN'T GIVE IT MUCH THOUGHT...
BUT BEFORE I KNEW IT...
...HE STARTED SHOWING UP EVERYWHERE.
DATE ME
FRIENDS FIRST
IT HIT ME THAT HE'S NOT--YOU KNOW--NORMAL.

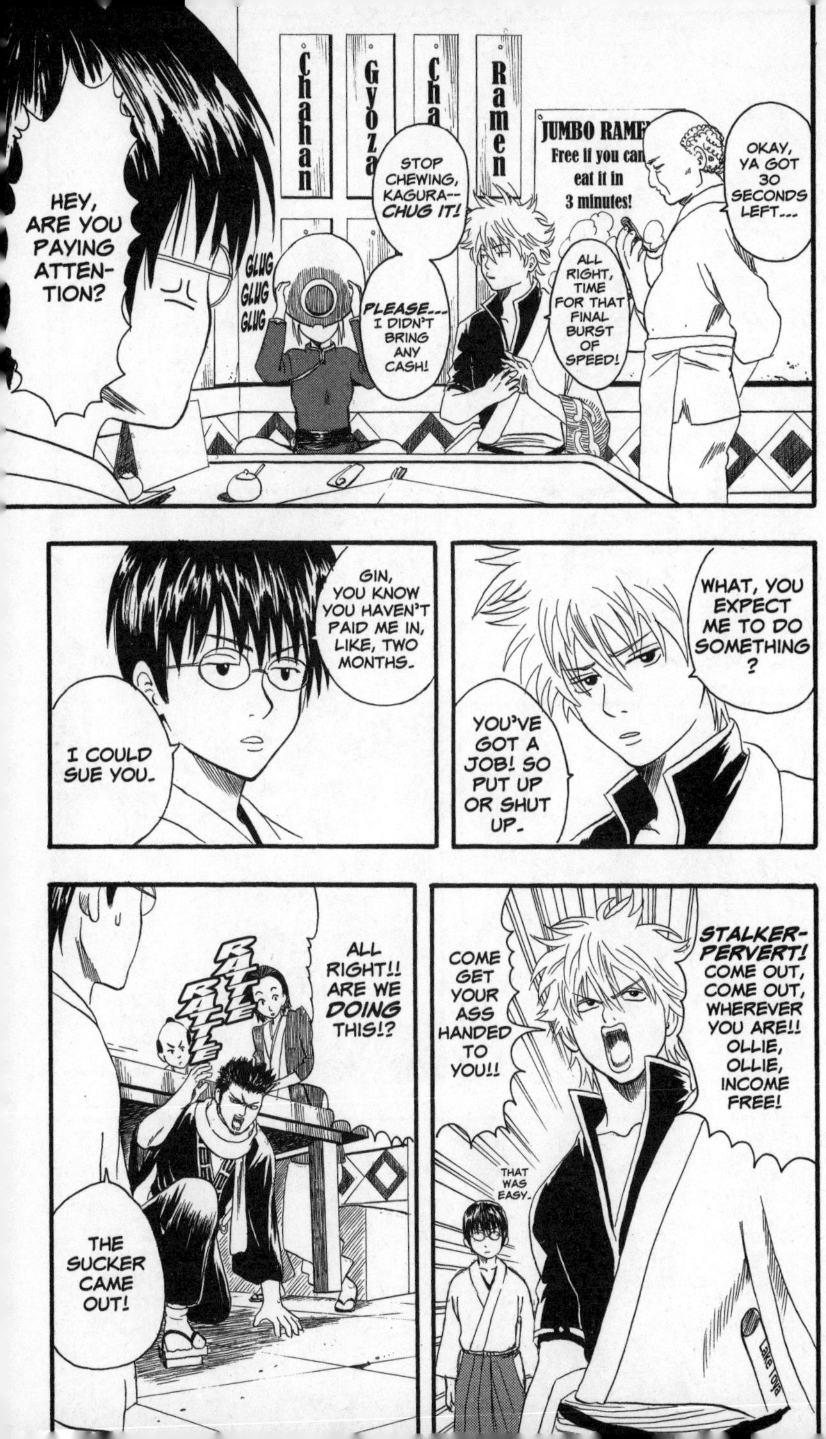
OKAY, YA GOT 30 SECONDS LEFT...
JUMBO RAME
Free if you ca
eat it in
3 minutes!
Ramen
Cha
Gyoza
Chahan
ALL RIGHT, TIME FOR THAT FINAL BURST OF SPEED!
STOP CHEWING, KAGURA-- *CHUG IT!*
PLEASE... I DIDN'T BRING ANY CASH!
GLUG GLUG GLUG
HEY, ARE YOU PAYING ATTEN-TION?
WHAT, YOU EXPECT ME TO DO SOMETHING?
YOU'VE GOT A JOB! SO PUT UP OR SHUT UP.
GIN, YOU KNOW YOU HAVEN'T PAID ME IN, LIKE, TWO MONTHS.
I COULD SUE YOU.
STALKER-PERVERT! COME OUT, COME OUT, WHEREVER YOU ARE!! OLLIE, OLLIE, INCOME FREE!
COME GET YOUR ASS HANDED TO YOU!!
THAT WAS EASY.
Lake Toya
ALL RIGHT!! ARE WE *DOING* THIS!?
RATTLE RATTLE
THE SUCKER CAME OUT!

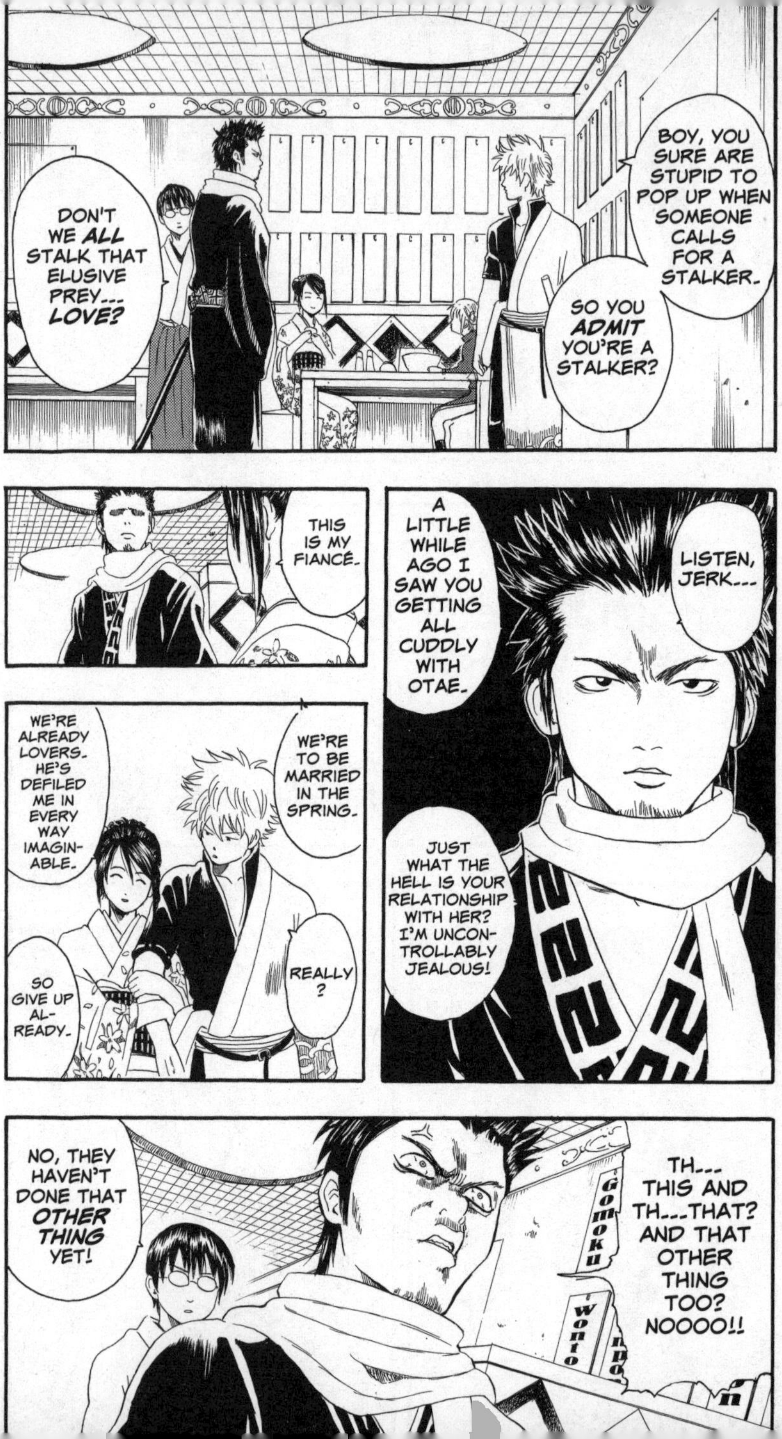
BOY, YOU SURE ARE STUPID TO POP UP WHEN SOMEONE CALLS FOR A STALKER.
SO YOU *ADMIT* YOU'RE A STALKER?
DON'T WE *ALL* STALK THAT ELUSIVE PREY... *LOVE?*
LISTEN, JERK...
A LITTLE WHILE AGO I SAW YOU GETTING ALL CUDDLY WITH OTAE.
JUST WHAT THE HELL IS YOUR RELATIONSHIP WITH HER? I'M UNCONTROLLABLY JEALOUS!
THIS IS MY FIANCÉ.
WE'RE TO BE MARRIED IN THE SPRING.
WE'RE ALREADY LOVERS. HE'S DEFILED ME IN EVERY WAY IMAGINABLE.
REALLY?
SO GIVE UP ALREADY.
TH... THIS AND TH...THAT? AND THAT OTHER THING TOO? NOOOO!!
Gomoku
NO, THEY HAVEN'T DONE THAT *OTHER THING* YET!

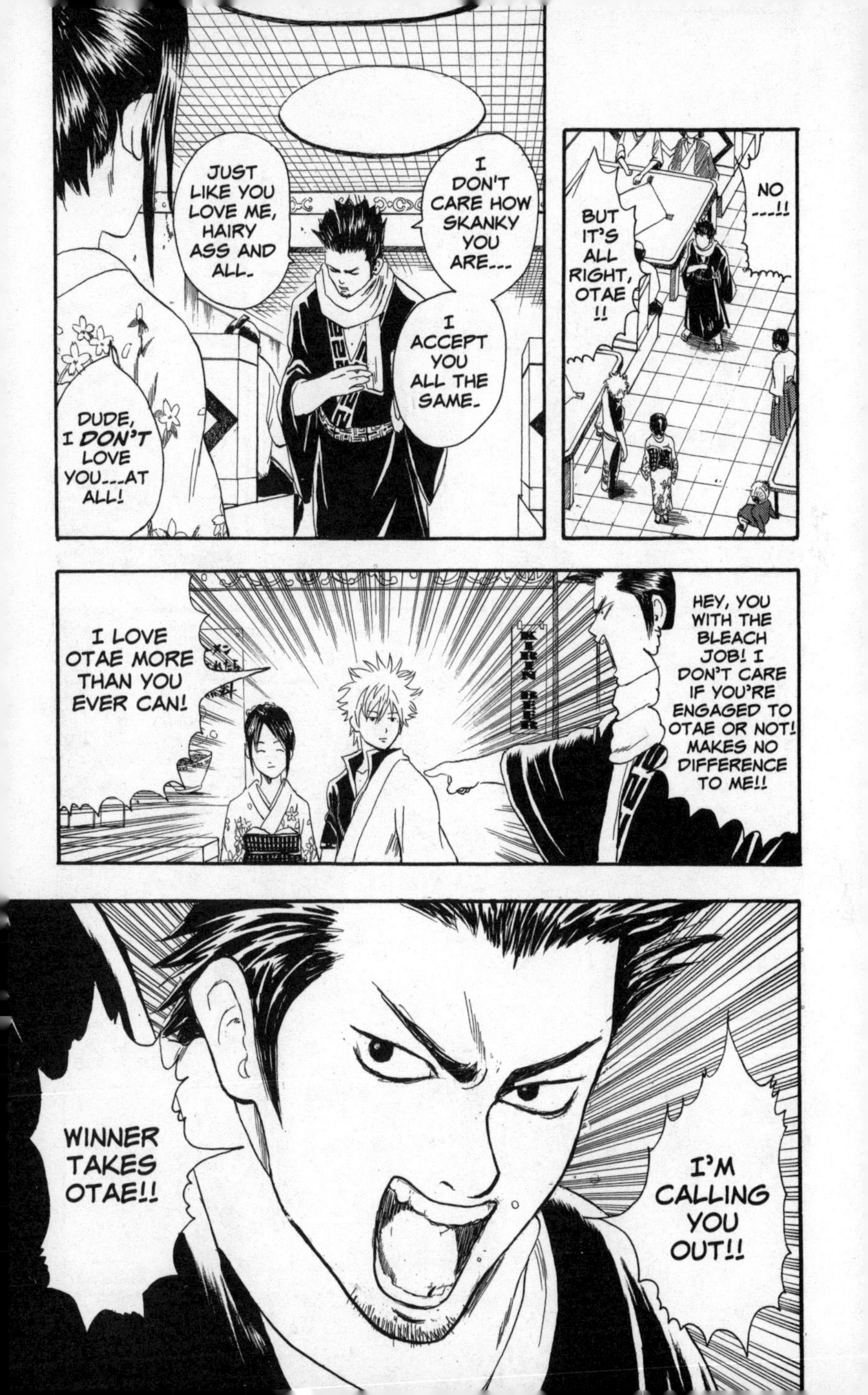
NO...!!
BUT IT'S ALL RIGHT, OTAE!!
I DON'T CARE HOW SKANKY YOU ARE...
I ACCEPT YOU ALL THE SAME.
JUST LIKE YOU LOVE ME, HAIRY ASS AND ALL.
DUDE, I *DON'T* LOVE YOU...AT ALL!
HEY, YOU WITH THE BLEACH JOB! I DON'T CARE IF YOU'RE ENGAGED TO OTAE OR NOT! MAKES NO DIFFERENCE TO ME!!
KIRIN BEER
I LOVE OTAE MORE THAN YOU EVER CAN!
I'M CALLING YOU OUT!!
WINNER TAKES OTAE!!

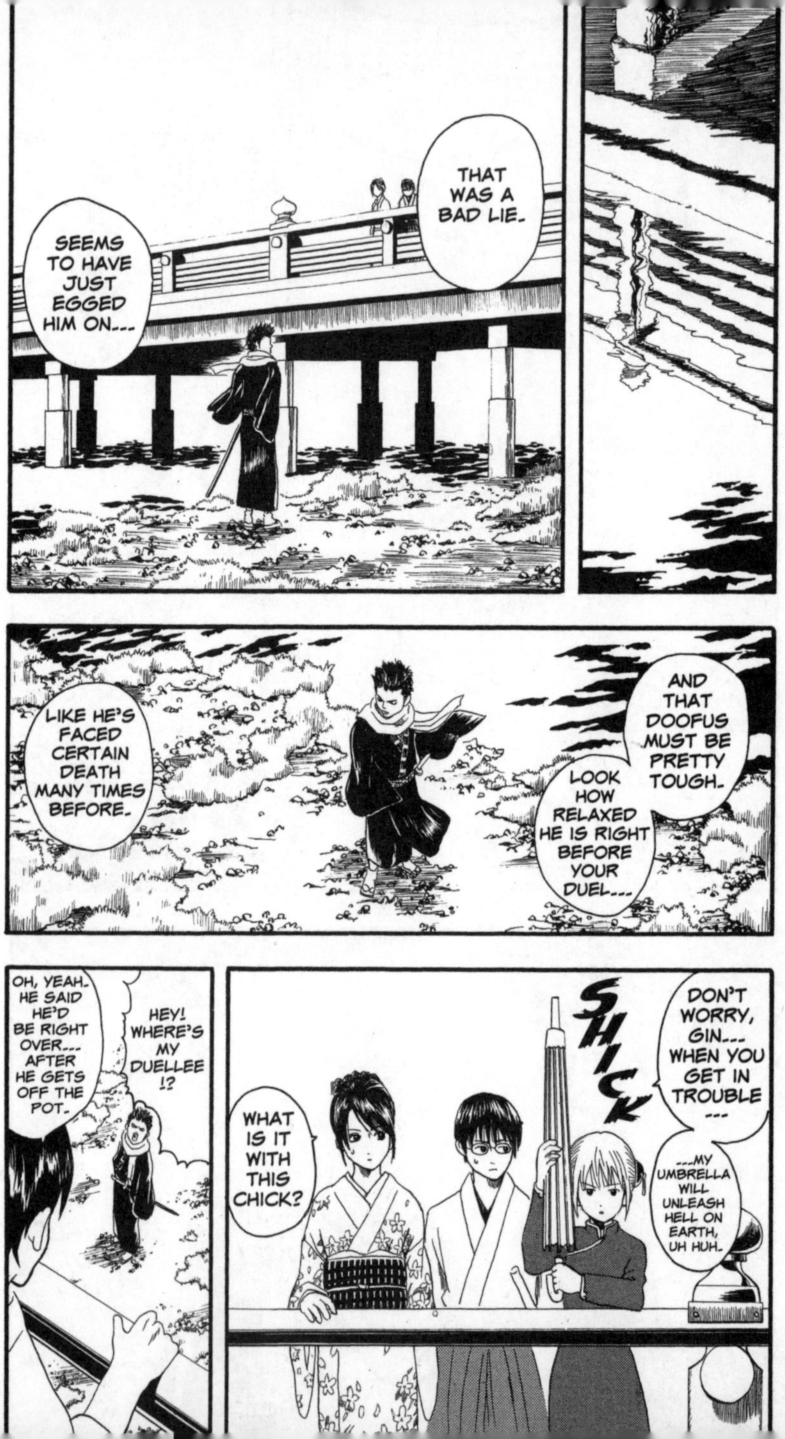
THAT WAS A BAD LIE.
SEEMS TO HAVE JUST EGGED HIM ON...
AND THAT DOOFUS MUST BE PRETTY TOUGH.
LOOK HOW RELAXED HE IS RIGHT BEFORE YOUR DUEL...
LIKE HE'S FACED CERTAIN DEATH MANY TIMES BEFORE.
SHICK
DON'T WORRY, GIN... WHEN YOU GET IN TROUBLE...
...MY UMBRELLA WILL UNLEASH HELL ON EARTH, UH HUH.
WHAT IS IT WITH THIS CHICK?
HEY! WHERE'S MY DUELLEE!?
OH, YEAH. HE SAID HE'D BE RIGHT OVER... AFTER HE GETS OFF THE POT.

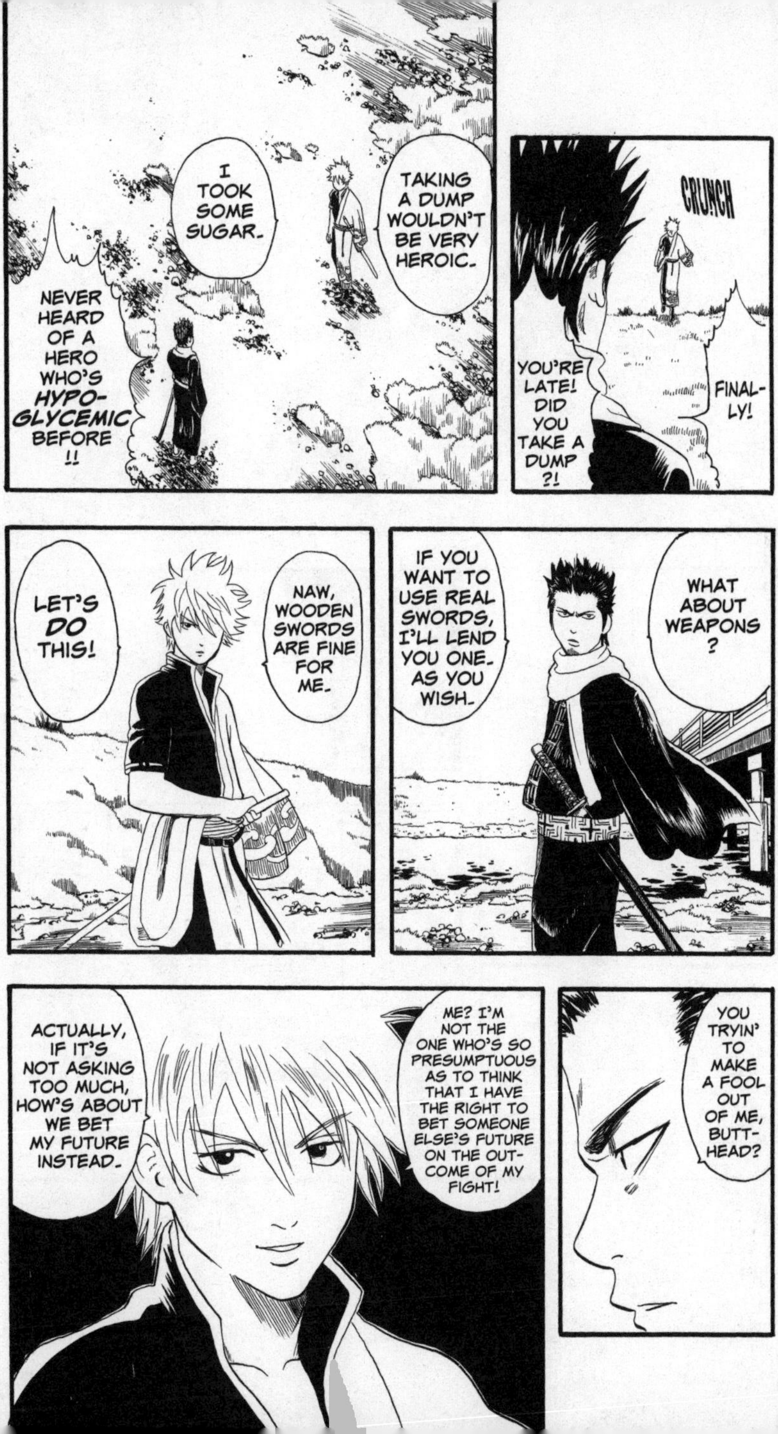
CRUNCH
FINAL-LY!
YOU'RE LATE! DID YOU TAKE A DUMP?!
TAKING A DUMP WOULDN'T BE VERY HEROIC.
I TOOK SOME SUGAR.
NEVER HEARD OF A HERO WHO'S *HYPOGLYCEMIC* BEFORE!!
WHAT ABOUT WEAPONS?
IF YOU WANT TO USE REAL SWORDS, I'LL LEND YOU ONE. AS YOU WISH.
NAW, WOODEN SWORDS ARE FINE FOR ME.
LET'S *DO* THIS!
YOU TRYIN' TO MAKE A FOOL OUT OF ME, BUTT-HEAD?
ME? I'M NOT THE ONE WHO'S SO PRESUMPTUOUS AS TO THINK THAT I HAVE THE RIGHT TO BET SOMEONE ELSE'S FUTURE ON THE OUTCOME OF MY FIGHT!
ACTUALLY, IF IT'S NOT ASKING TOO MUCH, HOW'S ABOUT WE BET MY FUTURE INSTEAD.

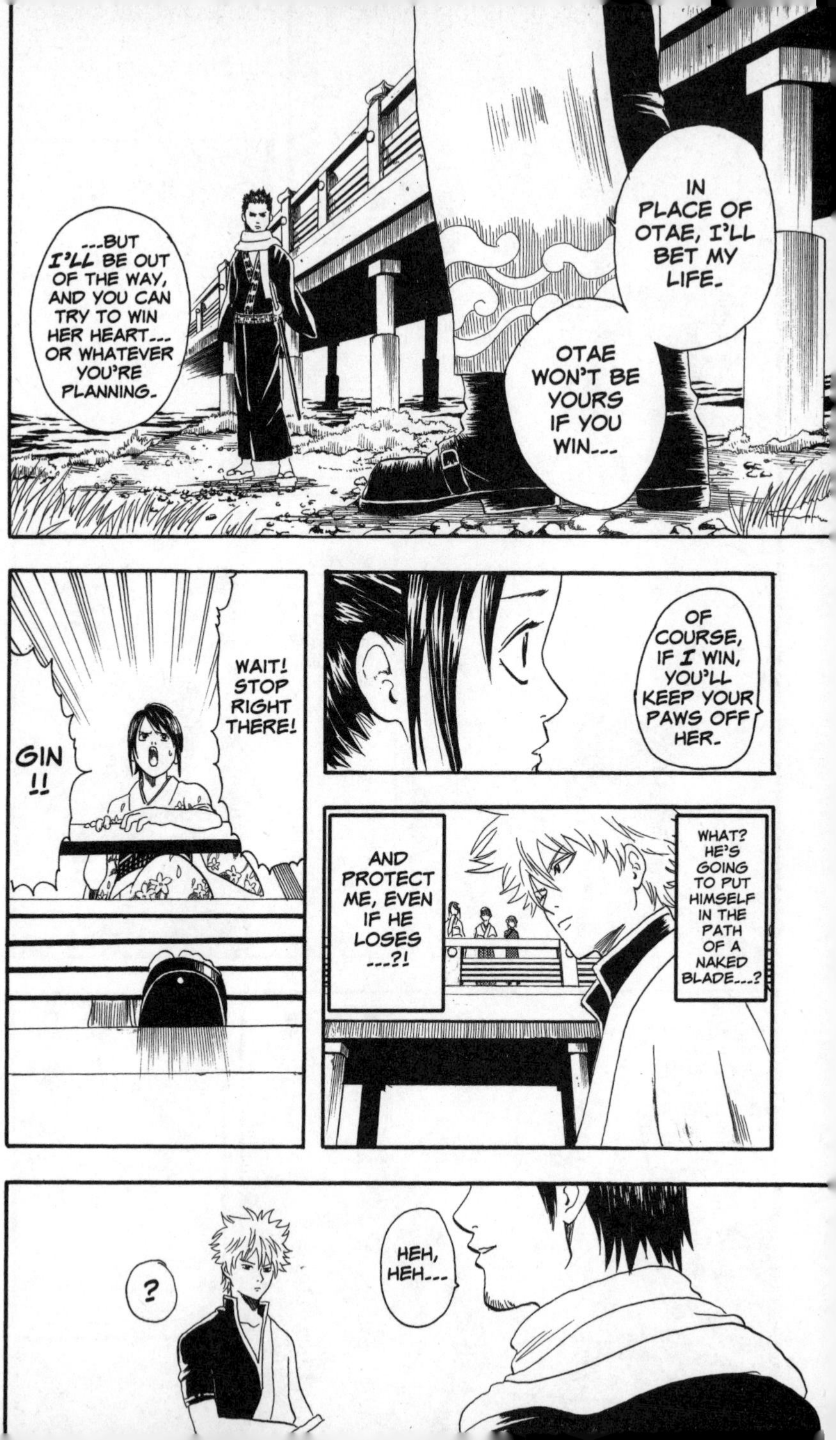
IN PLACE OF OTAE, I'LL BET MY LIFE.
OTAE WON'T BE YOURS IF YOU WIN...
...BUT I'LL BE OUT OF THE WAY, AND YOU CAN TRY TO WIN HER HEART... OR WHATEVER YOU'RE PLANNING.
OF COURSE, IF I WIN, YOU'LL KEEP YOUR PAWS OFF HER.
WHAT? HE'S GOING TO PUT HIMSELF IN THE PATH OF A NAKED BLADE...?
AND PROTECT ME, EVEN IF HE LOSES...?!
WAIT! STOP RIGHT THERE!
GIN!!
HEH, HEH...
?

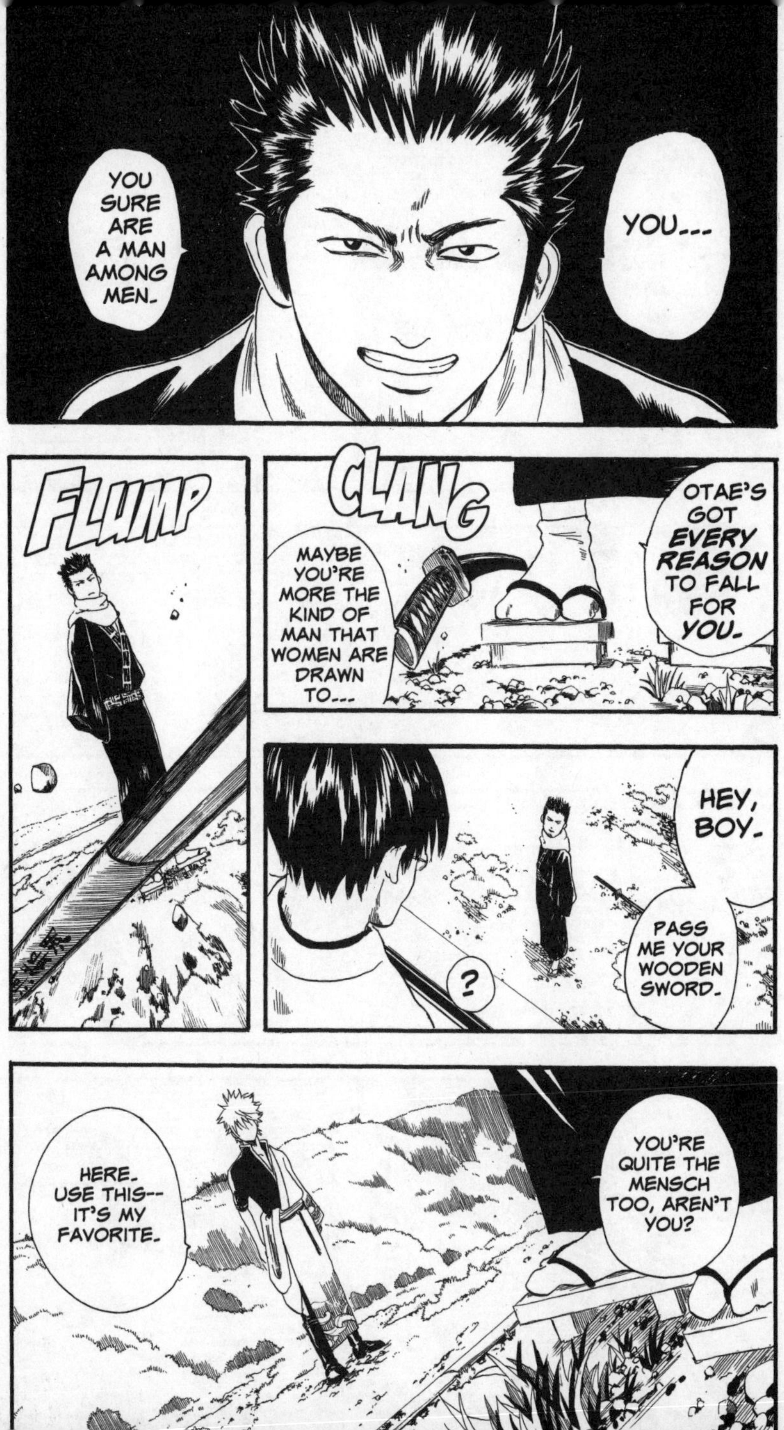
YOU...
YOU SURE ARE A MAN AMONG MEN.
OTAE'S GOT EVERY REASON TO FALL FOR YOU.
CLANG
MAYBE YOU'RE MORE THE KIND OF MAN THAT WOMEN ARE DRAWN TO...
HEY, BOY.
PASS ME YOUR WOODEN SWORD.
?
FLUMP
YOU'RE QUITE THE MENSCH TOO, AREN'T YOU?
HERE. USE THIS-- IT'S MY FAVORITE.

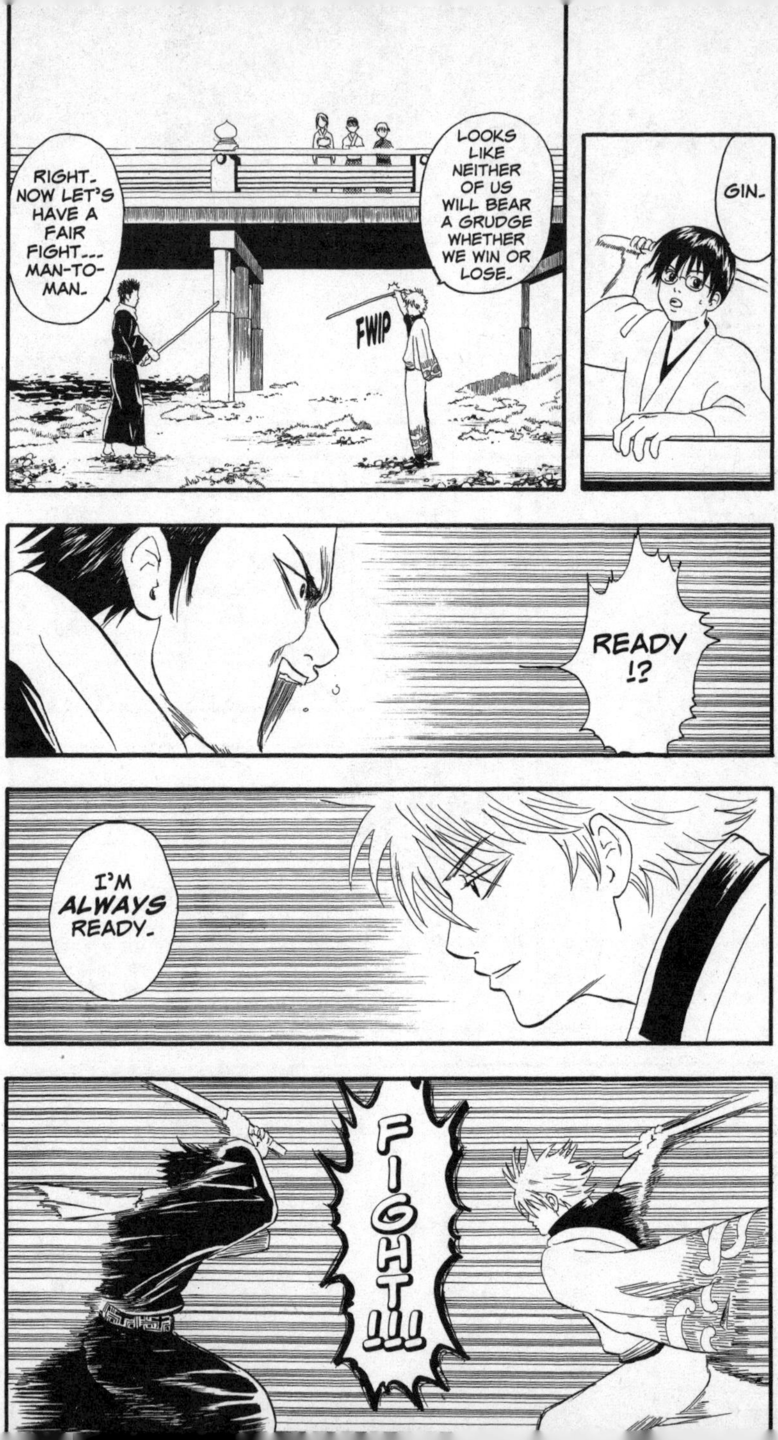

GIN.
LOOKS LIKE NEITHER OF US WILL BEAR A GRUDGE WHETHER WE WIN OR LOSE.
RIGHT. NOW LET'S HAVE A FAIR FIGHT... MAN-TO-MAN.
FWIP
READY!?
I'M ALWAYS READY.
FIGHT!!!

READ THIS WAY

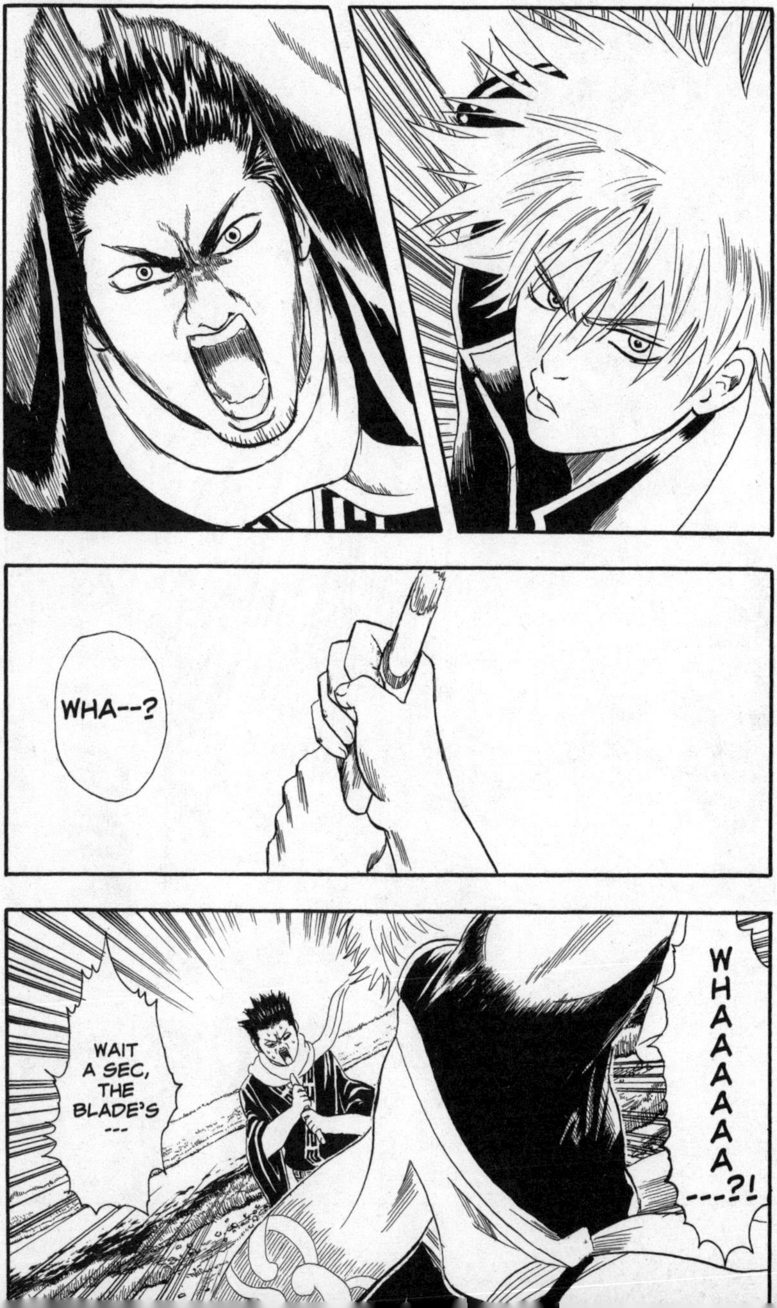
WHA--?
WHAAAAAA---?!
WAIT A SEC, THE BLADE'S ---

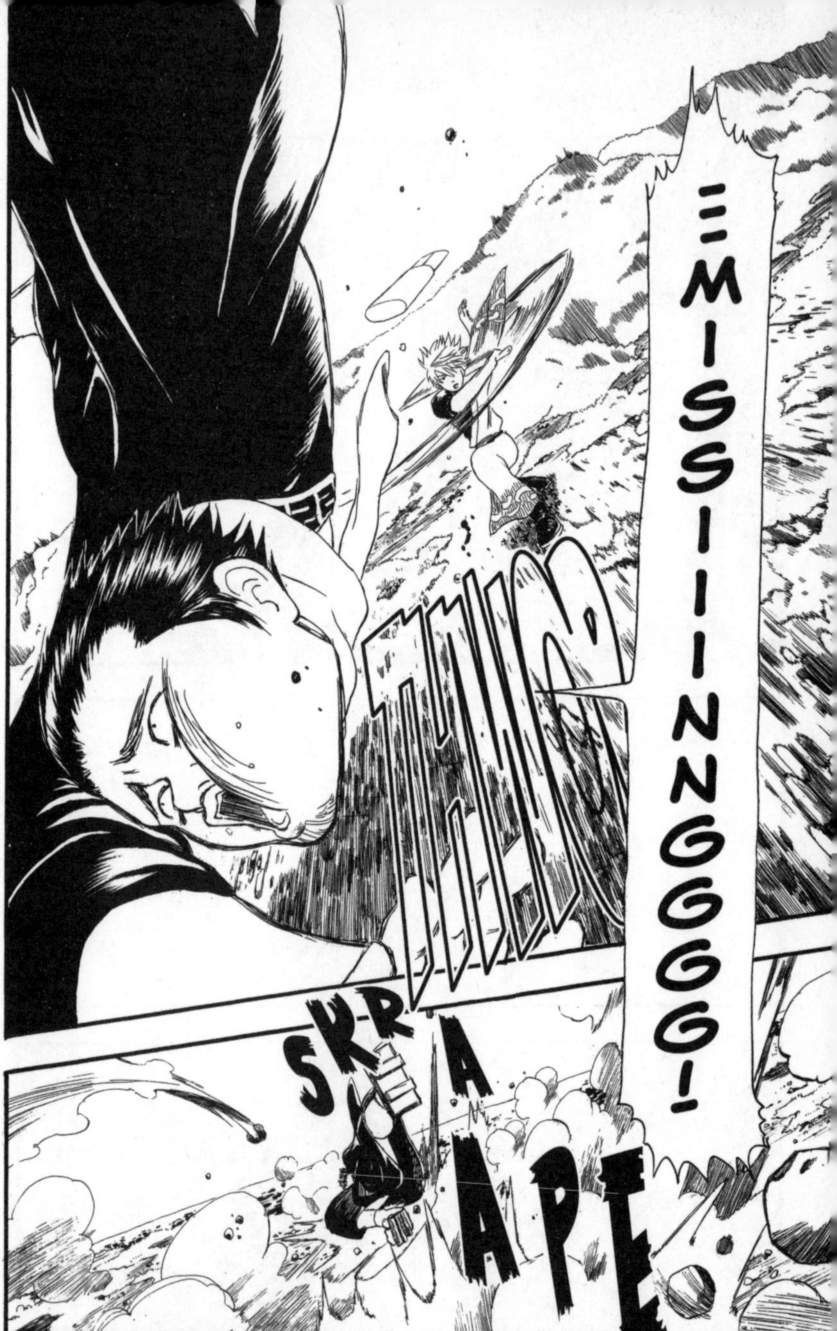
SKR-R-A-APE

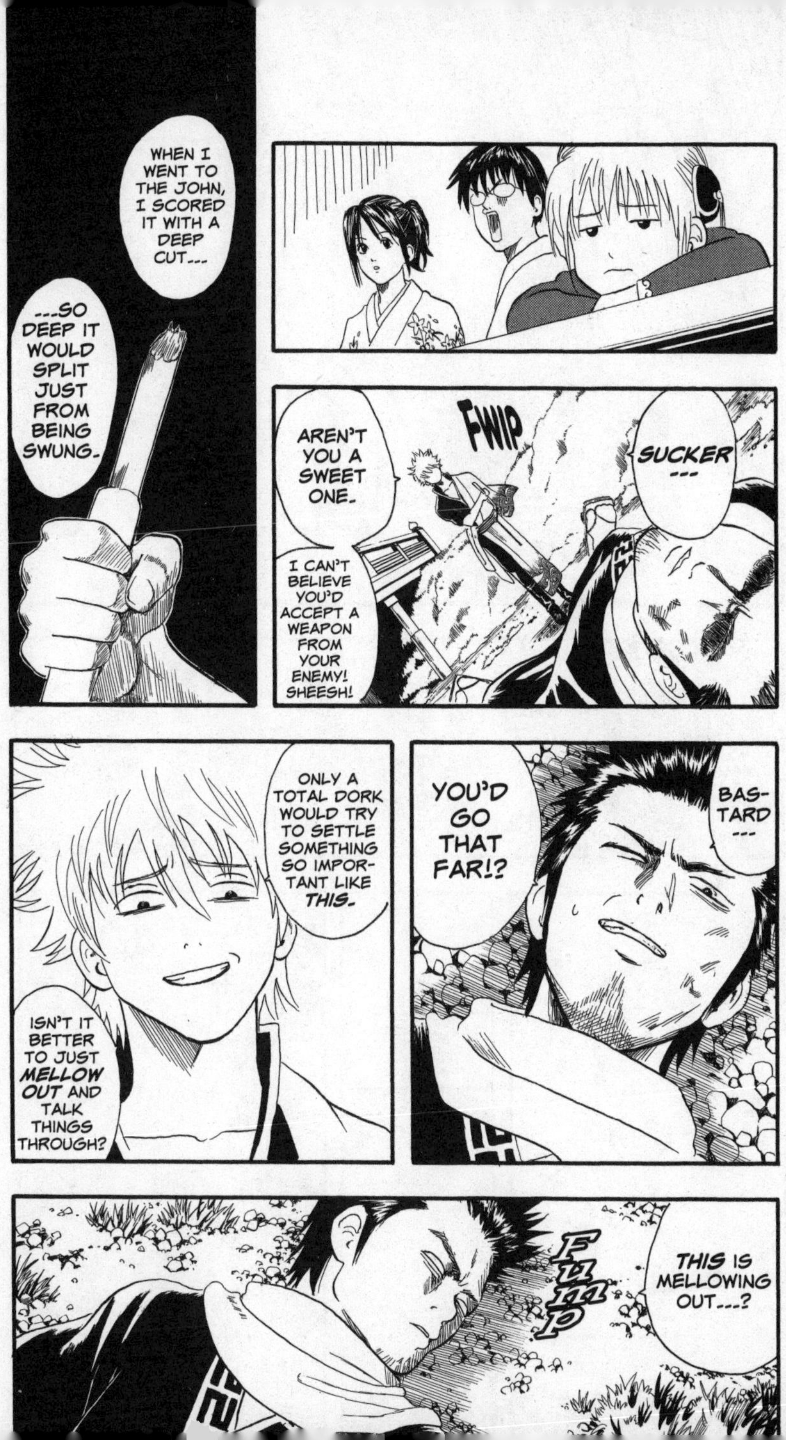
SUCKER...
FWIP
AREN'T YOU A SWEET ONE.
I CAN'T BELIEVE YOU'D ACCEPT A WEAPON FROM YOUR ENEMY! SHEESH!
WHEN I WENT TO THE JOHN, I SCORED IT WITH A DEEP CUT...
...SO DEEP IT WOULD SPLIT JUST FROM BEING SWUNG.
BAS-TARD...
YOU'D GO THAT FAR!?
ONLY A TOTAL DORK WOULD TRY TO SETTLE SOMETHING SO IMPOR-TANT LIKE THIS.
ISN'T IT BETTER TO JUST MELLOW OUT AND TALK THINGS THROUGH?
THIS IS MELLOWING OUT...?
FUMP

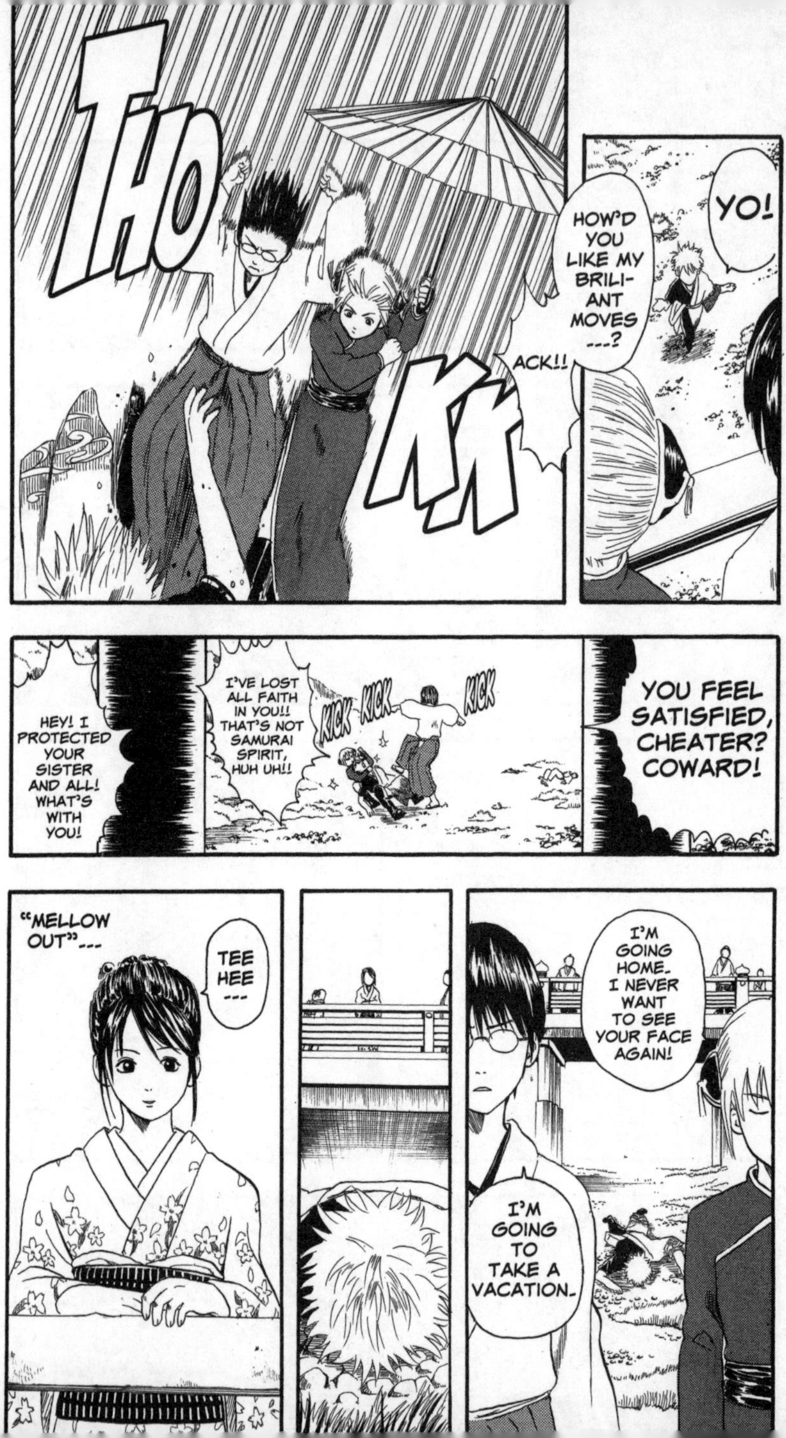
YO!
HOW'D YOU LIKE MY BRILI-ANT MOVES...?
ACK!!
THO
KK
YOU FEEL SATISFIED, CHEATER? COWARD!
KICK KICK KICK
I'VE LOST ALL FAITH IN YOU!! THAT'S NOT SAMURAI SPIRIT, HUH UH!!
HEY! I PROTECTED YOUR SISTER AND ALL! WHAT'S WITH YOU!
I'M GOING HOME. I NEVER WANT TO SEE YOUR FACE AGAIN!
I'M GOING TO TAKE A VACATION.
TEE HEE...
"MELLOW OUT"...

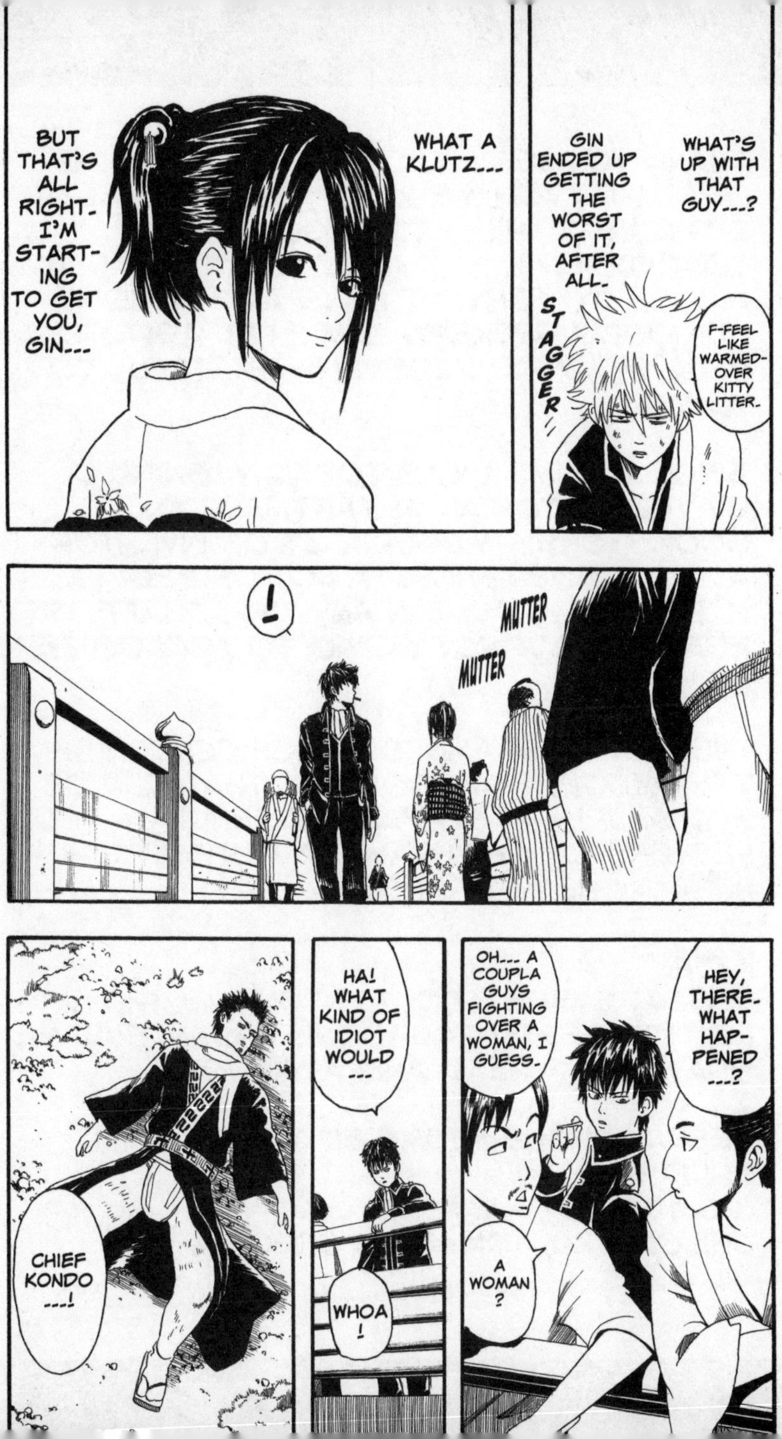
WHAT'S UP WITH THAT GUY...?
GIN ENDED UP GETTING THE WORST OF IT, AFTER ALL.
STAGGER
F-FEEL LIKE WARMED-OVER KITTY LITTER.
WHAT A KLUTZ...
BUT THAT'S ALL RIGHT. I'M STARTING TO GET YOU, GIN...
MUTTER
MUTTER
!
HEY, THERE. WHAT HAPPENED...?
OH... A COUPLA GUYS FIGHTING OVER A WOMAN, I GUESS.
A WOMAN?
HA! WHAT KIND OF IDIOT WOULD...
WHOA!
CHIEF KONDO...!

THANK YOU VERY MUCH FOR PURCHASING
GIN TAMA, VOLUME 2. TO TELL THE TRUTH,
I THOUGHT THIS TITLE WOULD GET
TORPEDOED RIGHT AWAY, BUT THANKS TO
ALL OF ITS FERVENT FANS AND VARIOUS
CURIOSITY SEEKERS, I'M STILL ABLE TO
PICK UP MY PEN. I'M VERY GRATEFUL TO
YOU ALL.

SINCE VOLUME 1 WAS TOTALLY IGNORED
BY THE EDITORIAL DEPARTMENT AND
BOOKSTORES, WE RAN OUT OF INVENTORY
AND INCONVENIENCED A LOT OF PEOPLE.
IT'S NOT MY FAULT IN ANY WAY, SHAPE, OR
FORM, SO I'M NOT GOING TO APOLOGIZE,
DAMN IT!

THE ONE TO BLAME IS MONCHICCHI ONISHI,
THE PROJECT MANAGER AT THAT DEN OF
EVIL SHUEISHA, SO PLEASE SEND ALL YOUR
LETTERS OF COMPLAINT DIRECTLY TO HIM.
HERE'S THE ADDRESS!

ATTN:
"LOOK, I MISSED OUT ON BUYING THE FIRST
EDITION OF *GIN TAMA*! ONISHI-SAN, PLEASE
SHAVE YOUR HEAD AND APOLOGIZE."

WEEKLY SHONEN JUMP EDITORIAL DEPT.
SHUEISHA
2-5-10 HITOTSUBASHI
CHIYODA-KU, TOKYO 101-8050 JAPAN

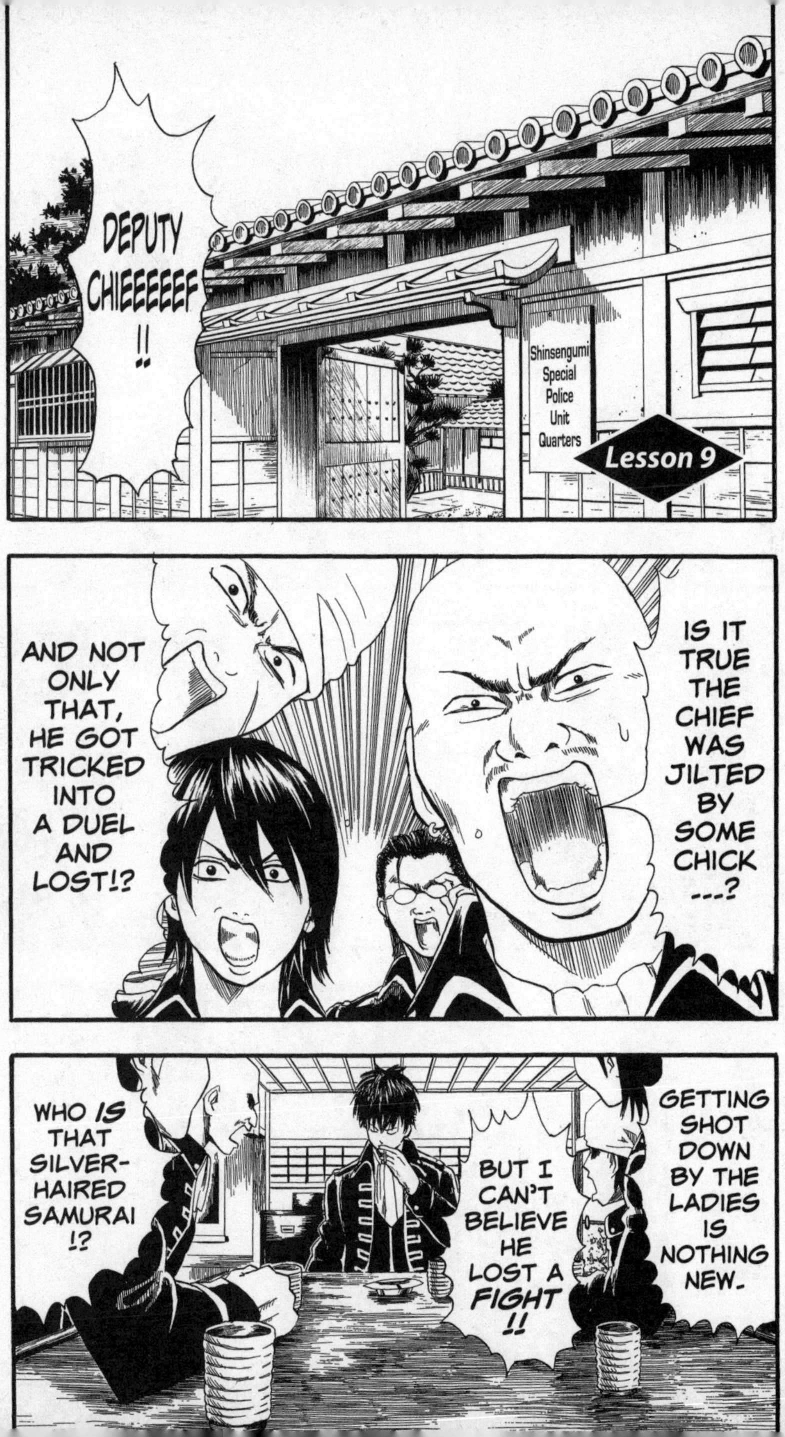
DEPUTY CHIEEEEEF !!
Shinsengumi Special Police Unit Quarters
Lesson 9
IS IT TRUE THE CHIEF WAS JILTED BY SOME CHICK...?
AND NOT ONLY THAT, HE GOT TRICKED INTO A DUEL AND LOST!?
GETTING SHOT DOWN BY THE LADIES IS NOTHING NEW.
BUT I CAN'T BELIEVE HE LOST A *FIGHT*!!
WHO *IS* THAT SILVER-HAIRED SAMURAI!?

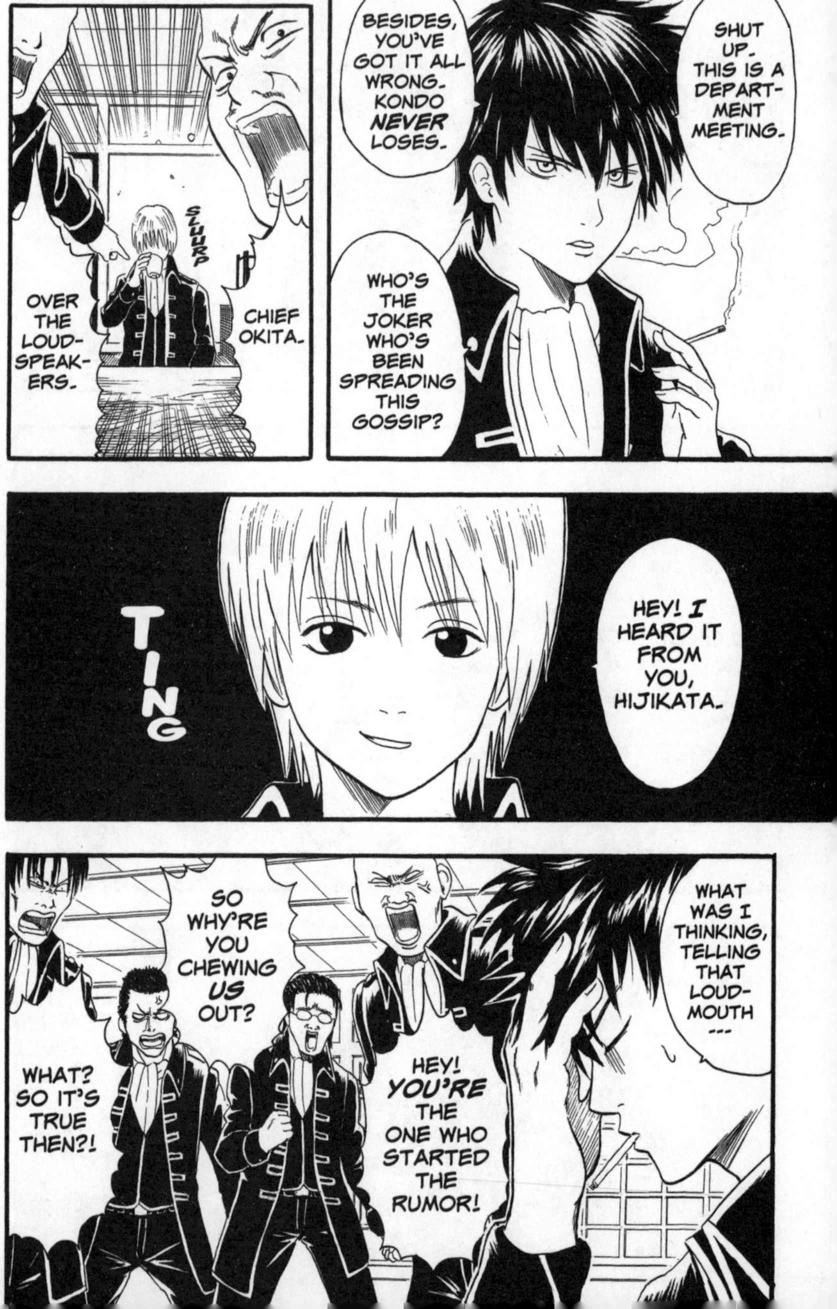
SHUT UP. THIS IS A DEPART-MENT MEETING.
BESIDES, YOU'VE GOT IT ALL WRONG. KONDO NEVER LOSES.
WHO'S THE JOKER WHO'S BEEN SPREADING THIS GOSSIP?
SLUURP
CHIEF OKITA.
OVER THE LOUD-SPEAK-ERS.
HEY! I HEARD IT FROM YOU, HIJIKATA.
TING
WHAT WAS I THINKING, TELLING THAT LOUD-MOUTH ---
SO WHY'RE YOU CHEWING US OUT?
HEY! YOU'RE THE ONE WHO STARTED THE RUMOR!
WHAT? SO IT'S TRUE THEN?!

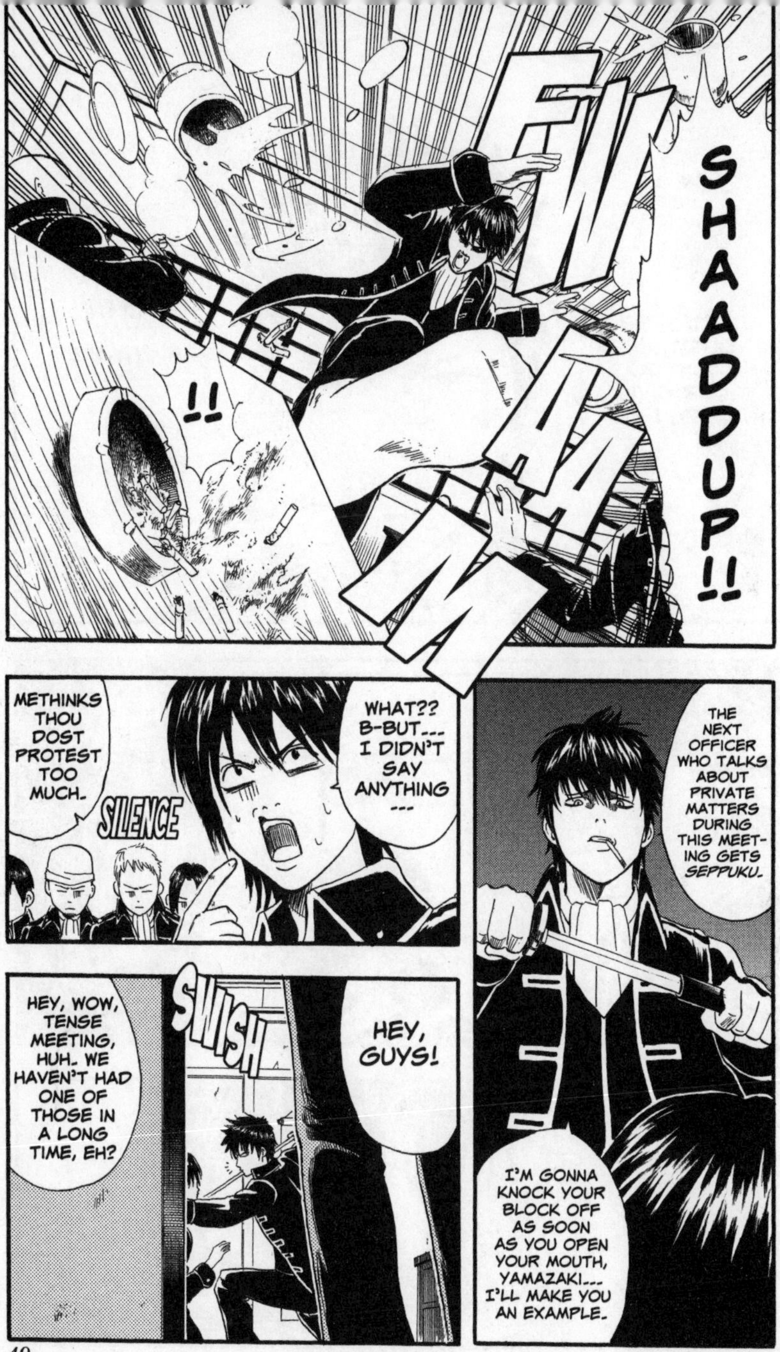
SHAADDUP!!
FWAAM
!!
THE NEXT OFFICER WHO TALKS ABOUT PRIVATE MATTERS DURING THIS MEET-ING GETS SEPPUKU.
I'M GONNA KNOCK YOUR BLOCK OFF AS SOON AS YOU OPEN YOUR MOUTH, YAMAZAKI... I'LL MAKE YOU AN EXAMPLE.
WHAT?? B-BUT... I DIDN'T SAY ANYTHING...
METHINKS THOU DOST PROTEST TOO MUCH.
SILENCE
HEY, GUYS!
SWISH
HEY, WOW, TENSE MEETING, HUH. WE HAVEN'T HAD ONE OF THOSE IN A LONG TIME, EH?

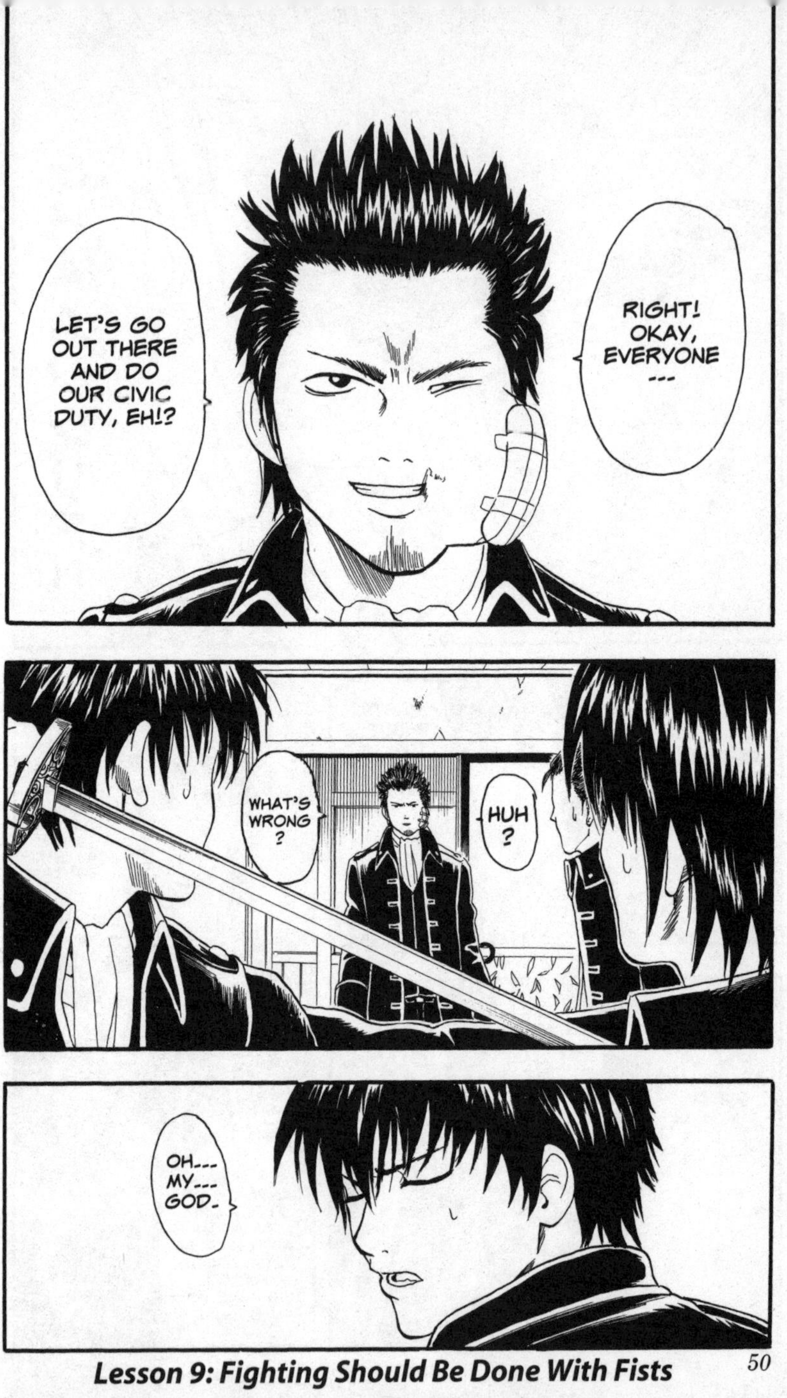
RIGHT! OKAY, EVERYONE ---
LET'S GO OUT THERE AND DO OUR CIVIC DUTY, EH!?
HUH ?
WHAT'S WRONG ?
OH--- MY--- GOD-

Lesson 9: Fighting Should Be Done With Fists

READ THIS WAY

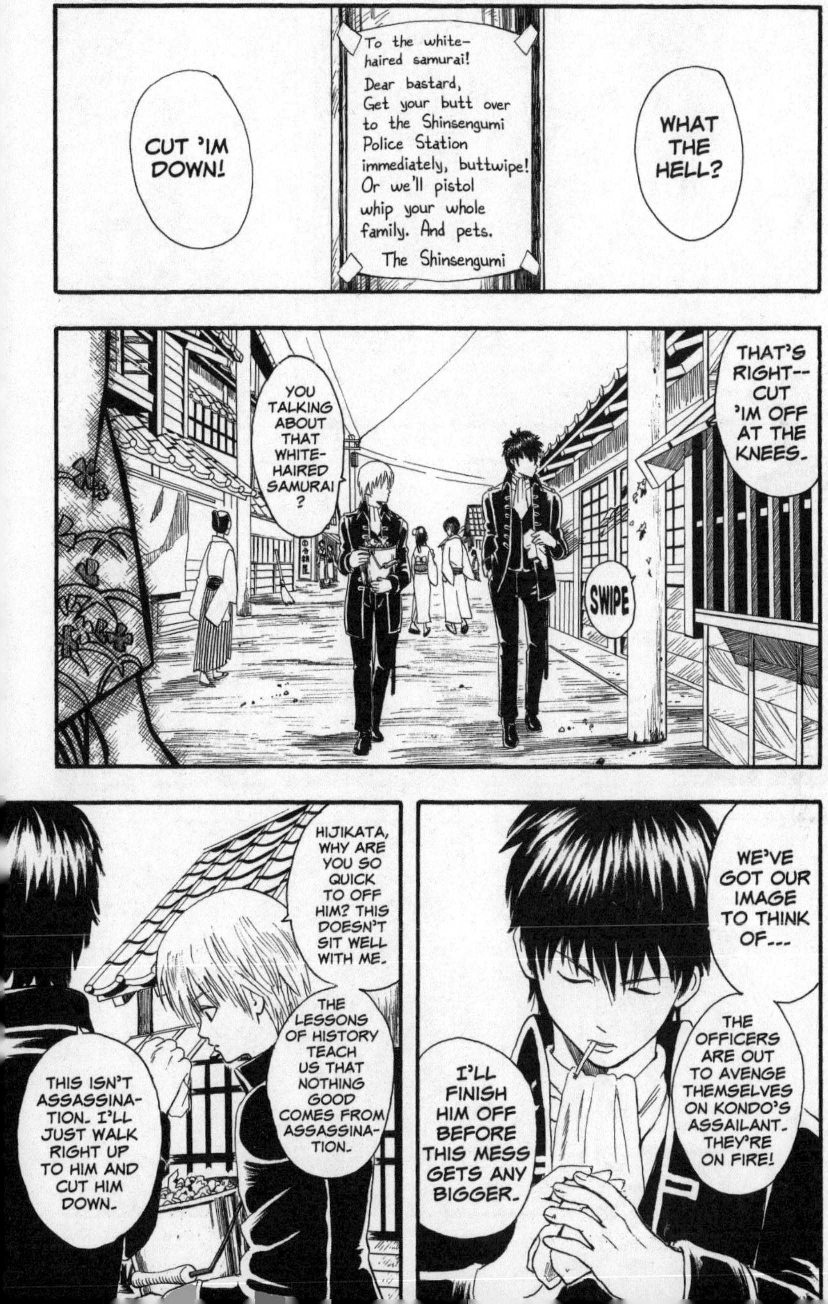
WHAT THE HELL?
To the white-haired samurai! Dear bastard, Get your butt over to the Shinsengumi Police Station immediately, buttwipe! Or we'll pistol whip your whole family. And pets. The Shinsengumi
CUT 'IM DOWN!
THAT'S RIGHT-- CUT 'IM OFF AT THE KNEES.
SWIPE
YOU TALKING ABOUT THAT WHITE-HAIRED SAMURAI?
WE'VE GOT OUR IMAGE TO THINK OF...
THE OFFICERS ARE OUT TO AVENGE THEMSELVES ON KONDO'S ASSAILANT. THEY'RE ON FIRE!
I'LL FINISH HIM OFF BEFORE THIS MESS GETS ANY BIGGER.
HIJIKATA, WHY ARE YOU SO QUICK TO OFF HIM? THIS DOESN'T SIT WELL WITH ME.
THE LESSONS OF HISTORY TEACH US THAT NOTHING GOOD COMES FROM ASSASSINATION.
THIS ISN'T ASSASSINATION. I'LL JUST WALK RIGHT UP TO HIM AND CUT HIM DOWN.

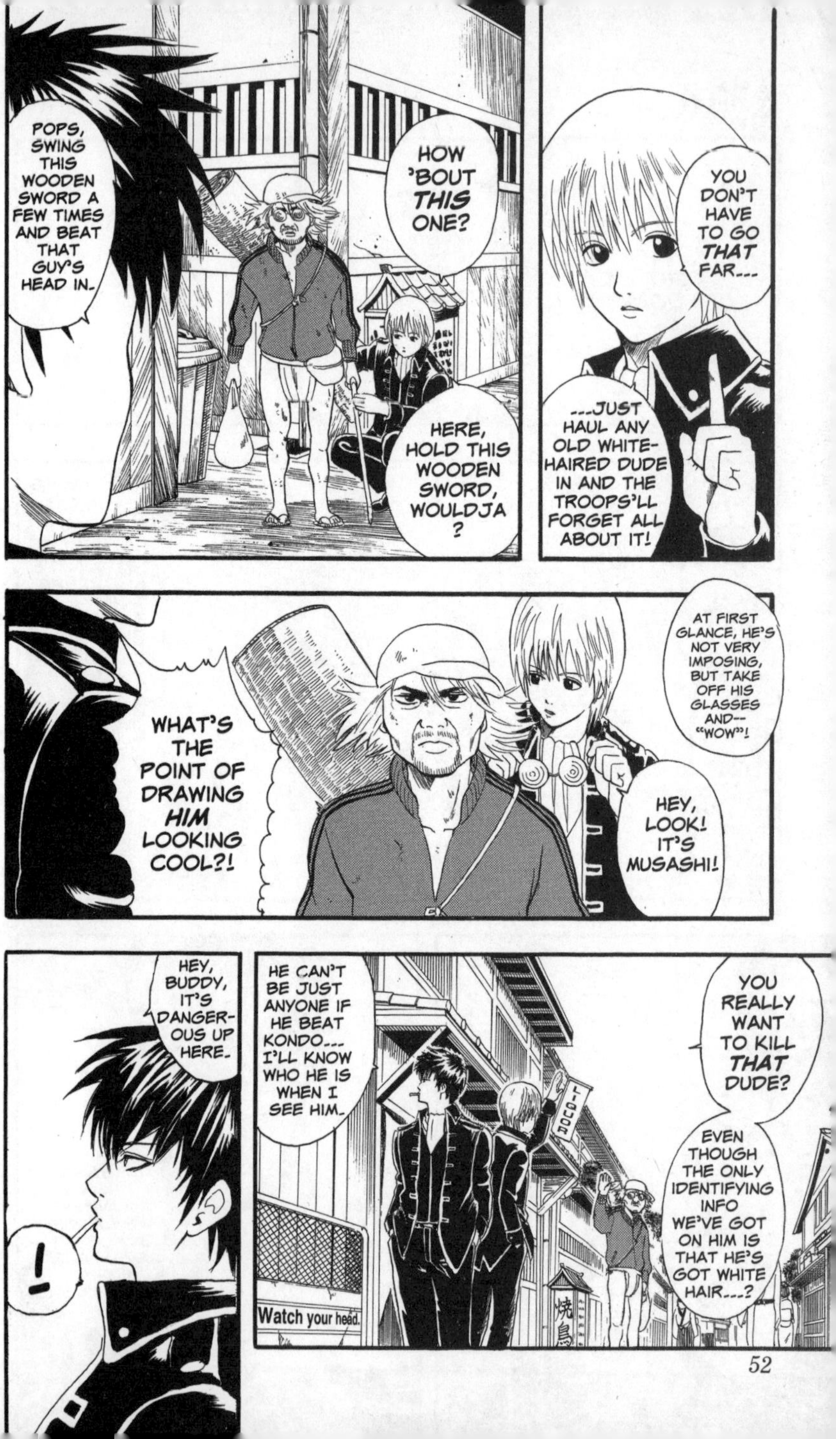
YOU DON'T HAVE TO GO *THAT* FAR...
...JUST HAUL ANY OLD WHITE-HAIRED DUDE IN AND THE TROOPS'LL FORGET ALL ABOUT IT!
HOW 'BOUT *THIS* ONE?
HERE, HOLD THIS WOODEN SWORD, WOULDJA?
POPS, SWING THIS WOODEN SWORD A FEW TIMES AND BEAT THAT GUY'S HEAD IN.
AT FIRST GLANCE, HE'S NOT VERY IMPOSING, BUT TAKE OFF HIS GLASSES AND-- "WOW"!
HEY, LOOK! IT'S MUSASHI!
WHAT'S THE POINT OF DRAWING *HIM* LOOKING COOL?!
YOU REALLY WANT TO KILL *THAT* DUDE?
EVEN THOUGH THE ONLY IDENTIFYING INFO WE'VE GOT ON HIM IS THAT HE'S GOT WHITE HAIR...?
HE CAN'T BE JUST ANYONE IF HE BEAT KONDO... I'LL KNOW WHO HE IS WHEN I SEE HIM.
LIQUOR
Watch your head.
HEY, BUDDY, IT'S DANGER-OUS UP HERE.
!

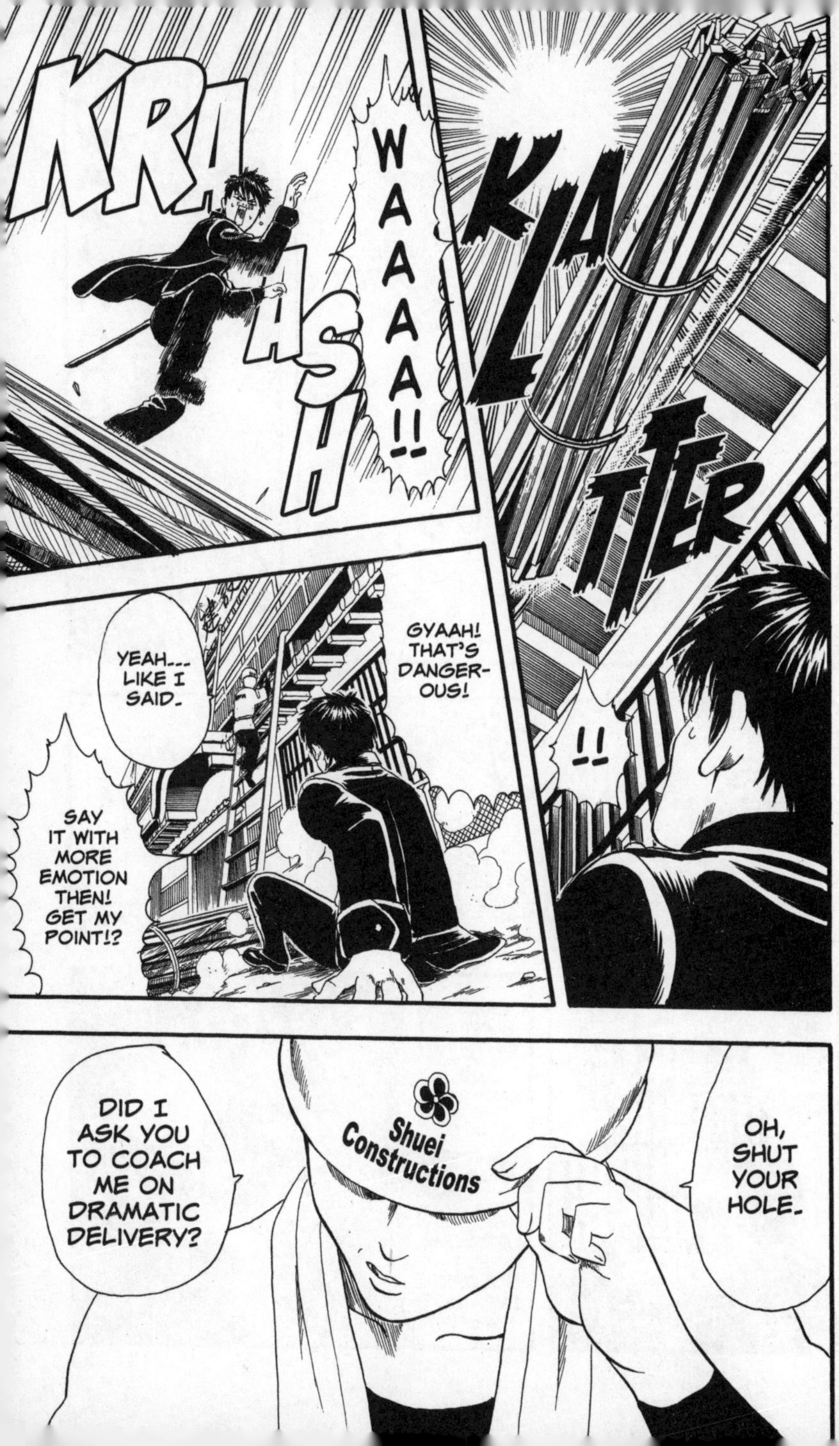

KLATTER
!!
KRASH
WAAAA!!
GYAAH! THAT'S DANGER-OUS!
YEAH... LIKE I SAID.
SAY IT WITH MORE EMOTION THEN! GET MY POINT!?
OH, SHUT YOUR HOLE.
Shuei Constructions
DID I ASK YOU TO COACH ME ON DRAMATIC DELIVERY?

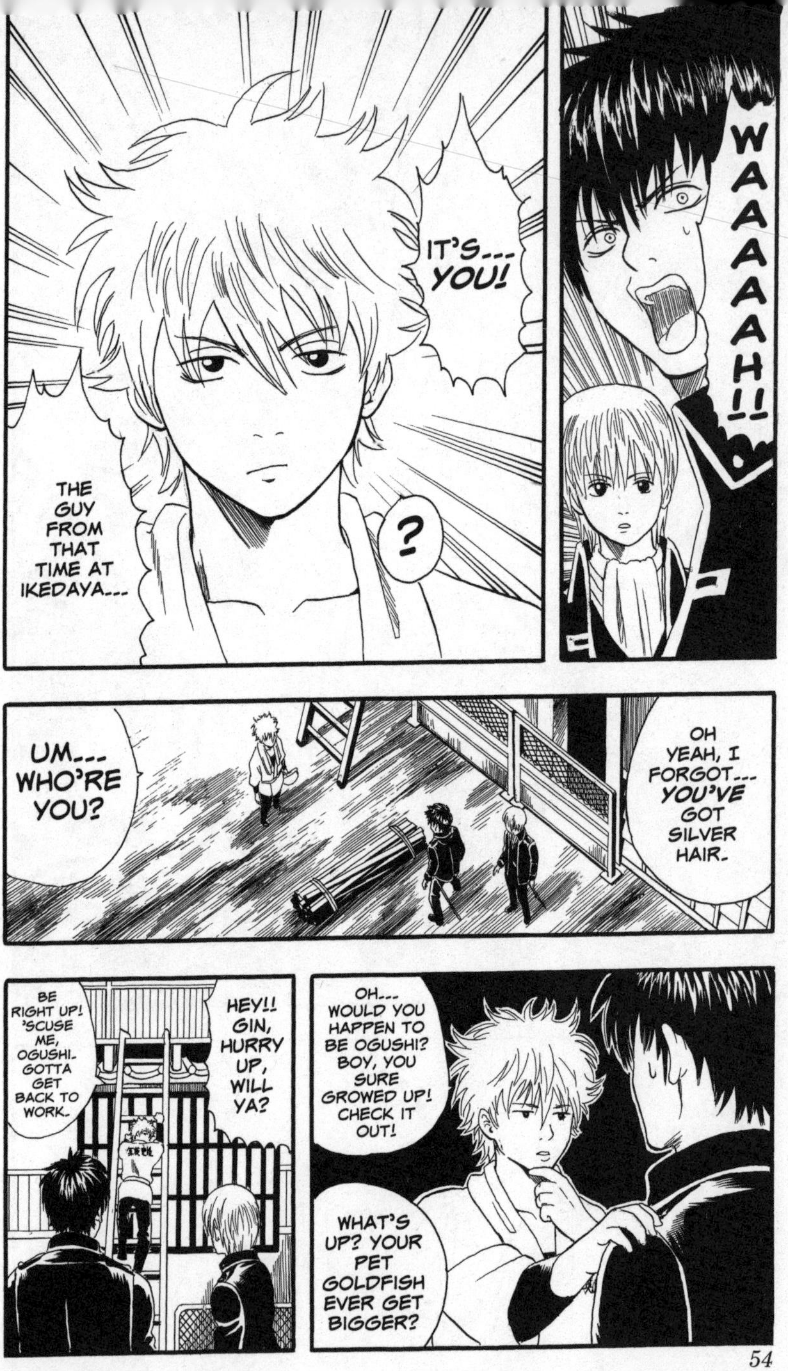
WAAAAAAH!!
IT'S... YOU!
?
THE GUY FROM THAT TIME AT IKEDAYA...
OH YEAH, I FORGOT... YOU'VE GOT SILVER HAIR.
UM... WHO'RE YOU?
OH... WOULD YOU HAPPEN TO BE OGUSHI? BOY, YOU SURE GROWED UP! CHECK IT OUT!
WHAT'S UP? YOUR PET GOLDFISH EVER GET BIGGER?
HEY!! GIN, HURRY UP, WILL YA?
BE RIGHT UP! 'SCUSE ME, OGUSHI. GOTTA GET BACK TO WORK.

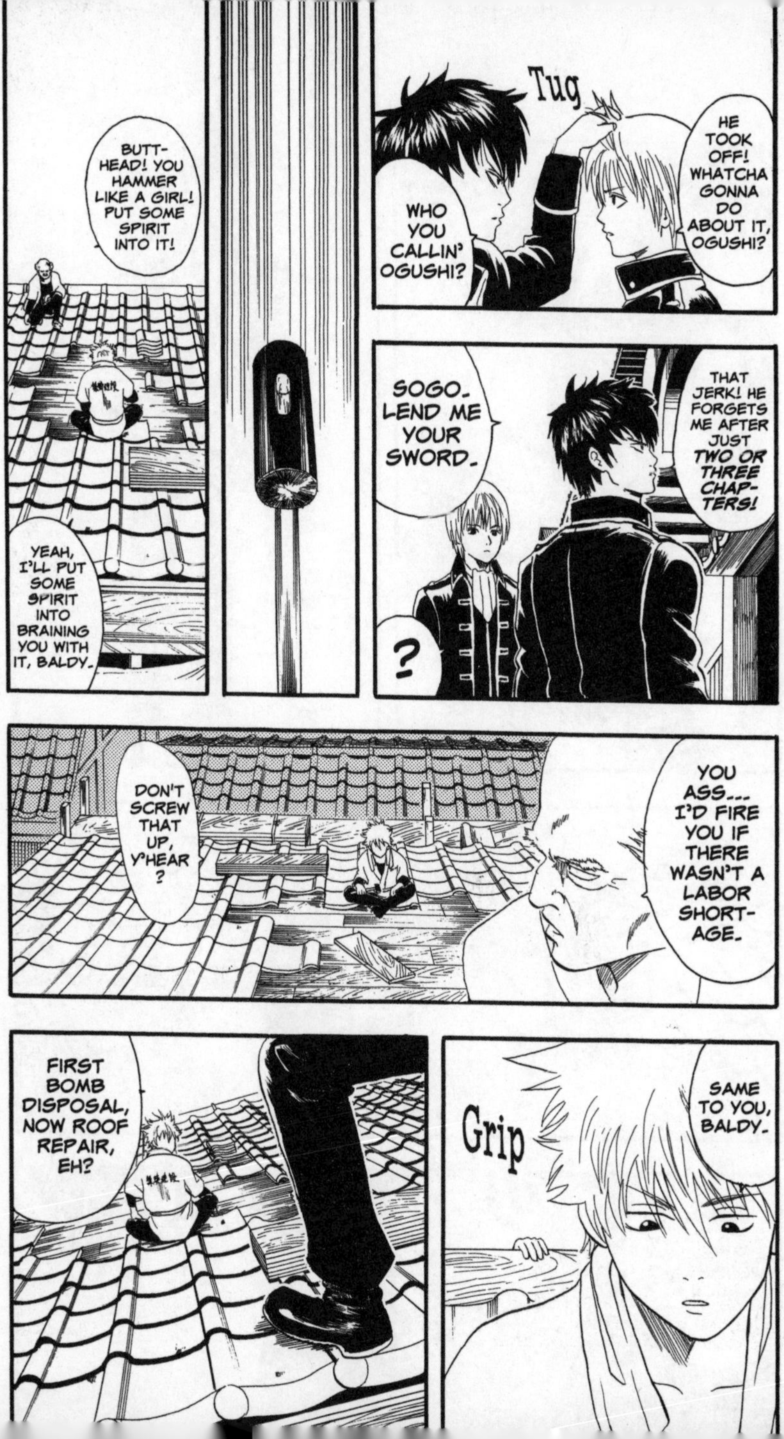
HE TOOK OFF! WHATCHA GONNA DO ABOUT IT, OGUSHI?
Tug
WHO YOU CALLIN' OGUSHI?
THAT JERK! HE FORGETS ME AFTER JUST TWO OR THREE CHAPTERS!
SOGO. LEND ME YOUR SWORD.
?
BUTT-HEAD! YOU HAMMER LIKE A GIRL! PUT SOME SPIRIT INTO IT!
YEAH, I'LL PUT SOME SPIRIT INTO BRAINING YOU WITH IT, BALDY.
YOU ASS... I'D FIRE YOU IF THERE WASN'T A LABOR SHORTAGE.
DON'T SCREW THAT UP, Y'HEAR?
SAME TO YOU, BALDY.
Grip
FIRST BOMB DISPOSAL, NOW ROOF REPAIR, EH?

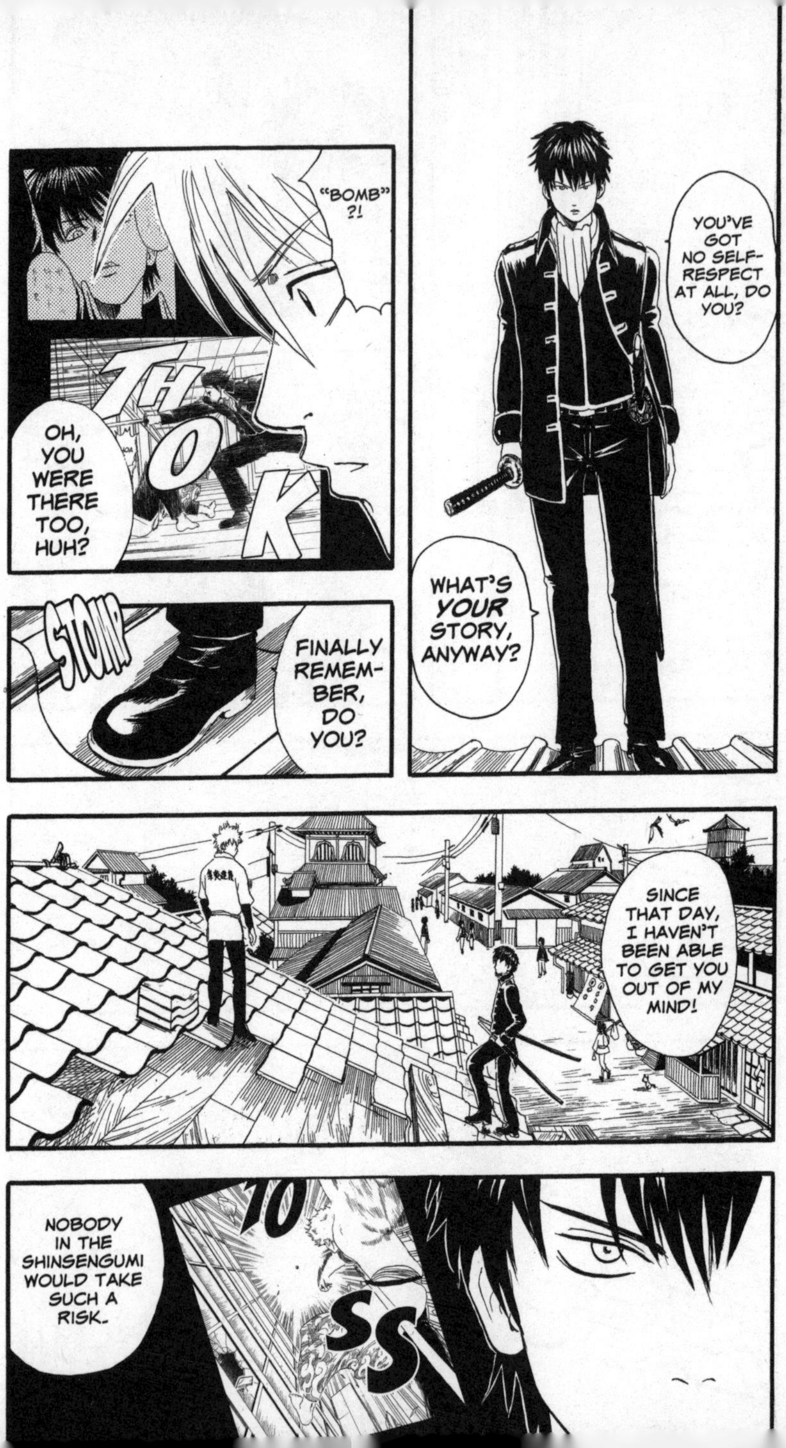
YOU'VE GOT NO SELF-RESPECT AT ALL, DO YOU?
WHAT'S YOUR STORY, ANYWAY?
"BOMB" ?!
THOK
OH, YOU WERE THERE TOO, HUH?
STOMP
FINALLY REMEMBER, DO YOU?
SINCE THAT DAY, I HAVEN'T BEEN ABLE TO GET YOU OUT OF MY MIND!
NOBODY IN THE SHINSENGUMI WOULD TAKE SUCH A RISK.
TOSS

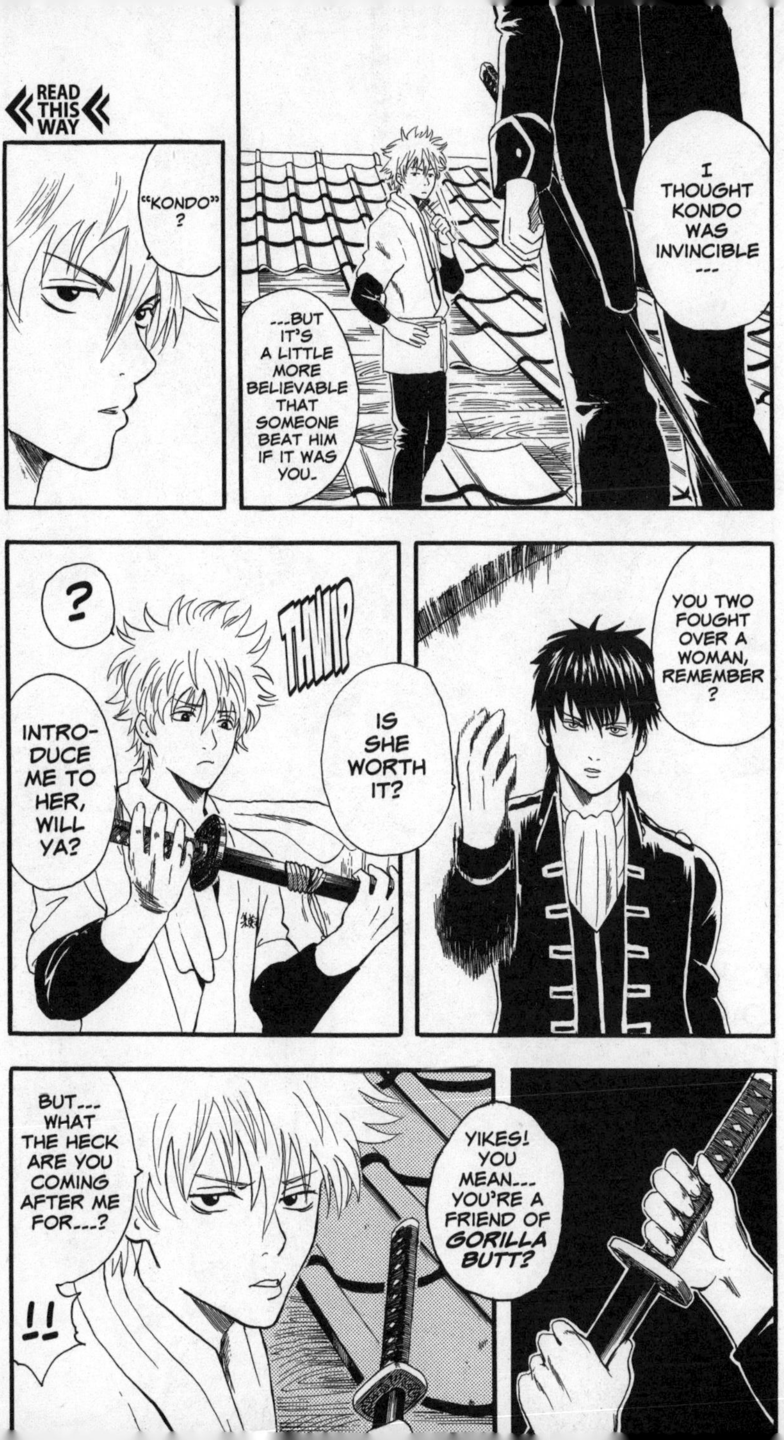

READ THIS WAY
I THOUGHT KONDO WAS INVINCIBLE ---
---BUT IT'S A LITTLE MORE BELIEVABLE THAT SOMEONE BEAT HIM IF IT WAS YOU.
“KONDO”?
YOU TWO FOUGHT OVER A WOMAN, REMEMBER?
THWIP
IS SHE WORTH IT?
?
INTRO-DUCE ME TO HER, WILL YA?
YIKES! YOU MEAN... YOU'RE A FRIEND OF *GORILLA BUTT*?
BUT... WHAT THE HECK ARE YOU COMING AFTER ME FOR...?
!!

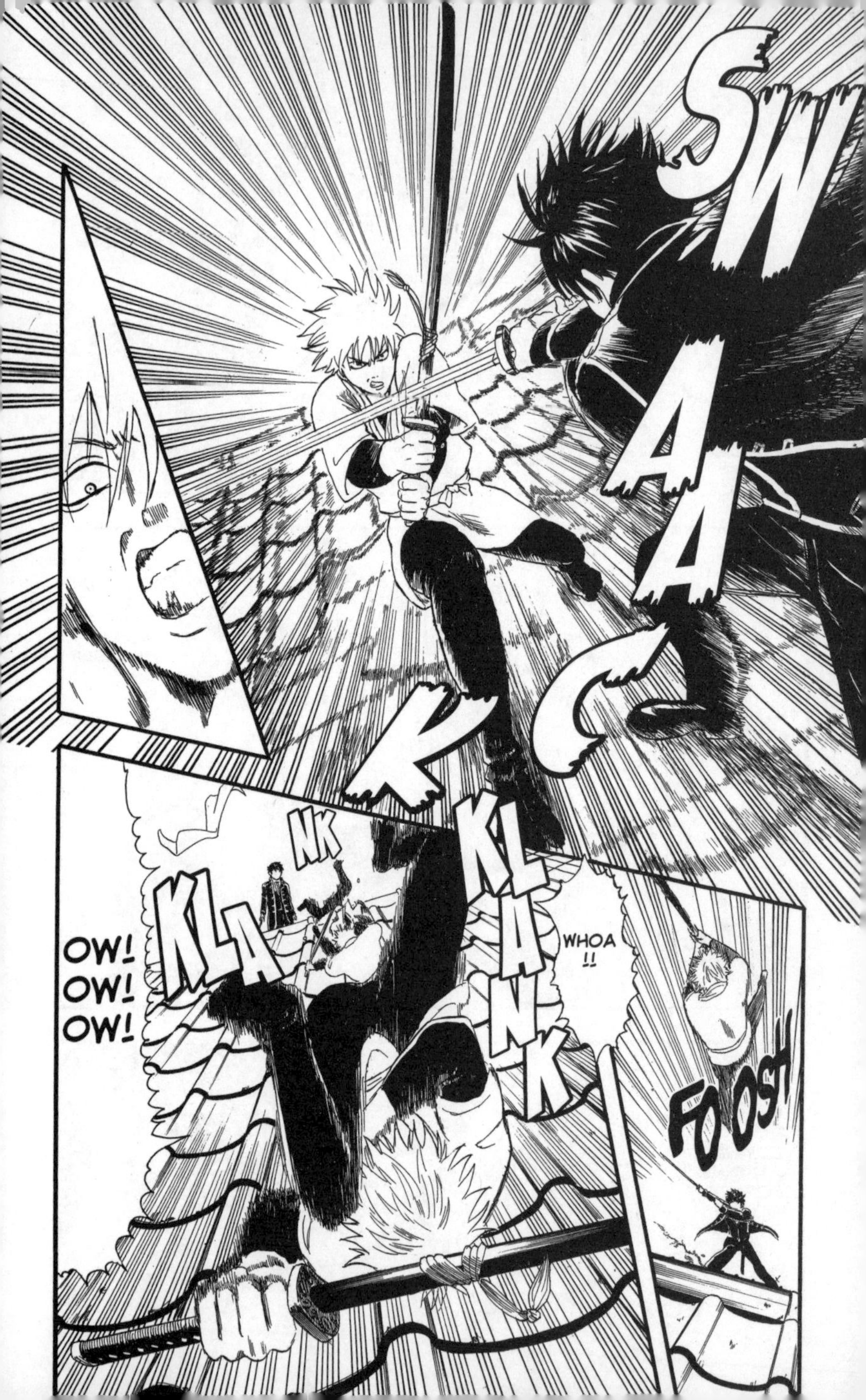
SWAACK
FOOSH
WHOA !!
KLANK
KLA
NK
OW! OW! OW!

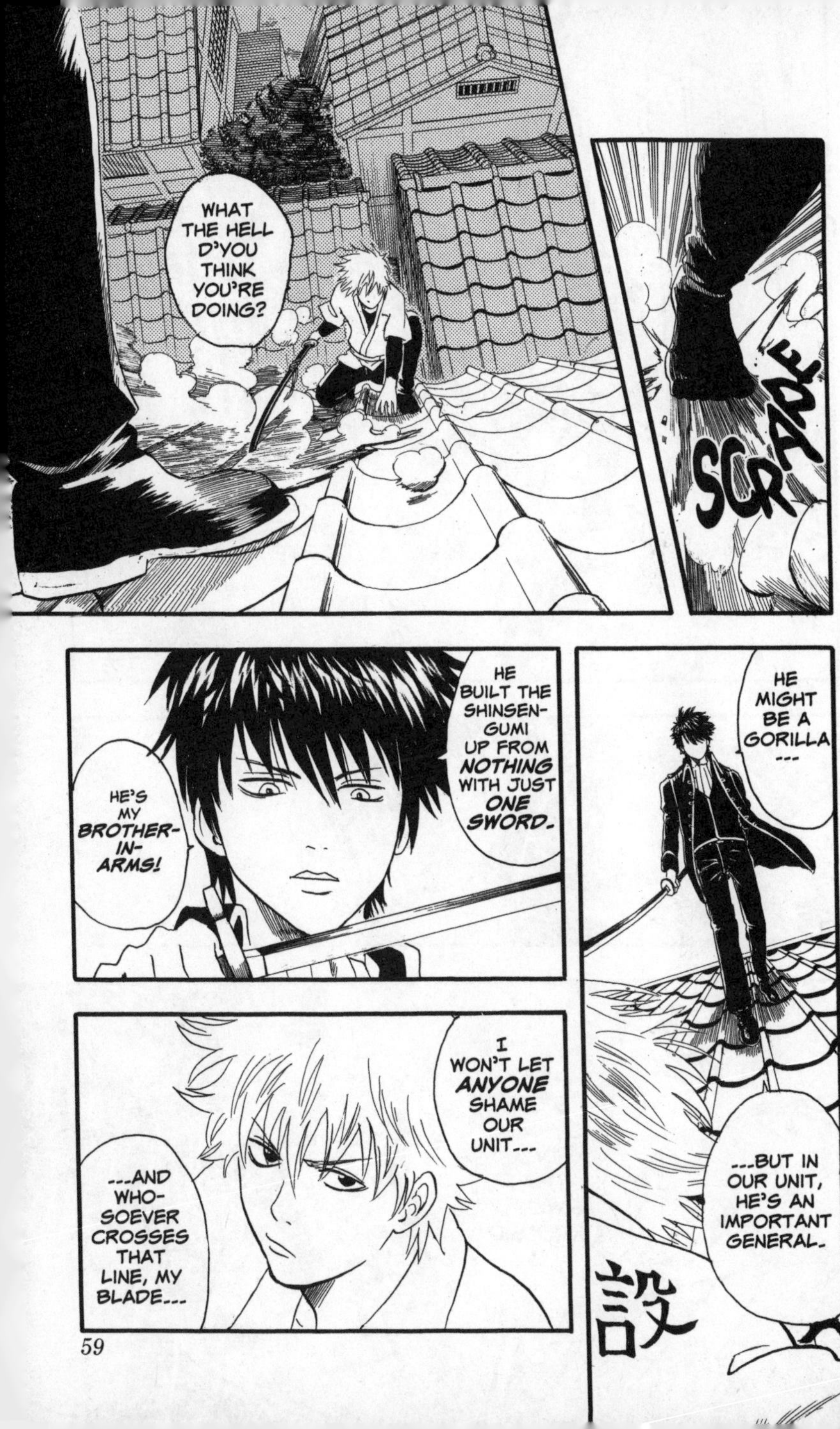
SCRAPE
WHAT THE HELL D'YOU THINK YOU'RE DOING?
HE MIGHT BE A GORILLA...
...BUT IN OUR UNIT, HE'S AN IMPORTANT GENERAL.
設
HE BUILT THE SHINSEN-GUMI UP FROM *NOTHING* WITH JUST *ONE SWORD*.
HE'S MY *BROTHER-IN-ARMS!*
I WON'T LET *ANYONE* SHAME OUR UNIT...
...AND WHO-SOEVER CROSSES THAT LINE, MY BLADE...

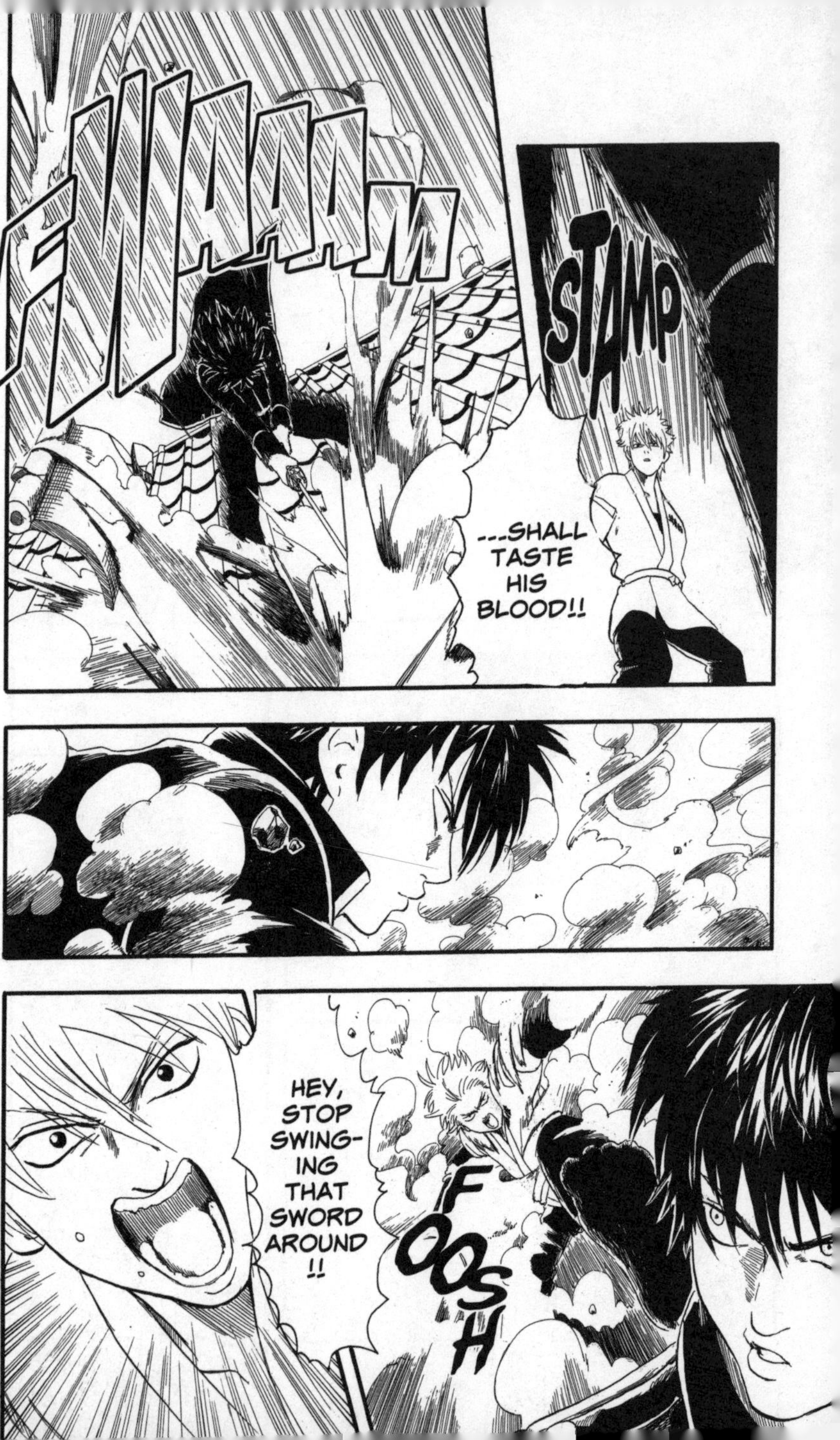
STAMP
---SHALL TASTE HIS BLOOD!!
FWAAAM
FOOSH
HEY, STOP SWING-ING THAT SWORD AROUND!!

READ THIS WAY

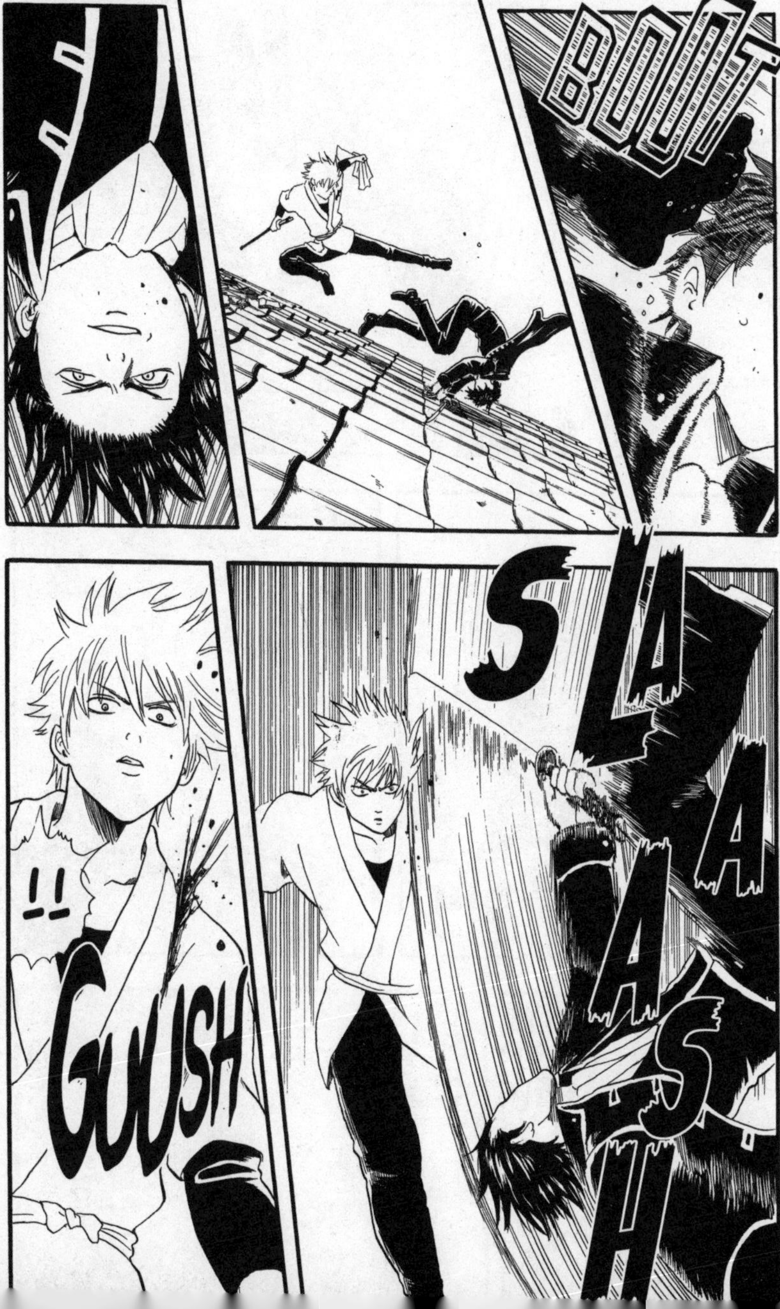
BOOOT
SLAAASH
!!
GUSH

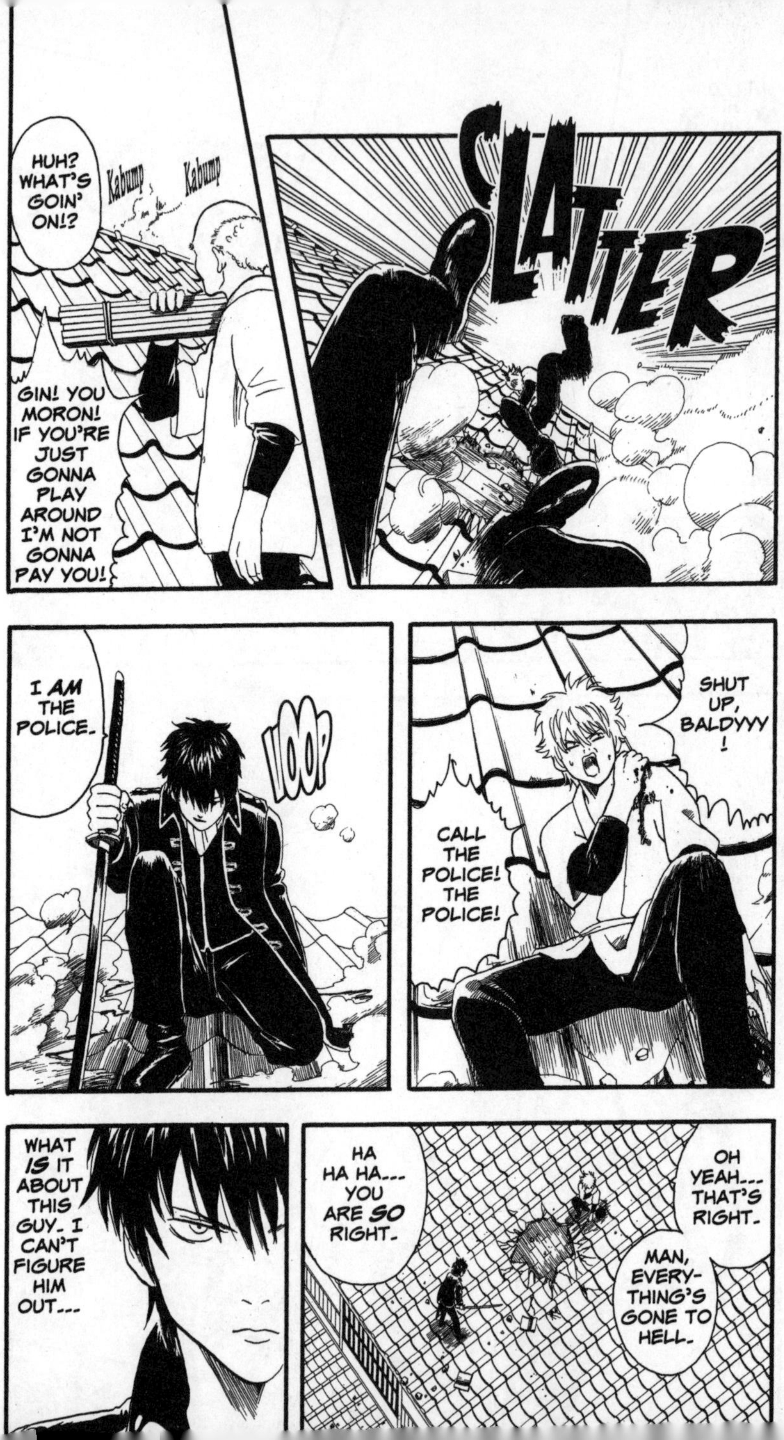
CLATTER
Kabump
Kabump
HUH? WHAT'S GOIN' ON!?
GIN! YOU MORON! IF YOU'RE JUST GONNA PLAY AROUND I'M NOT GONNA PAY YOU!
SHUT UP, BALDYYY!
CALL THE POLICE! THE POLICE!
VOOP
I *AM* THE POLICE.
OH YEAH... THAT'S RIGHT.
HA HA HA... YOU ARE *SO* RIGHT.
MAN, EVERYTHING'S GONE TO HELL.
WHAT *IS* IT ABOUT THIS GUY. I CAN'T FIGURE HIM OUT...

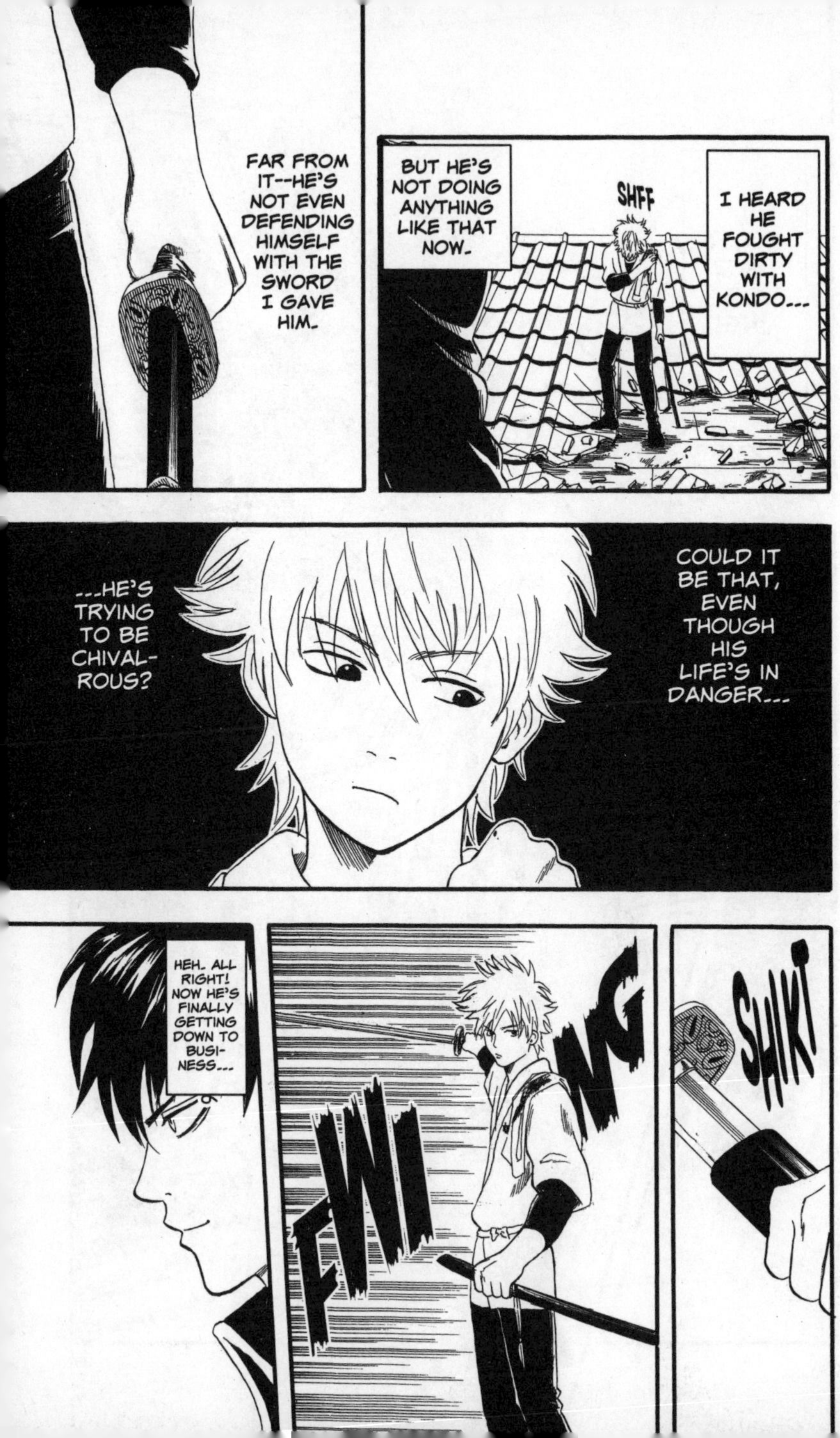
I HEARD HE FOUGHT DIRTY WITH KONDO...
SHFF
BUT HE'S NOT DOING ANYTHING LIKE THAT NOW.
FAR FROM IT--HE'S NOT EVEN DEFENDING HIMSELF WITH THE SWORD I GAVE HIM.
COULD IT BE THAT, EVEN THOUGH HIS LIFE'S IN DANGER...
...HE'S TRYING TO BE CHIVAL-ROUS?
SHIKI
FWING
HEH. ALL RIGHT! NOW HE'S FINALLY GETTING DOWN TO BUSI-NESS...

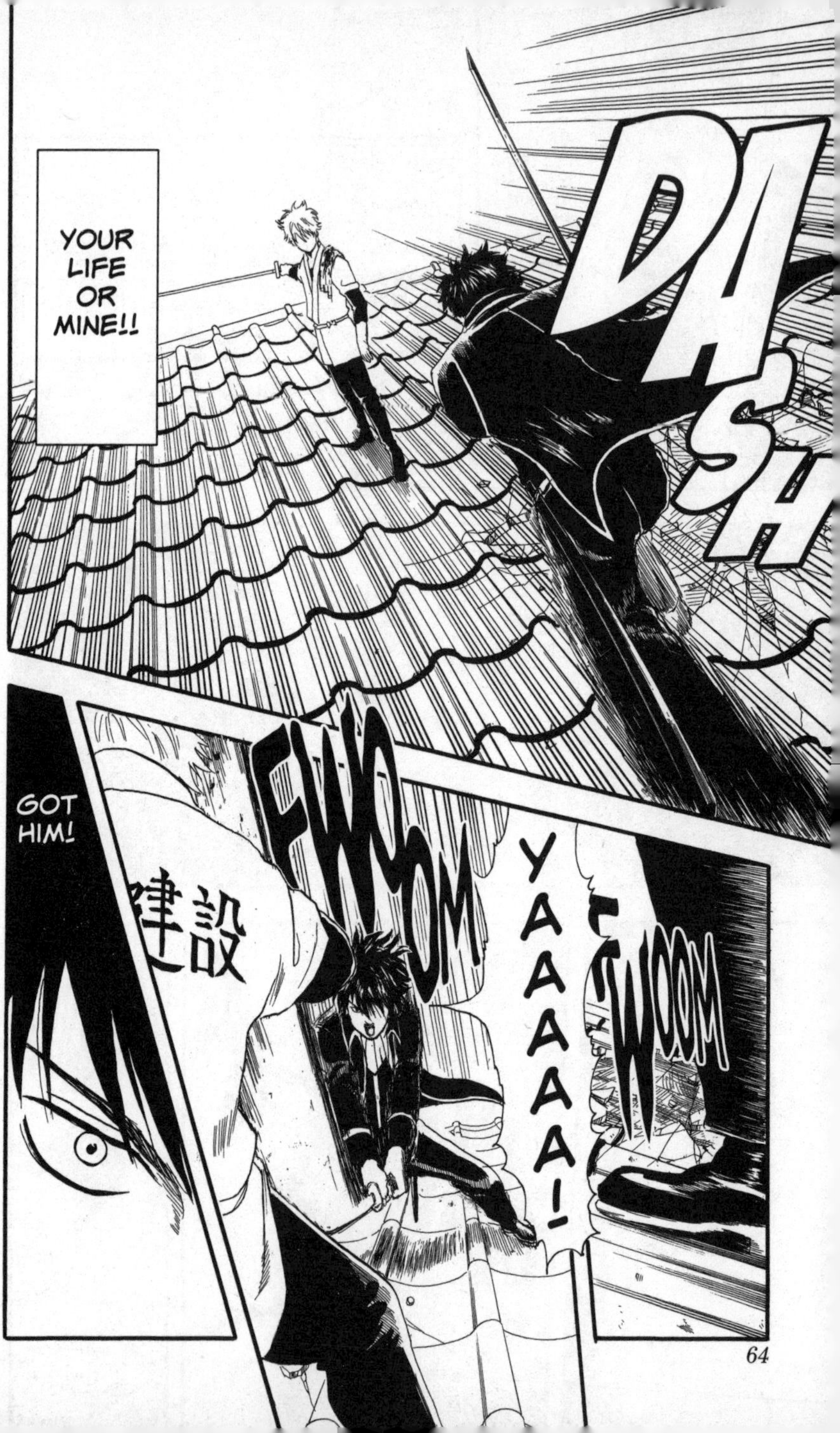
DASH
YOUR LIFE OR MINE!!
WOOM
YAAAAA!
FWOOM
建設
GOT HIM!

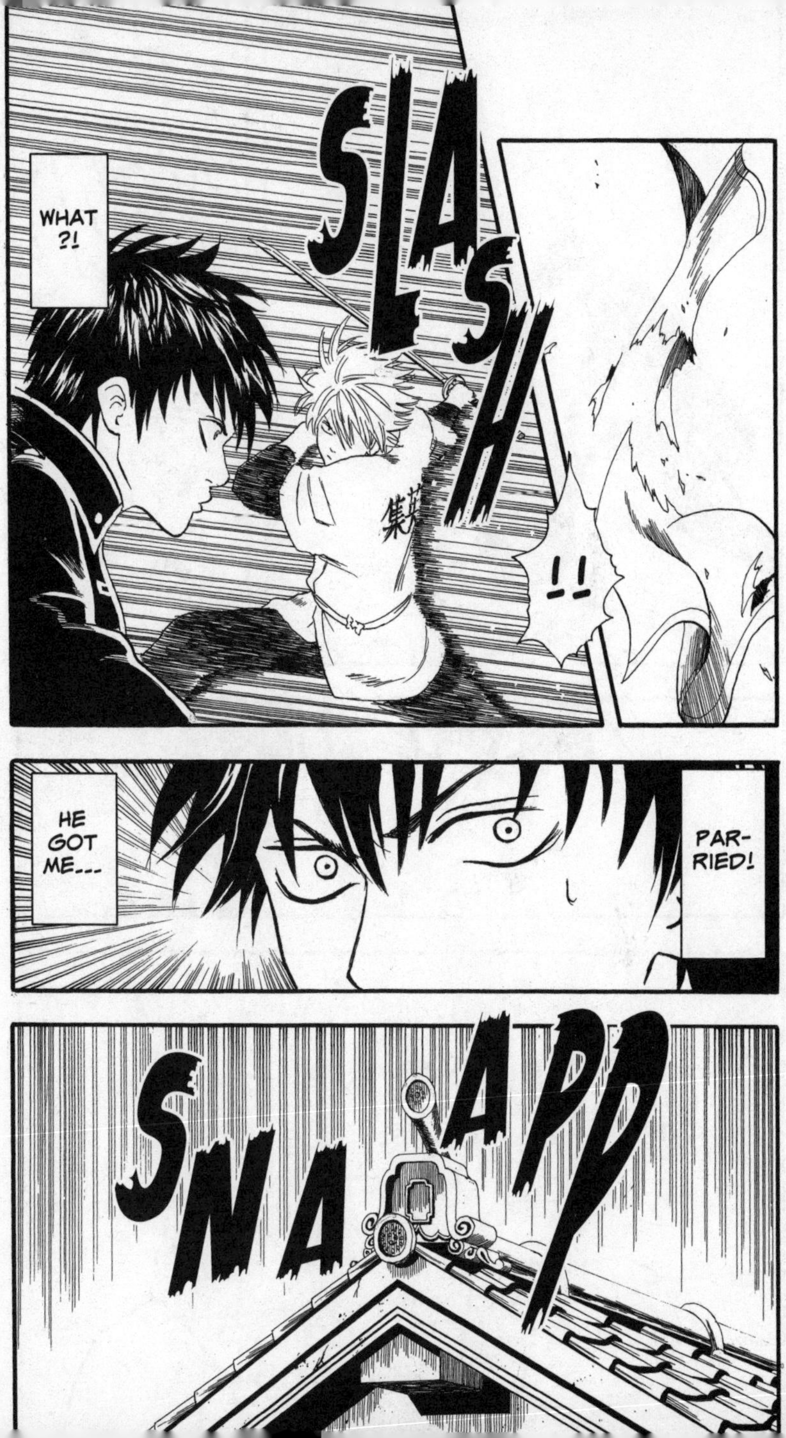
!!
SLASH
WHAT?!
PAR-RIED!
HE GOT ME...
SNAAPP

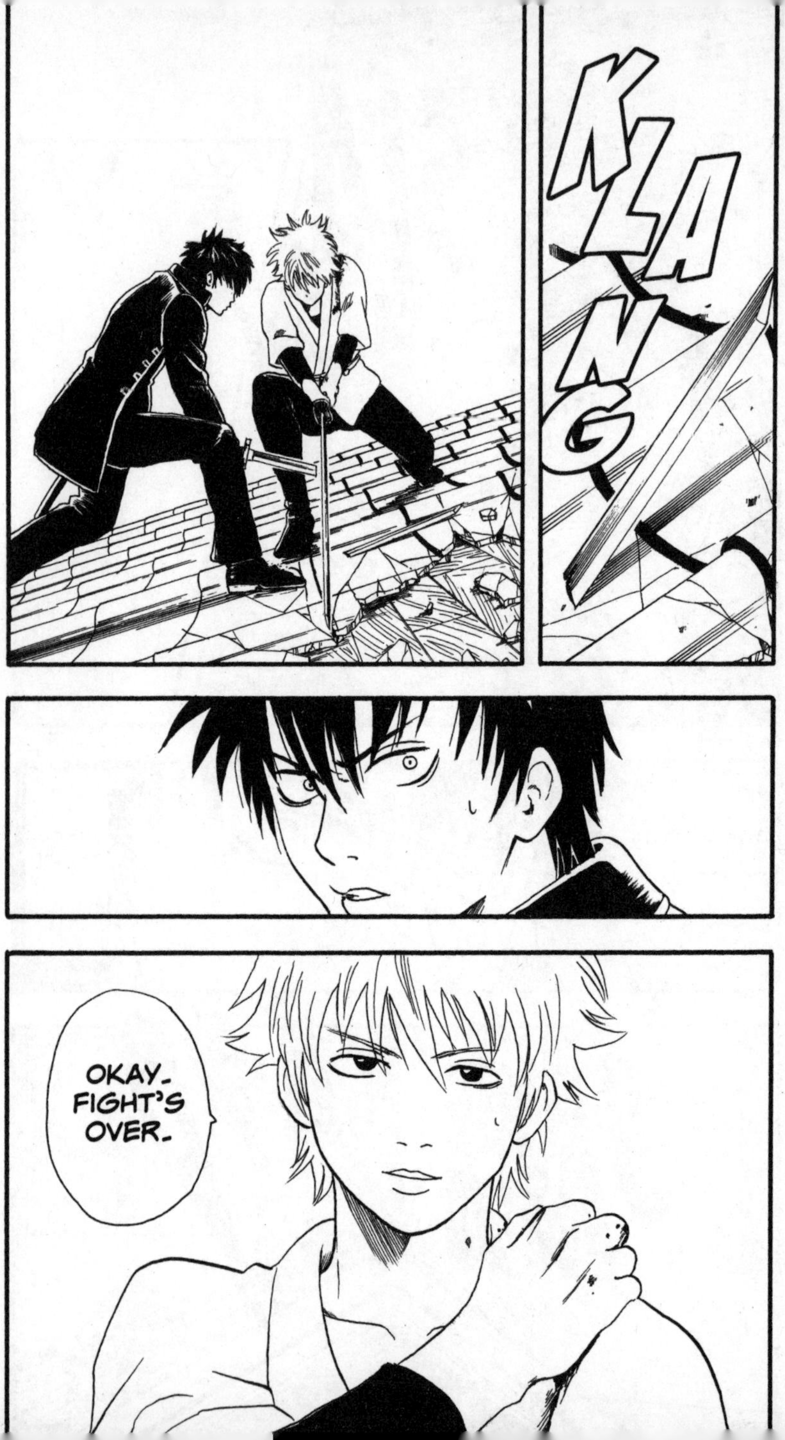
KLANG
OKAY... FIGHT'S OVER...

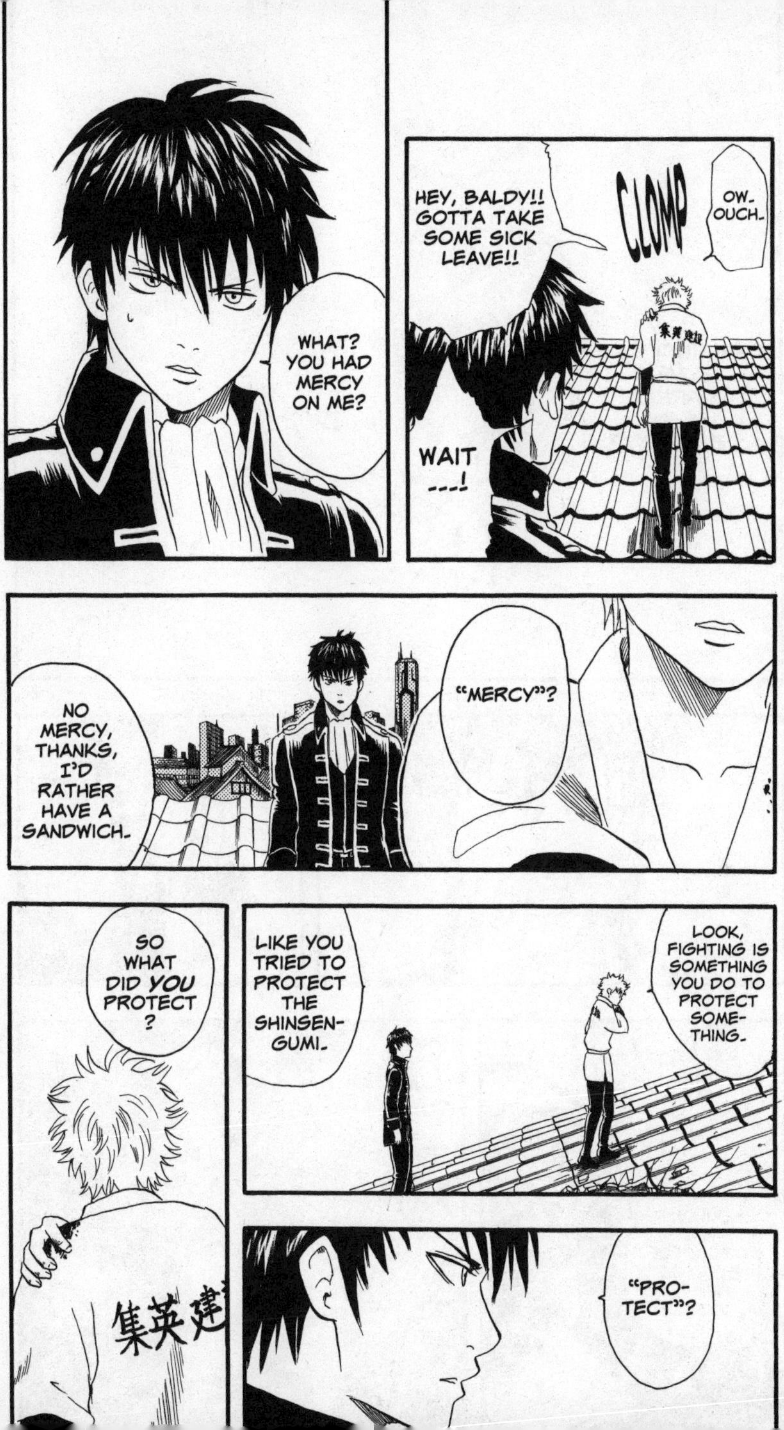
OW... OUCH...
CLOMP
HEY, BALDY!! GOTTA TAKE SOME SICK LEAVE!!
WAIT---!
WHAT? YOU HAD MERCY ON ME?
"MERCY"?
NO MERCY, THANKS, I'D RATHER HAVE A SANDWICH.
LOOK, FIGHTING IS SOMETHING YOU DO TO PROTECT SOME-THING.
LIKE YOU TRIED TO PROTECT THE SHINSEN-GUMI.
"PRO-TECT"?
SO WHAT DID *YOU* PROTECT?
集英建

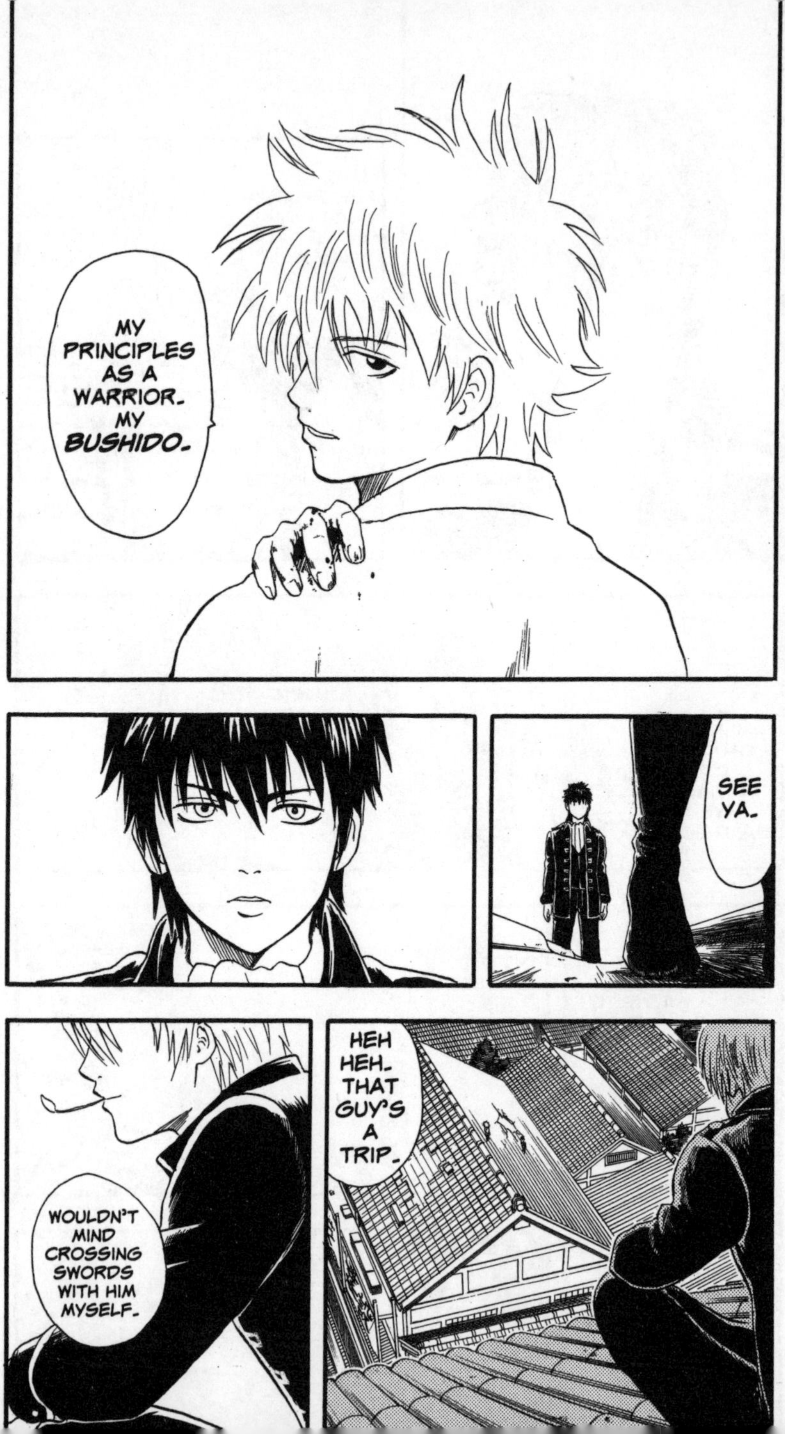
MY PRINCIPLES AS A WARRIOR... MY BUSHIDO...
SEE YA...
HEH HEH... THAT GUY'S A TRIP...
WOULDN'T MIND CROSSING SWORDS WITH HIM MYSELF...

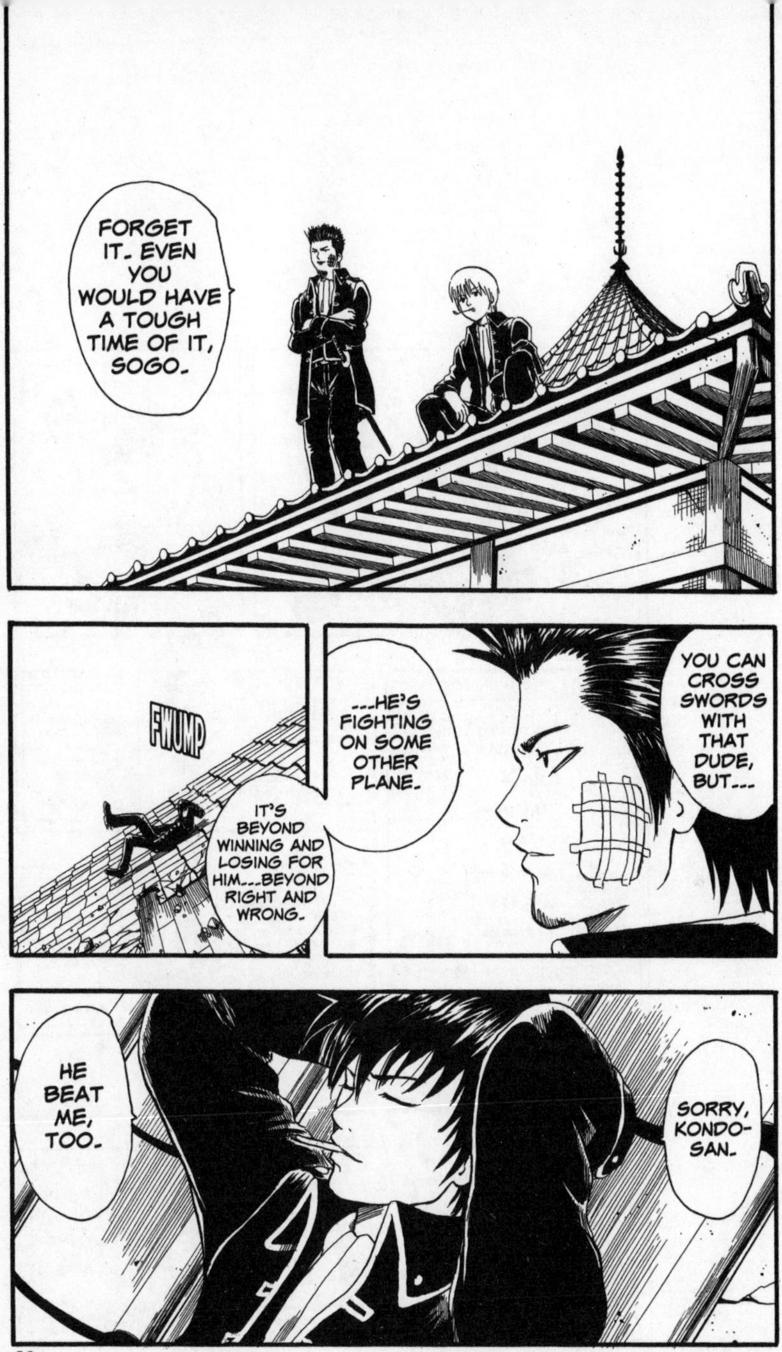
FORGET IT. EVEN YOU WOULD HAVE A TOUGH TIME OF IT, SOGO.
YOU CAN CROSS SWORDS WITH THAT DUDE, BUT...
...HE'S FIGHTING ON SOME OTHER PLANE.
IT'S BEYOND WINNING AND LOSING FOR HIM...BEYOND RIGHT AND WRONG.
FWUMP
SORRY, KONDO-SAN.
HE BEAT ME, TOO.

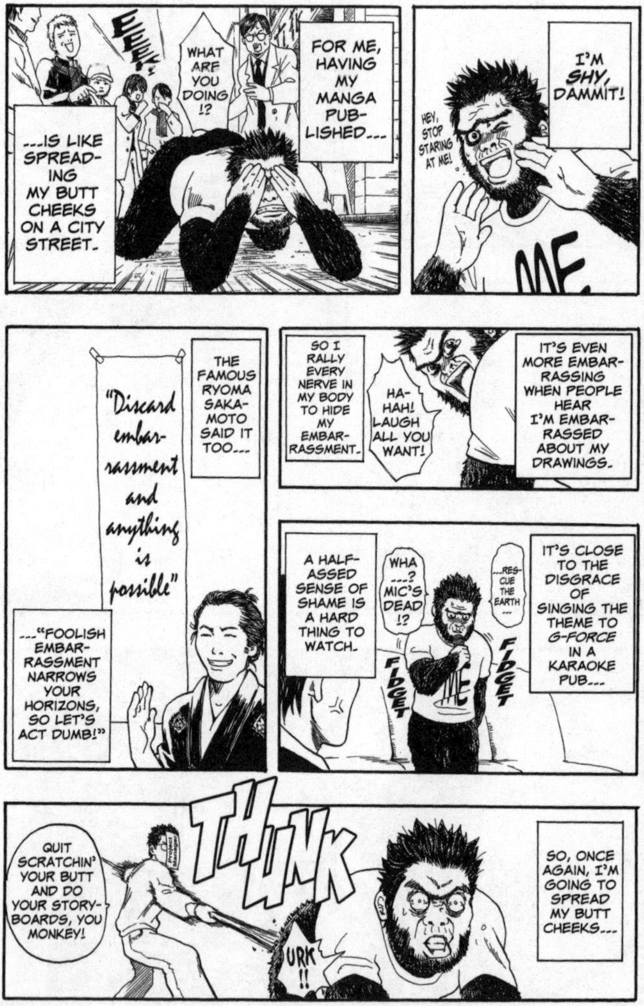
I'M SHY, DAMMIT!
HEY, STOP STARING AT ME!
FOR ME, HAVING MY MANGA PUB-LISHED...
WHAT ARE YOU DOING!?
EEEK!
...IS LIKE SPREAD-ING MY BUTT CHEEKS ON A CITY STREET.
IT'S EVEN MORE EMBAR-RASSING WHEN PEOPLE HEAR I'M EMBAR-RASSED ABOUT MY DRAWINGS.
HA-HAH! LAUGH ALL YOU WANT!
SO I RALLY EVERY NERVE IN MY BODY TO HIDE MY EMBAR-RASSMENT.
IT'S CLOSE TO THE DISGRACE OF SINGING THE THEME TO G-FORCE IN A KARAOKE PUB...
...RES-CUE THE EARTH...
FIDGET
FIDGET
WHA...? MIC'S DEAD!?
A HALF-ASSED SENSE OF SHAME IS A HARD THING TO WATCH.
THE FAMOUS RYOMA SAKA-MOTO SAID IT TOO...
"Discard embar-rassment and anything is possible"
..."FOOLISH EMBAR-RASSMENT NARROWS YOUR HORIZONS, SO LET'S ACT DUMB!"
SO, ONCE AGAIN, I'M GOING TO SPREAD MY BUTT CHEEKS...
THUNK
URK!!
Project Manager
QUIT SCRATCHIN' YOUR BUTT AND DO YOUR STORY-BOARDS, YOU MONKEY!

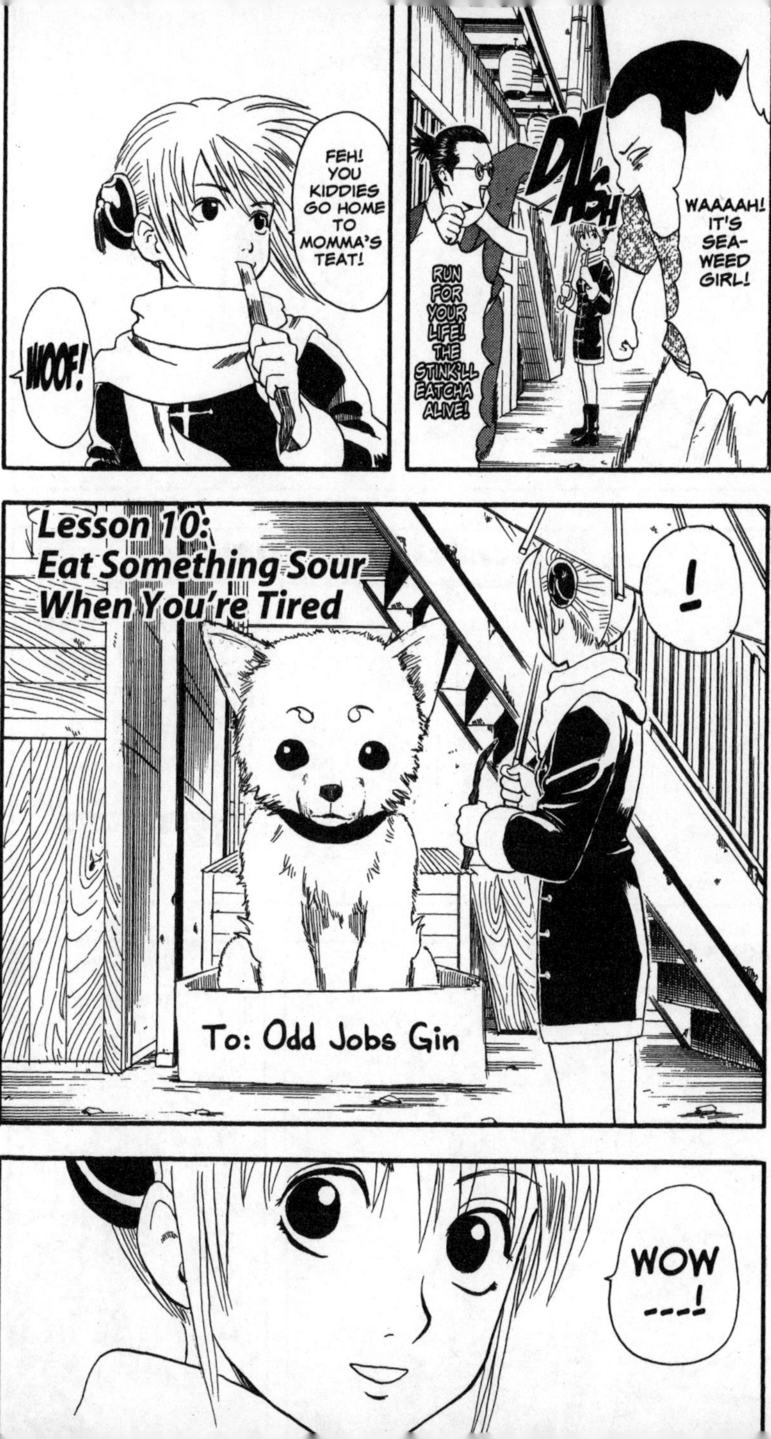
WAAAAH! IT'S SEA-WEED GIRL!
DASH
RUN FOR YOUR LIFE! THE STINK'LL EATCHA ALIVE!
FEH! YOU KIDDIES GO HOME TO MOMMA'S TEAT!
WOOF!
Lesson 10: Eat Something Sour When You're Tired
!
To: Odd Jobs Gin
WOW ---!

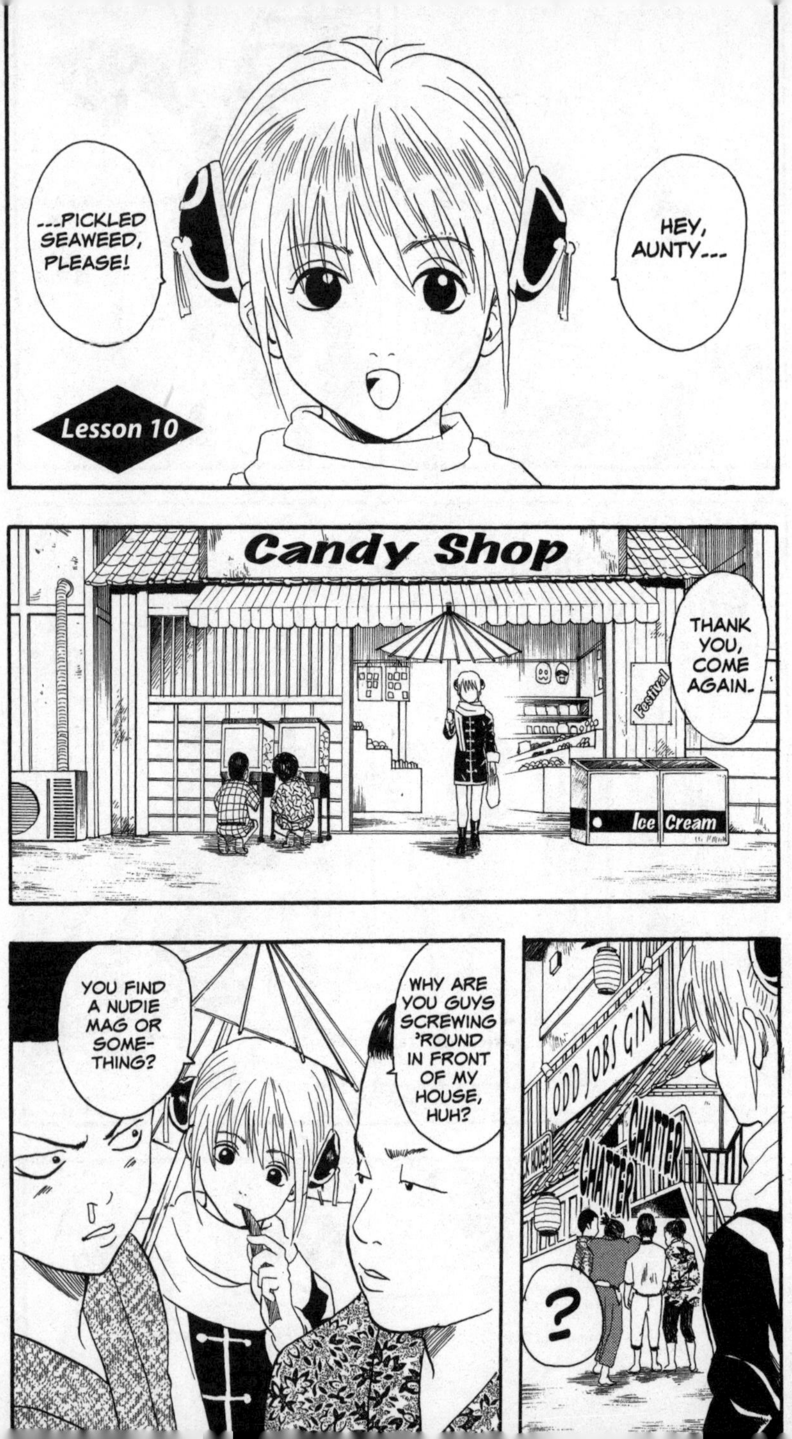
HEY, AUNTY...
...PICKLED SEAWEED, PLEASE!
Lesson 10
Candy Shop
THANK YOU, COME AGAIN.
Festival
Ice Cream
ODD JOBS GIN
CHATTER
CHATTER
?
WHY ARE YOU GUYS SCREWING 'ROUND IN FRONT OF MY HOUSE, HUH?
YOU FIND A NUDIE MAG OR SOME-THING?

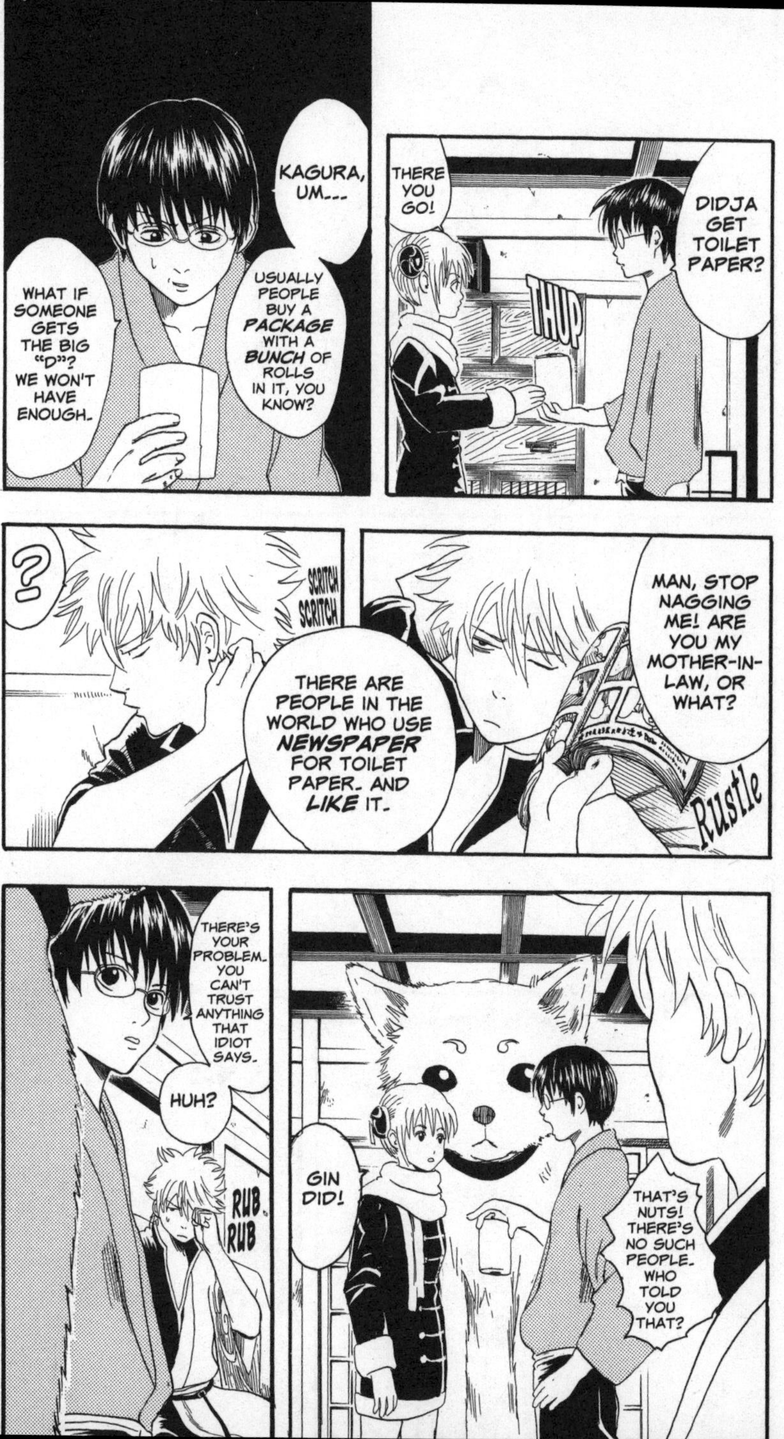
DIDJA GET TOILET PAPER?
THERE YOU GO!
THUP
KAGURA, UM...
USUALLY PEOPLE BUY A PACKAGE WITH A BUNCH OF ROLLS IN IT, YOU KNOW?
WHAT IF SOMEONE GETS THE BIG "D"? WE WON'T HAVE ENOUGH.
MAN, STOP NAGGING ME! ARE YOU MY MOTHER-IN-LAW, OR WHAT?
THERE ARE PEOPLE IN THE WORLD WHO USE NEWSPAPER FOR TOILET PAPER. AND LIKE IT.
Rustle
SCRITCH SCRITCH
?
THAT'S NUTS! THERE'S NO SUCH PEOPLE. WHO TOLD YOU THAT?
GIN DID!
THERE'S YOUR PROBLEM. YOU CAN'T TRUST ANYTHING THAT IDIOT SAYS.
HUH?
RUB RUB

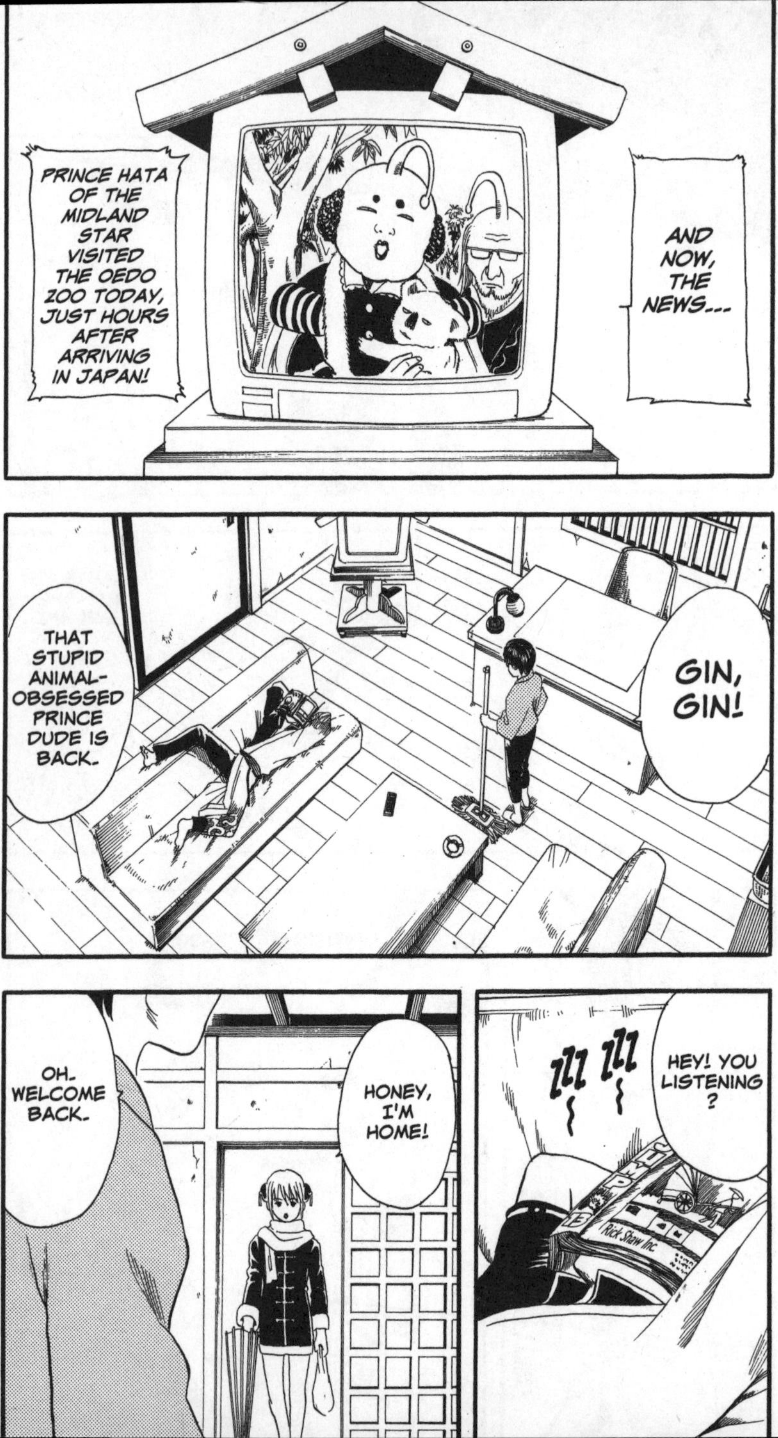
AND NOW, THE NEWS...
PRINCE HATA OF THE MIDLAND STAR VISITED THE OEDO ZOO TODAY, JUST HOURS AFTER ARRIVING IN JAPAN!
GIN, GIN!
THAT STUPID ANIMAL-OBSESSED PRINCE DUDE IS BACK.
HEY! YOU LISTENING?
ZZZ ZZZ
Rick Shaw Inc.
HONEY, I'M HOME!
OH. WELCOME BACK.

READ THIS WAY

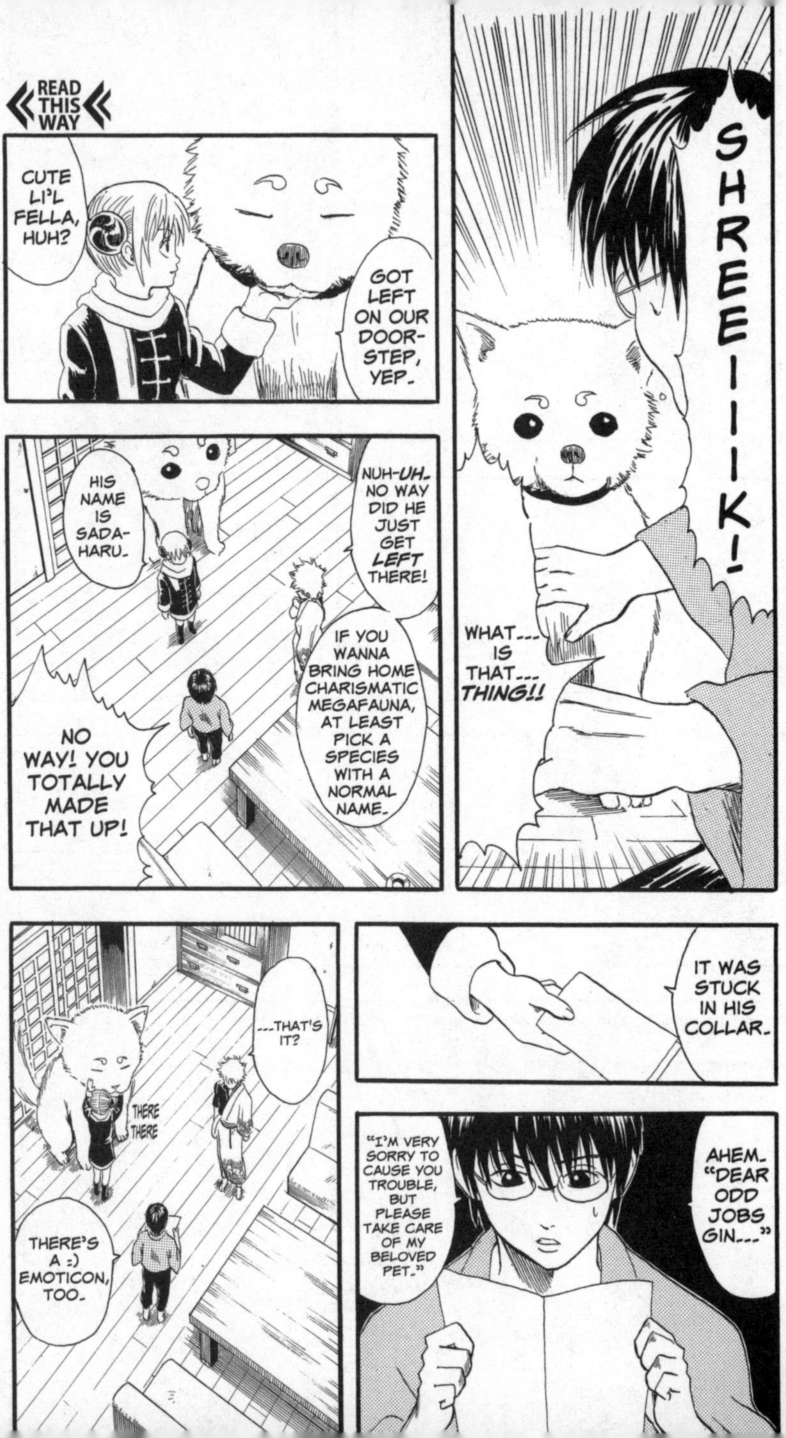
SHREEIIIK!
WHAT... IS THAT... THING!!
CUTE LI'L FELLA, HUH?
GOT LEFT ON OUR DOOR-STEP, YEP.
NUH-UH. NO WAY DID HE JUST GET LEFT THERE!
IF YOU WANNA BRING HOME CHARISMATIC MEGAFAUNA, AT LEAST PICK A SPECIES WITH A NORMAL NAME.
HIS NAME IS SADA-HARU.
NO WAY! YOU TOTALLY MADE THAT UP!
IT WAS STUCK IN HIS COLLAR.
AHEM. "DEAR ODD JOBS GIN..."
"I'M VERY SORRY TO CAUSE YOU TROUBLE, BUT PLEASE TAKE CARE OF MY BELOVED PET."
...THAT'S IT?
THERE THERE
THERE'S A :) EMOTICON, TOO.

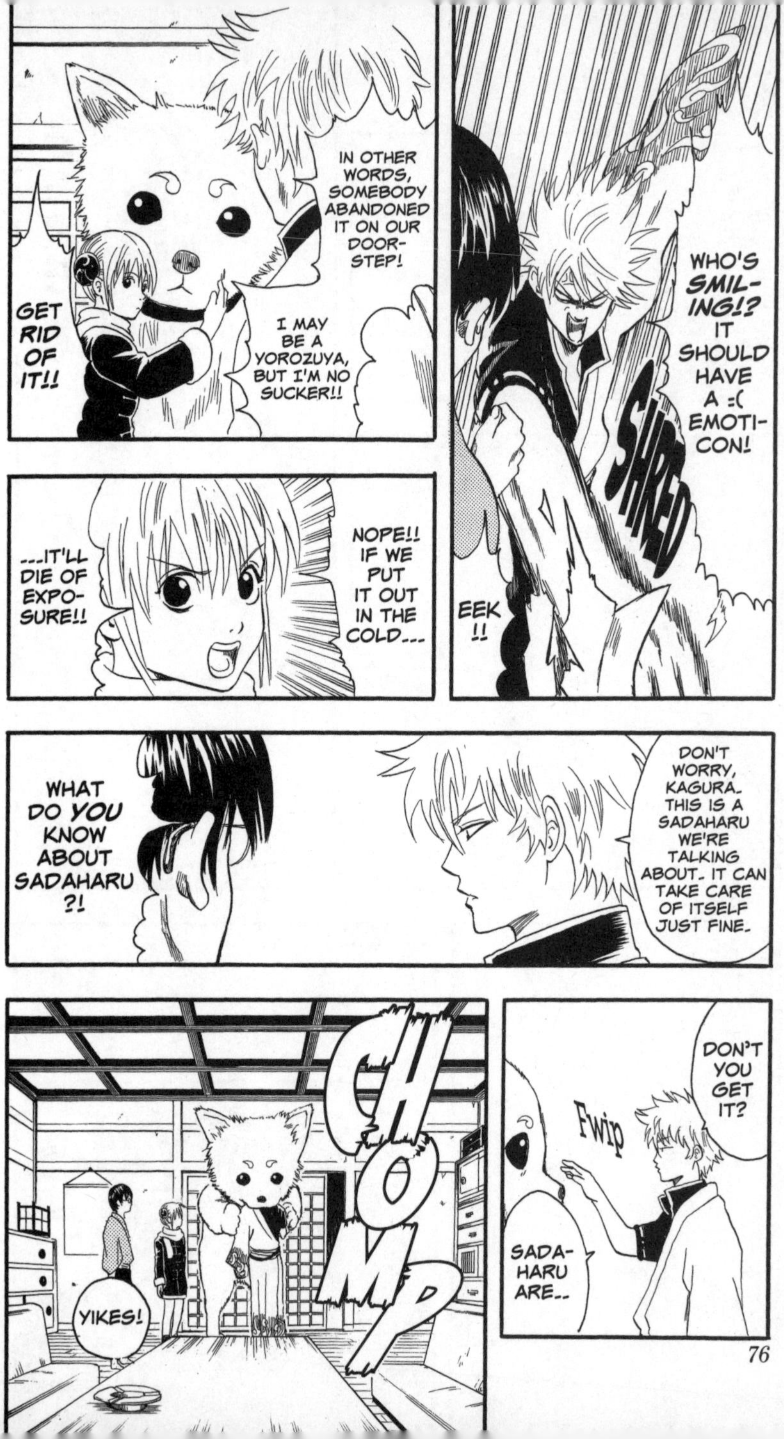
WHO'S SMILING!? IT SHOULD HAVE A :(EMOTICON!
SHRED
EEK!!
IN OTHER WORDS, SOMEBODY ABANDONED IT ON OUR DOORSTEP!
I MAY BE A YOROZUYA, BUT I'M NO SUCKER!!
GET RID OF IT!!
NOPE!! IF WE PUT IT OUT IN THE COLD...
...IT'LL DIE OF EXPOSURE!!
DON'T WORRY, KAGURA. THIS IS A SADAHARU WE'RE TALKING ABOUT. IT CAN TAKE CARE OF ITSELF JUST FINE.
WHAT DO YOU KNOW ABOUT SADAHARU?!
DON'T YOU GET IT?
Fwip
SADAHARU ARE...
CHOMP
YIKES!

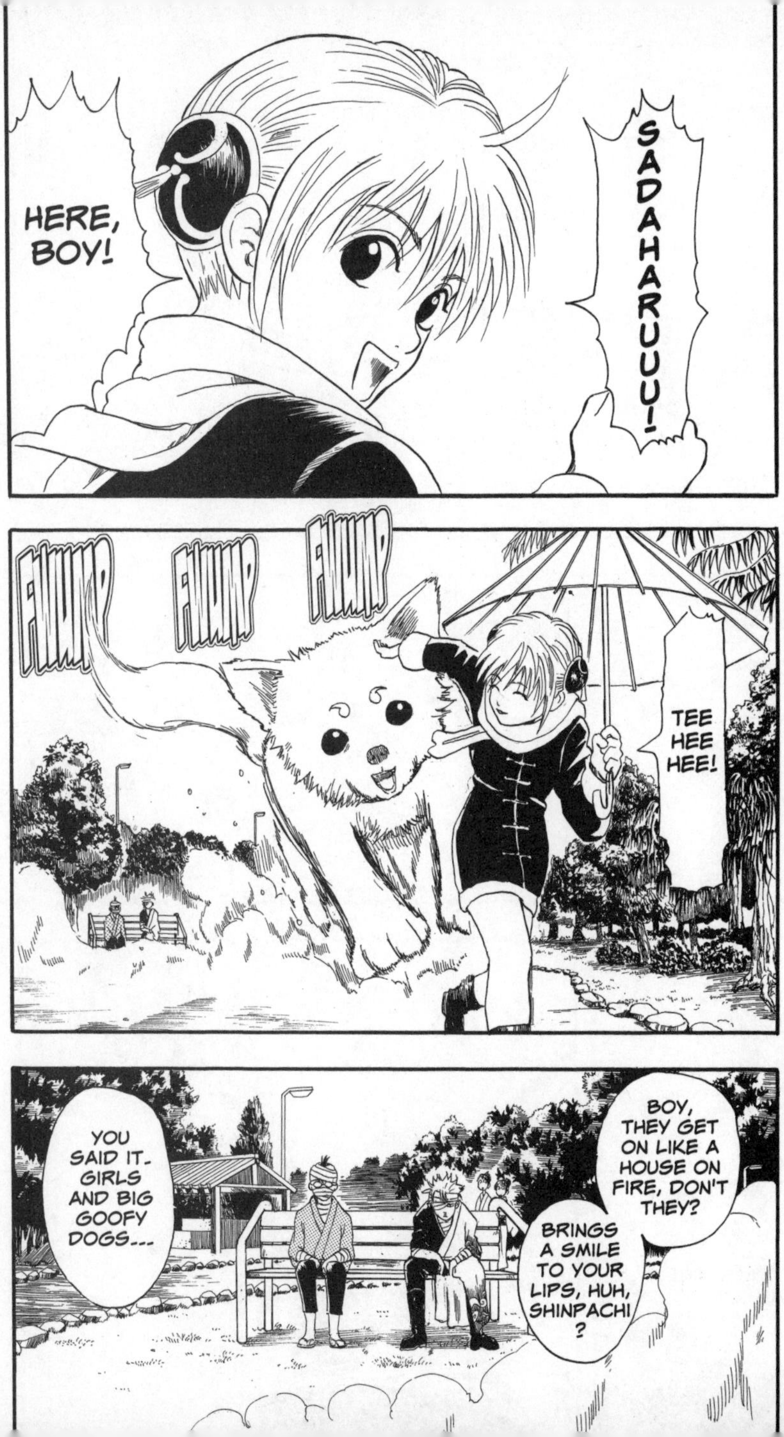
SADAHARUUU!
HERE, BOY!
FWUMP
FWUMP
FWUMP
TEE HEE HEE!
BOY, THEY GET ON LIKE A HOUSE ON FIRE, DON'T THEY?
BRINGS A SMILE TO YOUR LIPS, HUH, SHINPACHI?
YOU SAID IT. GIRLS AND BIG GOOFY DOGS...

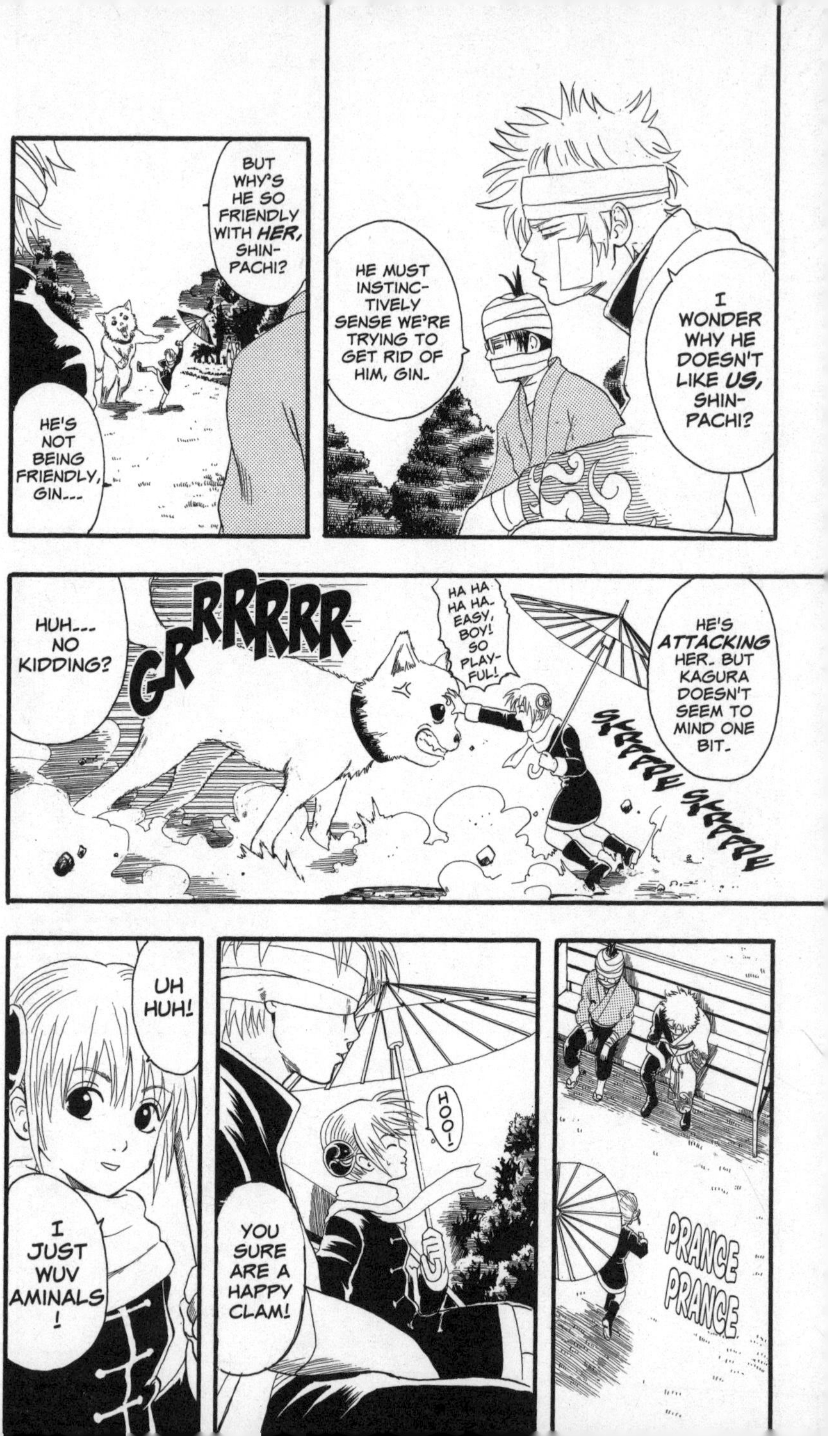
I WONDER WHY HE DOESN'T LIKE US, SHINPACHI?
HE MUST INSTINCTIVELY SENSE WE'RE TRYING TO GET RID OF HIM, GIN.
BUT WHY'S HE SO FRIENDLY WITH HER, SHINPACHI?
HE'S NOT BEING FRIENDLY, GIN...
HE'S ATTACKING HER. BUT KAGURA DOESN'T SEEM TO MIND ONE BIT.
SKRAPPE SKRAPPE
HA HA HA HA. EASY, BOY! SO PLAYFUL!
GRRRRRRR
HUH... NO KIDDING?
PRANCE PRANCE
HOO!
YOU SURE ARE A HAPPY CLAM!
UH HUH!
I JUST WUV AMINALS!

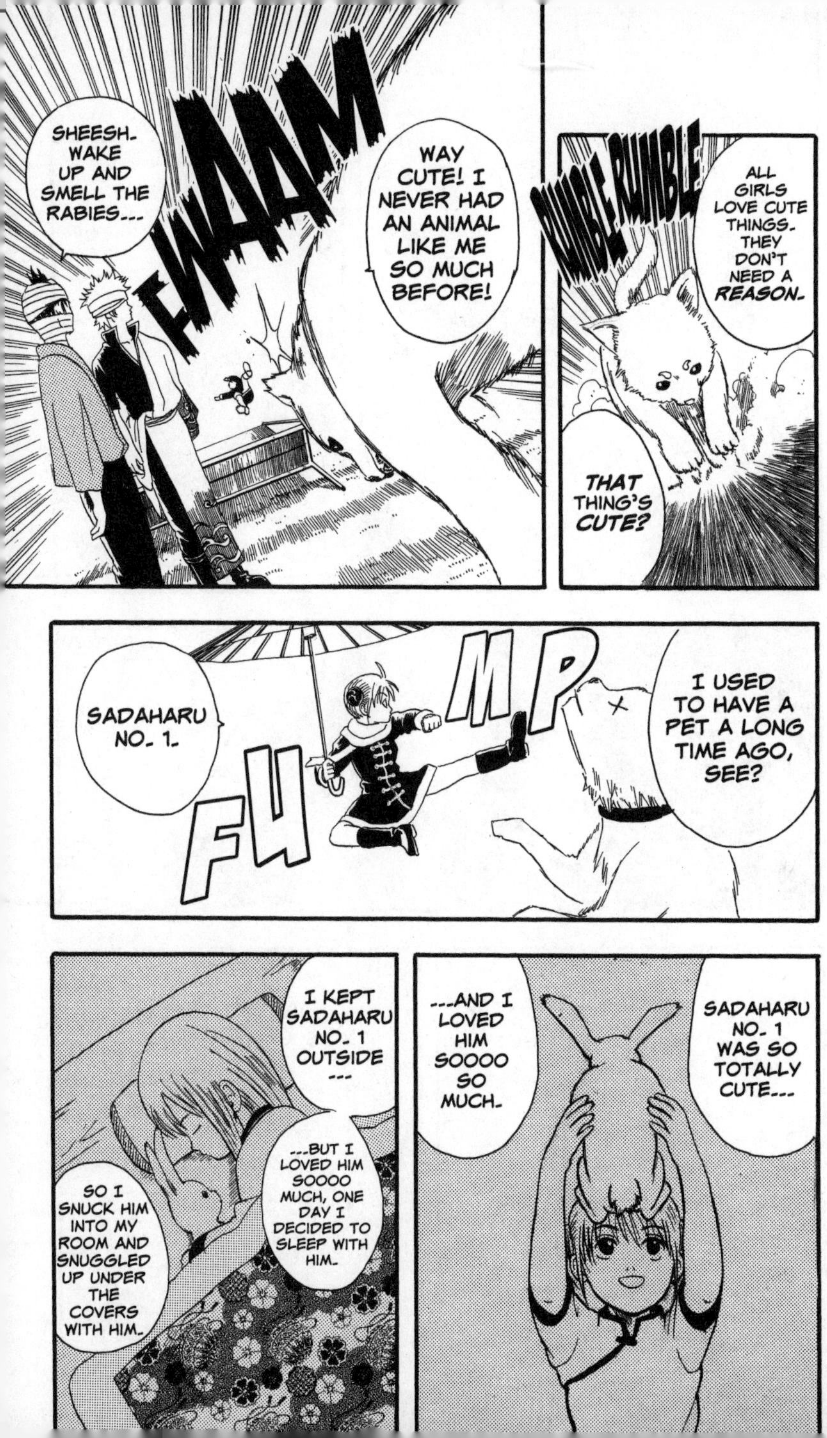
ALL GIRLS LOVE CUTE THINGS. THEY DON'T NEED A REASON.
RUMBLE RUMBLE
THAT THING'S CUTE?
WAY CUTE! I NEVER HAD AN ANIMAL LIKE ME SO MUCH BEFORE!
WHAM
SHEESH. WAKE UP AND SMELL THE RABIES...
I USED TO HAVE A PET A LONG TIME AGO, SEE?
FUMP
SADAHARU NO. 1.
SADAHARU NO. 1 WAS SO TOTALLY CUTE...
...AND I LOVED HIM SOOOO SO MUCH.
I KEPT SADAHARU NO. 1 OUTSIDE...
...BUT I LOVED HIM SOOOO MUCH, ONE DAY I DECIDED TO SLEEP WITH HIM.
SO I SNUCK HIM INTO MY ROOM AND SNUGGLED UP UNDER THE COVERS WITH HIM.

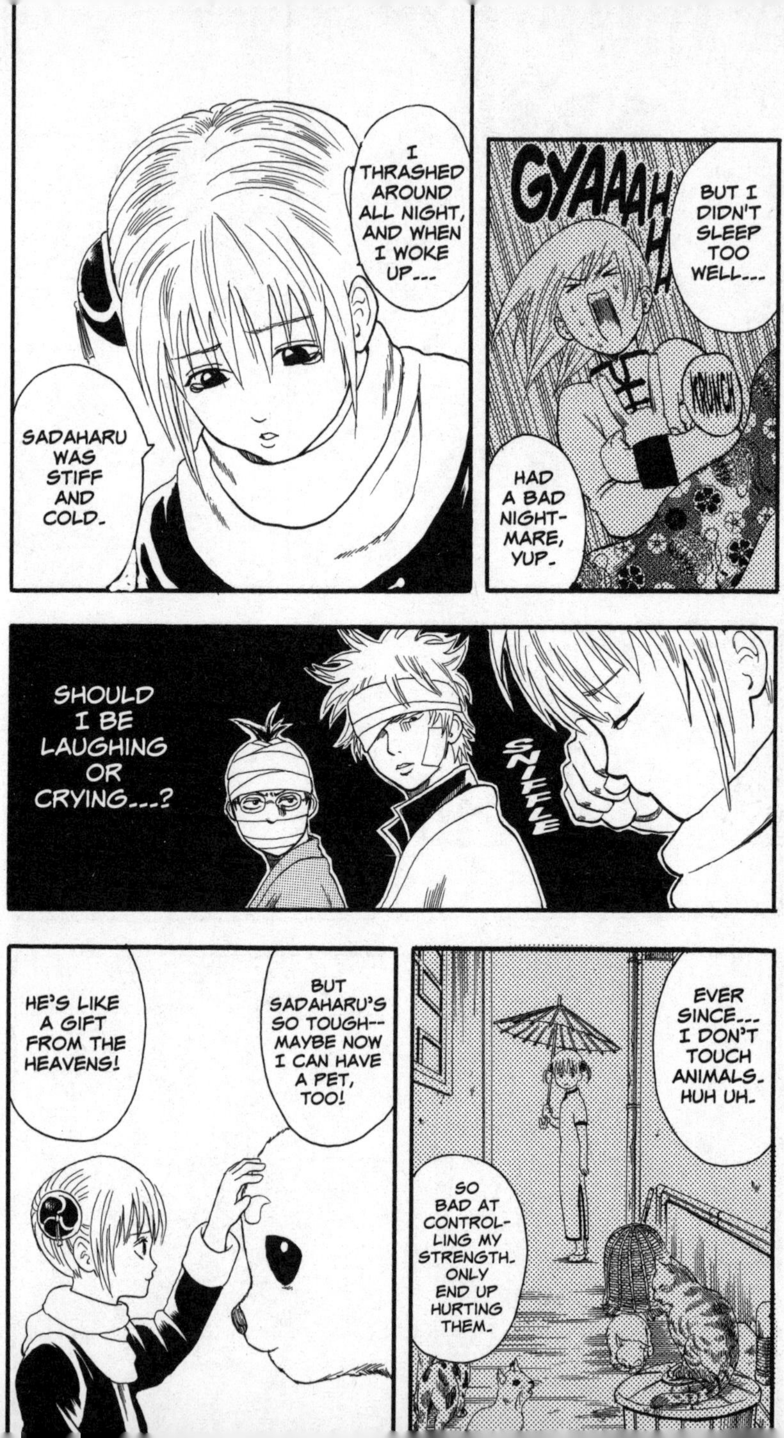
GYAAAHH
BUT I DIDN'T SLEEP TOO WELL...
KRUNCH
HAD A BAD NIGHT-MARE, YUP.
I THRASHED AROUND ALL NIGHT, AND WHEN I WOKE UP...
SADAHARU WAS STIFF AND COLD.
SNIFFLE
SHOULD I BE LAUGHING OR CRYING...?
EVER SINCE... I DON'T TOUCH ANIMALS. HUH UH.
SO BAD AT CONTROL-LING MY STRENGTH. ONLY END UP HURTING THEM.
BUT SADAHARU'S SO TOUGH-- MAYBE NOW I CAN HAVE A PET, TOO!
HE'S LIKE A GIFT FROM THE HEAVENS!

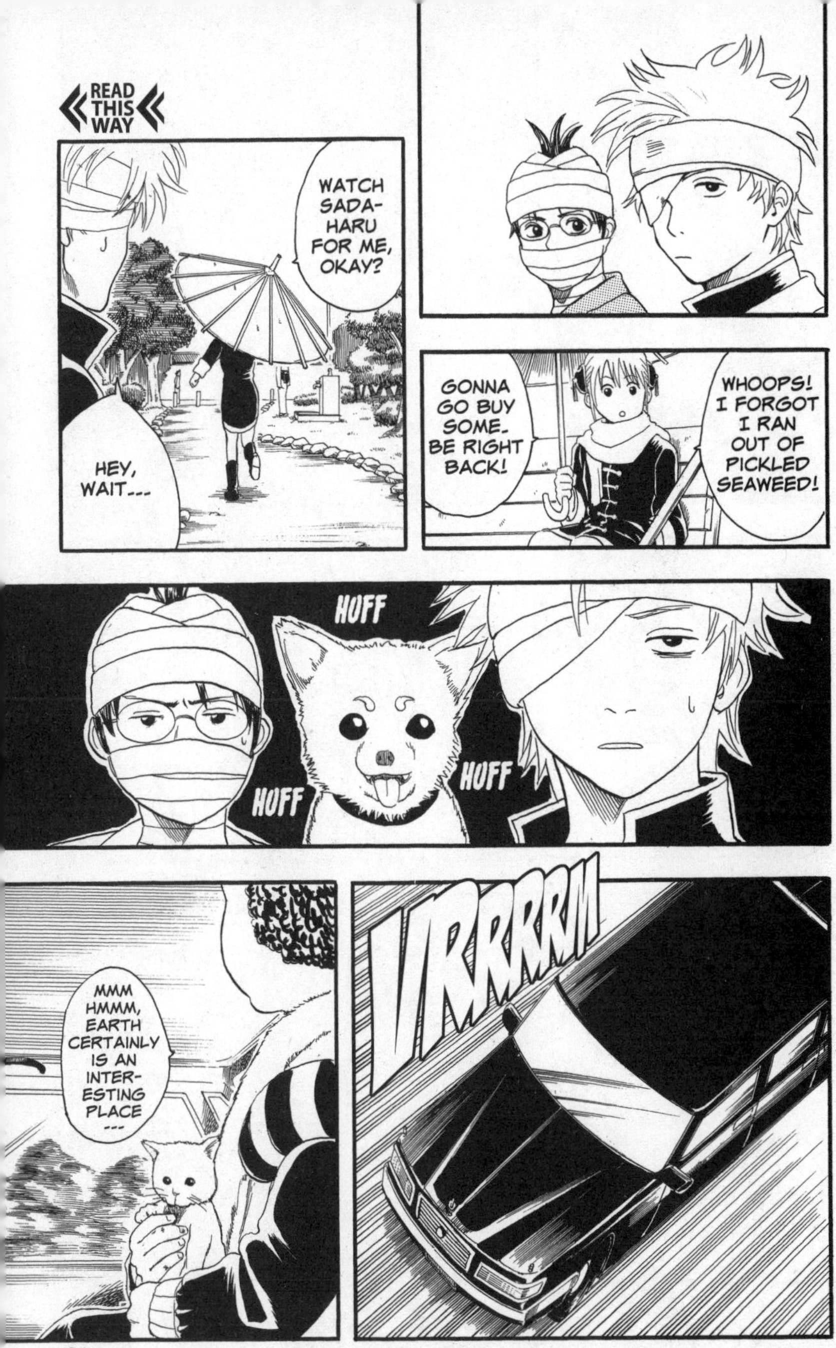
READ THIS WAY
WHOOPS! I FORGOT I RAN OUT OF PICKLED SEAWEED!
GONNA GO BUY SOME. BE RIGHT BACK!
WATCH SADA-HARU FOR ME, OKAY?
HEY, WAIT...
HUFF
HUFF
HUFF
VRRRRM
MMM HMMM, EARTH CERTAINLY IS AN INTER-ESTING PLACE...

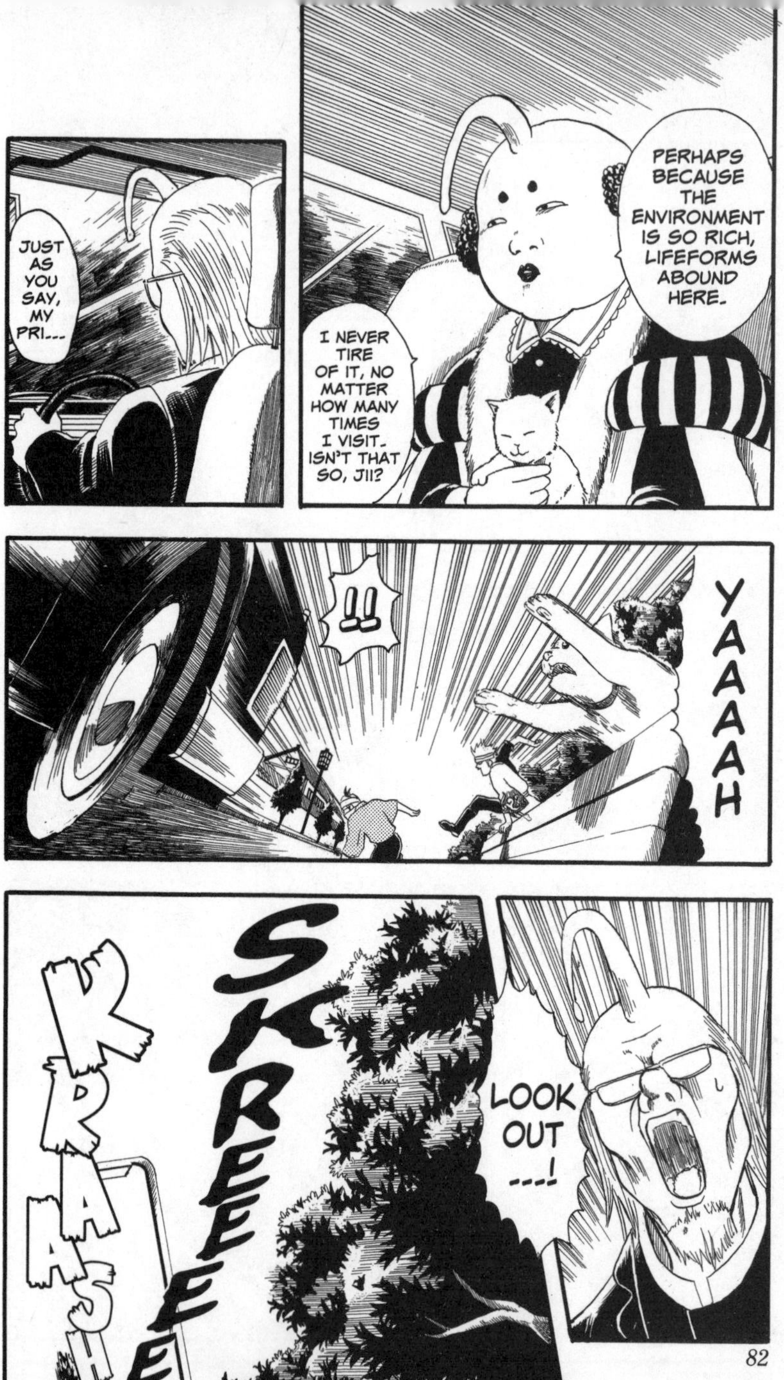
PERHAPS BECAUSE THE ENVIRONMENT IS SO RICH, LIFEFORMS ABOUND HERE.
I NEVER TIRE OF IT, NO MATTER HOW MANY TIMES I VISIT. ISN'T THAT SO, JII?
JUST AS YOU SAY, MY PRI...
YAAAAAH
!!
LOOK OUT ...!
SKREEEEE
KRAASH

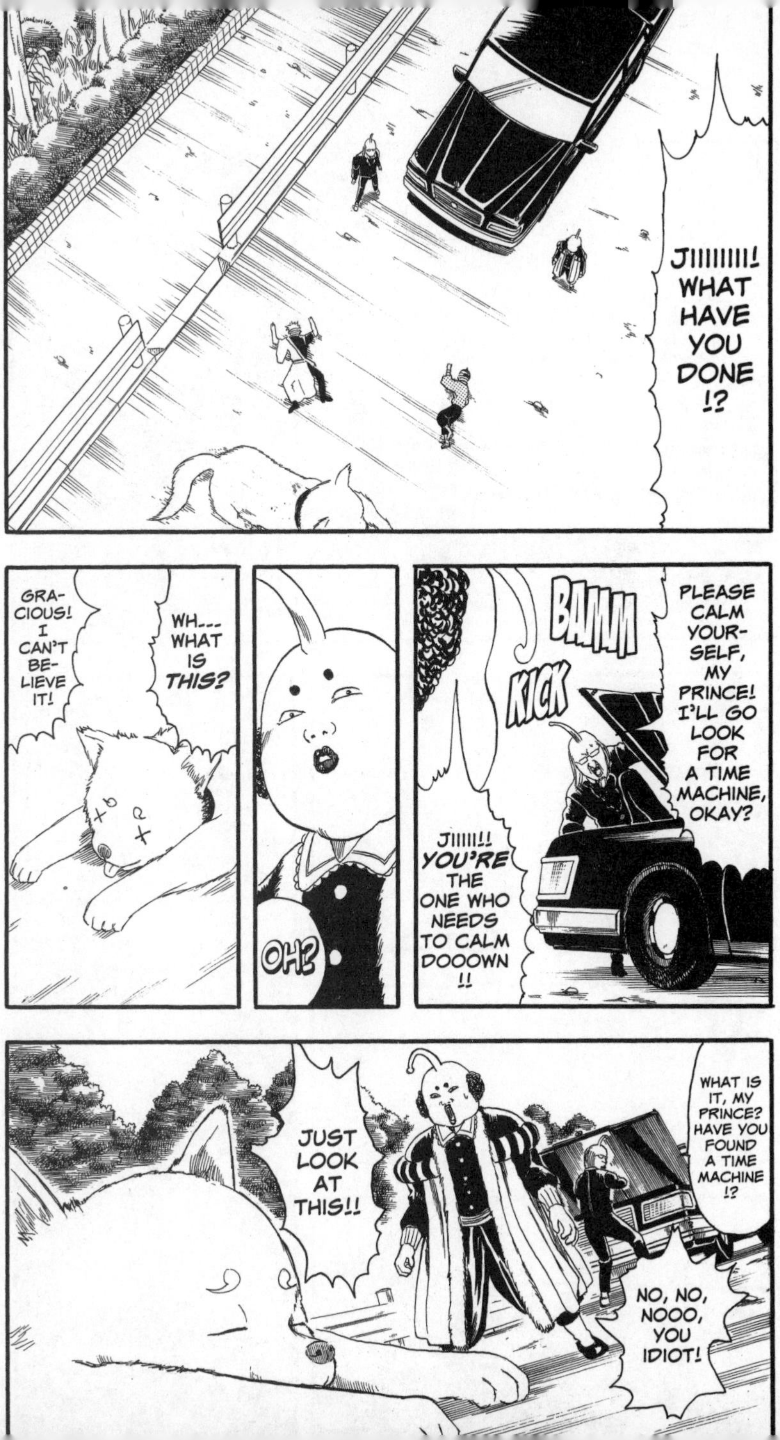
JIIIIIIII! WHAT HAVE YOU DONE!?
PLEASE CALM YOURSELF, MY PRINCE! I'LL GO LOOK FOR A TIME MACHINE, OKAY?
BAMM
KICK
JIIII!! YOU'RE THE ONE WHO NEEDS TO CALM DOOOWN!!
OH?
WH... WHAT IS THIS?
GRACIOUS! I CAN'T BELIEVE IT!
WHAT IS IT, MY PRINCE? HAVE YOU FOUND A TIME MACHINE!?
JUST LOOK AT THIS!!
NO, NO, NOOO, YOU IDIOT!

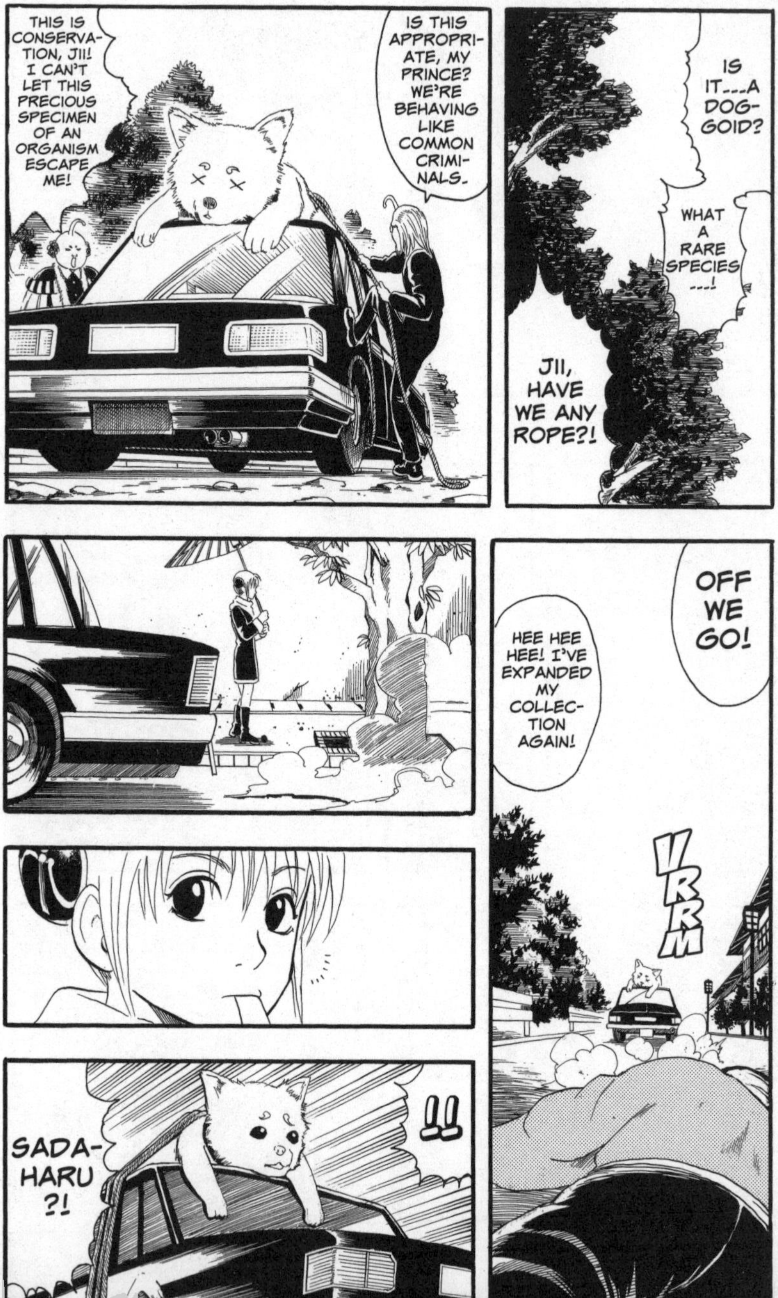
IS IT---A DOG-GOID?
WHAT A RARE SPECIES---!
JII, HAVE WE ANY ROPE?!
IS THIS APPROPRIATE, MY PRINCE? WE'RE BEHAVING LIKE COMMON CRIMINALS.
THIS IS CONSERVATION, JII! I CAN'T LET THIS PRECIOUS SPECIMEN OF AN ORGANISM ESCAPE ME!
OFF WE GO!
HEE HEE HEE! I'VE EXPANDED MY COLLECTION AGAIN!
VRRM
!!
SADAHARU ?!

READ THIS WAY

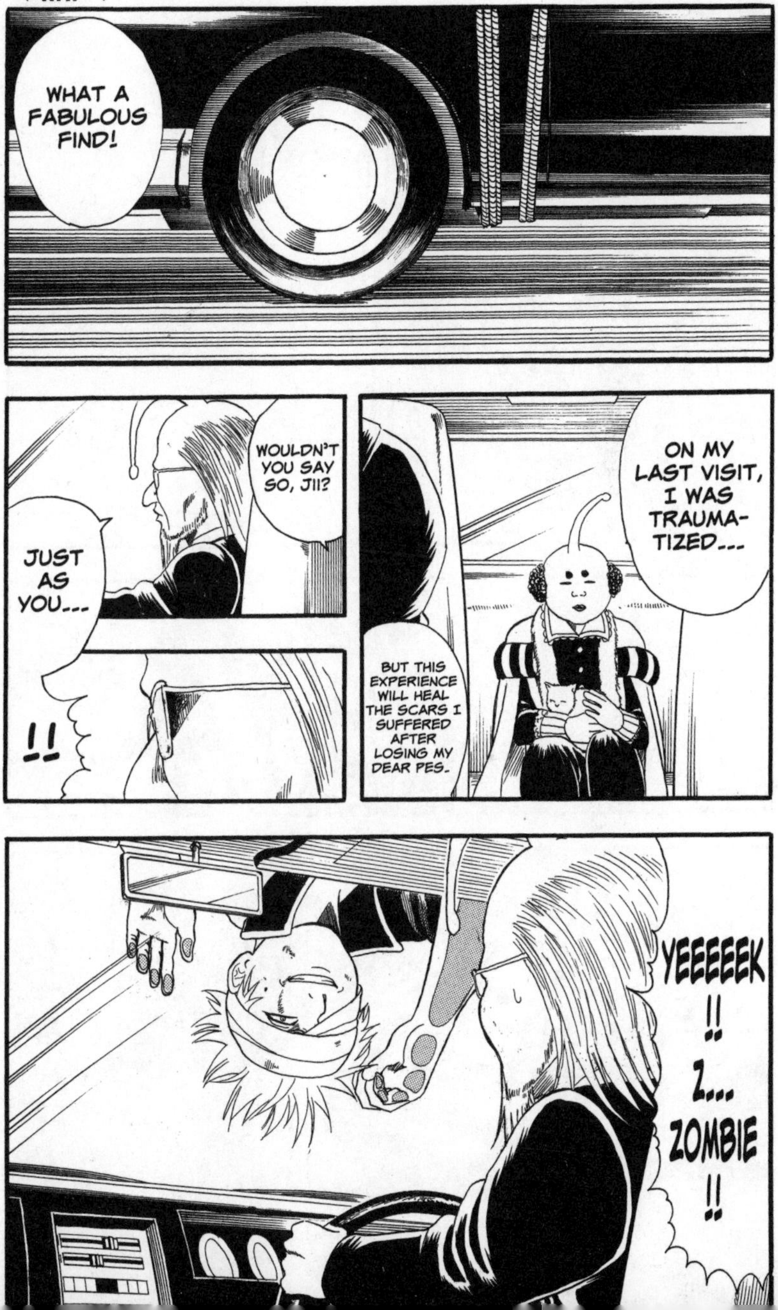
WHAT A FABULOUS FIND!
ON MY LAST VISIT, I WAS TRAUMA-TIZED...
BUT THIS EXPERIENCE WILL HEAL THE SCARS I SUFFERED AFTER LOSING MY DEAR PES.
WOULDN'T YOU SAY SO, JII?
JUST AS YOU...
!!
YEEEEEK!!
Z... ZOMBIE!!

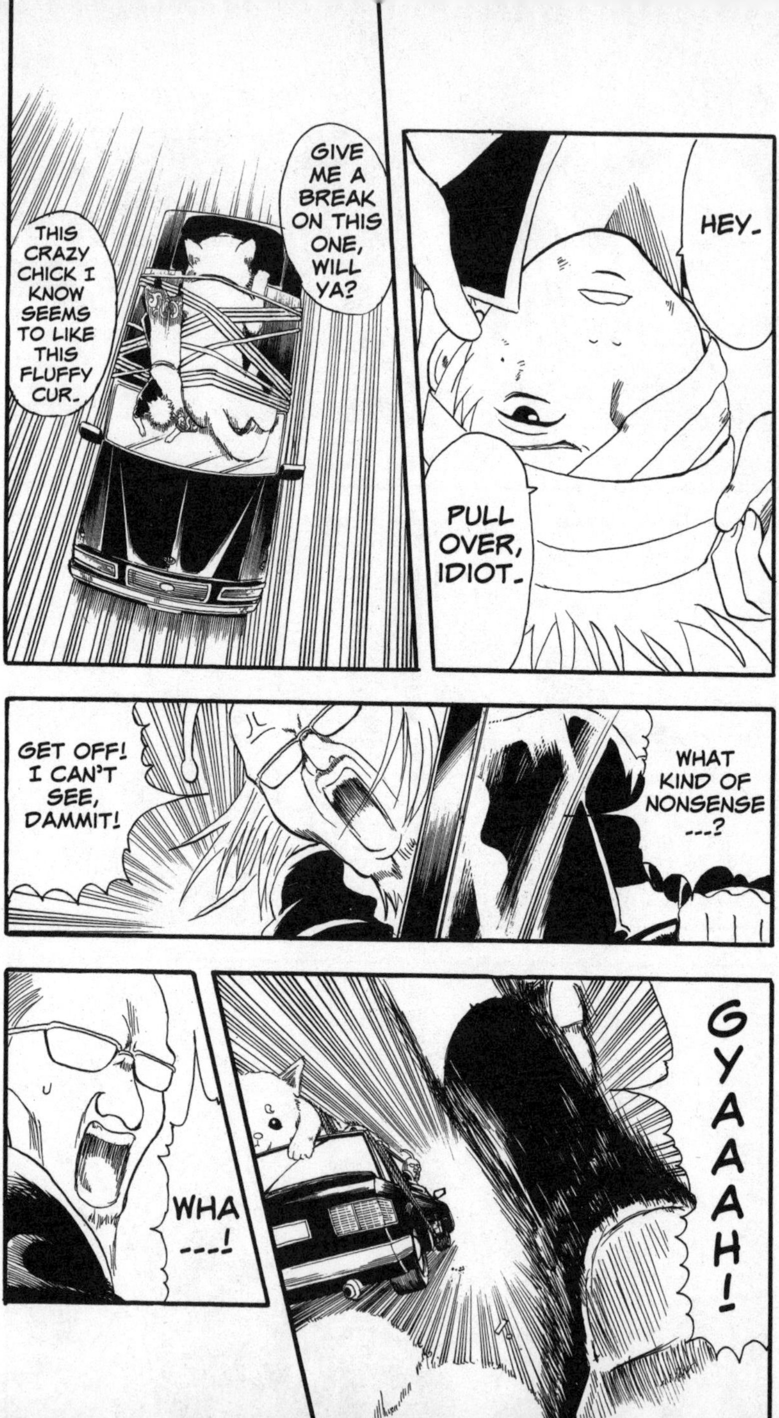

HEY...
PULL OVER, IDIOT...
GIVE ME A BREAK ON THIS ONE, WILL YA?
THIS CRAZY CHICK I KNOW SEEMS TO LIKE THIS FLUFFY CUR...
WHAT KIND OF NONSENSE---?
GET OFF! I CAN'T SEE, DAMMIT!
GYAAAAH!
WHA---!

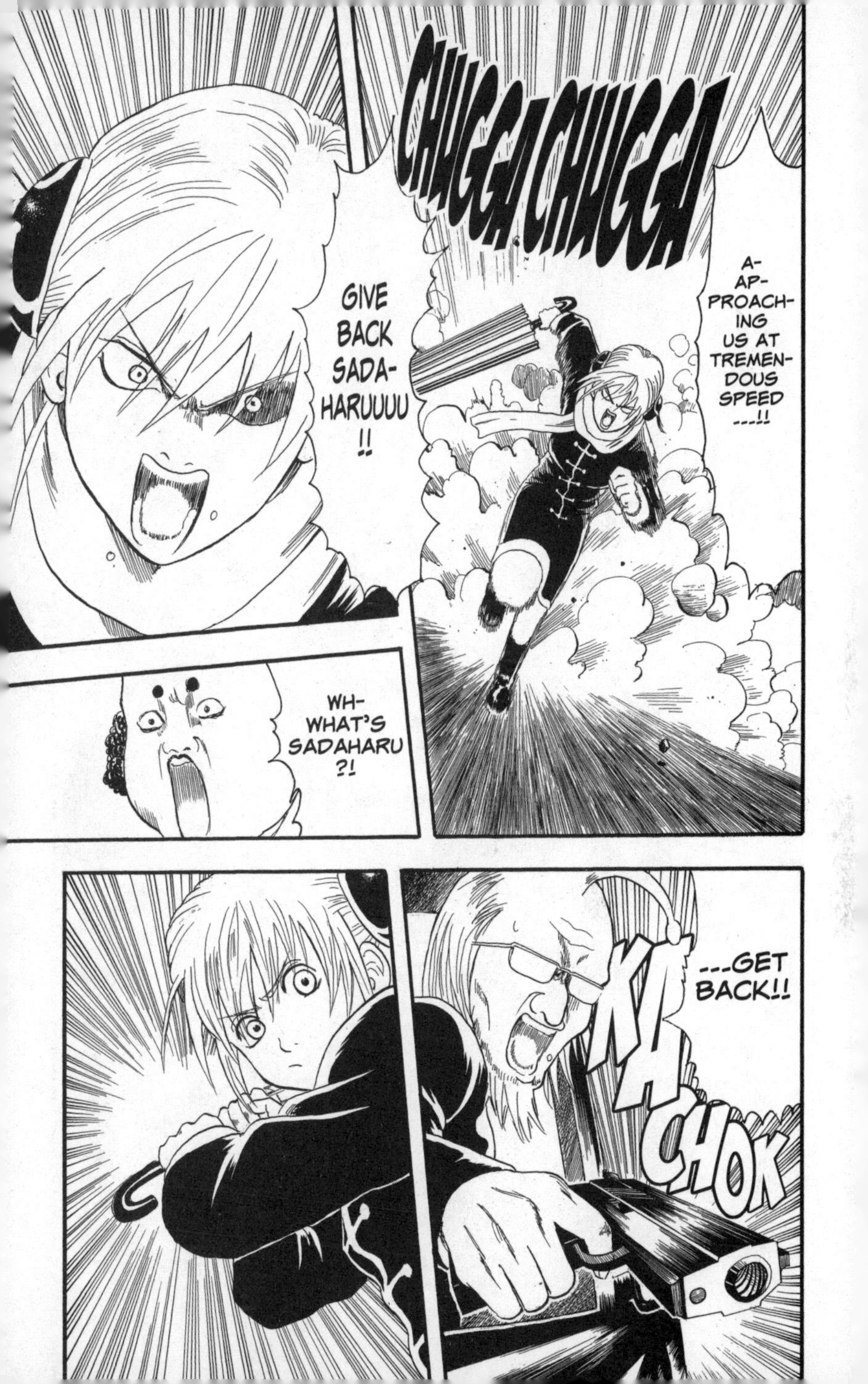

CHUGGA CHUGGA
A-AP-PROACHING US AT TREMENDOUS SPEED ...!!
GIVE BACK SADAHARUUUU!!
WH-WHAT'S SADAHARU?!
...GET BACK!!
KA-CHOK

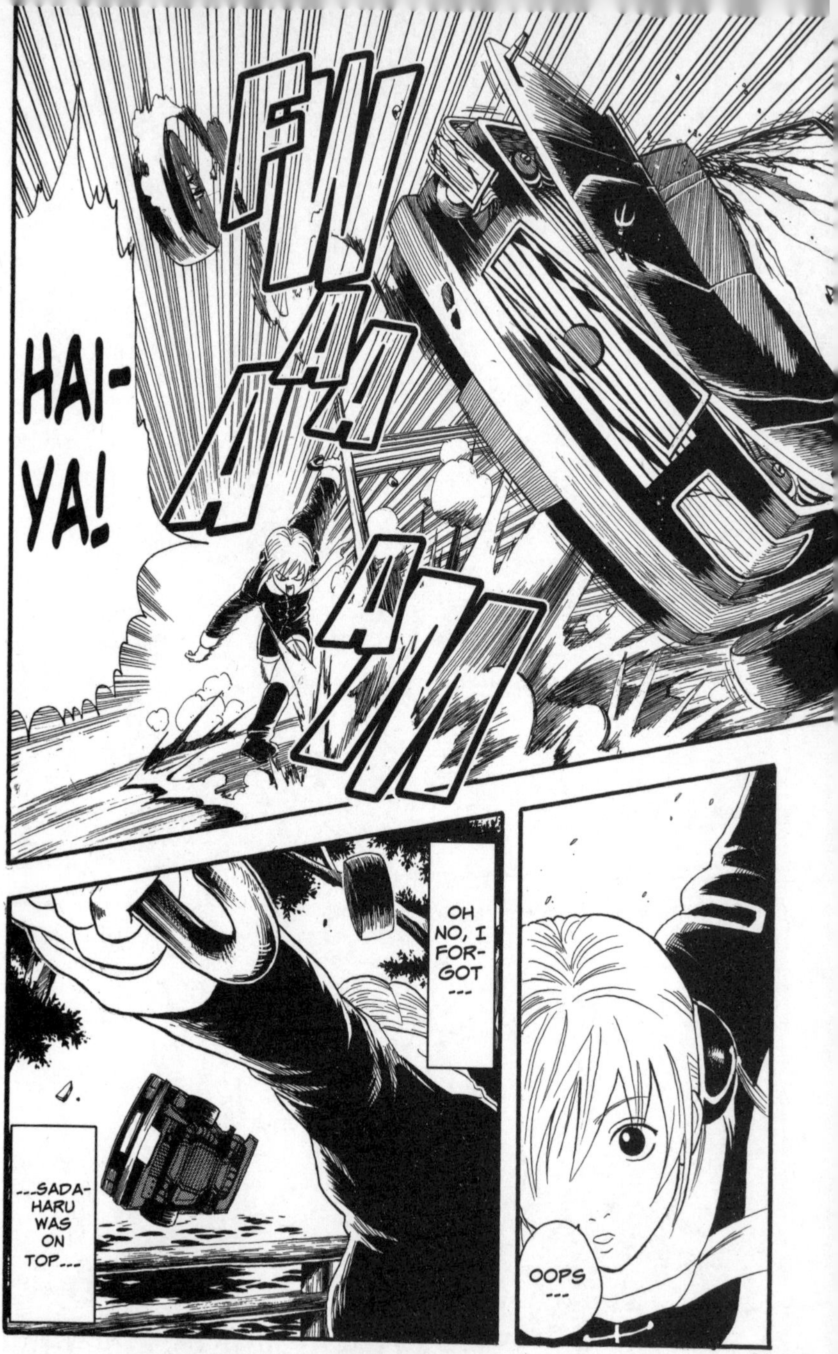
FWAAAAM
HAI-YA!
OOPS...
OH NO, I FORGOT...
...SADAHARU WAS ON TOP...

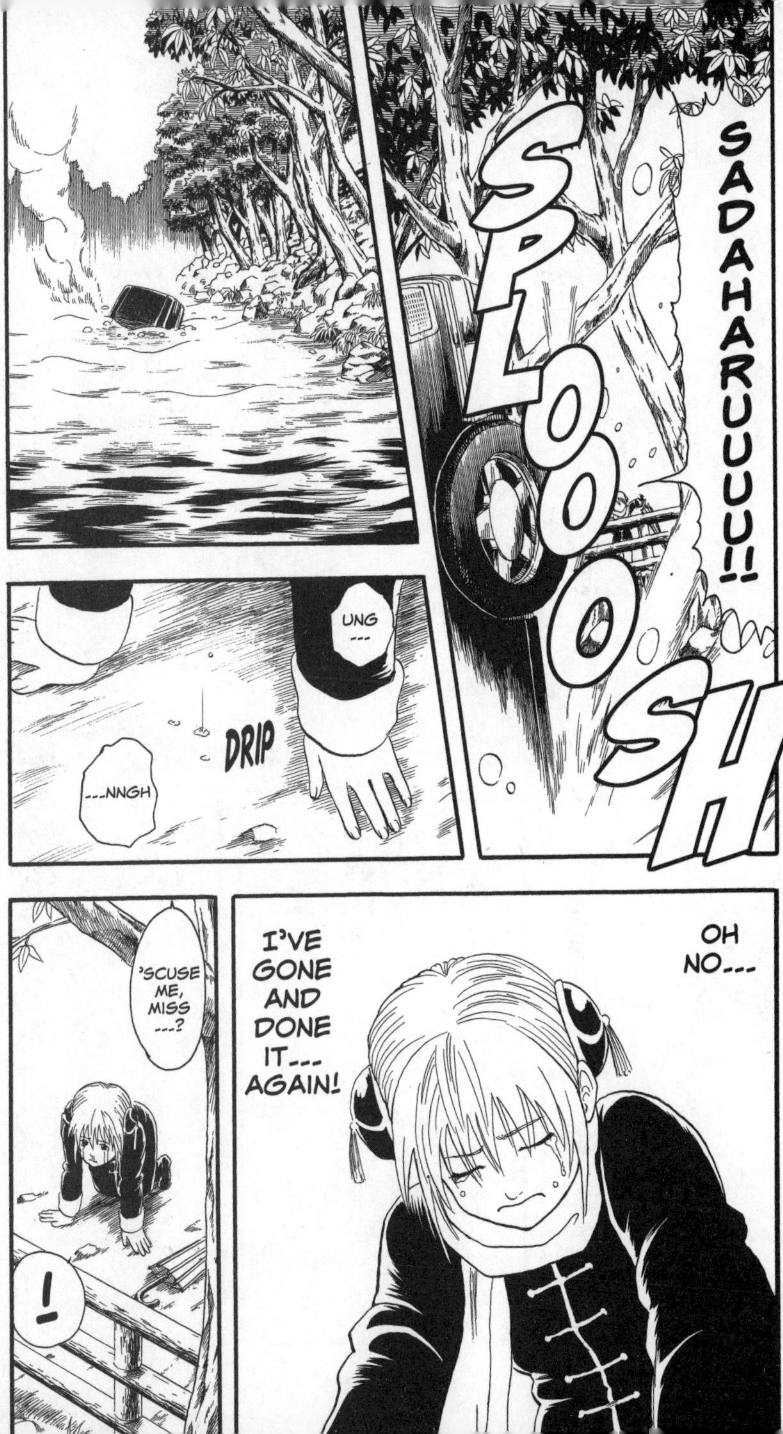
SADAHARUUUUU!!
SPLOOOOSH
UNG...
DRIP
...NNGH
OH NO...
I'VE GONE AND DONE IT... AGAIN!
'SCUSE ME, MISS...?
!

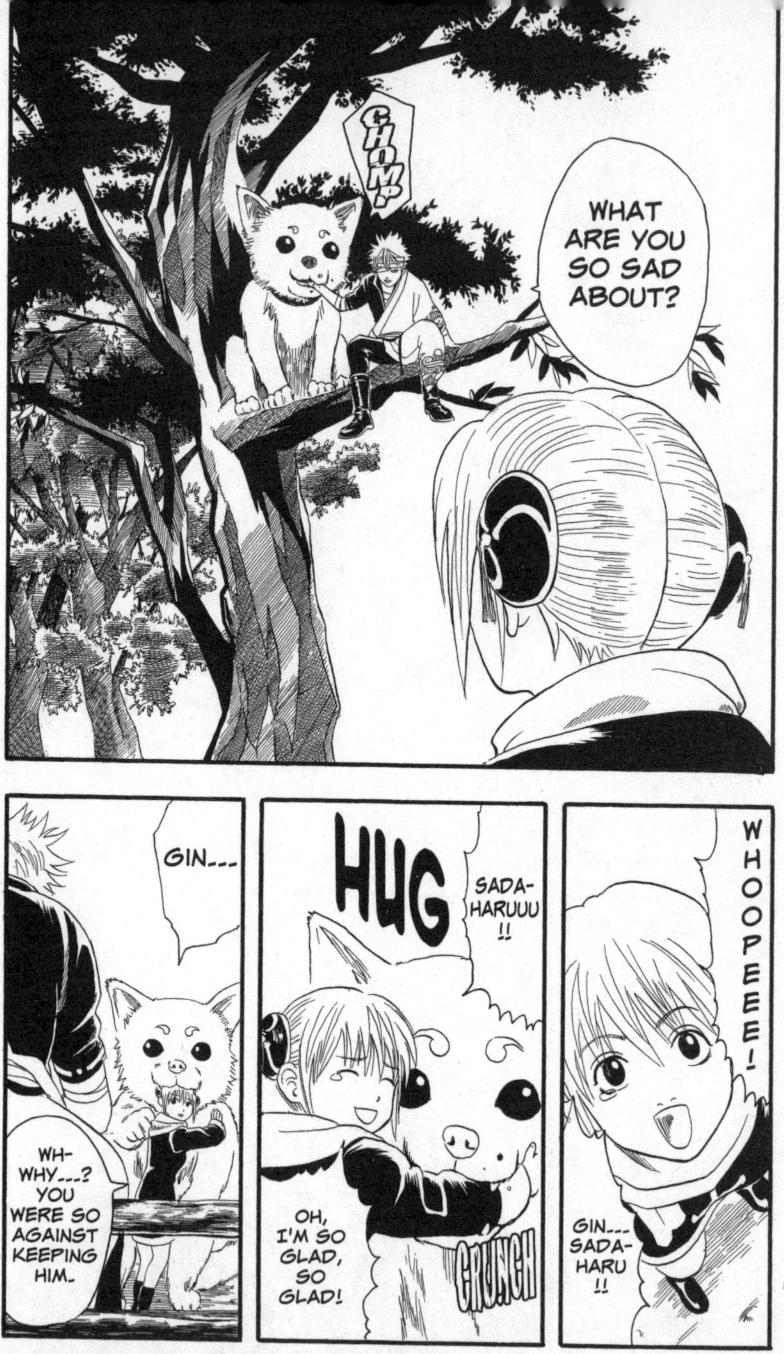
CHOMP!
WHAT ARE YOU SO SAD ABOUT?
WHOOPEEE!
GIN... SADA-HARU!!
SADA-HARUUU!!
HUG
OH, I'M SO GLAD, SO GLAD!
CRUNCH
GIN...
WH- WHY...? YOU WERE SO AGAINST KEEPING HIM.

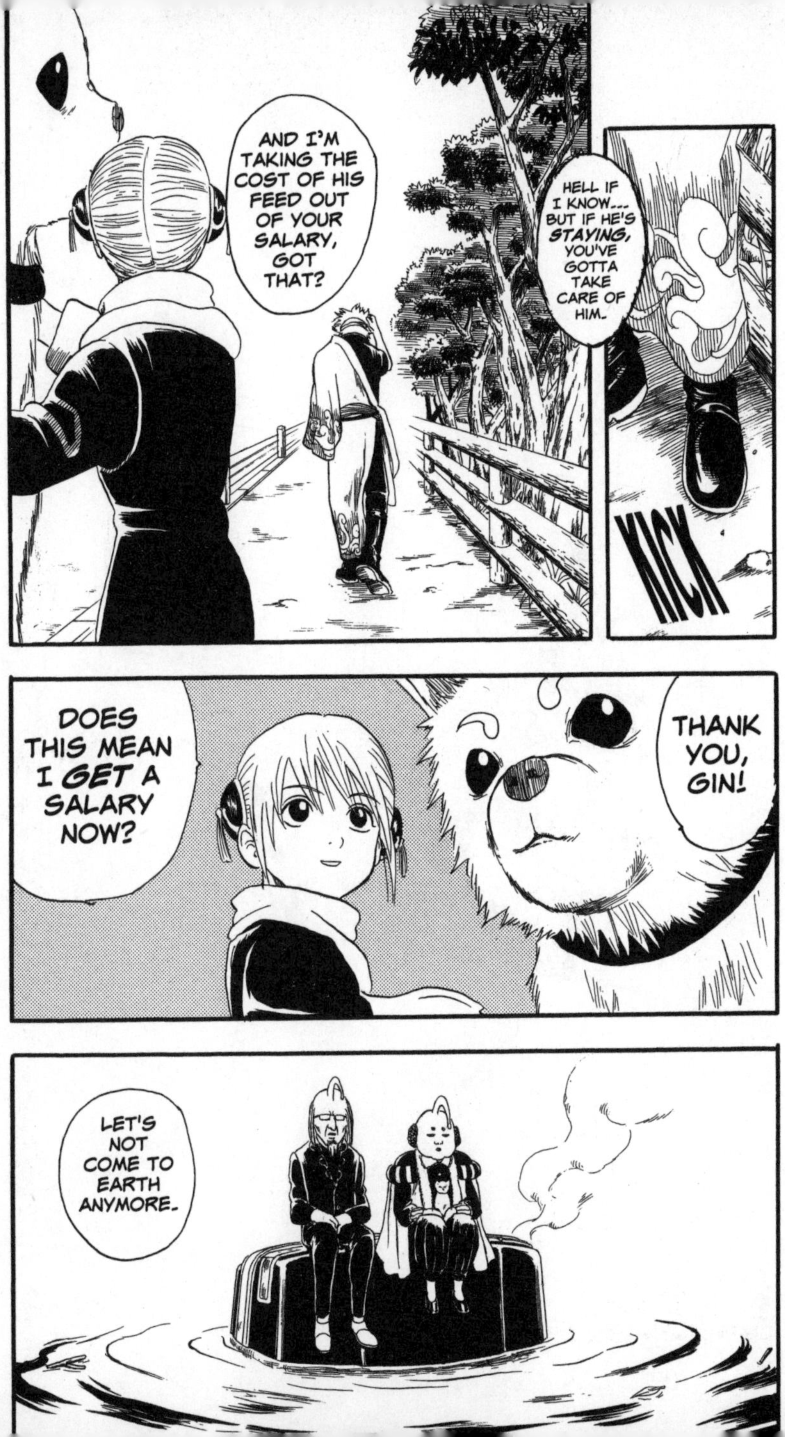
KICK
HELL IF I KNOW... BUT IF HE'S *STAYING,* YOU'VE GOTTA TAKE CARE OF HIM.
AND I'M TAKING THE COST OF HIS FEED OUT OF YOUR SALARY, GOT THAT?
THANK YOU, GIN!
DOES THIS MEAN I *GET* A SALARY NOW?
LET'S NOT COME TO EARTH ANYMORE.

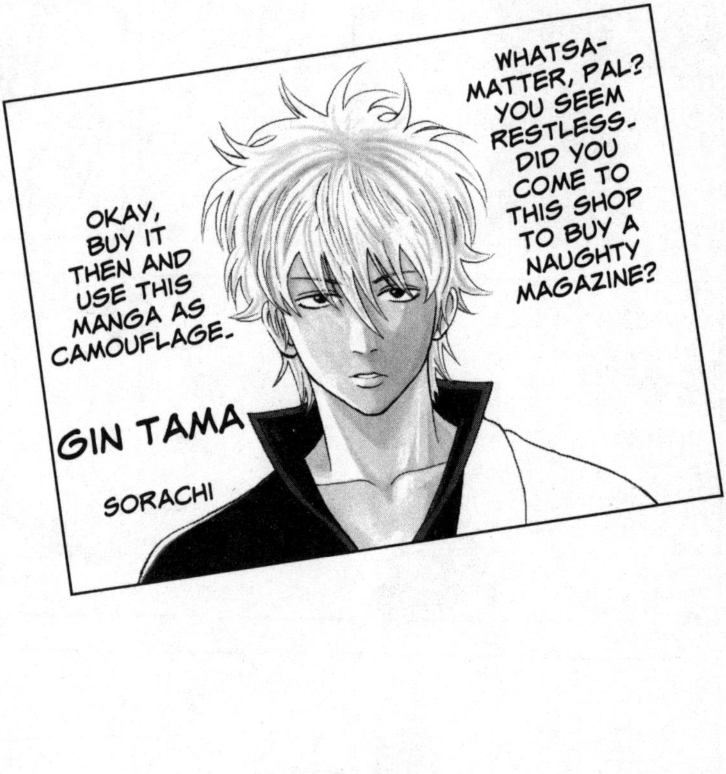
WHATSA-MATTER, PAL? YOU SEEM RESTLESS. DID YOU COME TO THIS SHOP TO BUY A NAUGHTY MAGAZINE?
OKAY, BUY IT THEN AND USE THIS MANGA AS CAMOUFLAGE.
GIN TAMA
SORACHI

Lesson 11

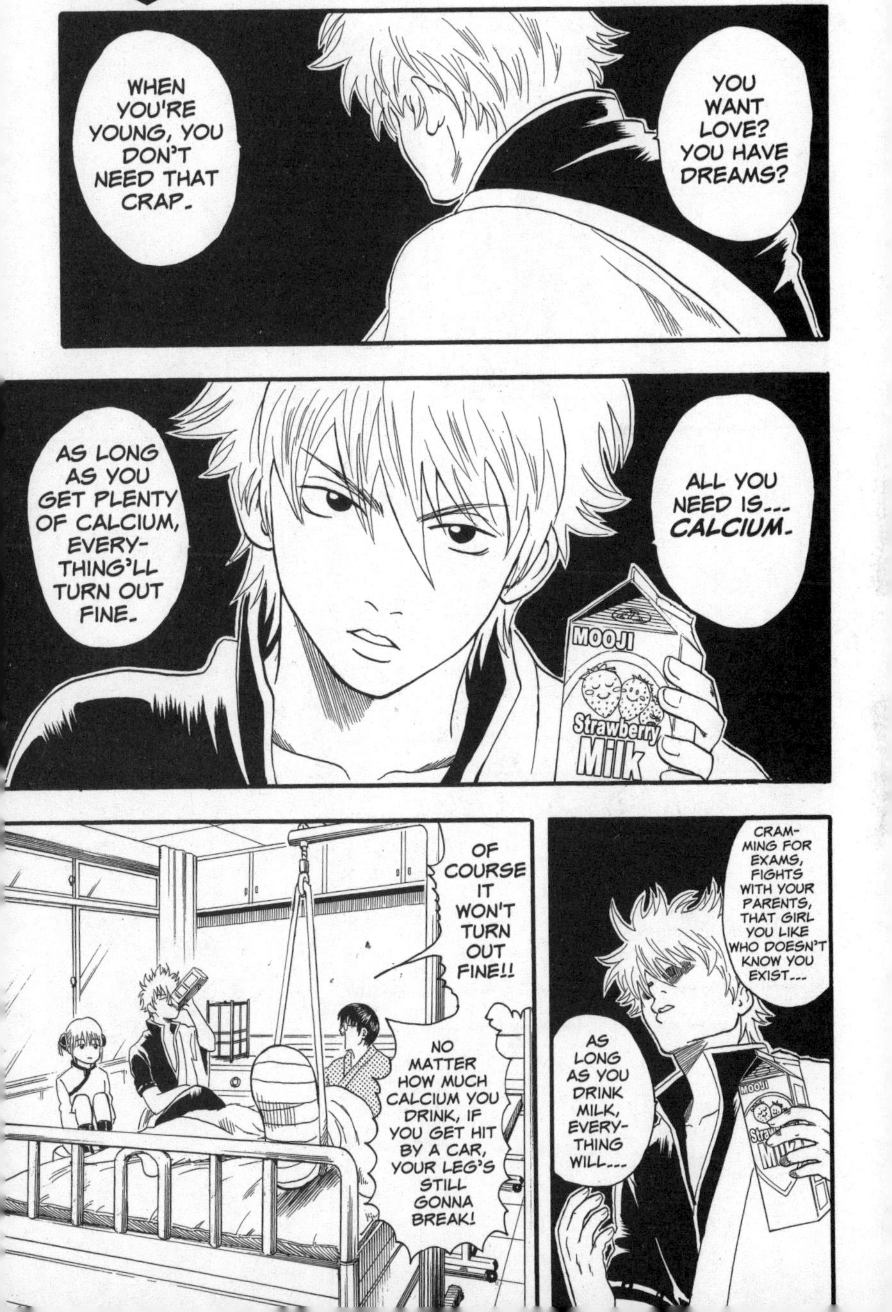
YOU WANT LOVE? YOU HAVE DREAMS?
WHEN YOU'RE YOUNG, YOU DON'T NEED THAT CRAP.
ALL YOU NEED IS... *CALCIUM*.
AS LONG AS YOU GET PLENTY OF CALCIUM, EVERYTHING'LL TURN OUT FINE.
MOOJI
Strawberry Milk
CRAMMING FOR EXAMS, FIGHTS WITH YOUR PARENTS, THAT GIRL YOU LIKE WHO DOESN'T KNOW YOU EXIST...
AS LONG AS YOU DRINK MILK, EVERYTHING WILL...
OF COURSE IT WON'T TURN OUT FINE!!
NO MATTER HOW MUCH CALCIUM YOU DRINK, IF YOU GET HIT BY A CAR, YOUR LEG'S STILL GONNA BREAK!

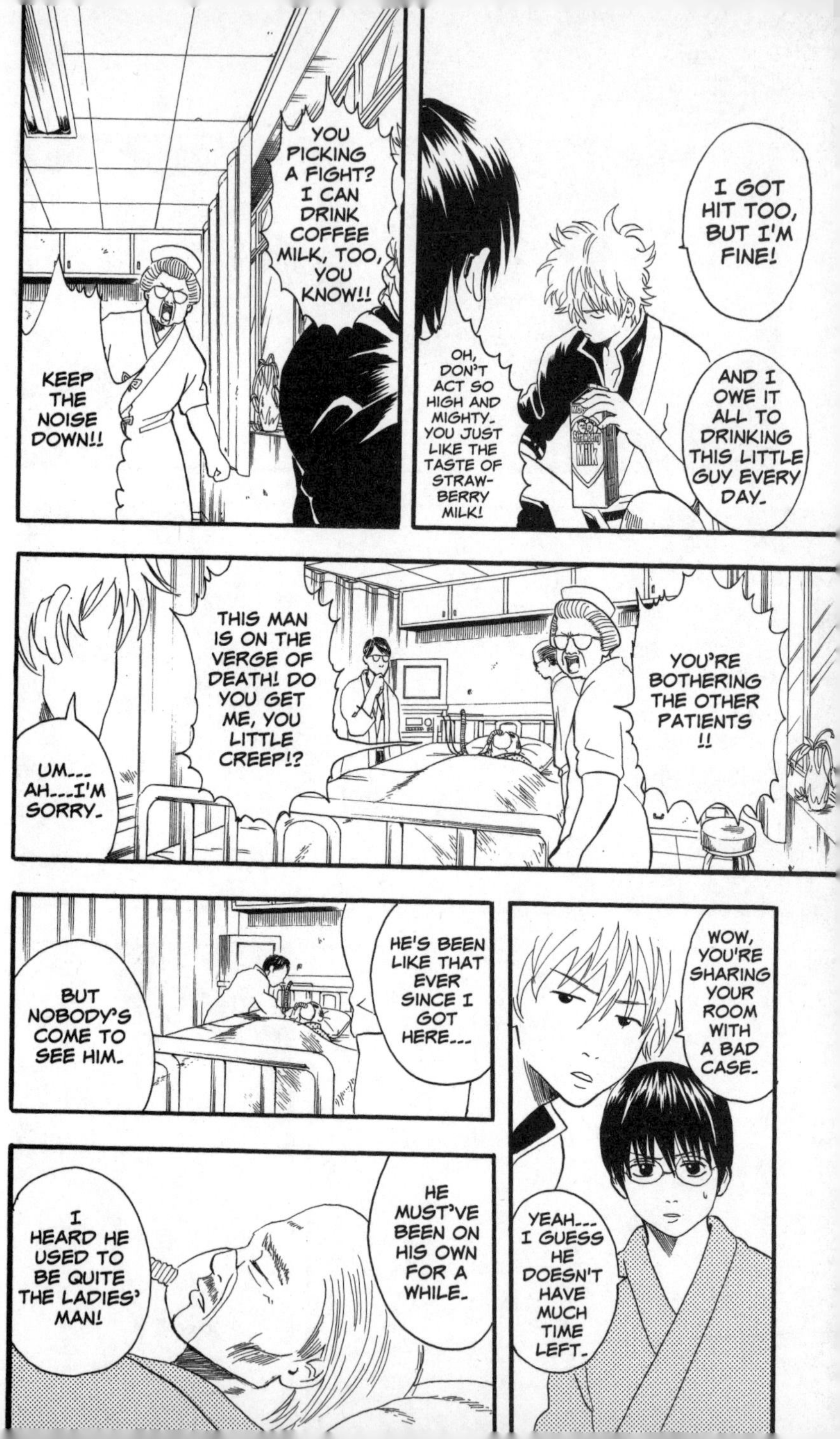
I GOT HIT TOO, BUT I'M FINE!
AND I OWE IT ALL TO DRINKING THIS LITTLE GUY EVERY DAY.
Milk
OH, DON'T ACT SO HIGH AND MIGHTY. YOU JUST LIKE THE TASTE OF STRAW-BERRY MILK!
YOU PICKING A FIGHT? I CAN DRINK COFFEE MILK, TOO, YOU KNOW!!
KEEP THE NOISE DOWN!!
YOU'RE BOTHERING THE OTHER PATIENTS!!
THIS MAN IS ON THE VERGE OF DEATH! DO YOU GET ME, YOU LITTLE CREEP!?
UM... AH...I'M SORRY.
WOW, YOU'RE SHARING YOUR ROOM WITH A BAD CASE.
YEAH... I GUESS HE DOESN'T HAVE MUCH TIME LEFT.
HE'S BEEN LIKE THAT EVER SINCE I GOT HERE...
BUT NOBODY'S COME TO SEE HIM.
HE MUST'VE BEEN ON HIS OWN FOR A WHILE.
I HEARD HE USED TO BE QUITE THE LADIES' MAN!

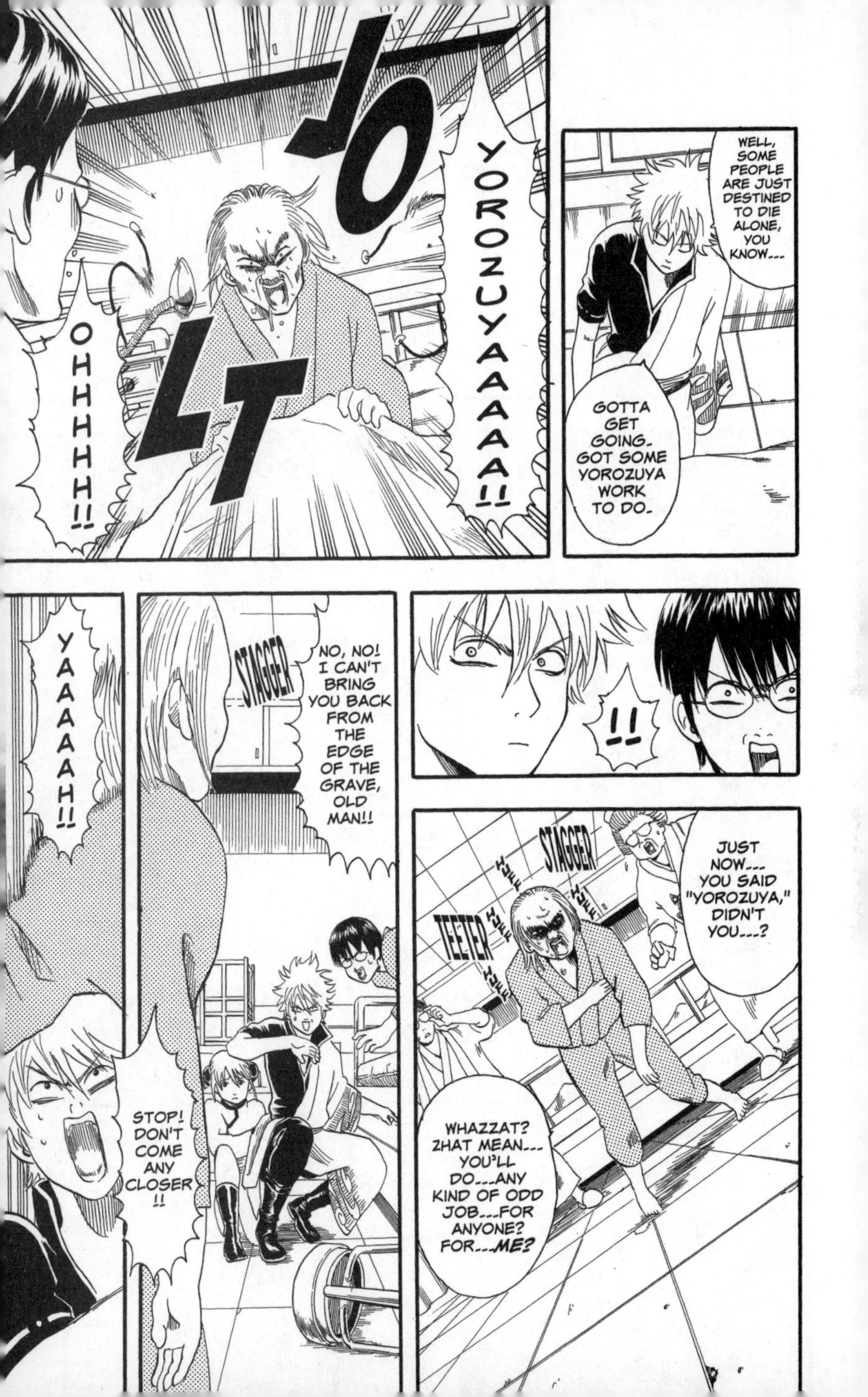

WELL, SOME PEOPLE ARE JUST DESTINED TO DIE ALONE, YOU KNOW...
GOTTA GET GOING. GOT SOME YOROZUYA WORK TO DO.
JOLT
YOROZUYAAAAAA!!
OHHHHHH!!
!!
STAGGER
JUST NOW... YOU SAID "YOROZUYA," DIDN'T YOU...?
HUFF HUFF
TEETER
HUFF HUFF
WHAZZAT? ZHAT MEAN... YOU'LL DO... ANY KIND OF ODD JOB... FOR ANYONE? FOR... ME?
STAGGER
NO, NO! I CAN'T BRING YOU BACK FROM THE EDGE OF THE GRAVE, OLD MAN!!
STOP! DON'T COME ANY CLOSER!!
YAAAAAAAH!!

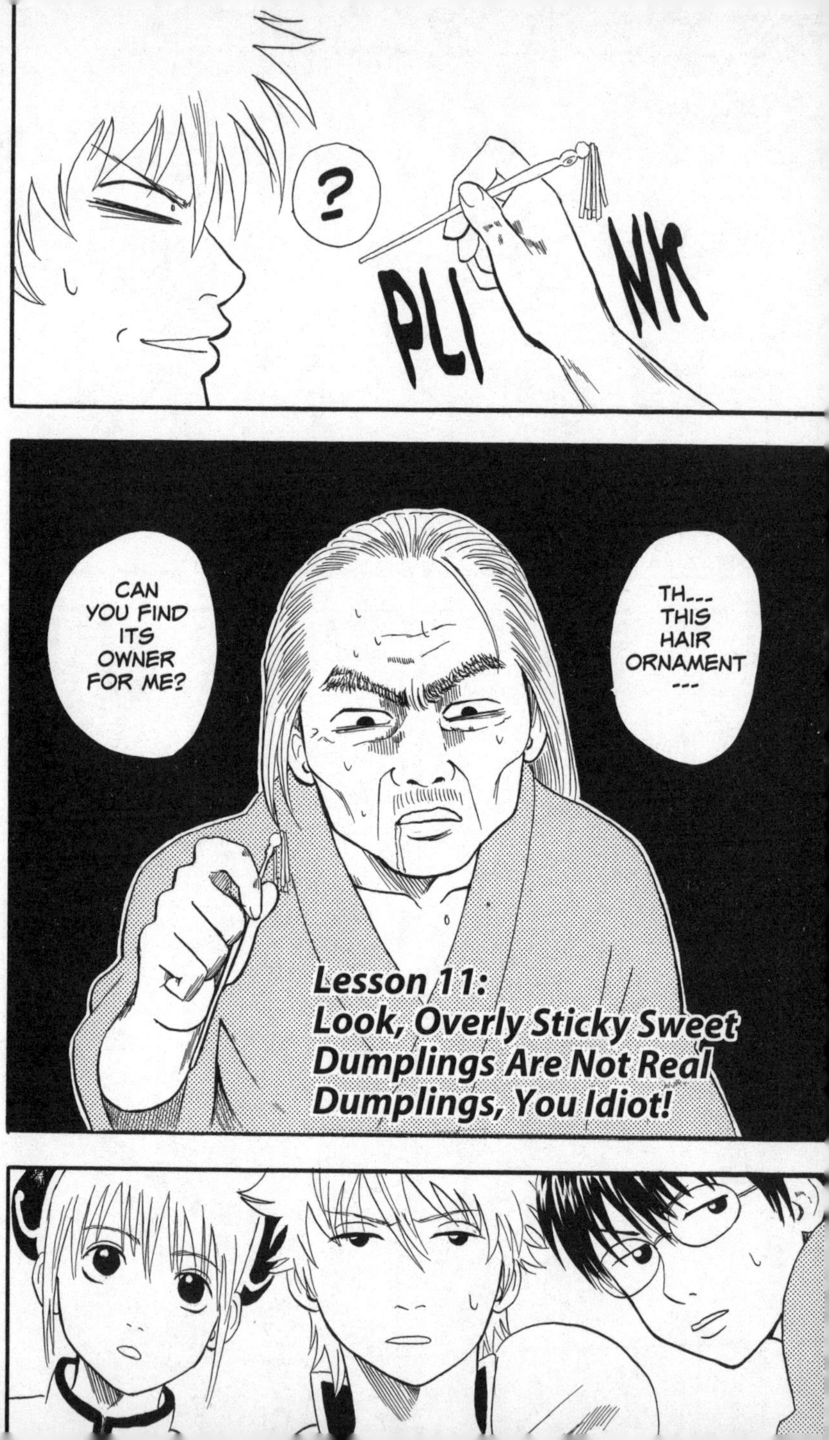
?
PLINK
TH... THIS HAIR ORNAMENT...
CAN YOU FIND ITS OWNER FOR ME?
Lesson 11: Look, Overly Sticky Sweet Dumplings Are Not Real Dumplings, You Idiot!

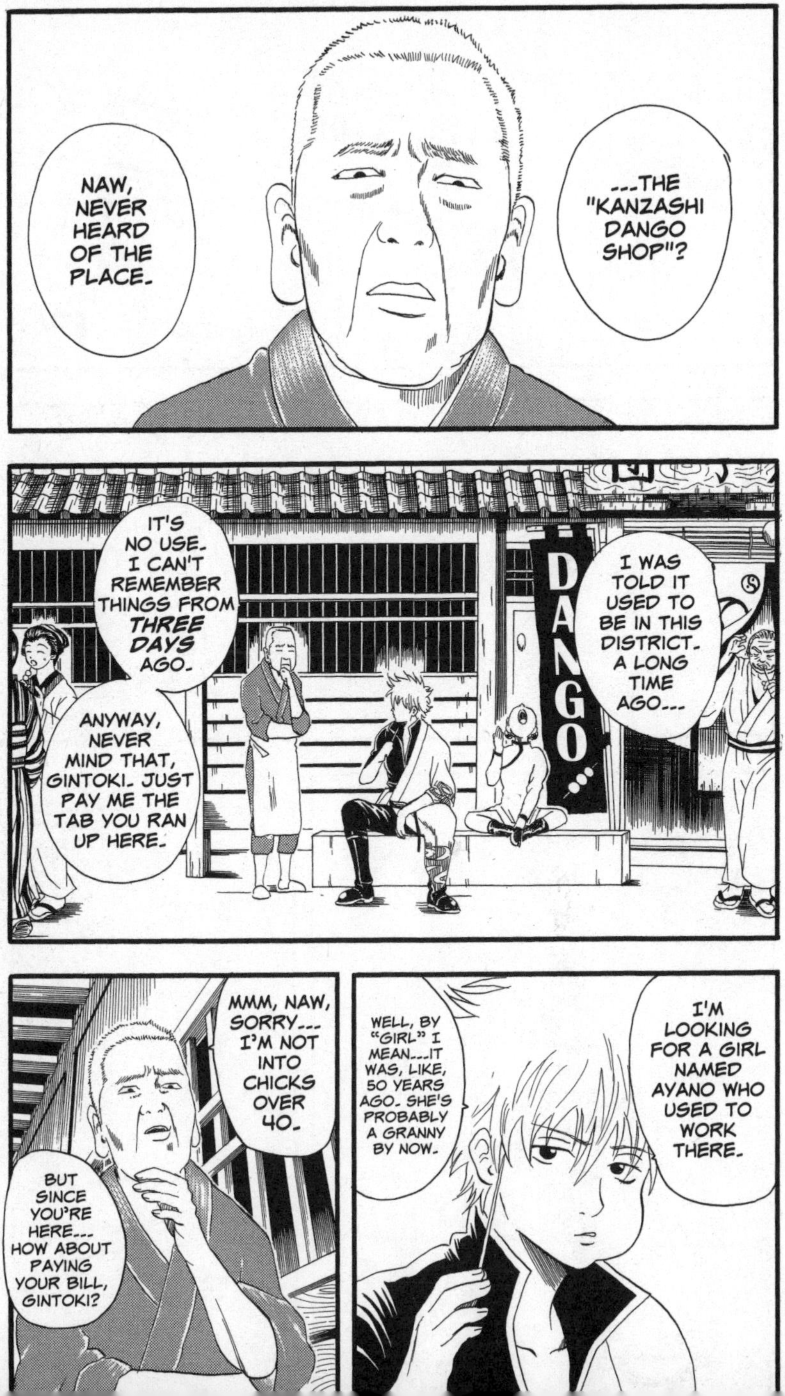
...THE "KANZASHI DANGO SHOP"?
NAW, NEVER HEARD OF THE PLACE.
I WAS TOLD IT USED TO BE IN THIS DISTRICT. A LONG TIME AGO...
DANGO
IT'S NO USE. I CAN'T REMEMBER THINGS FROM *THREE DAYS* AGO.
ANYWAY, NEVER MIND THAT, GINTOKI. JUST PAY ME THE TAB YOU RAN UP HERE.
I'M LOOKING FOR A GIRL NAMED AYANO WHO USED TO WORK THERE.
WELL, BY "GIRL" I MEAN...IT WAS, LIKE, 50 YEARS AGO. SHE'S PROBABLY A GRANNY BY NOW.
MMM, NAW, SORRY... I'M NOT INTO CHICKS OVER 40.
BUT SINCE YOU'RE HERE... HOW ABOUT PAYING YOUR BILL, GINTOKI?

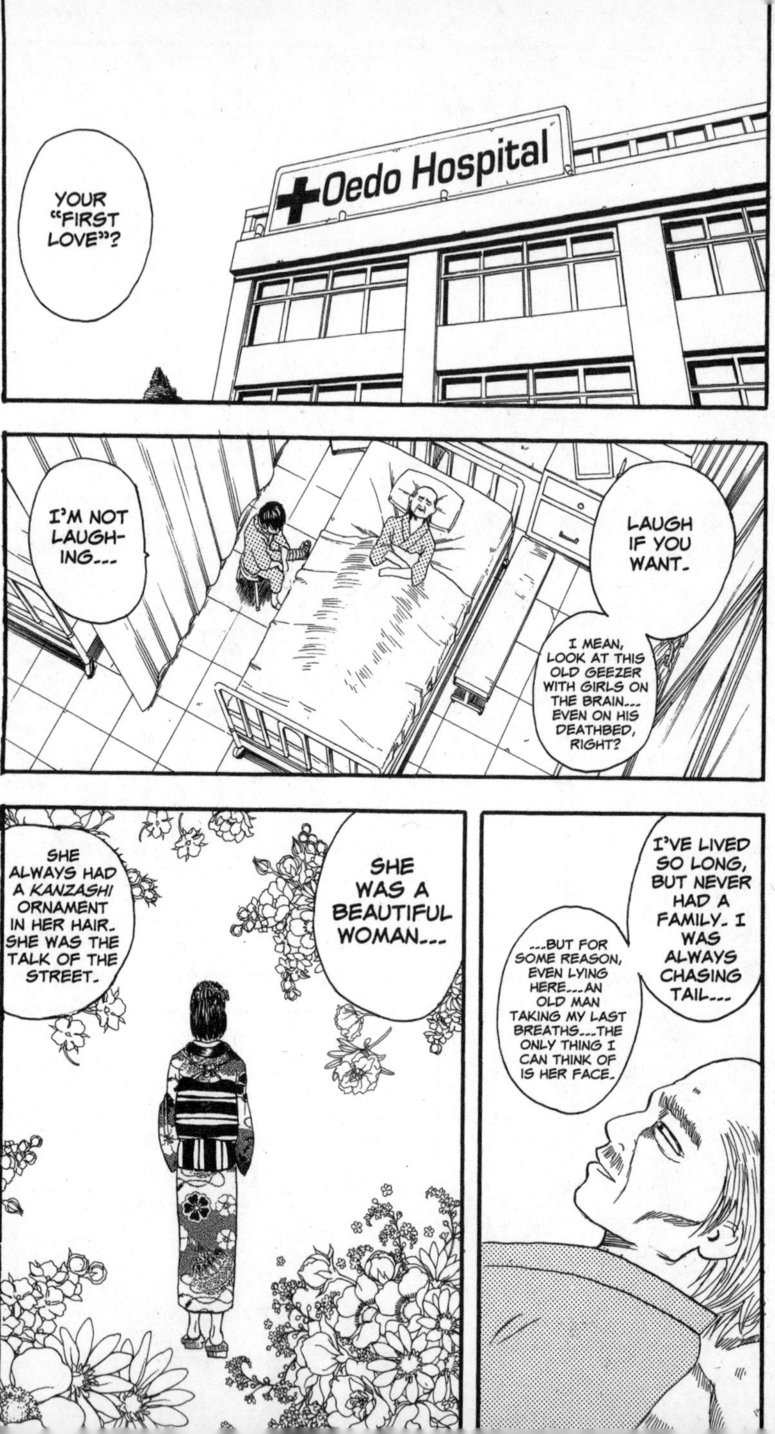

Oedo Hospital
YOUR "FIRST LOVE"?
LAUGH IF YOU WANT.
I MEAN, LOOK AT THIS OLD GEEZER WITH GIRLS ON THE BRAIN... EVEN ON HIS DEATHBED, RIGHT?
I'M NOT LAUGHING...
I'VE LIVED SO LONG, BUT NEVER HAD A FAMILY. I WAS ALWAYS CHASING TAIL...
...BUT FOR SOME REASON, EVEN LYING HERE... AN OLD MAN TAKING MY LAST BREATHS... THE ONLY THING I CAN THINK OF IS HER FACE.
SHE WAS A BEAUTIFUL WOMAN...
SHE ALWAYS HAD A *KANZASHI* ORNAMENT IN HER HAIR. SHE WAS THE TALK OF THE STREET.

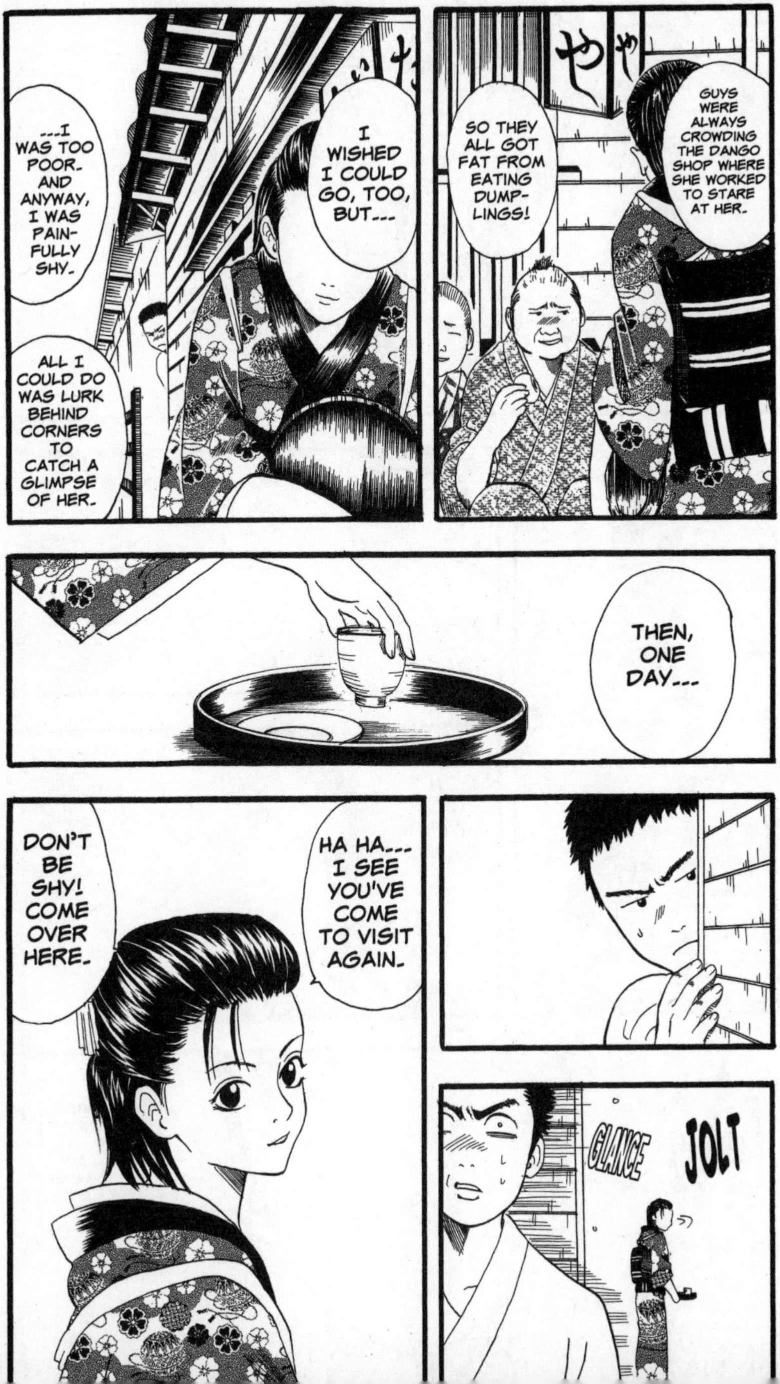
GUYS WERE ALWAYS CROWDING THE DANGO SHOP WHERE SHE WORKED TO STARE AT HER.
SO THEY ALL GOT FAT FROM EATING DUMP-LINGS!
I WISHED I COULD GO, TOO, BUT...
...I WAS TOO POOR. AND ANYWAY, I WAS PAIN-FULLY SHY.
ALL I COULD DO WAS LURK BEHIND CORNERS TO CATCH A GLIMPSE OF HER.
THEN, ONE DAY...
GLANCE
JOLT
HA HA... I SEE YOU'VE COME TO VISIT AGAIN.
DON'T BE SHY! COME OVER HERE.

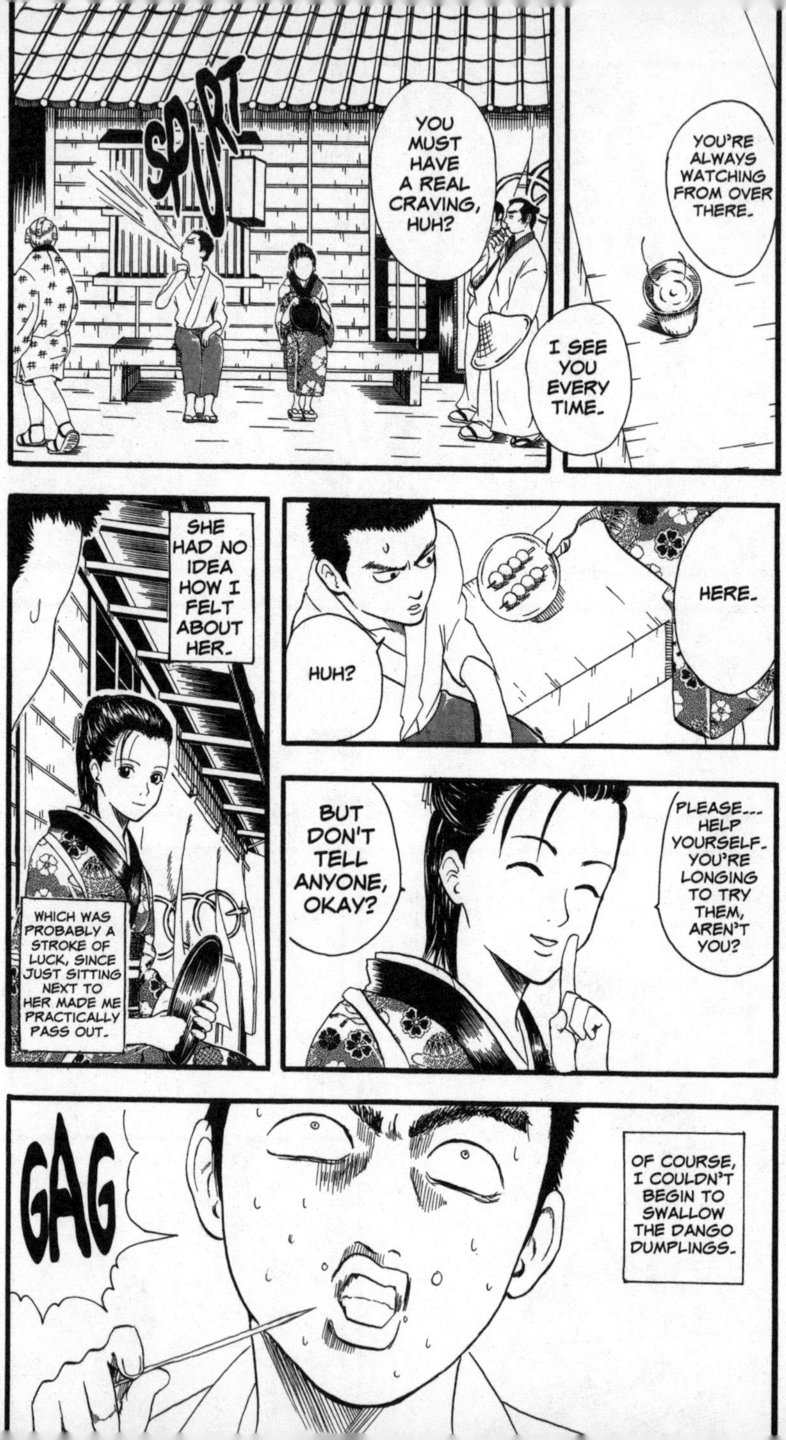
YOU'RE ALWAYS WATCHING FROM OVER THERE.
I SEE YOU EVERY TIME.
YOU MUST HAVE A REAL CRAVING, HUH?
SPURT
HERE.
HUH?
PLEASE... HELP YOURSELF. YOU'RE LONGING TO TRY THEM, AREN'T YOU?
BUT DON'T TELL ANYONE, OKAY?
SHE HAD NO IDEA HOW I FELT ABOUT HER.
WHICH WAS PROBABLY A STROKE OF LUCK, SINCE JUST SITTING NEXT TO HER MADE ME PRACTICALLY PASS OUT.
OF COURSE, I COULDN'T BEGIN TO SWALLOW THE DANGO DUMPLINGS.
GAG

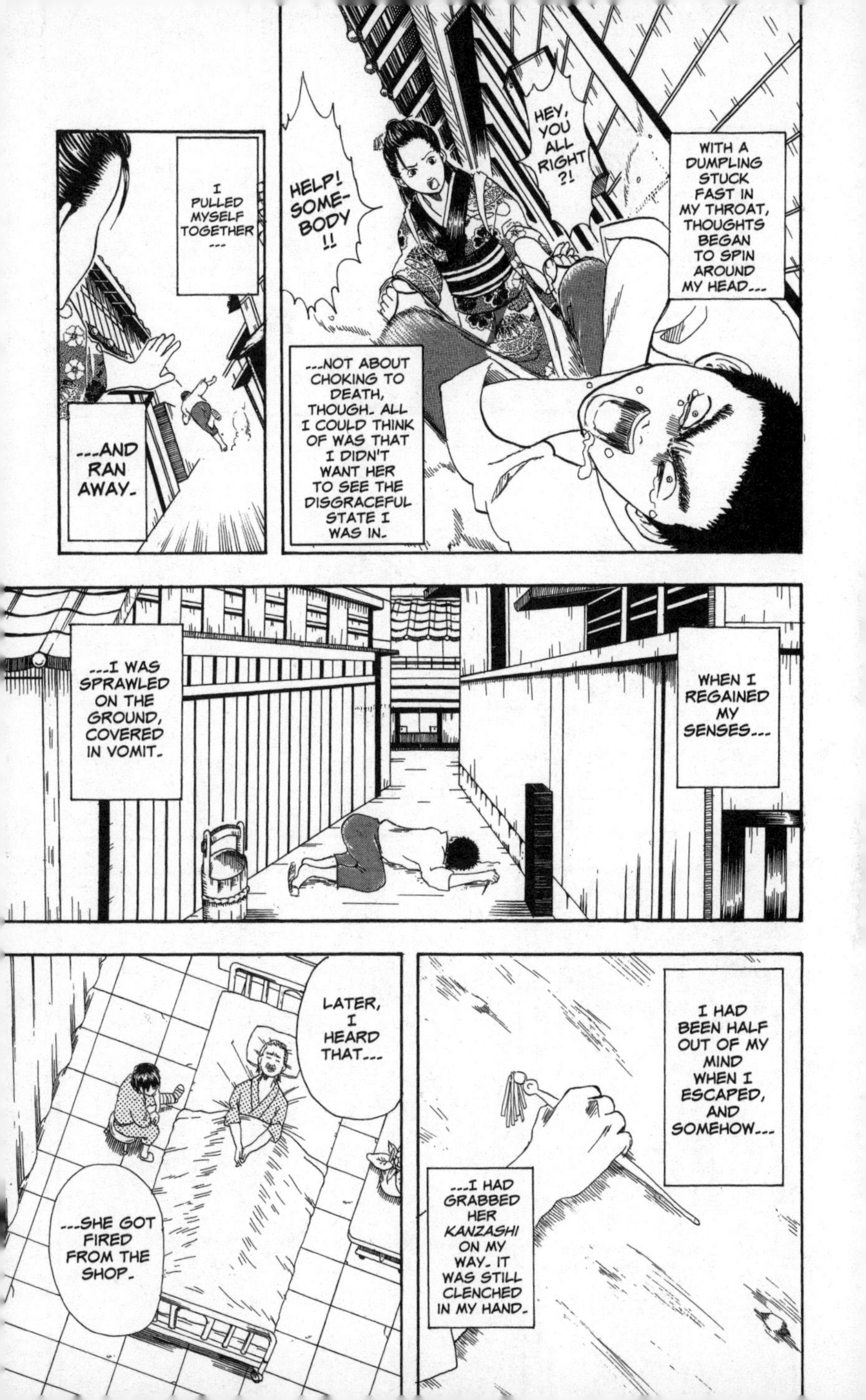
WITH A DUMPLING STUCK FAST IN MY THROAT, THOUGHTS BEGAN TO SPIN AROUND MY HEAD...
HEY, YOU ALL RIGHT?!
HELP! SOMEBODY!!
...NOT ABOUT CHOKING TO DEATH, THOUGH. ALL I COULD THINK OF WAS THAT I DIDN'T WANT HER TO SEE THE DISGRACEFUL STATE I WAS IN.
I PULLED MYSELF TOGETHER...
...AND RAN AWAY.
WHEN I REGAINED MY SENSES...
...I WAS SPRAWLED ON THE GROUND, COVERED IN VOMIT.
I HAD BEEN HALF OUT OF MY MIND WHEN I ESCAPED, AND SOMEHOW...
...I HAD GRABBED HER *KANZASHI* ON MY WAY. IT WAS STILL CLENCHED IN MY HAND.
LATER, I HEARD THAT...
...SHE GOT FIRED FROM THE SHOP.

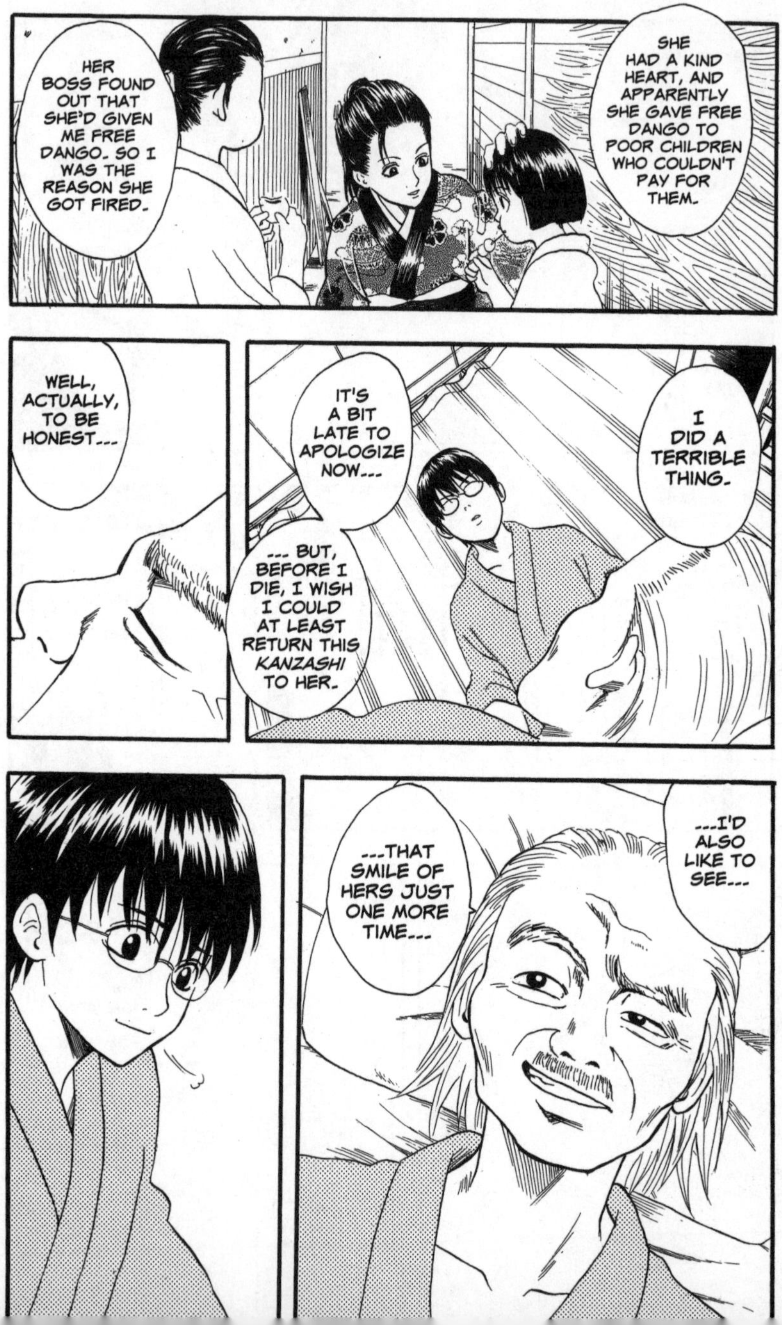
SHE HAD A KIND HEART, AND APPARENTLY SHE GAVE FREE DANGO TO POOR CHILDREN WHO COULDN'T PAY FOR THEM.
HER BOSS FOUND OUT THAT SHE'D GIVEN ME FREE DANGO. SO I WAS THE REASON SHE GOT FIRED.
I DID A TERRIBLE THING.
IT'S A BIT LATE TO APOLOGIZE NOW...
... BUT, BEFORE I DIE, I WISH I COULD AT LEAST RETURN THIS *KANZASHI* TO HER.
WELL, ACTUALLY, TO BE HONEST...
...I'D ALSO LIKE TO SEE...
...THAT SMILE OF HERS JUST ONE MORE TIME...

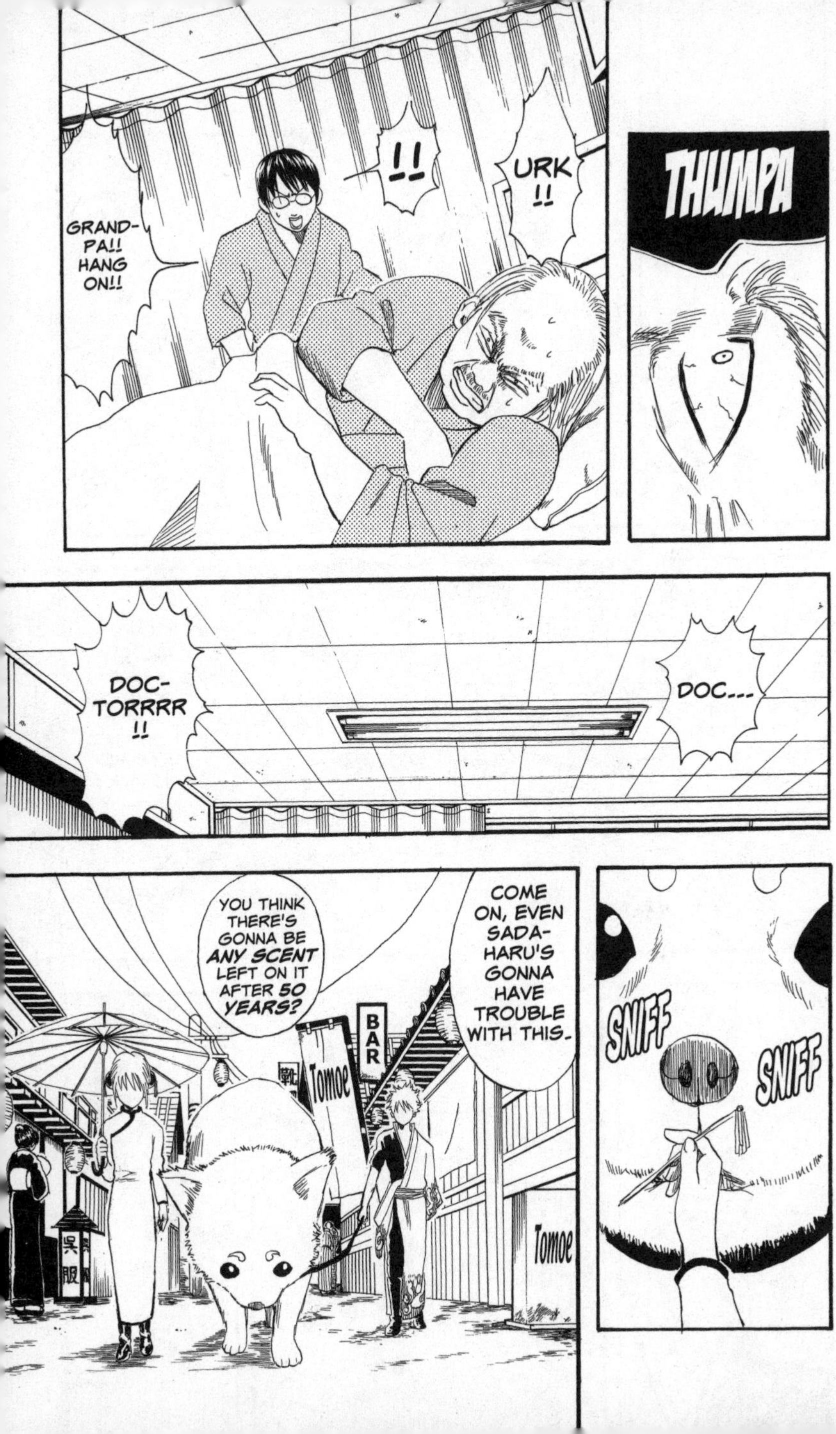
THUMPA
URK !!
!!
GRAND-PA!! HANG ON!!
DOC...
DOC-TORRRR !!
SNIFF
SNIFF
COME ON, EVEN SADA-HARU'S GONNA HAVE TROUBLE WITH THIS.
YOU THINK THERE'S GONNA BE ANY SCENT LEFT ON IT AFTER 50 YEARS?
BAR
Tomoe
Tomoe

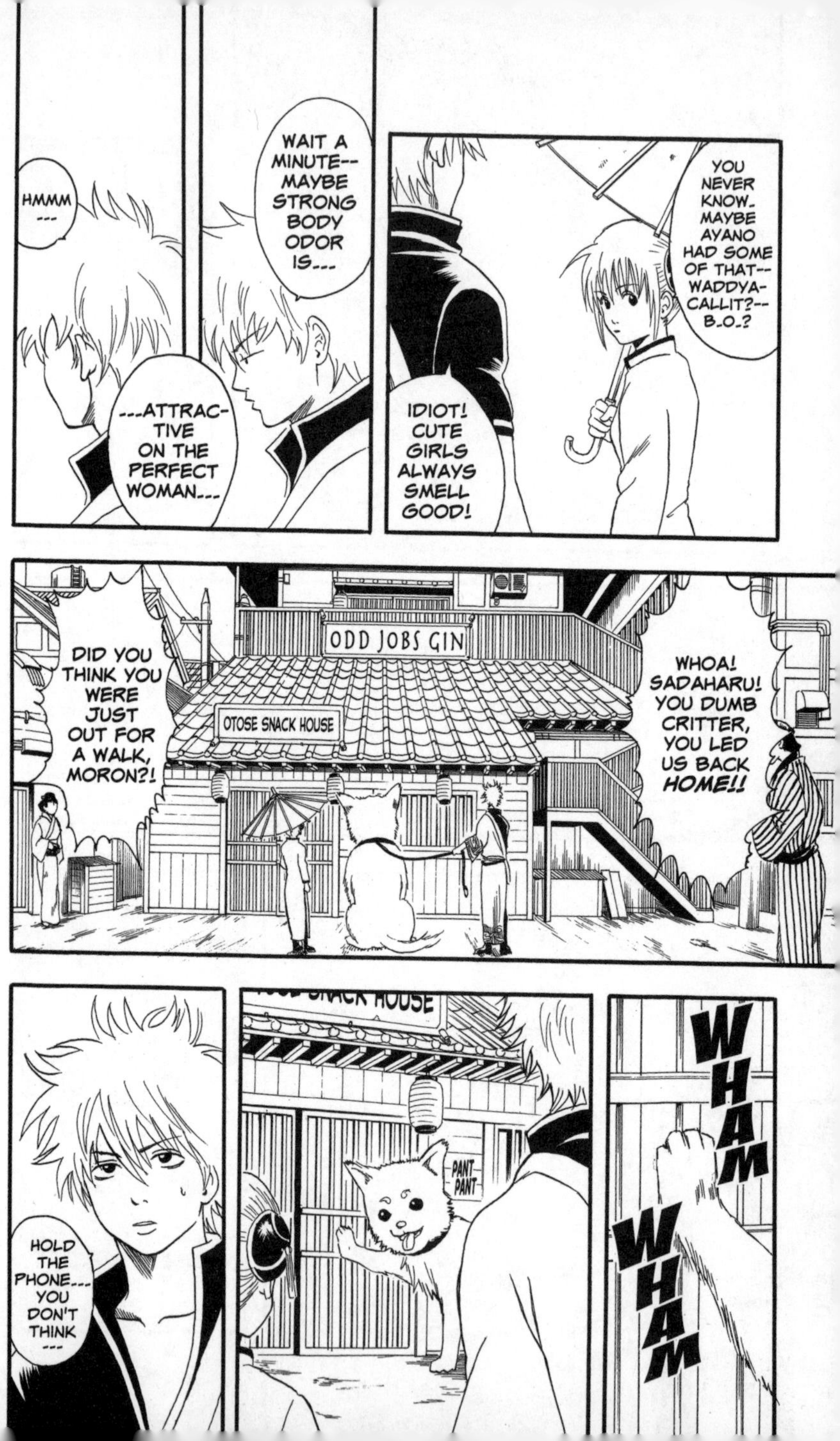

YOU NEVER KNOW... MAYBE AYANO HAD SOME OF THAT--WADDYA-CALLIT?--B.O.?
IDIOT! CUTE GIRLS ALWAYS SMELL GOOD!
WAIT A MINUTE-- MAYBE STRONG BODY ODOR IS...
...ATTRACTIVE ON THE PERFECT WOMAN...
HMMM...
ODD JOBS GIN
OTOSE SNACK HOUSE
WHOA! SADAHARU! YOU DUMB CRITTER, YOU LED US BACK HOME!!
DID YOU THINK YOU WERE JUST OUT FOR A WALK, MORON?!
WHAM
WHAM
SNACK HOUSE
PANT PANT
HOLD THE PHONE... YOU DON'T THINK...

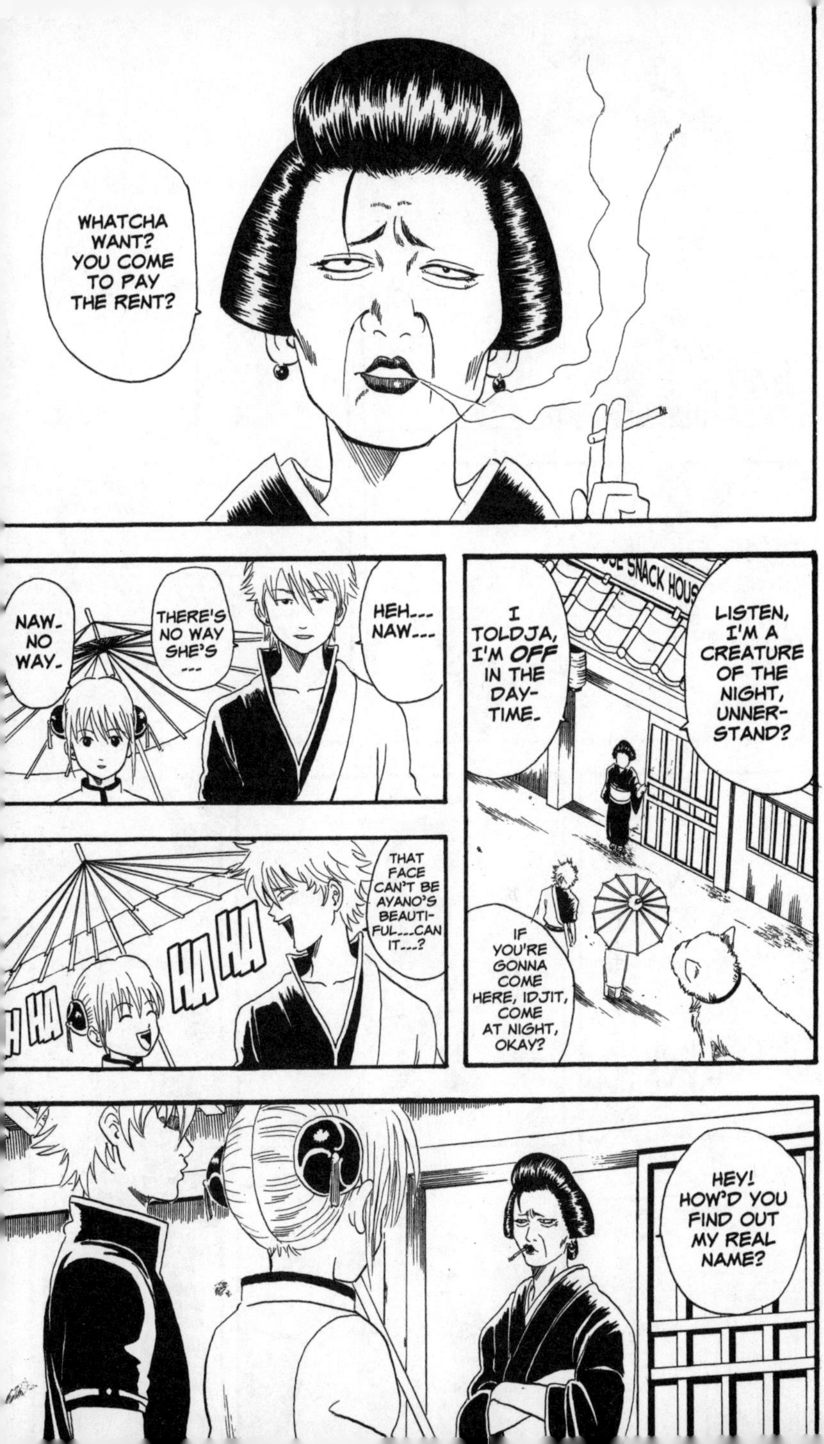
WHATCHA WANT? YOU COME TO PAY THE RENT?
LISTEN, I'M A CREATURE OF THE NIGHT, UNNER-STAND?
I TOLDJA, I'M *OFF* IN THE DAY-TIME.
IF YOU'RE GONNA COME HERE, IDJIT, COME AT NIGHT, OKAY?
HEH... NAW...
THERE'S NO WAY SHE'S ---
NAW. NO WAY.
THAT FACE CAN'T BE AYANO'S BEAUTI-FUL...CAN IT...?
HA HA
HEY! HOW'D YOU FIND OUT MY REAL NAME?

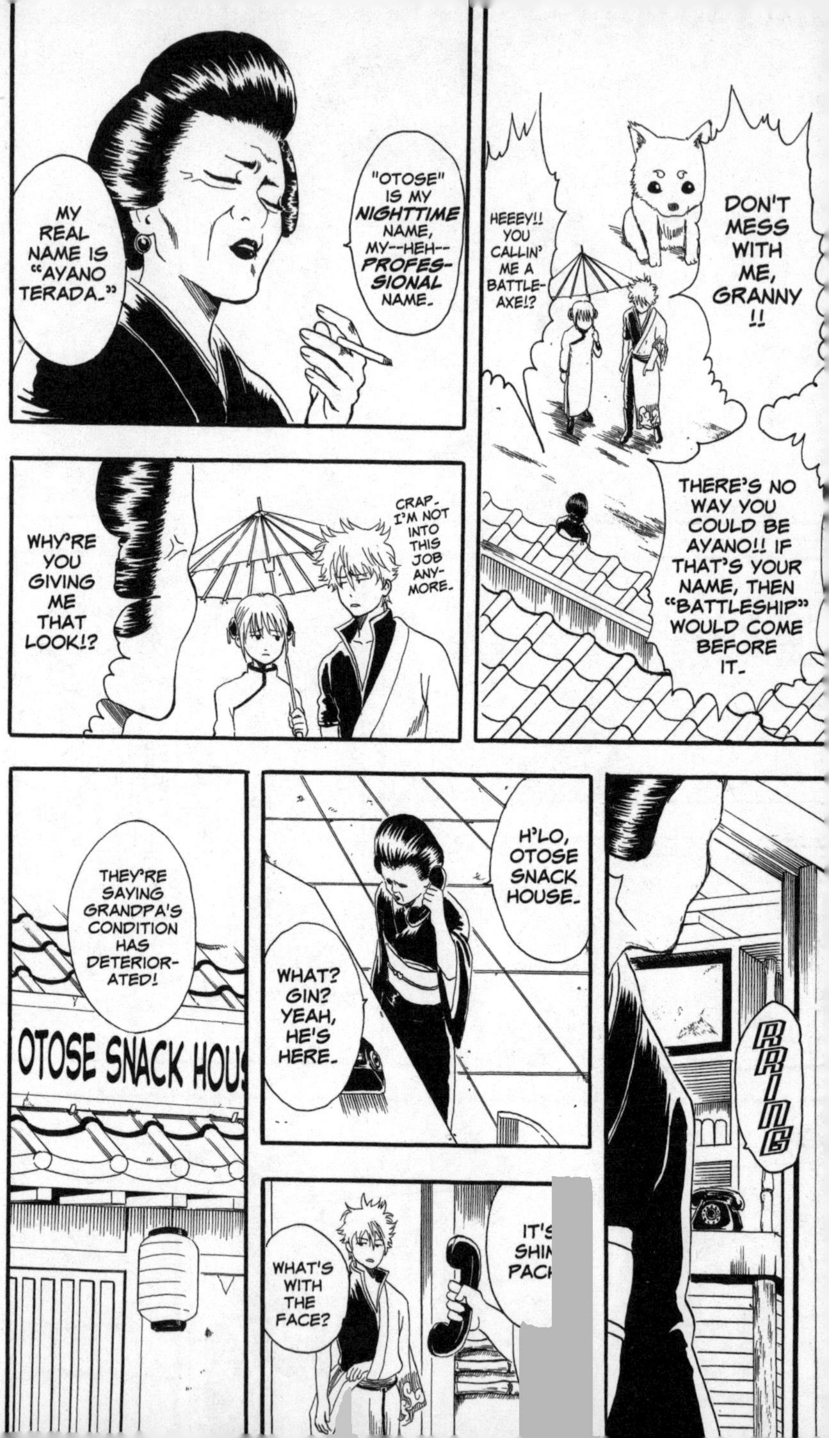
"OTOSE" IS MY NIGHTTIME NAME, MY--HEH--PROFESSIONAL NAME.
MY REAL NAME IS "AYANO TERADA."
WHY'RE YOU GIVING ME THAT LOOK!?
CRAP. I'M NOT INTO THIS JOB ANYMORE.
DON'T MESS WITH ME, GRANNY!!
HEEEY!! YOU CALLIN' ME A BATTLE-AXE!?
THERE'S NO WAY YOU COULD BE AYANO!! IF THAT'S YOUR NAME, THEN "BATTLESHIP" WOULD COME BEFORE IT.
RRING
H'LO, OTOSE SNACK HOUSE.
WHAT? GIN? YEAH, HE'S HERE.
IT'S SHIN PACK
WHAT'S WITH THE FACE?
OTOSE SNACK HOUS
THEY'RE SAYING GRANDPA'S CONDITION HAS DETERIORATED!

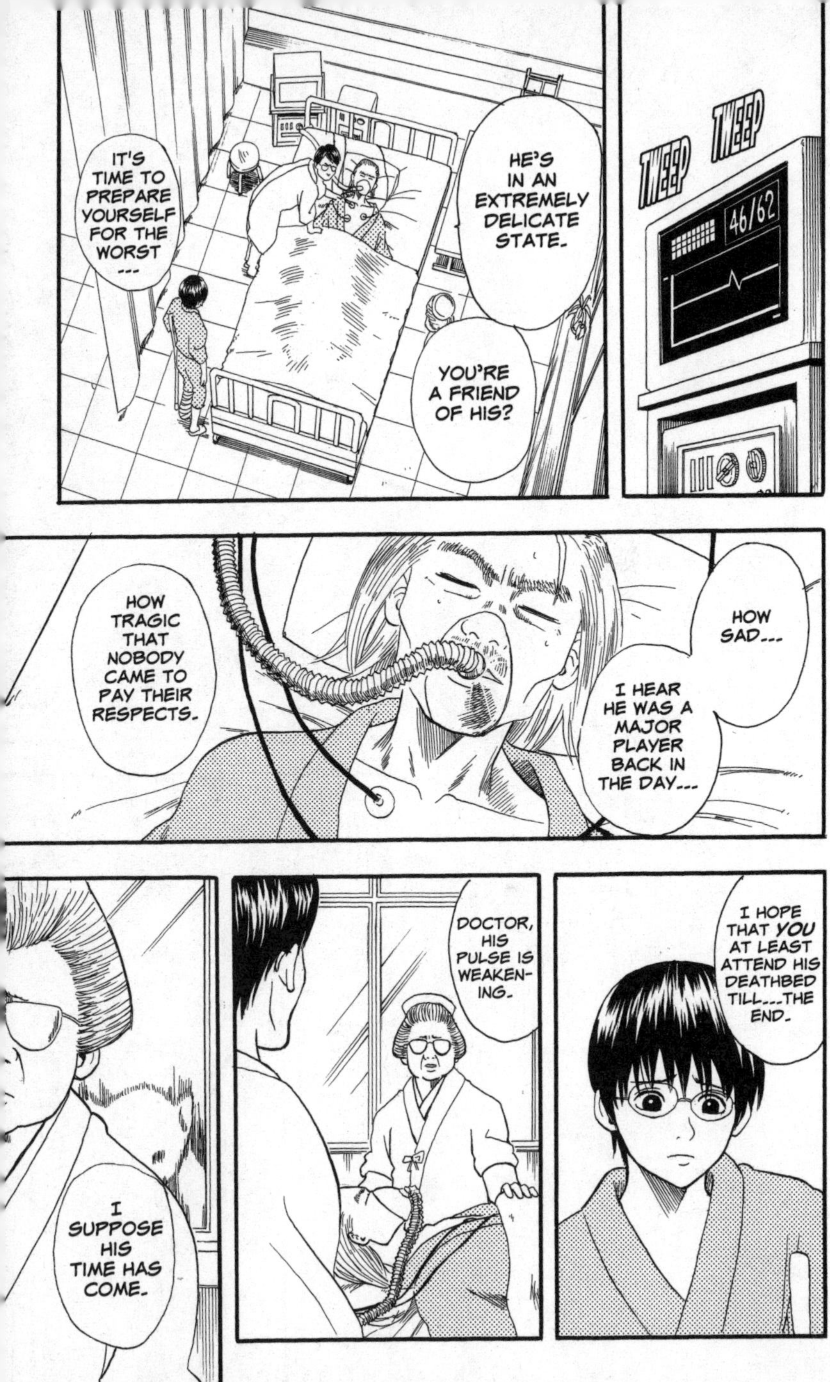
TWEEP TWEEP
46/62
HE'S IN AN EXTREMELY DELICATE STATE.
YOU'RE A FRIEND OF HIS?
IT'S TIME TO PREPARE YOURSELF FOR THE WORST...
HOW SAD...
I HEAR HE WAS A MAJOR PLAYER BACK IN THE DAY...
HOW TRAGIC THAT NOBODY CAME TO PAY THEIR RESPECTS.
I HOPE THAT *YOU* AT LEAST ATTEND HIS DEATHBED TILL...THE END.
DOCTOR, HIS PULSE IS WEAKEN-ING.
I SUPPOSE HIS TIME HAS COME.

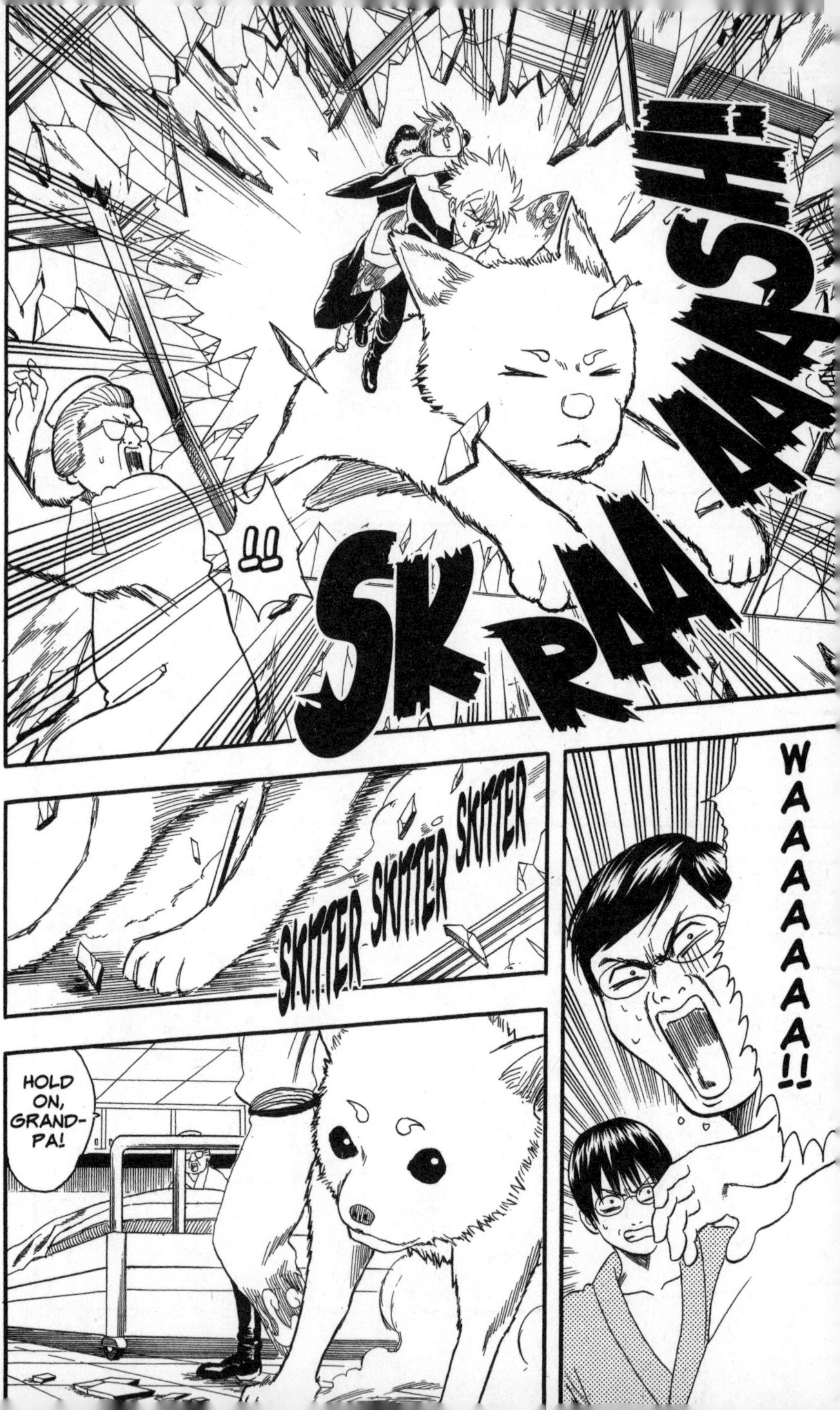
!!
SKRAAAASH!!
WAAAAAAAA!!
SKITTER SKITTER SKITTER
HOLD ON, GRANDPA!

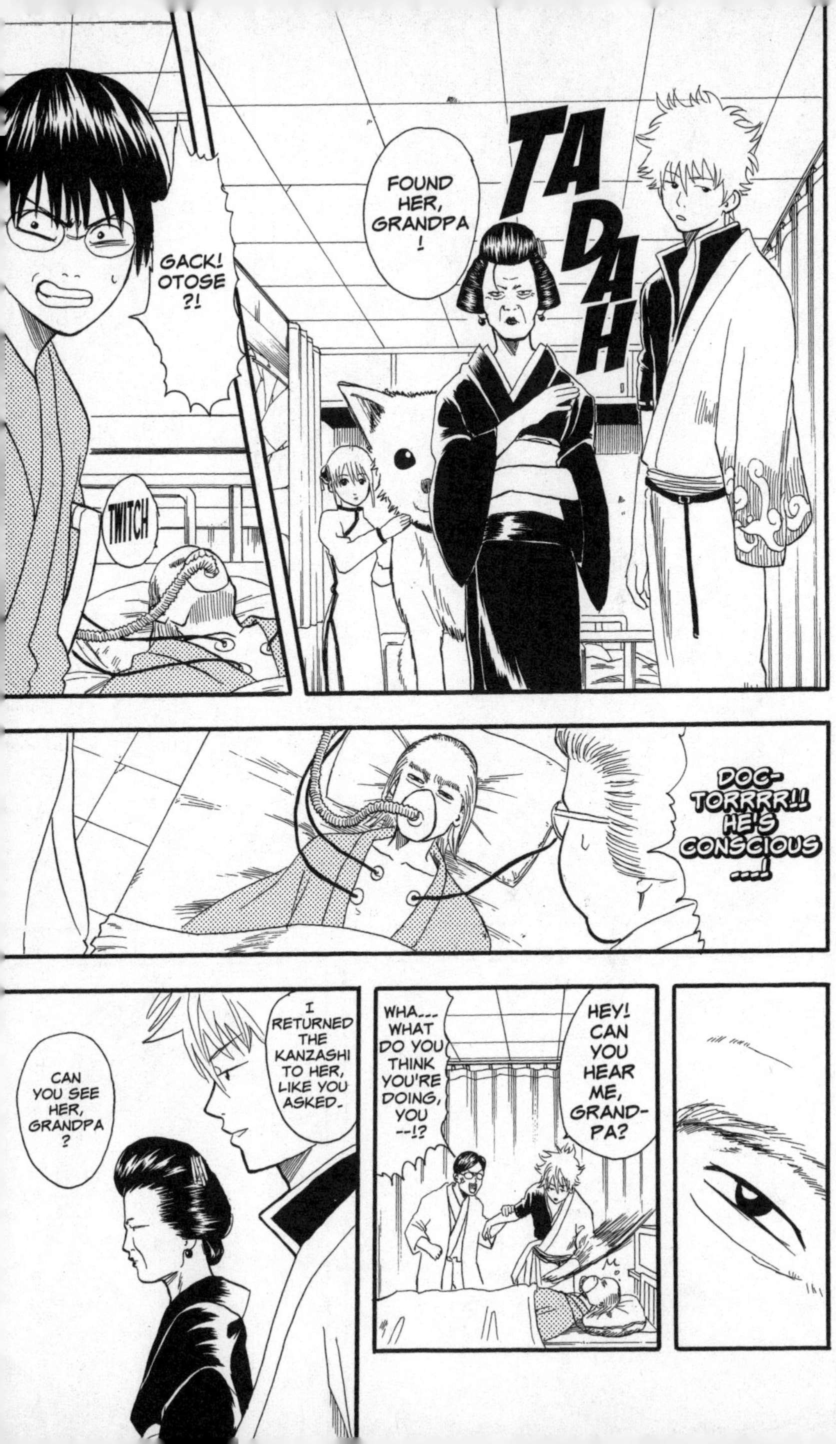
TADAH
FOUND HER, GRANDPA!
GACK! OTOSE?!
TWITCH
DOC-TORRRR!! HE'S CONSCIOUS...!
HEY! CAN YOU HEAR ME, GRANDPA?
WHA... WHAT DO YOU THINK YOU'RE DOING, YOU--!?
I RETURNED THE KANZASHI TO HER, LIKE YOU ASKED.
CAN YOU SEE HER, GRANDPA?

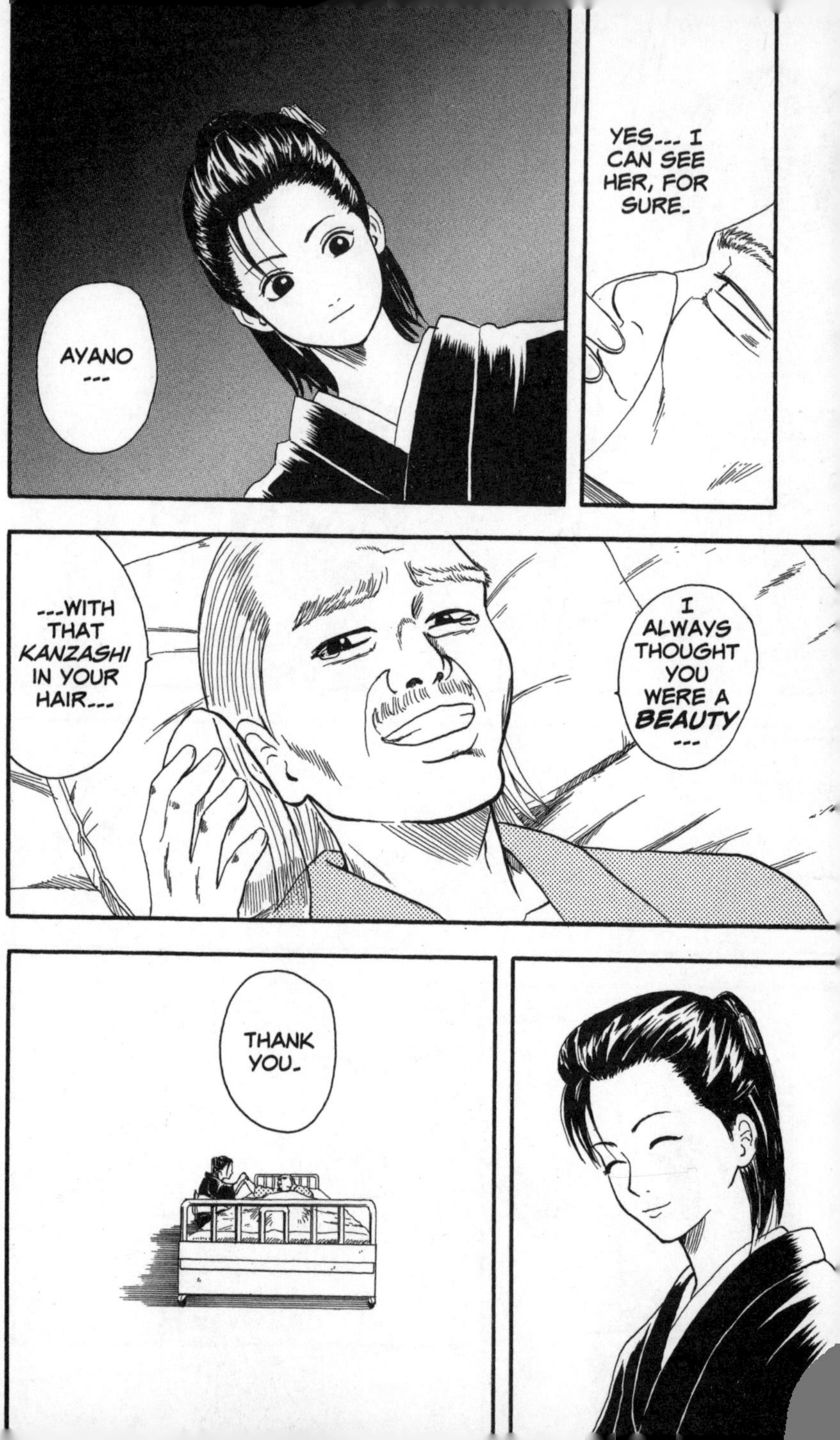
YES... I CAN SEE HER, FOR SURE.
AYANO...
I ALWAYS THOUGHT YOU WERE A BEAUTY...
...WITH THAT KANZASHI IN YOUR HAIR...
THANK YOU.

READ THIS WAY

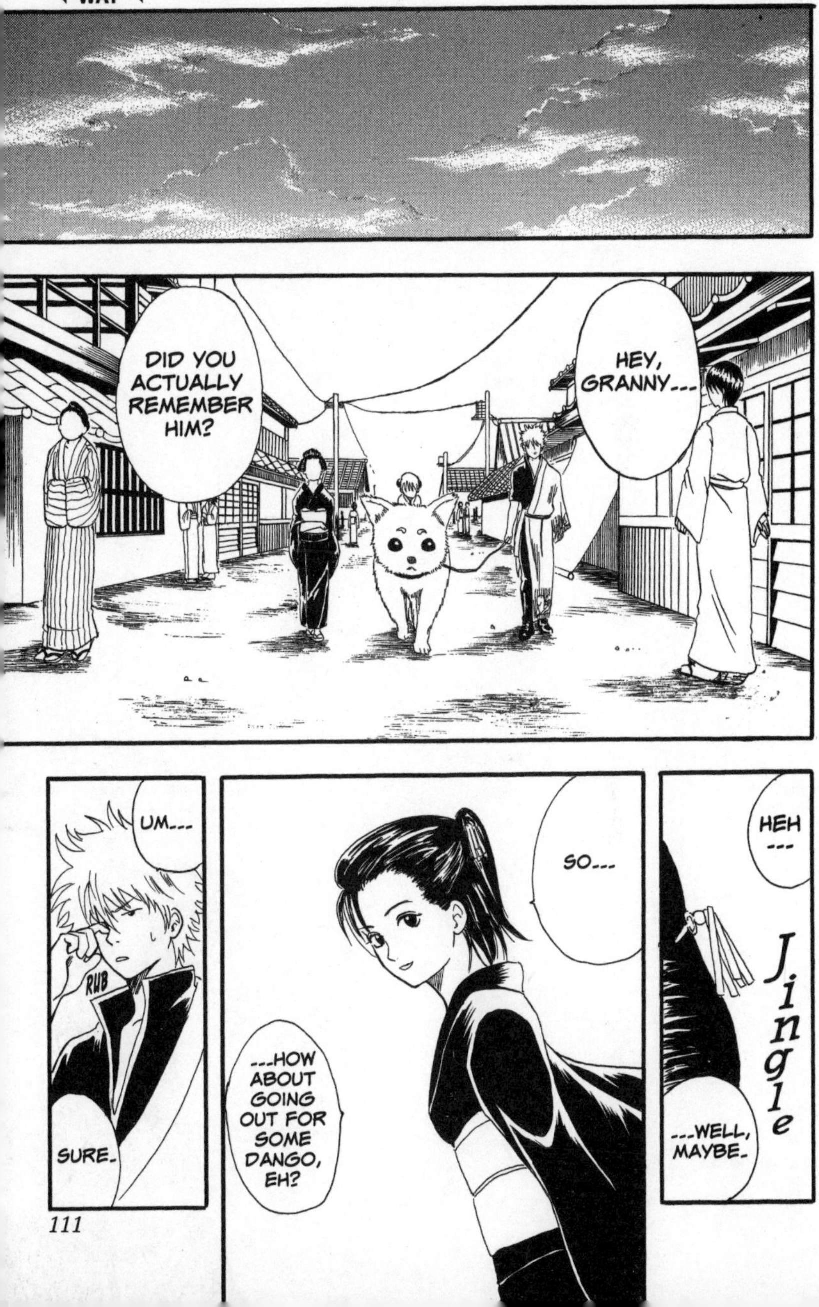
HEY, GRANNY...
DID YOU ACTUALLY REMEMBER HIM?
HEH...
Jingle
...WELL, MAYBE.
SO...
...HOW ABOUT GOING OUT FOR SOME DANGO, EH?
UM...
RUB
SURE.

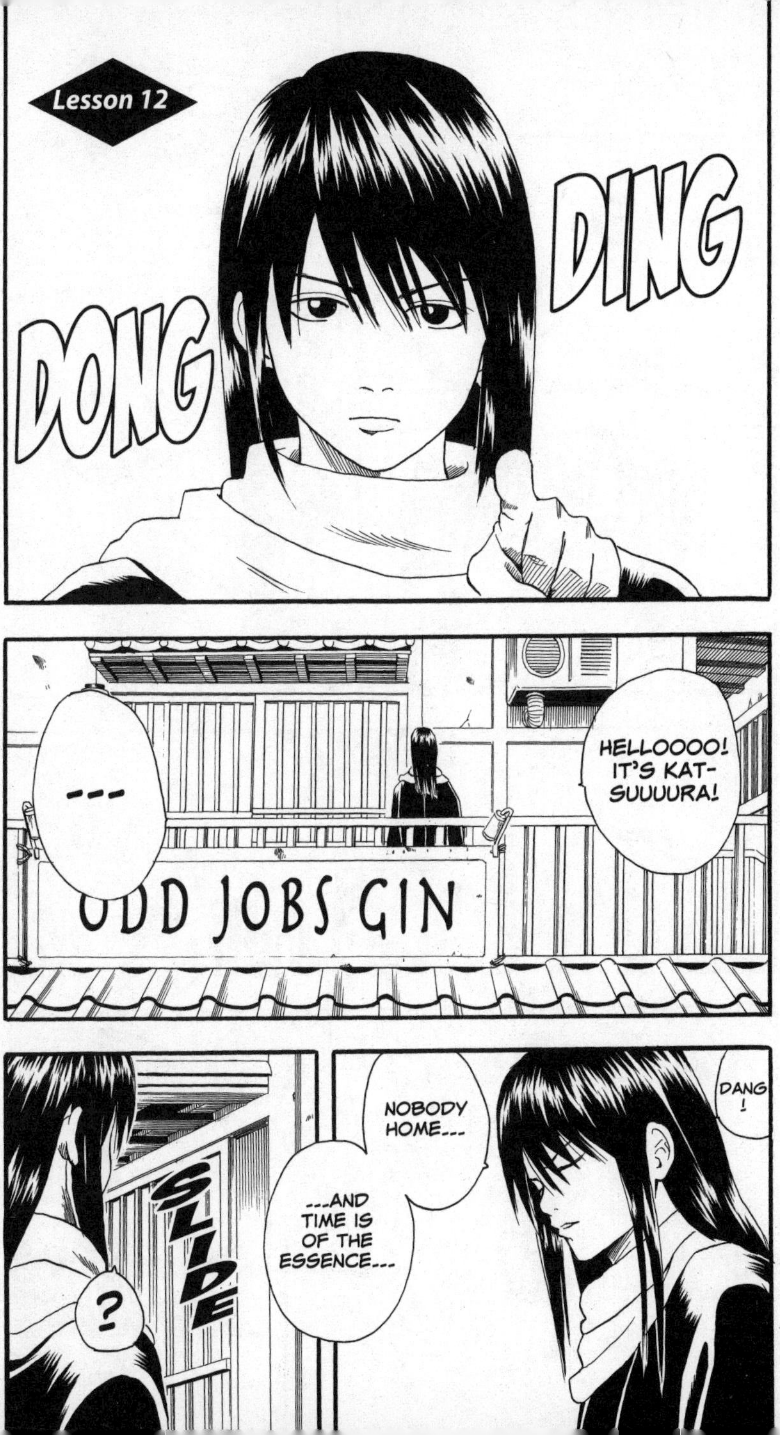
Lesson 12
DING
DONG
HELLOOOO! IT'S KAT-SUUUURA!
...
DANG!
NOBODY HOME...
...AND TIME IS OF THE ESSENCE...
SLIDE
?
ODD JOBS GIN

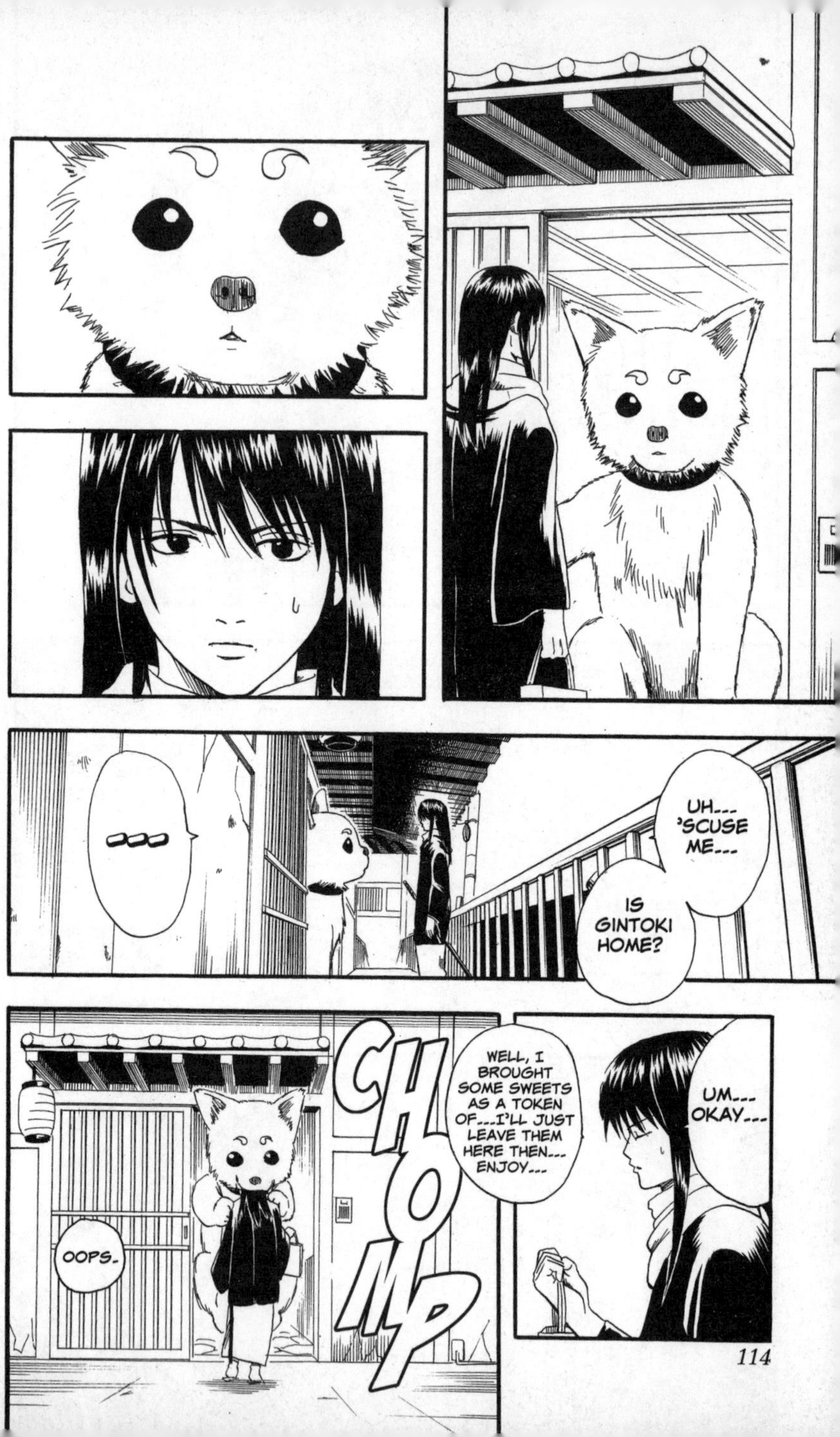

UH... 'SCUSE ME...
IS GINTOKI HOME?
......
UM... OKAY...
WELL, I BROUGHT SOME SWEETS AS A TOKEN OF...I'LL JUST LEAVE THEM HERE THEN... ENJOY...
CHOMP
OOPS.

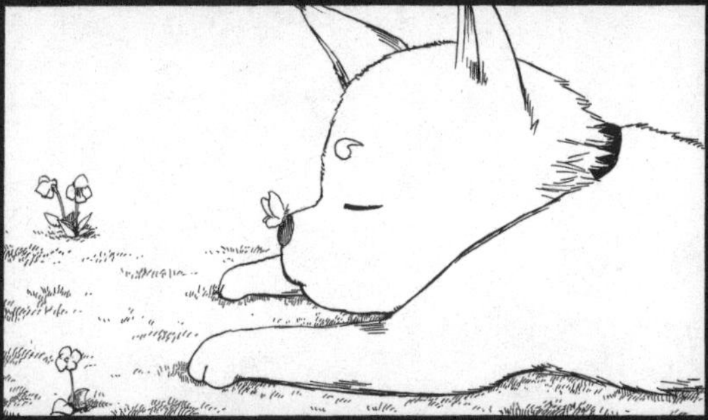

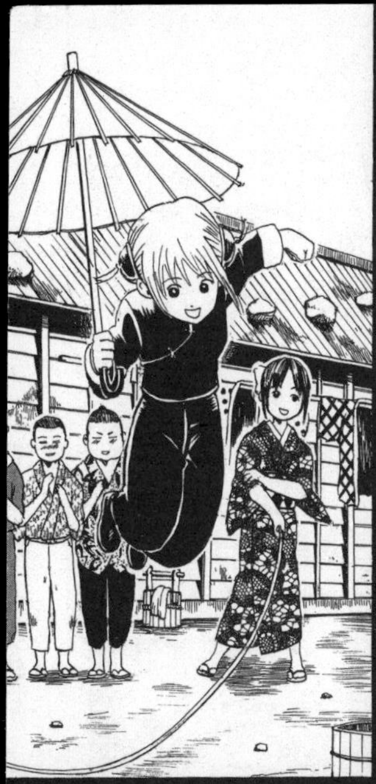

Lesson 12

Young Girls Across the Country, Get Home Before Curfew

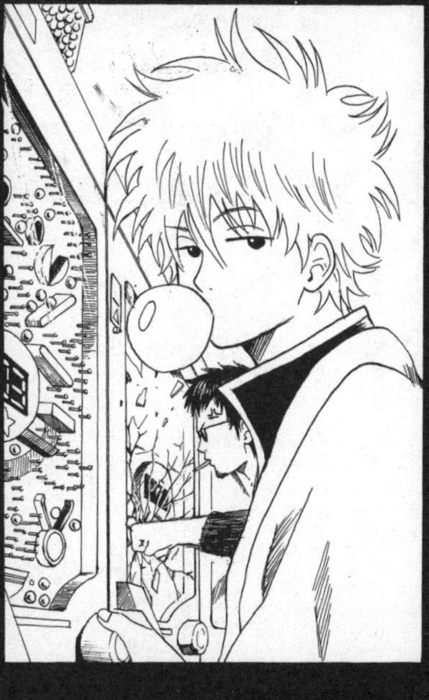

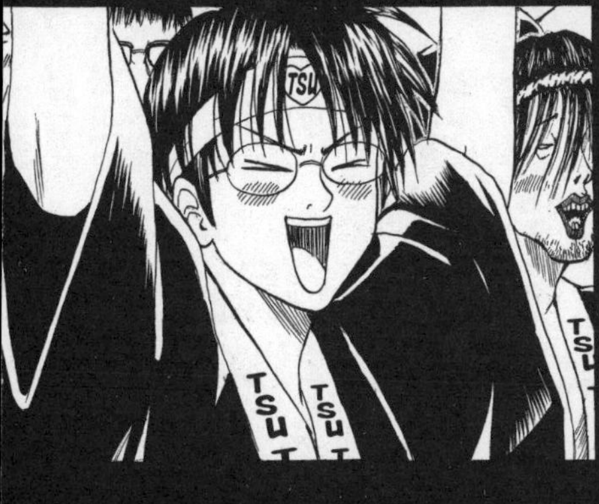
TSU
TSU
TSU
TSU

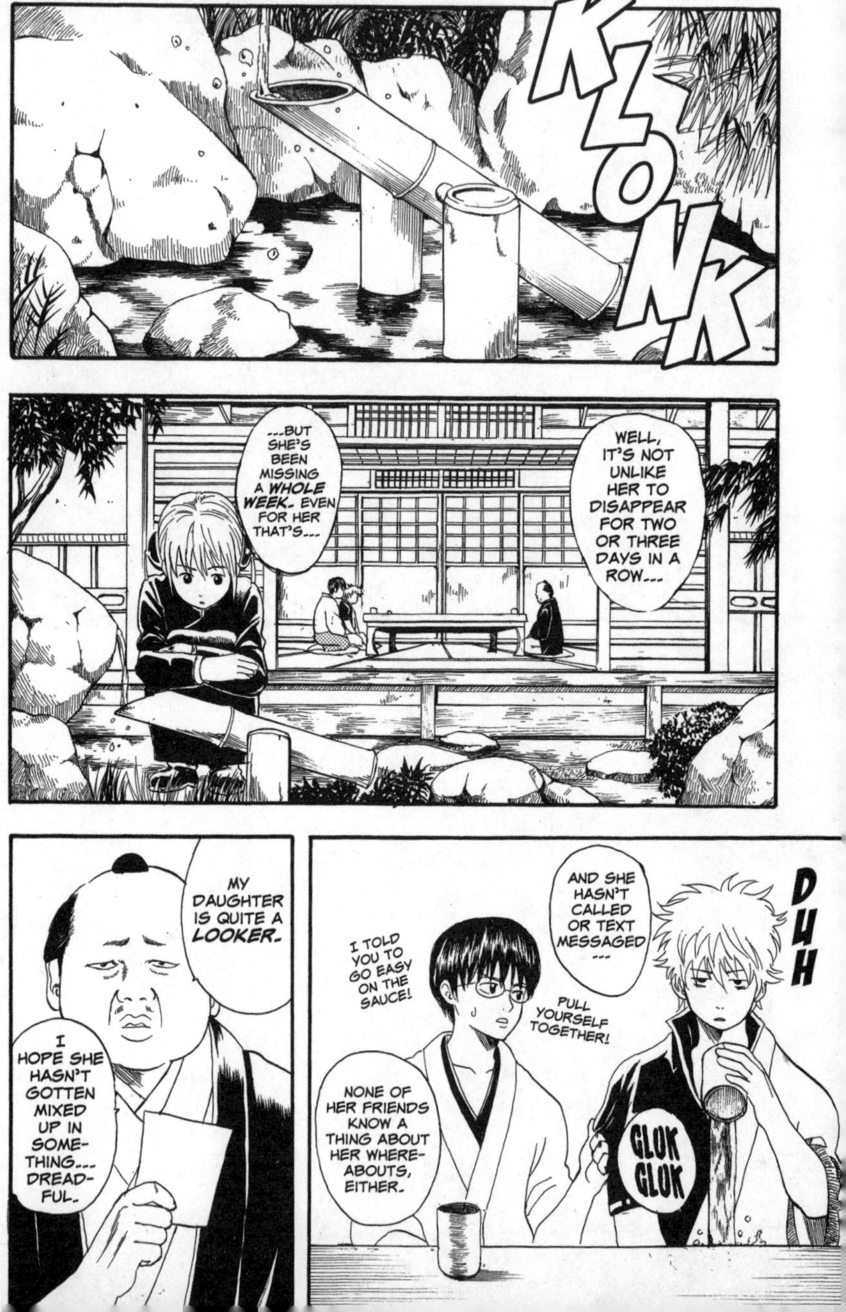
KLONK
WELL, IT'S NOT UNLIKE HER TO DISAPPEAR FOR TWO OR THREE DAYS IN A ROW...
...BUT SHE'S BEEN MISSING A ***WHOLE WEEK.*** EVEN FOR HER THAT'S...
DUH
AND SHE HASN'T CALLED OR TEXT MESSAGED ...
PULL YOURSELF TOGETHER!
I TOLD YOU TO GO EASY ON THE SAUCE!
GLOK GLOK
NONE OF HER FRIENDS KNOW A THING ABOUT HER WHEREABOUTS, EITHER.
MY DAUGHTER IS QUITE A ***LOOKER.***
I HOPE SHE HASN'T GOTTEN MIXED UP IN SOMETHING... DREADFUL.

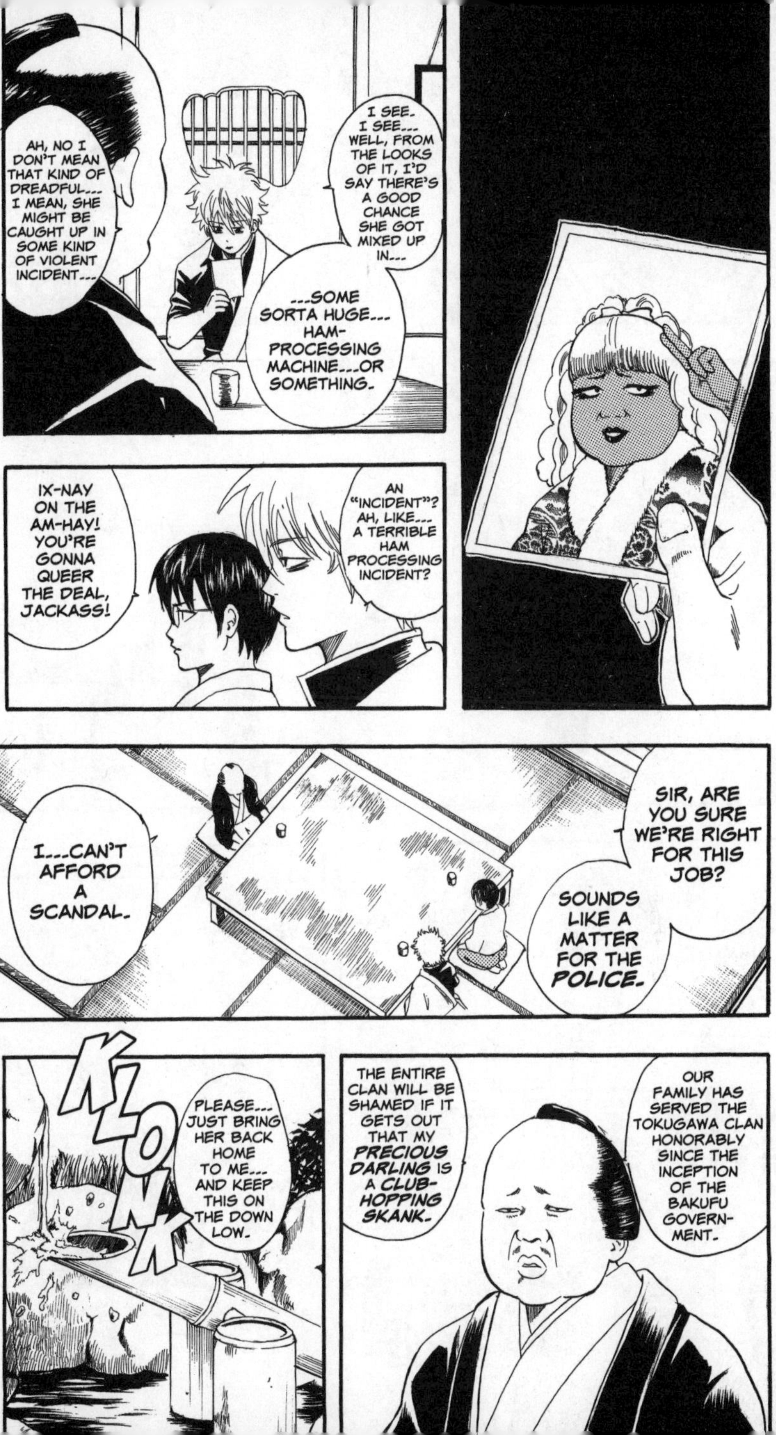
I SEE. I SEE... WELL, FROM THE LOOKS OF IT, I'D SAY THERE'S A GOOD CHANCE SHE GOT MIXED UP IN...
...SOME SORTA HUGE... HAM-PROCESSING MACHINE...OR SOMETHING.
AH, NO I DON'T MEAN THAT KIND OF DREADFUL... I MEAN, SHE MIGHT BE CAUGHT UP IN SOME KIND OF VIOLENT INCIDENT...
AN "INCIDENT"? AH, LIKE... A TERRIBLE HAM PROCESSING INCIDENT?
IX-NAY ON THE AM-HAY! YOU'RE GONNA QUEER THE DEAL, JACKASS!
SIR, ARE YOU SURE WE'RE RIGHT FOR THIS JOB?
SOUNDS LIKE A MATTER FOR THE *POLICE*.
I...CAN'T AFFORD A SCANDAL.
OUR FAMILY HAS SERVED THE TOKUGAWA CLAN HONORABLY SINCE THE INCEPTION OF THE BAKUFU GOVERNMENT.
THE ENTIRE CLAN WILL BE SHAMED IF IT GETS OUT THAT MY *PRECIOUS DARLING* IS A *CLUB-HOPPING SKANK*.
PLEASE... JUST BRING HER BACK HOME TO ME... AND KEEP THIS ON THE DOWN LOW.
KLONK

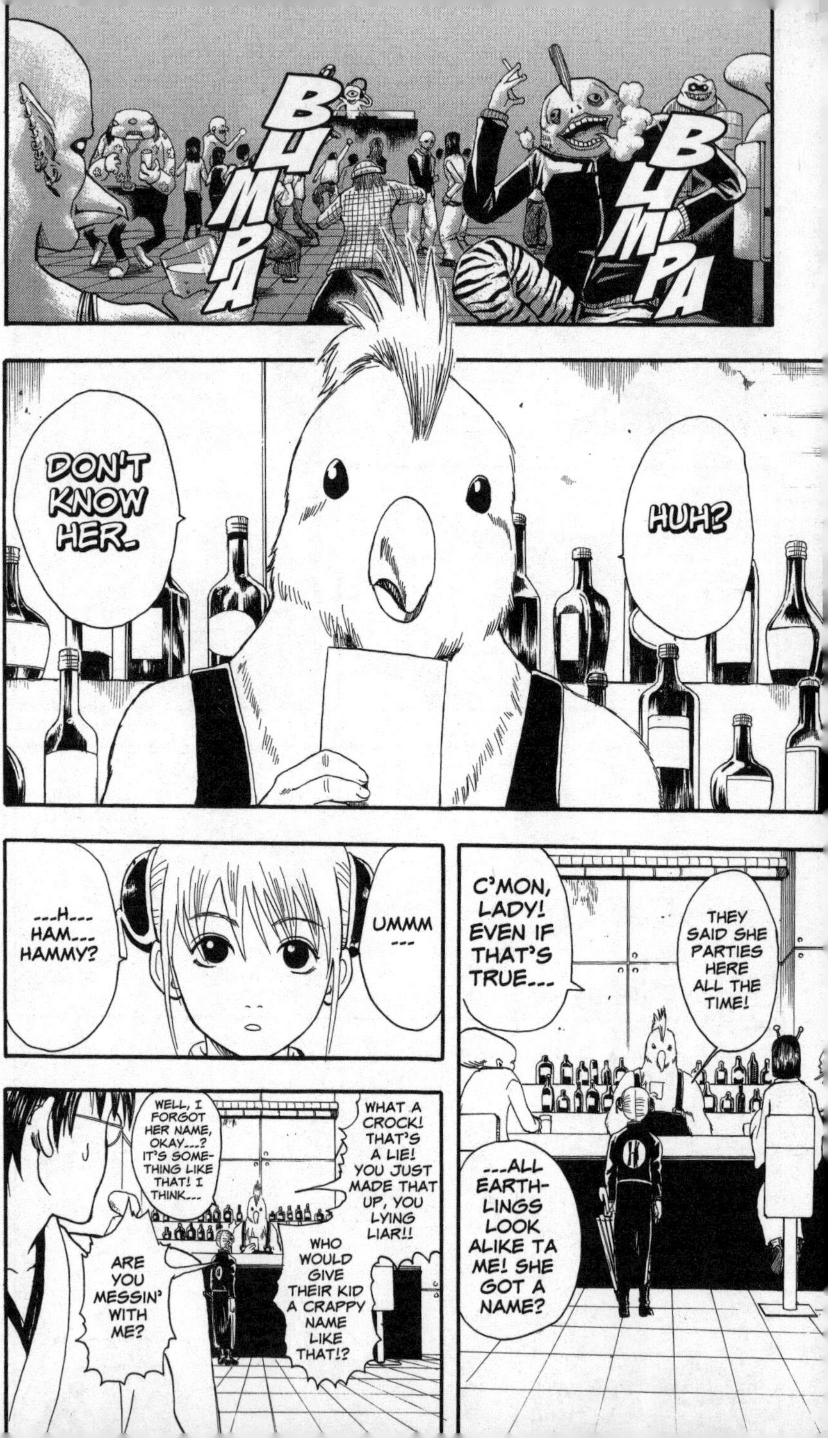
BUMPA
BUMPA
HUH?
DON'T KNOW HER...
THEY SAID SHE PARTIES HERE ALL THE TIME!
C'MON, LADY! EVEN IF THAT'S TRUE...
...ALL EARTH-LINGS LOOK ALIKE TA ME! SHE GOT A NAME?
UMMM...
...H... HAM... HAMMY?
WHAT A CROCK! THAT'S A LIE! YOU JUST MADE THAT UP, YOU LYING LIAR!!
WELL, I FORGOT HER NAME, OKAY...? IT'S SOME-THING LIKE THAT! I THINK...
WHO WOULD GIVE THEIR KID A CRAPPY NAME LIKE THAT!?
ARE YOU MESSIN' WITH ME?

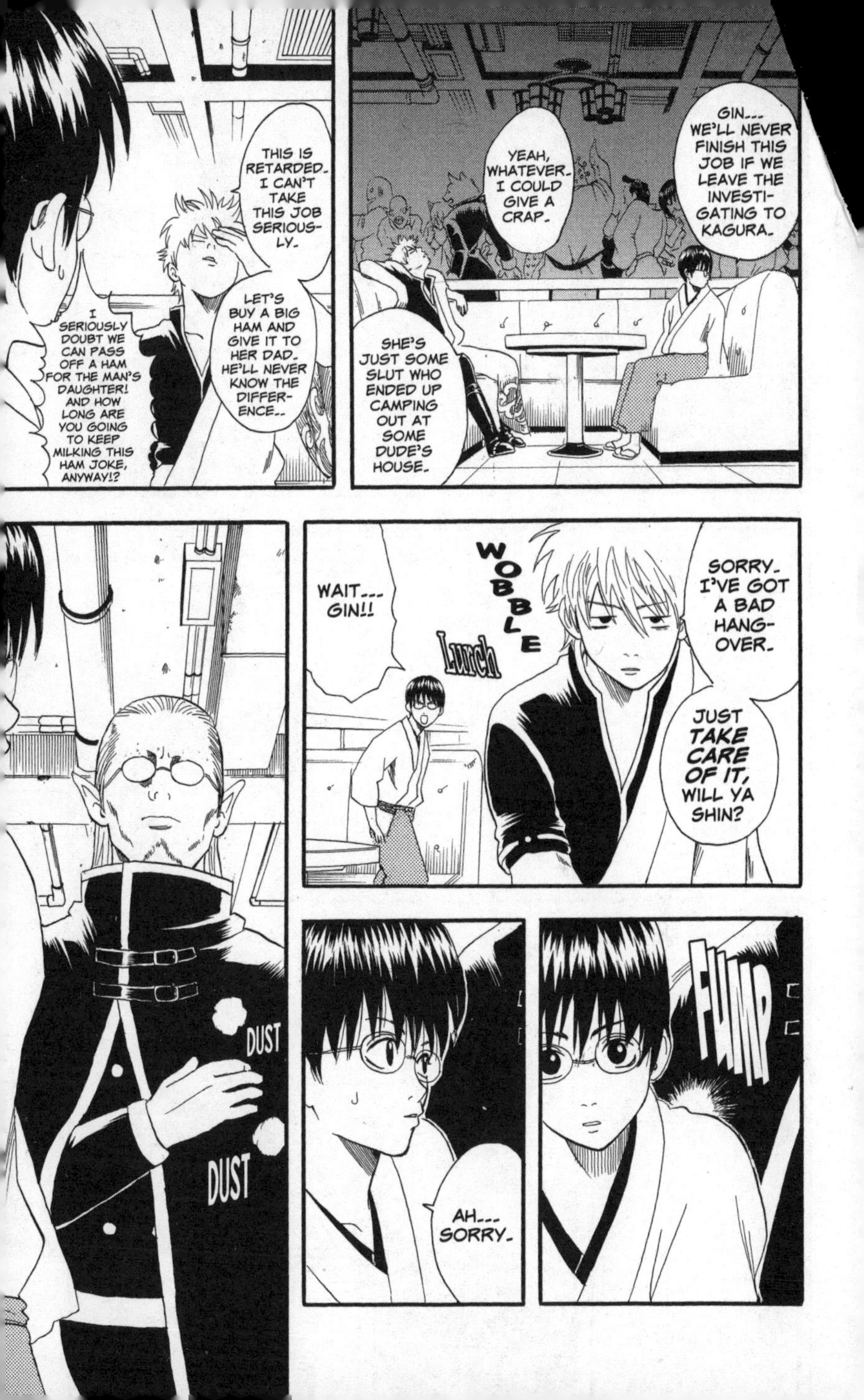
GIN... WE'LL NEVER FINISH THIS JOB IF WE LEAVE THE INVESTI-GATING TO KAGURA.
YEAH, WHATEVER. I COULD GIVE A CRAP.
SHE'S JUST SOME SLUT WHO ENDED UP CAMPING OUT AT SOME DUDE'S HOUSE.
THIS IS RETARDED. I CAN'T TAKE THIS JOB SERIOUS-LY.
LET'S BUY A BIG HAM AND GIVE IT TO HER DAD. HE'LL NEVER KNOW THE DIFFER-ENCE..
I SERIOUSLY DOUBT WE CAN PASS OFF A HAM FOR THE MAN'S DAUGHTER! AND HOW LONG ARE YOU GOING TO KEEP MILKING THIS HAM JOKE, ANYWAY!?
SORRY. I'VE GOT A BAD HANG-OVER.
JUST TAKE CARE OF IT, WILL YA SHIN?
WOBBLE
Lurch
WAIT... GIN!!
FUMP
AH... SORRY.
DUST
DUST

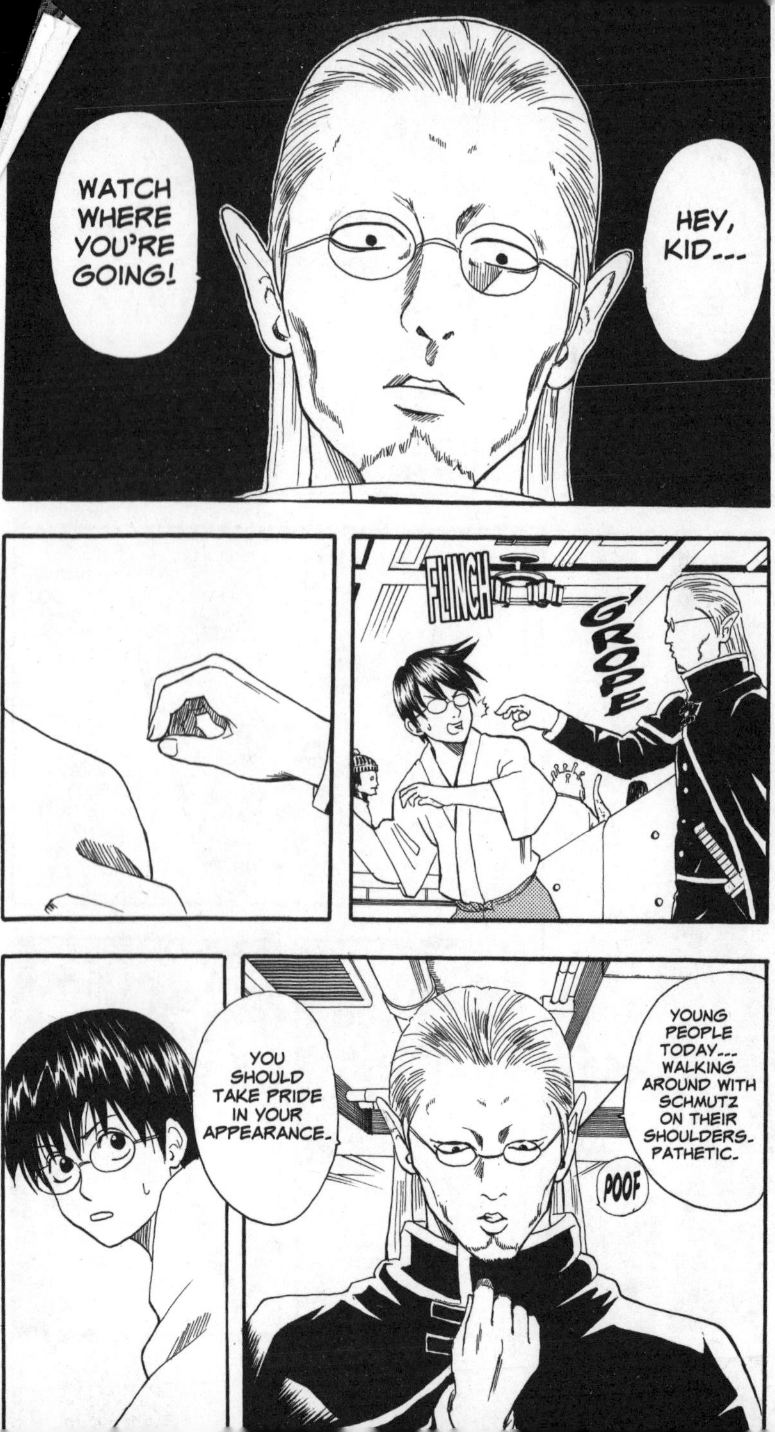
HEY, KID...
WATCH WHERE YOU'RE GOING!
FLINCH
GROPE
YOUNG PEOPLE TODAY... WALKING AROUND WITH SCHMUTZ ON THEIR SHOULDERS. PATHETIC.
POOF
YOU SHOULD TAKE PRIDE IN YOUR APPEARANCE.

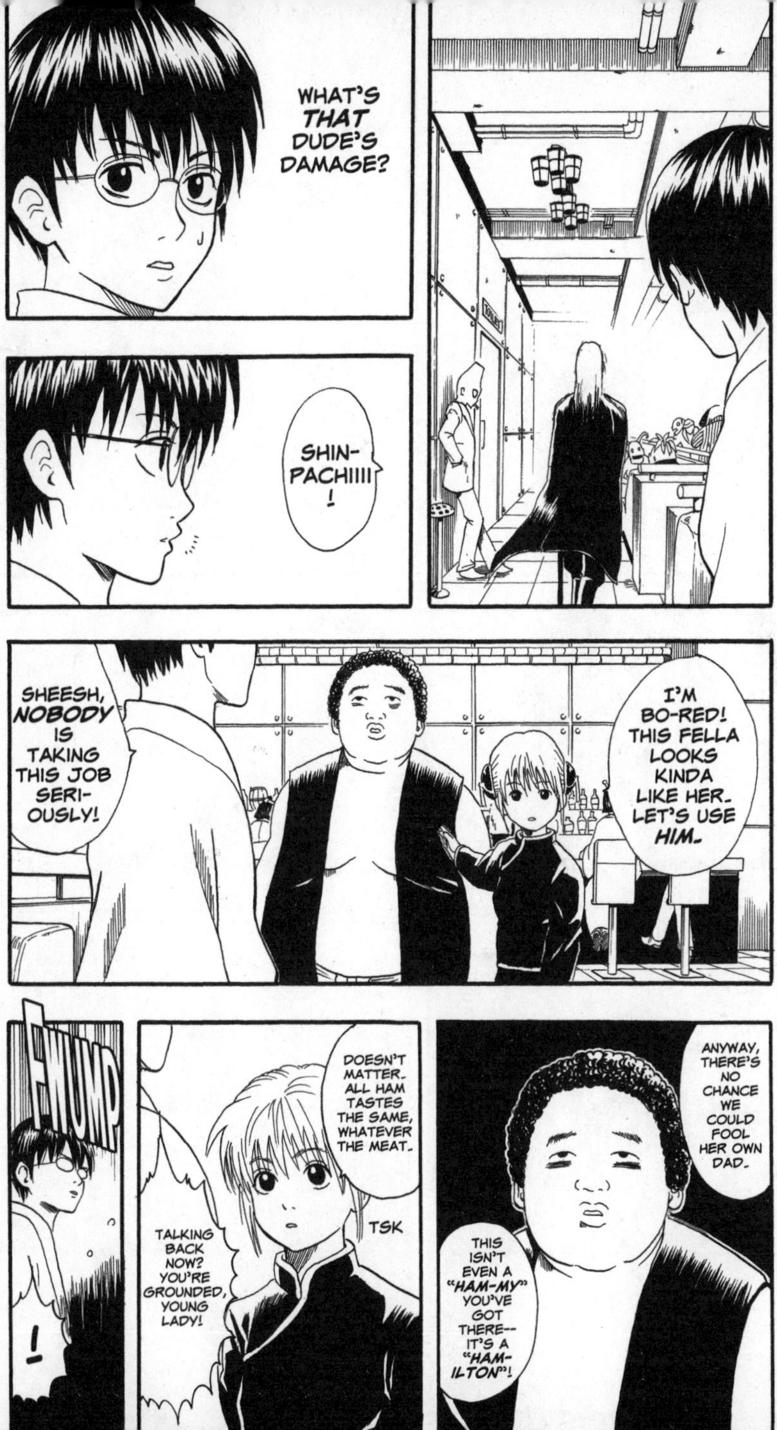
WHAT'S *THAT* DUDE'S DAMAGE?
SHIN-PACHI!!!!!
I'M BO-RED! THIS FELLA LOOKS KINDA LIKE HER. LET'S USE *HIM*.
SHEESH, *NOBODY* IS TAKING THIS JOB SERI-OUSLY!
ANYWAY, THERE'S NO CHANCE WE COULD FOOL HER OWN DAD.
THIS ISN'T EVEN A "*HAM-MY*" YOU'VE GOT THERE-- IT'S A "*HAM-ILTON*"!
DOESN'T MATTER. ALL HAM TASTES THE SAME, WHATEVER THE MEAT.
TSK
TALKING BACK NOW? YOU'RE GROUNDED, YOUNG LADY!
FWUMP
!

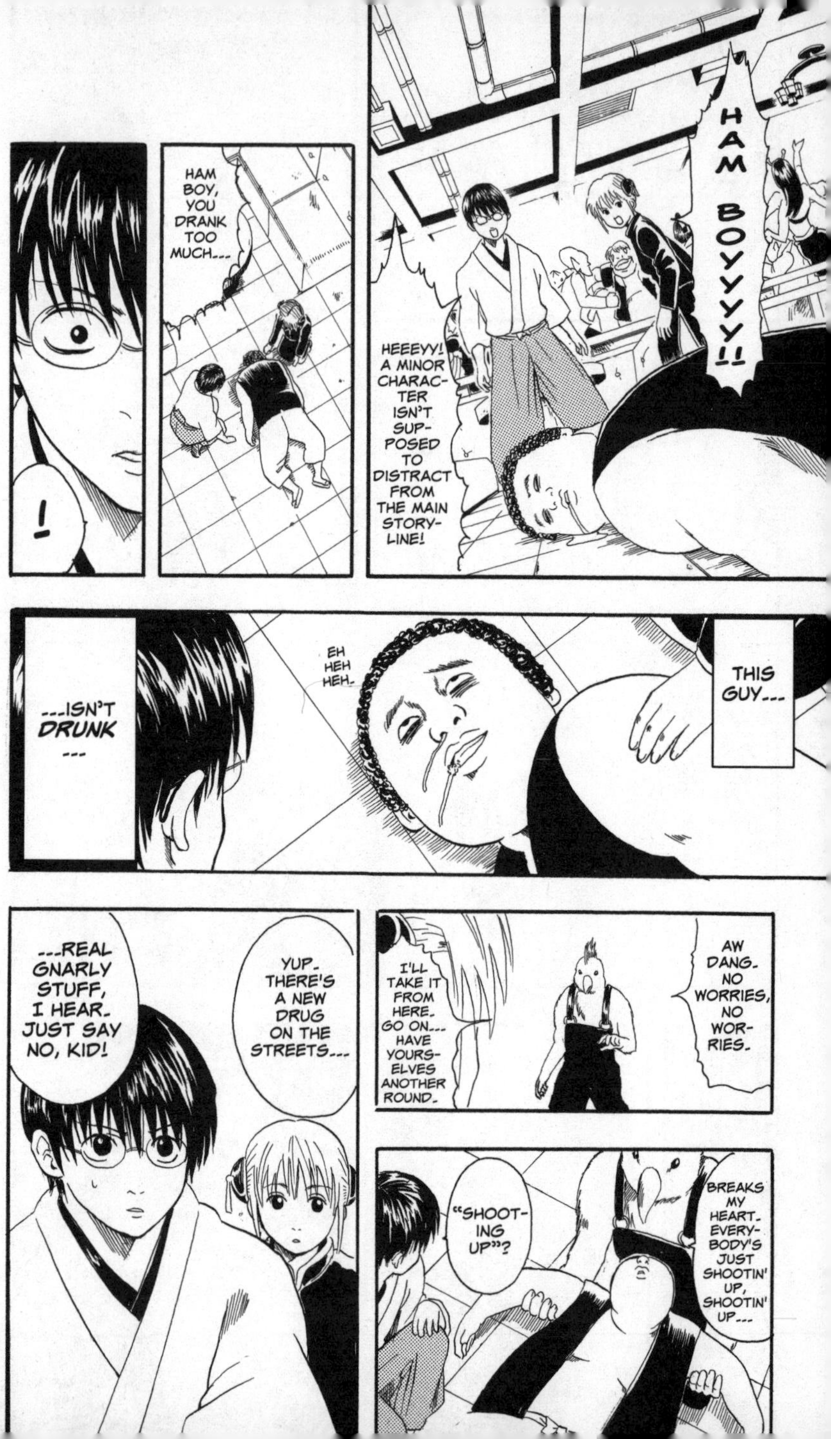
HAM BOYYYYY!!
HEEEYY! A MINOR CHARACTER ISN'T SUPPOSED TO DISTRACT FROM THE MAIN STORYLINE!
HAM BOY, YOU DRANK TOO MUCH...
!
THIS GUY...
EH HEH HEH.
...ISN'T DRUNK ...
AW DANG. NO WORRIES, NO WORRIES.
I'LL TAKE IT FROM HERE. GO ON... HAVE YOURSELVES ANOTHER ROUND.
BREAKS MY HEART. EVERYBODY'S JUST SHOOTIN' UP, SHOOTIN' UP...
"SHOOTING UP"?
YUP. THERE'S A NEW DRUG ON THE STREETS...
...REAL GNARLY STUFF, I HEAR. JUST SAY NO, KID!

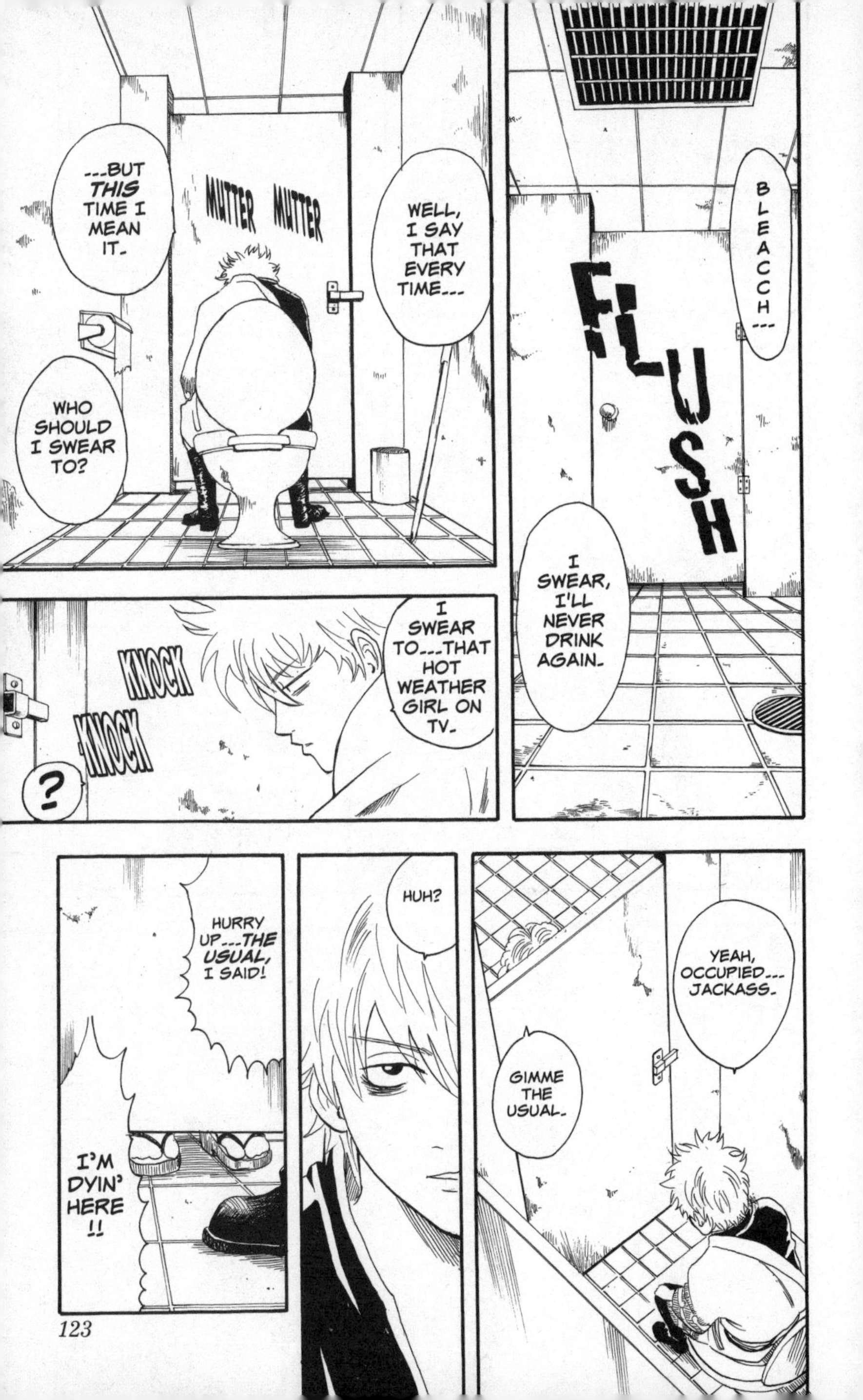
BLEACCH...
FLUSH
I SWEAR, I'LL NEVER DRINK AGAIN.
WELL, I SAY THAT EVERY TIME...
MUTTER MUTTER
...BUT THIS TIME I MEAN IT.
WHO SHOULD I SWEAR TO?
I SWEAR TO...THAT HOT WEATHER GIRL ON TV.
KNOCK KNOCK
?
YEAH, OCCUPIED... JACKASS.
GIMME THE USUAL.
HUH?
HURRY UP...THE USUAL, I SAID!
I'M DYIN' HERE!!

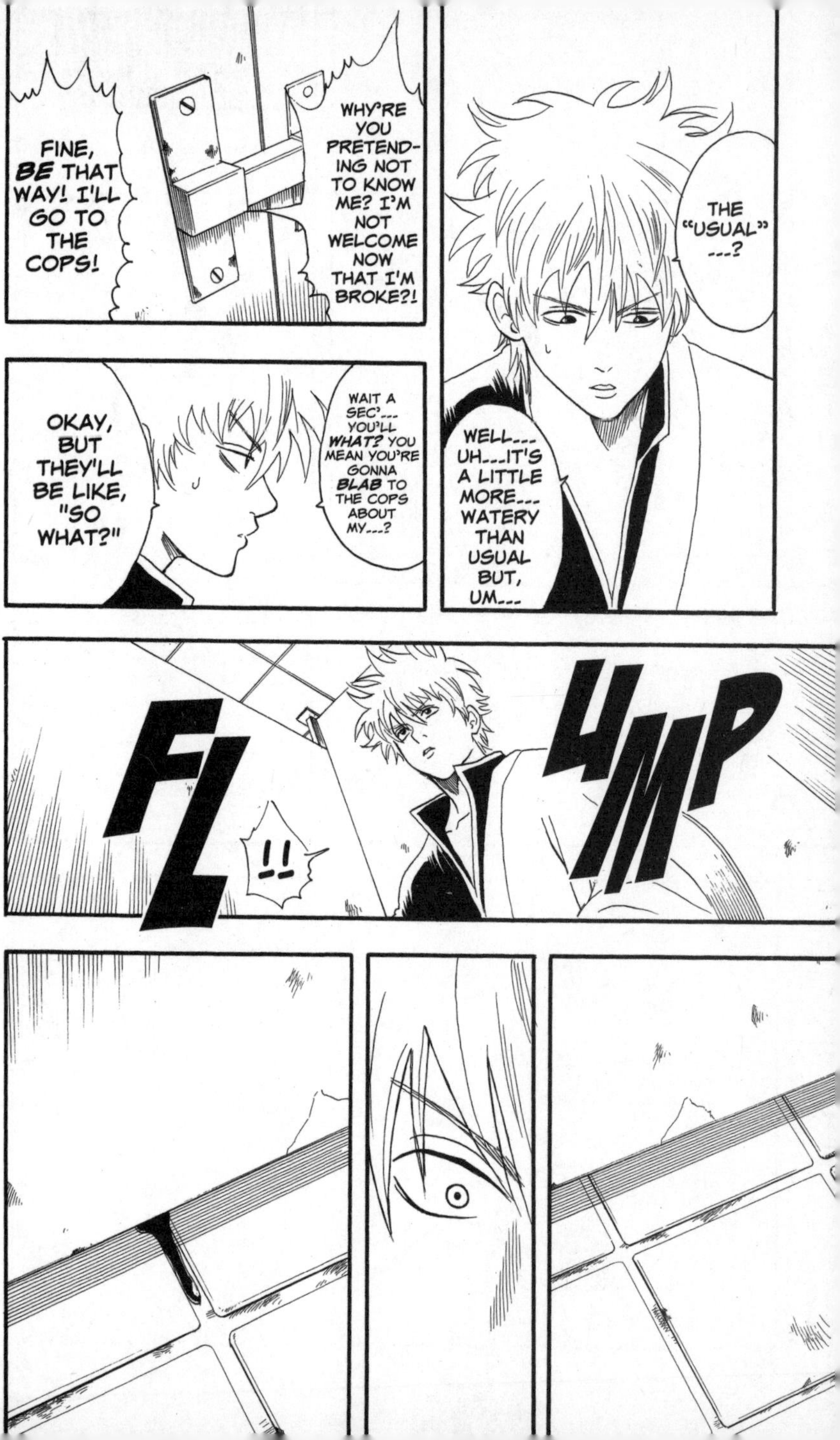
THE "USUAL"---?
WELL--- UH---IT'S A LITTLE MORE--- WATERY THAN USUAL BUT, UM---
WHY'RE YOU PRETENDING NOT TO KNOW ME? I'M NOT WELCOME NOW THAT I'M BROKE?!
FINE, BE THAT WAY! I'LL GO TO THE COPS!
WAIT A SEC'--- YOU'LL WHAT? YOU MEAN YOU'RE GONNA BLAB TO THE COPS ABOUT MY---?
OKAY, BUT THEY'LL BE LIKE, "SO WHAT?"
FLUMP
!!

READ THIS WAY

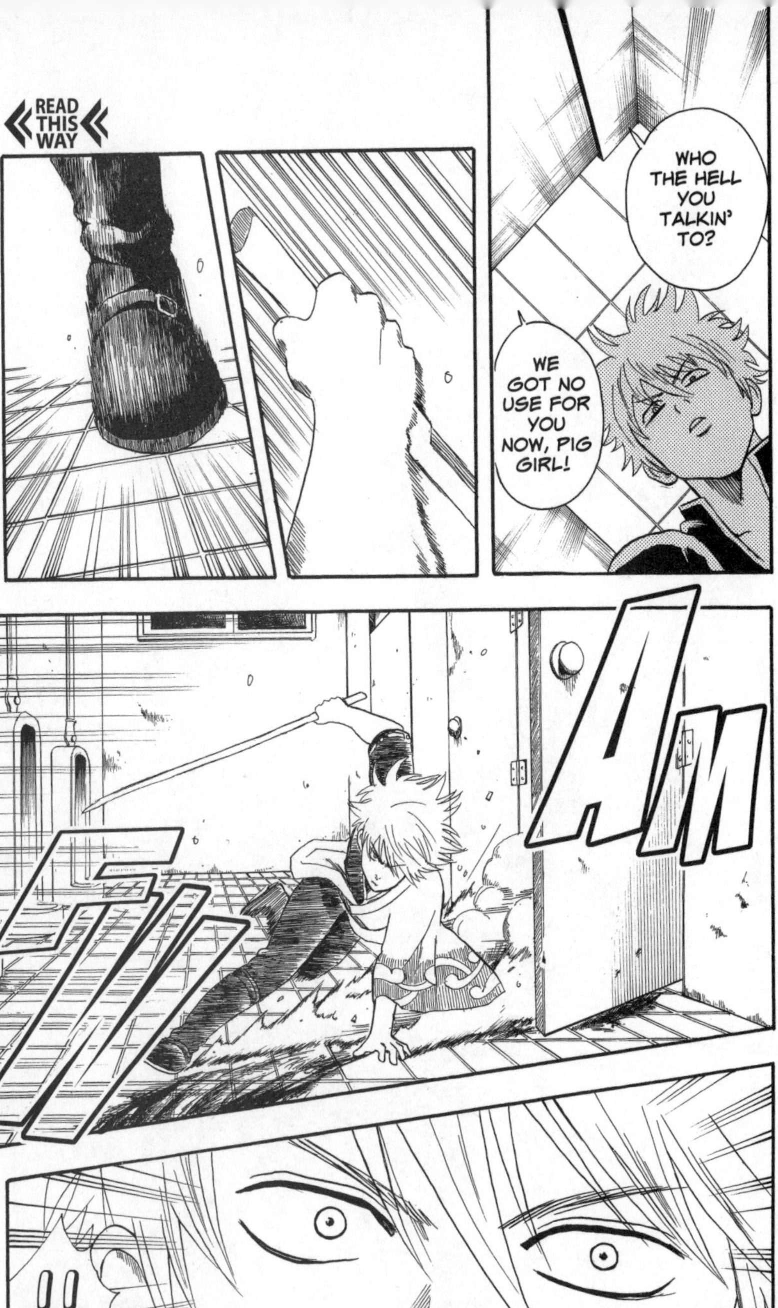
WHO THE HELL YOU TALKIN' TO?
WE GOT NO USE FOR YOU NOW, PIG GIRL!
AM

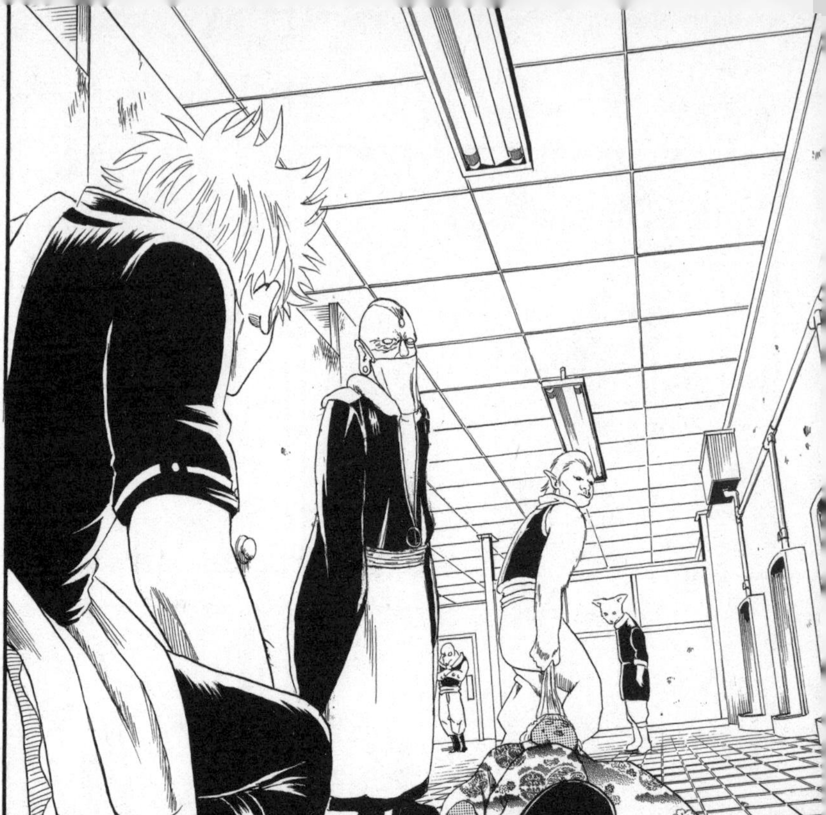
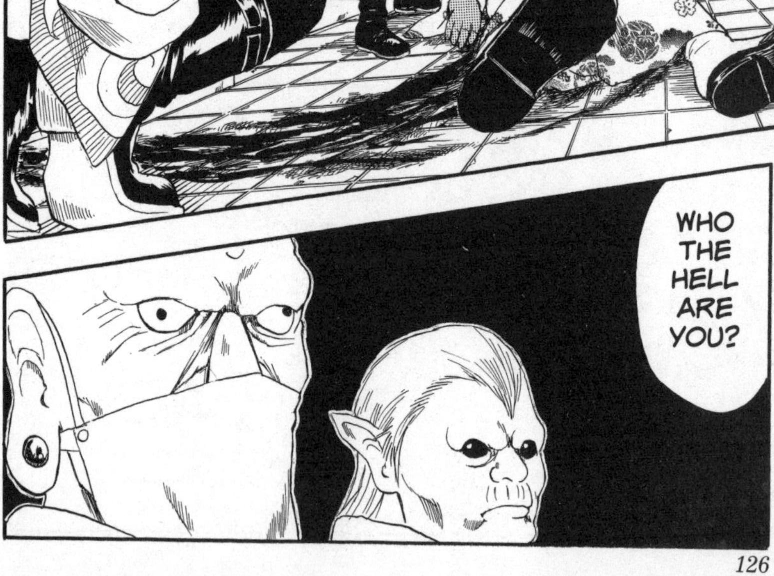
WHO THE HELL ARE YOU?

READ THIS WAY

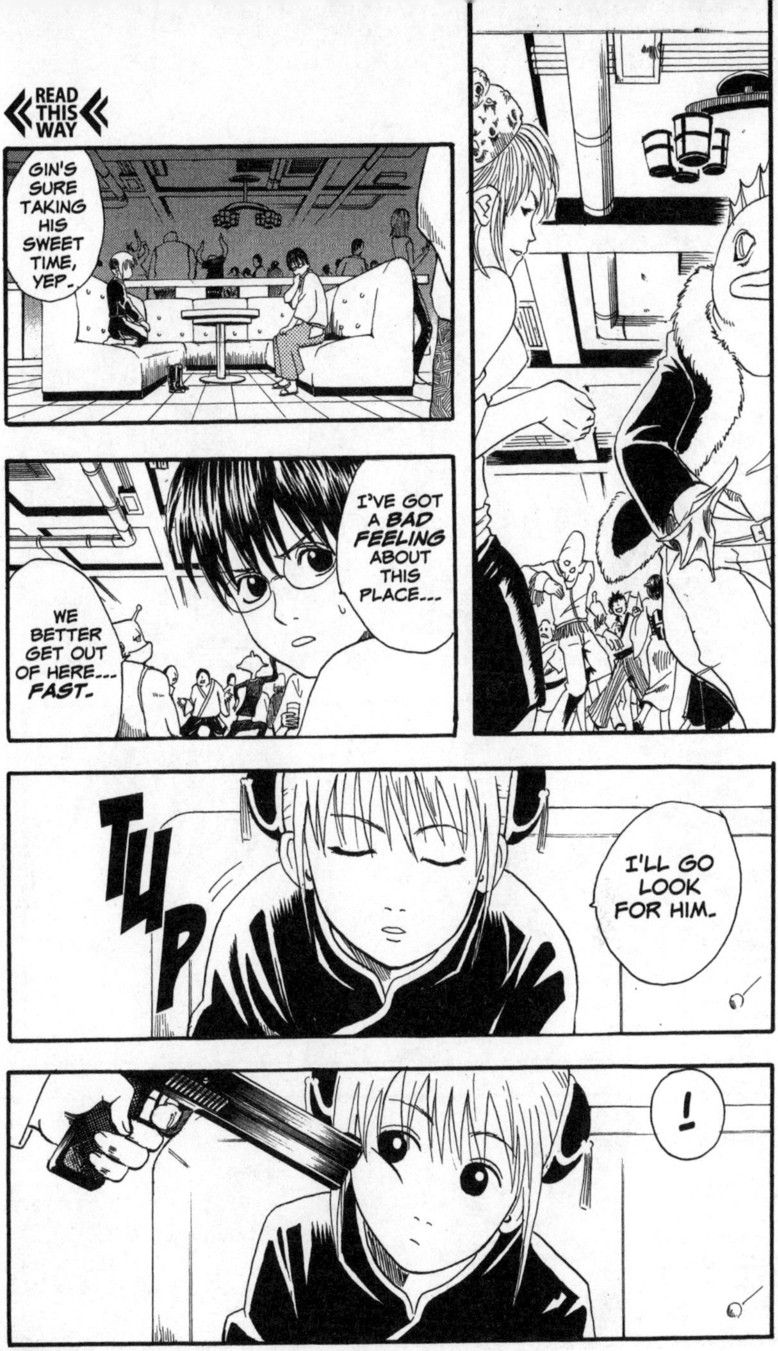
GIN'S SURE TAKING HIS SWEET TIME, YEP.
I'VE GOT A BAD FEELING ABOUT THIS PLACE...
WE BETTER GET OUT OF HERE... FAST.
I'LL GO LOOK FOR HIM.
TUP
!

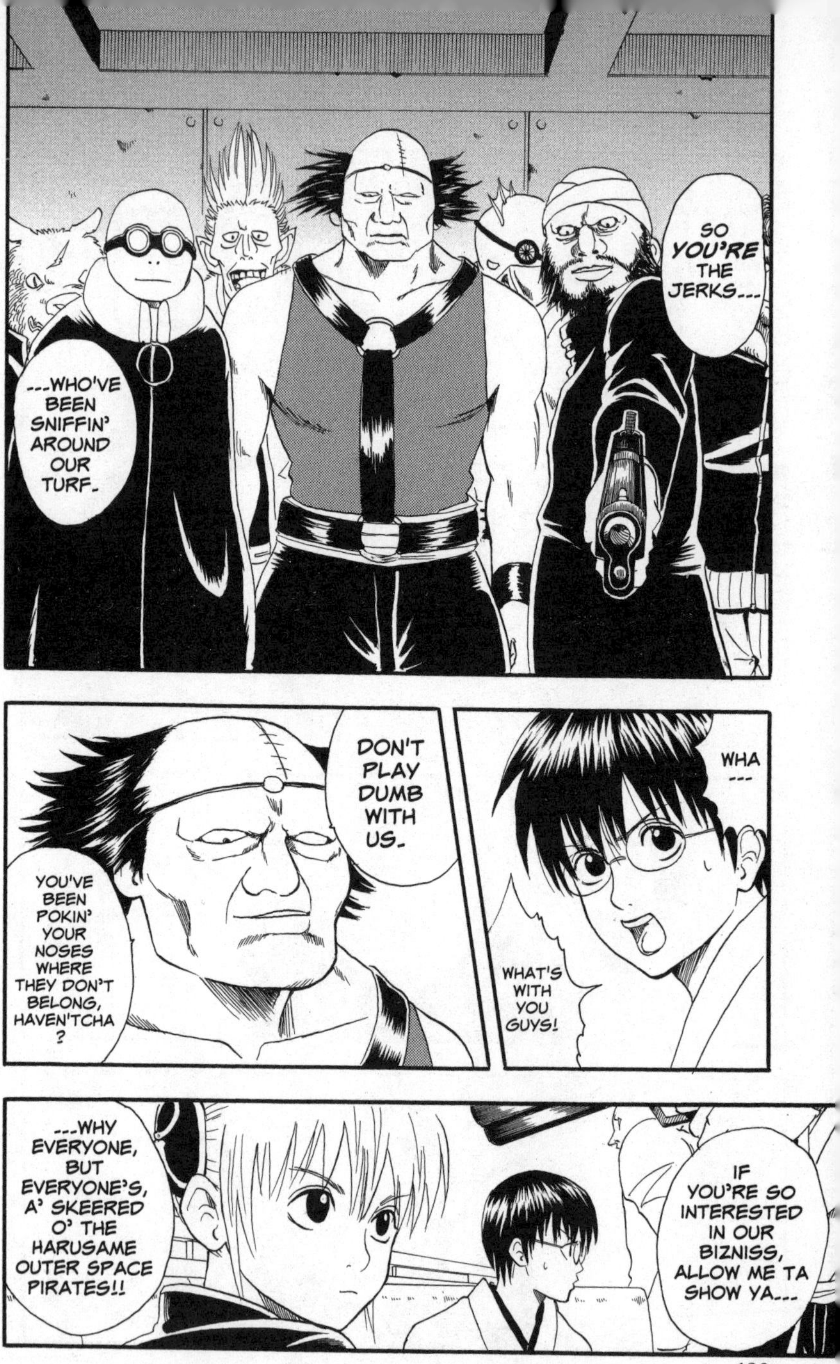
SO YOU'RE THE JERKS...
...WHO'VE BEEN SNIFFIN' AROUND OUR TURF.
WHA--
WHAT'S WITH YOU GUYS!
DON'T PLAY DUMB WITH US.
YOU'VE BEEN POKIN' YOUR NOSES WHERE THEY DON'T BELONG, HAVEN'TCHA?
IF YOU'RE SO INTERESTED IN OUR BIZNISS, ALLOW ME TA SHOW YA...
...WHY EVERYONE, BUT EVERYONE'S, A' SKEERED O' THE HARUSAME OUTER SPACE PIRATES!!

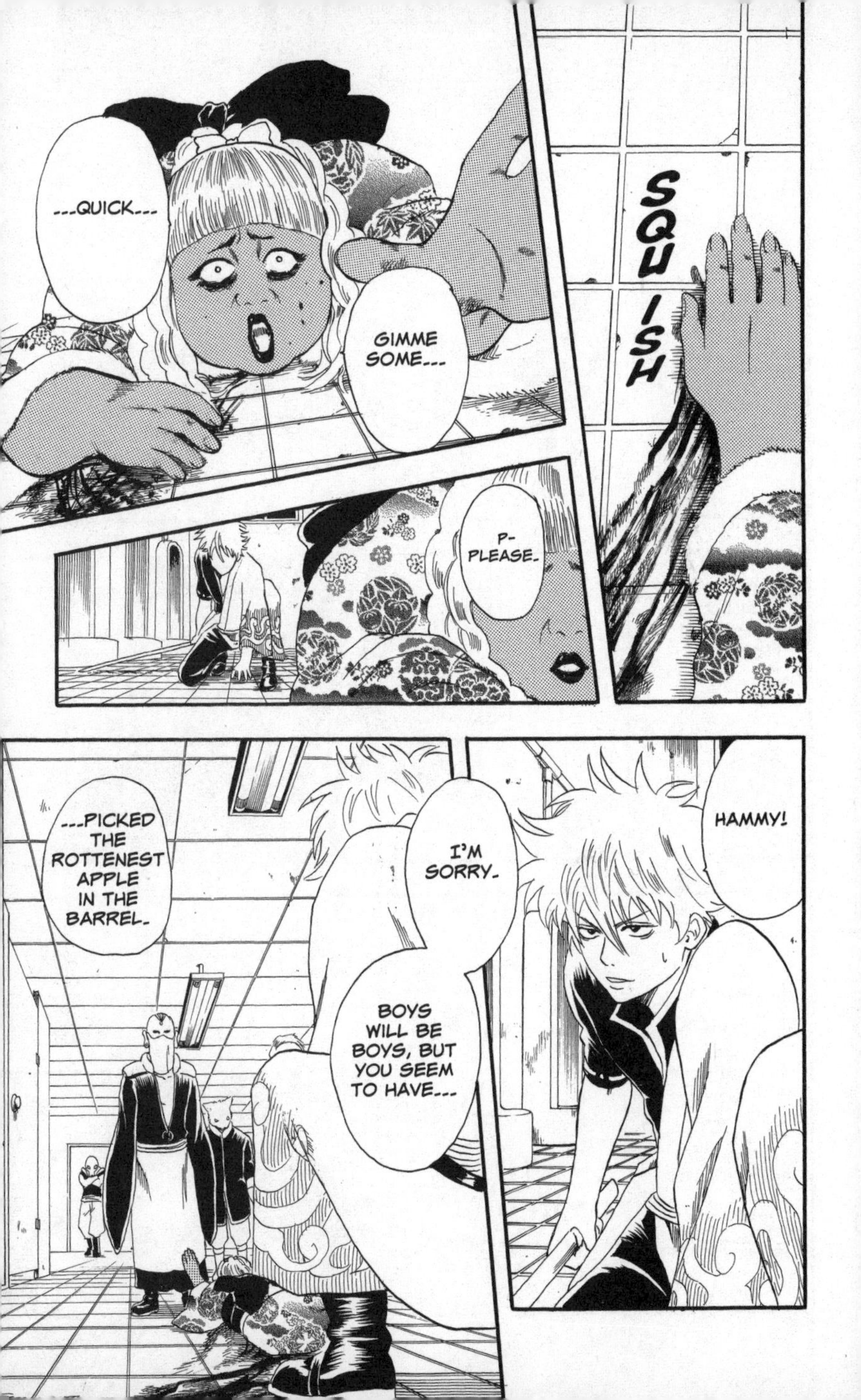
SQUISH
GIMME SOME...
...QUICK...
P-PLEASE.
HAMMY!
I'M SORRY.
BOYS WILL BE BOYS, BUT YOU SEEM TO HAVE...
...PICKED THE ROTTENEST APPLE IN THE BARREL.

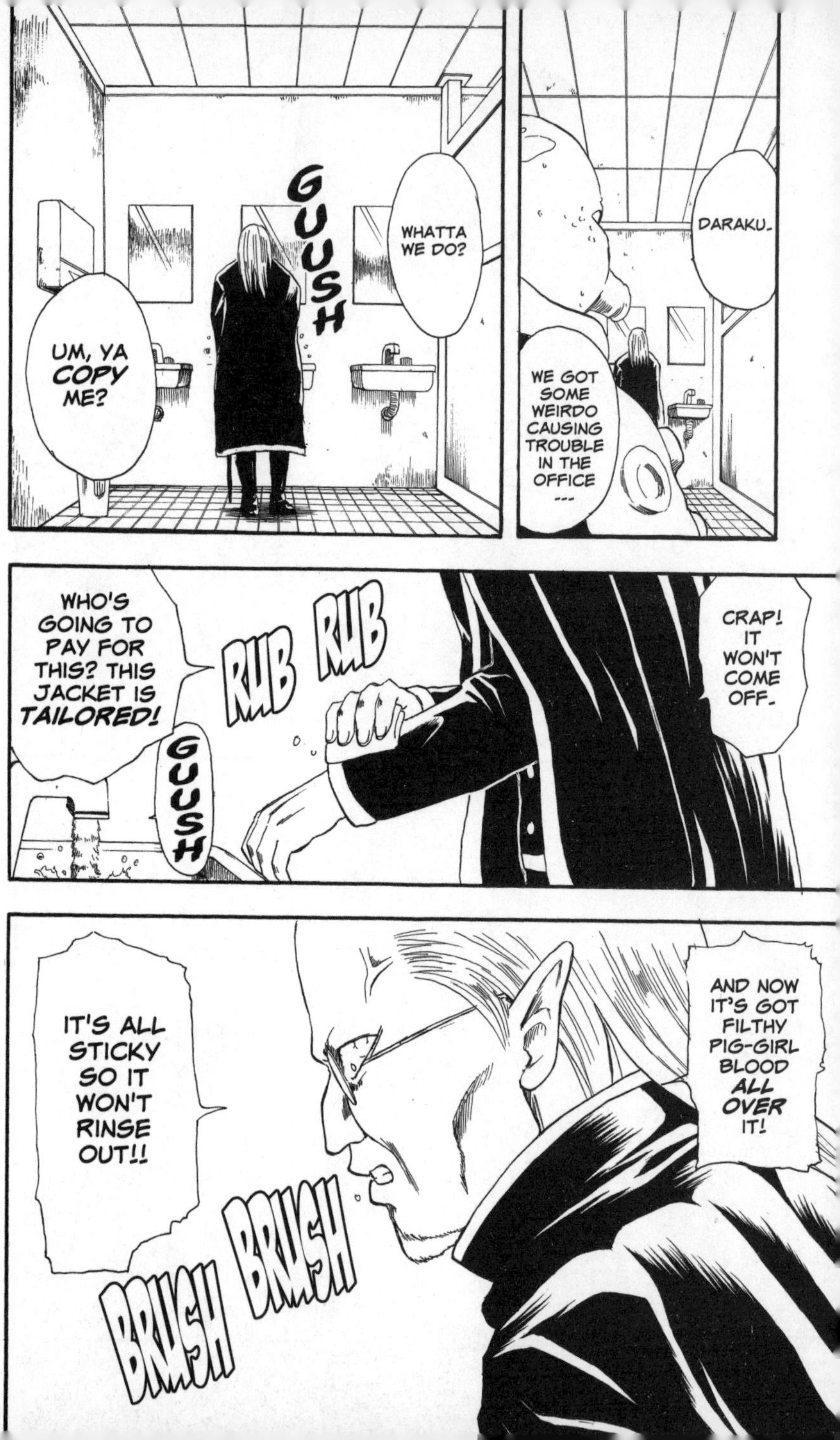
DARAKU_
WE GOT SOME WEIRDO CAUSING TROUBLE IN THE OFFICE ---
WHATTA WE DO?
GUUSH
UM, YA COPY ME?
CRAP! IT WON'T COME OFF_
RUB RUB
WHO'S GOING TO PAY FOR THIS? THIS JACKET IS TAILORED!
GUUSH
AND NOW IT'S GOT FILTHY PIG-GIRL BLOOD ALL OVER IT!
IT'S ALL STICKY SO IT WON'T RINSE OUT!!
BRUSH BRUSH

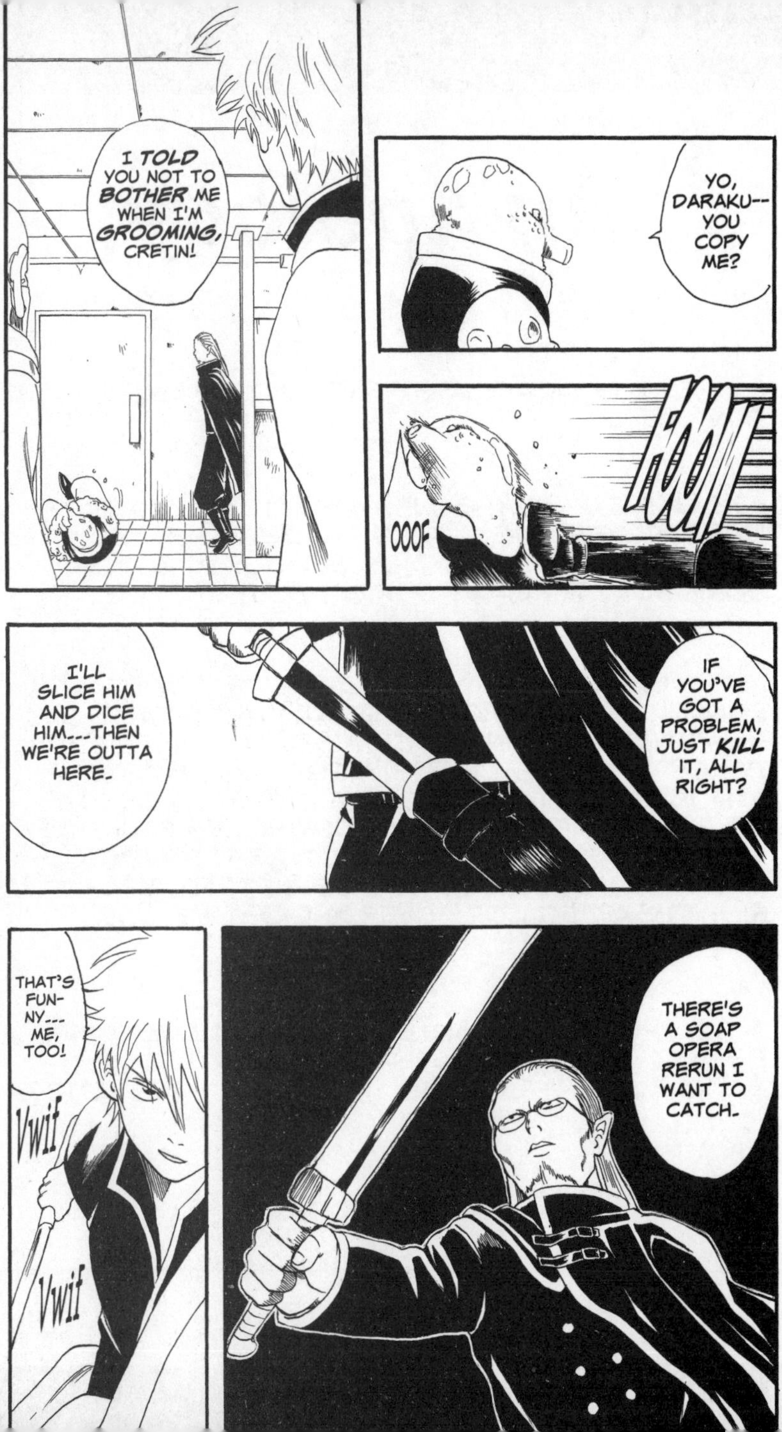
YO, DARAKU-- YOU COPY ME?
FOOM
OOOF
I *TOLD* YOU NOT TO *BOTHER* ME WHEN I'M *GROOMING*, CRETIN!
IF YOU'VE GOT A PROBLEM, JUST *KILL* IT, ALL RIGHT?
I'LL SLICE HIM AND DICE HIM...THEN WE'RE OUTTA HERE.
THERE'S A SOAP OPERA RERUN I WANT TO CATCH.
THAT'S FUN-NY... ME, TOO!
Vwif
Vwif

An Apology

VOLUME 2 IS AN APOLOGY-FEST, SO I'D LIKE TO ADD THIS ONE...

BECAUSE I USED THE UNSAVORY TITLE *GIN TAMA**, I'VE BEEN GETTING TONS OF MAIL SAYING, "YO, IT'S SO EMBARRASSING. I CAN'T BUY IT, YOU ROTTEN GORILLA." I'M REALLY SORRY ABOUT THAT.

IN THE BEGINNING, MY STRATEGY WAS TO GET HIGH SCHOOL GIRLS ACROSS THE COUNTRY TO BLITHELY SAY THINGS LIKE "HEY, DIDJA SEE THIS WEEK'S *GIN TAMA?*" AND THUS CREATE A CONVIVIAL, FOLKSY ATMOSPHERE IN JAPAN, BUT THIS TURNED OUT TO BE A BIG FLOP. IT WAS NOBODY ELSE'S FAULT BUT MINE. SO DON'T BEAT UP THE OTHERS. IF YOU'RE GONNA KILL SOMEONE, TAKE ME INSTEAD. YEAH, I'M RIGHT HERE, SO COME OVER AND GET ME, YOU BASTAAAAAARDS!!

* THE CHINESE CHARACTERS FOR "GIN TAMA" CAN BE READ TO MEAN "SILVER SPIRIT" OR "GOLDEN BALLS," I.E., "TESTICLES"   --ED. NOTE

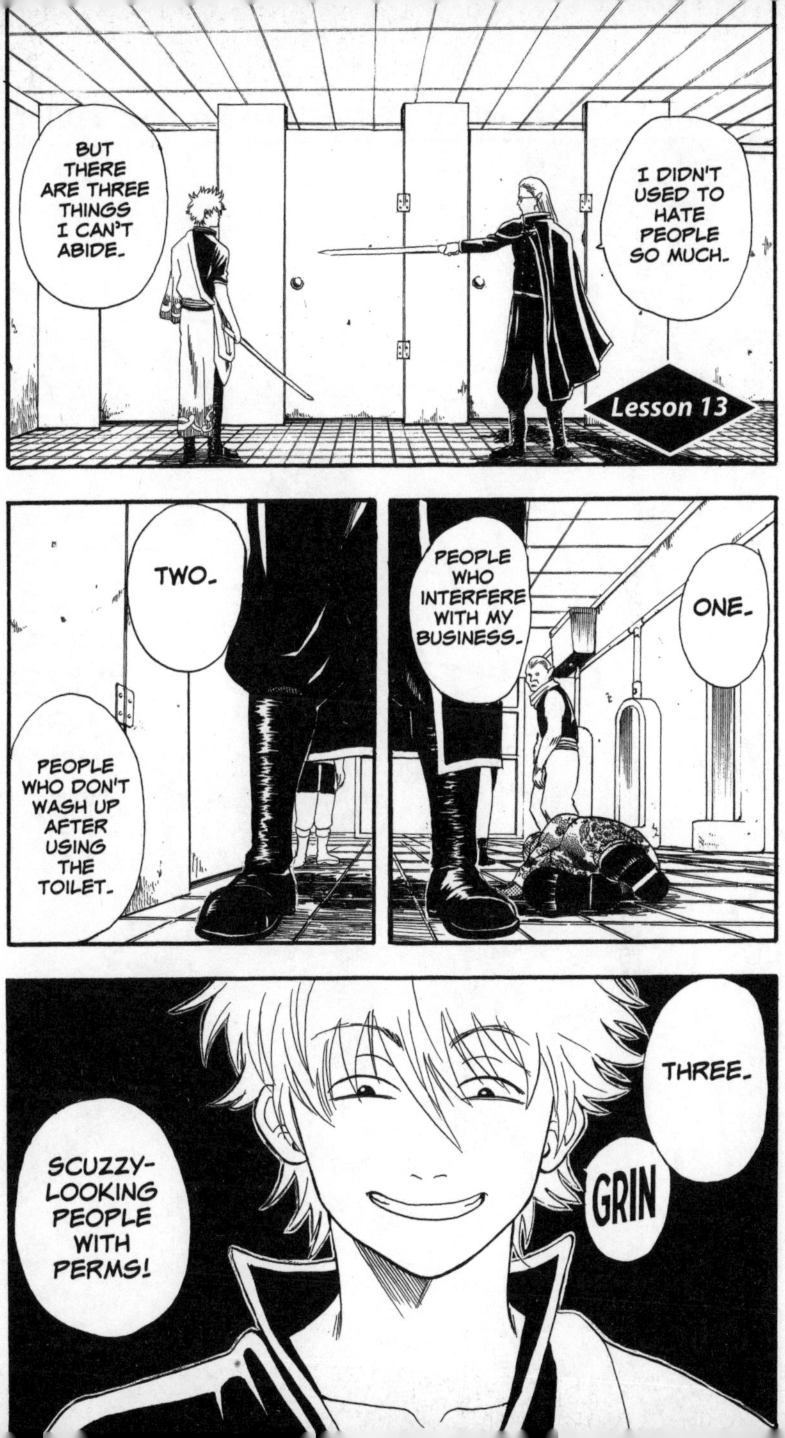
I DIDN'T USED TO HATE PEOPLE SO MUCH.
Lesson 13
BUT THERE ARE THREE THINGS I CAN'T ABIDE.
ONE.
PEOPLE WHO INTERFERE WITH MY BUSINESS.
TWO.
PEOPLE WHO DON'T WASH UP AFTER USING THE TOILET.
THREE.
GRIN
SCUZZY-LOOKING PEOPLE WITH PERMS!

Lesson 13: Only Dirty Things Are Born of Toilets

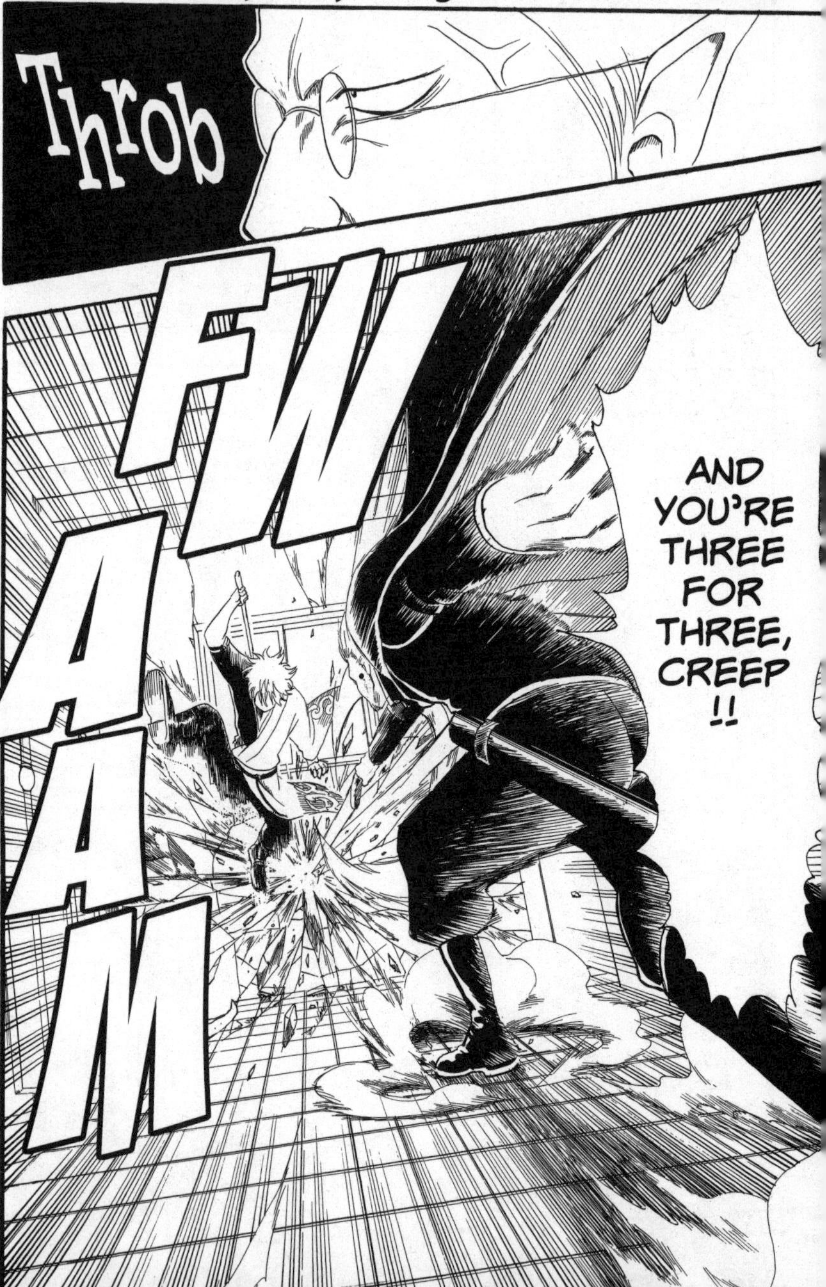
Throb
FWAAM
AND YOU'RE THREE FOR THREE, CREEP!!

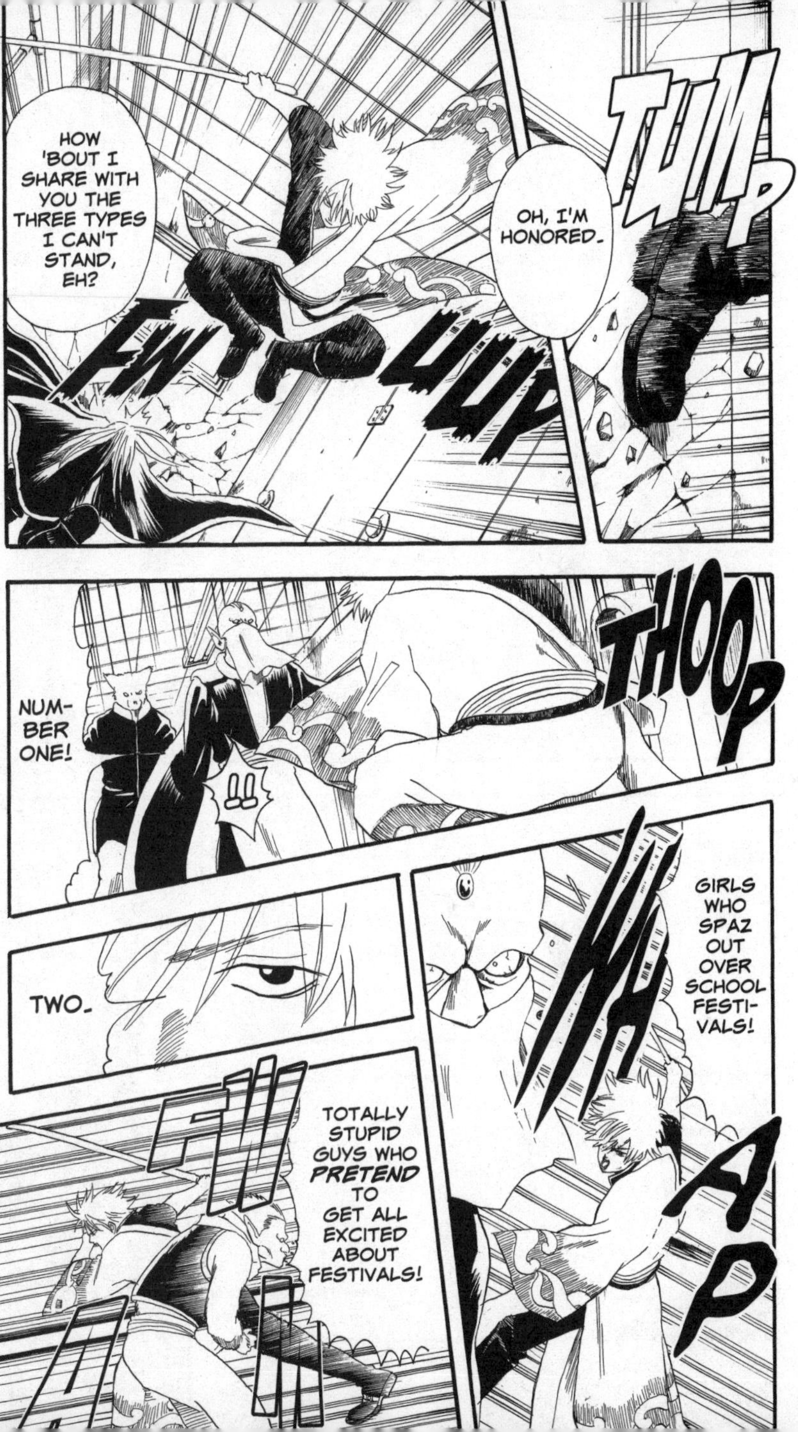
THUMP
OH, I'M HONORED.
HOW 'BOUT I SHARE WITH YOU THE THREE TYPES I CAN'T STAND, EH?
THOOP
NUMBER ONE!
!!
GIRLS WHO SPAZ OUT OVER SCHOOL FESTIVALS!
TWO.
TOTALLY STUPID GUYS WHO **PRETEND** TO GET ALL EXCITED ABOUT FESTIVALS!

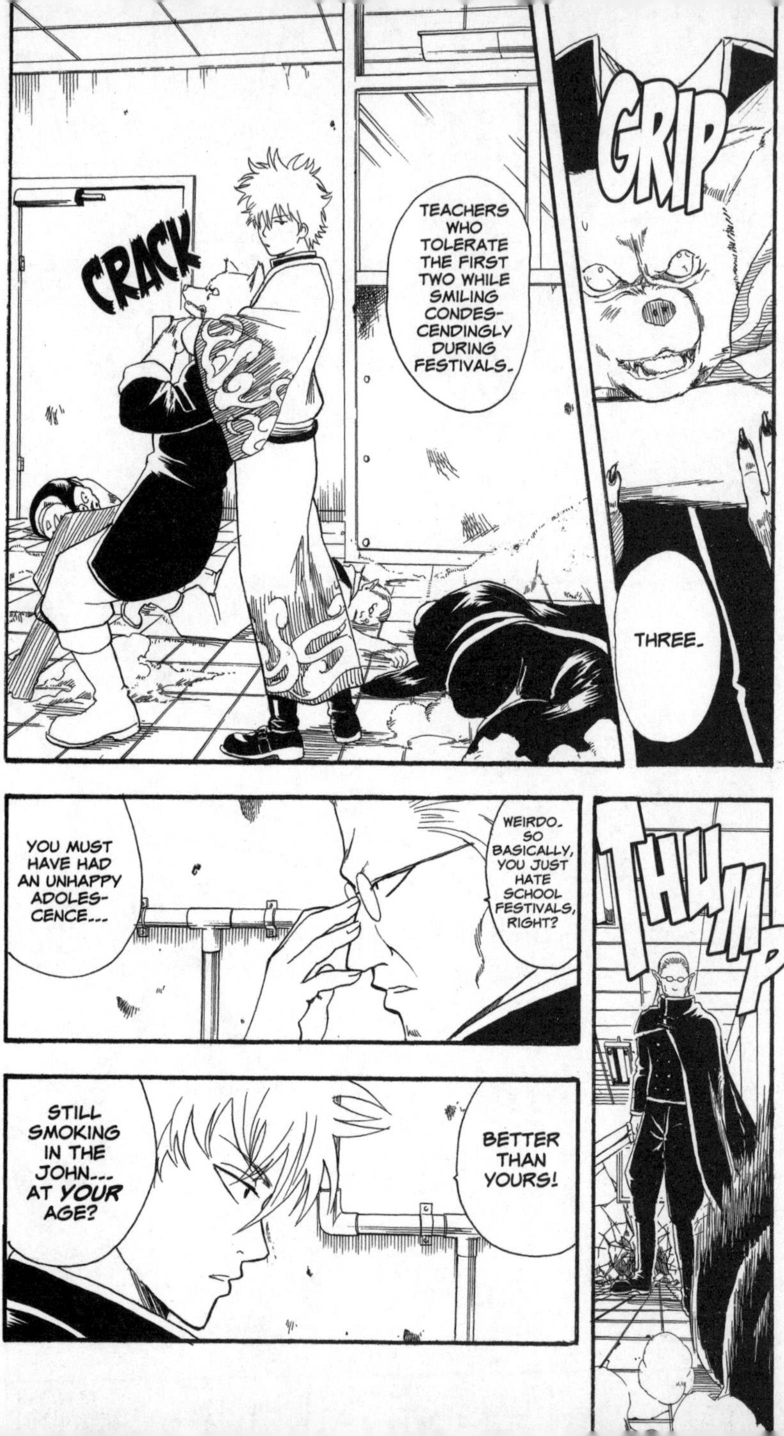
GRIP
THREE.
CRACK
TEACHERS WHO TOLERATE THE FIRST TWO WHILE SMILING CONDES-CENDINGLY DURING FESTIVALS.
THUMP
WEIRDO. SO BASICALLY, YOU JUST HATE SCHOOL FESTIVALS, RIGHT?
YOU MUST HAVE HAD AN UNHAPPY ADOLES-CENCE...
BETTER THAN YOURS!
STILL SMOKING IN THE JOHN... AT *YOUR* AGE?

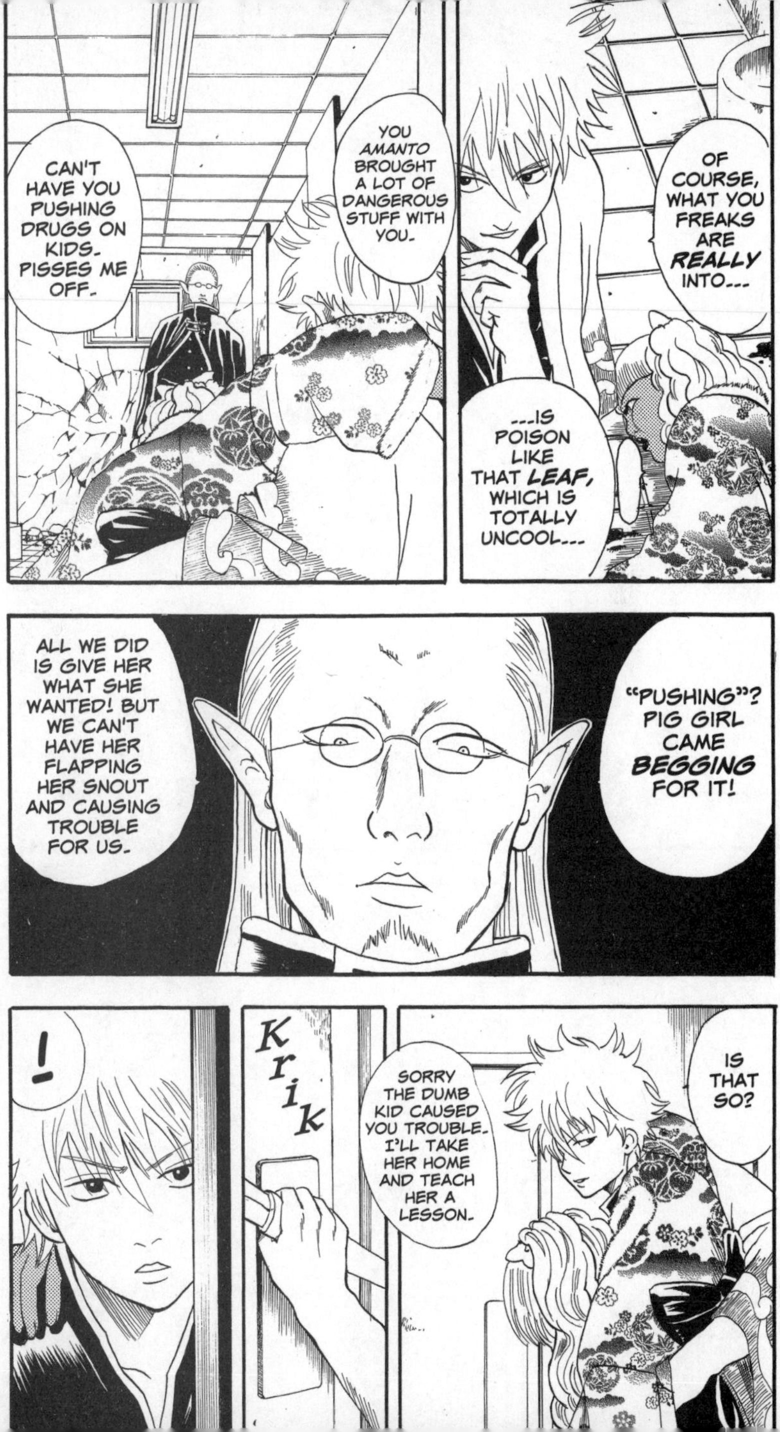
OF COURSE, WHAT YOU FREAKS ARE REALLY INTO...
...IS POISON LIKE THAT LEAF, WHICH IS TOTALLY UNCOOL...
YOU AMANTO BROUGHT A LOT OF DANGEROUS STUFF WITH YOU.
CAN'T HAVE YOU PUSHING DRUGS ON KIDS. PISSES ME OFF.
"PUSHING"? PIG GIRL CAME BEGGING FOR IT!
ALL WE DID IS GIVE HER WHAT SHE WANTED! BUT WE CAN'T HAVE HER FLAPPING HER SNOUT AND CAUSING TROUBLE FOR US.
IS THAT SO?
SORRY THE DUMB KID CAUSED YOU TROUBLE. I'LL TAKE HER HOME AND TEACH HER A LESSON.
Krik
!

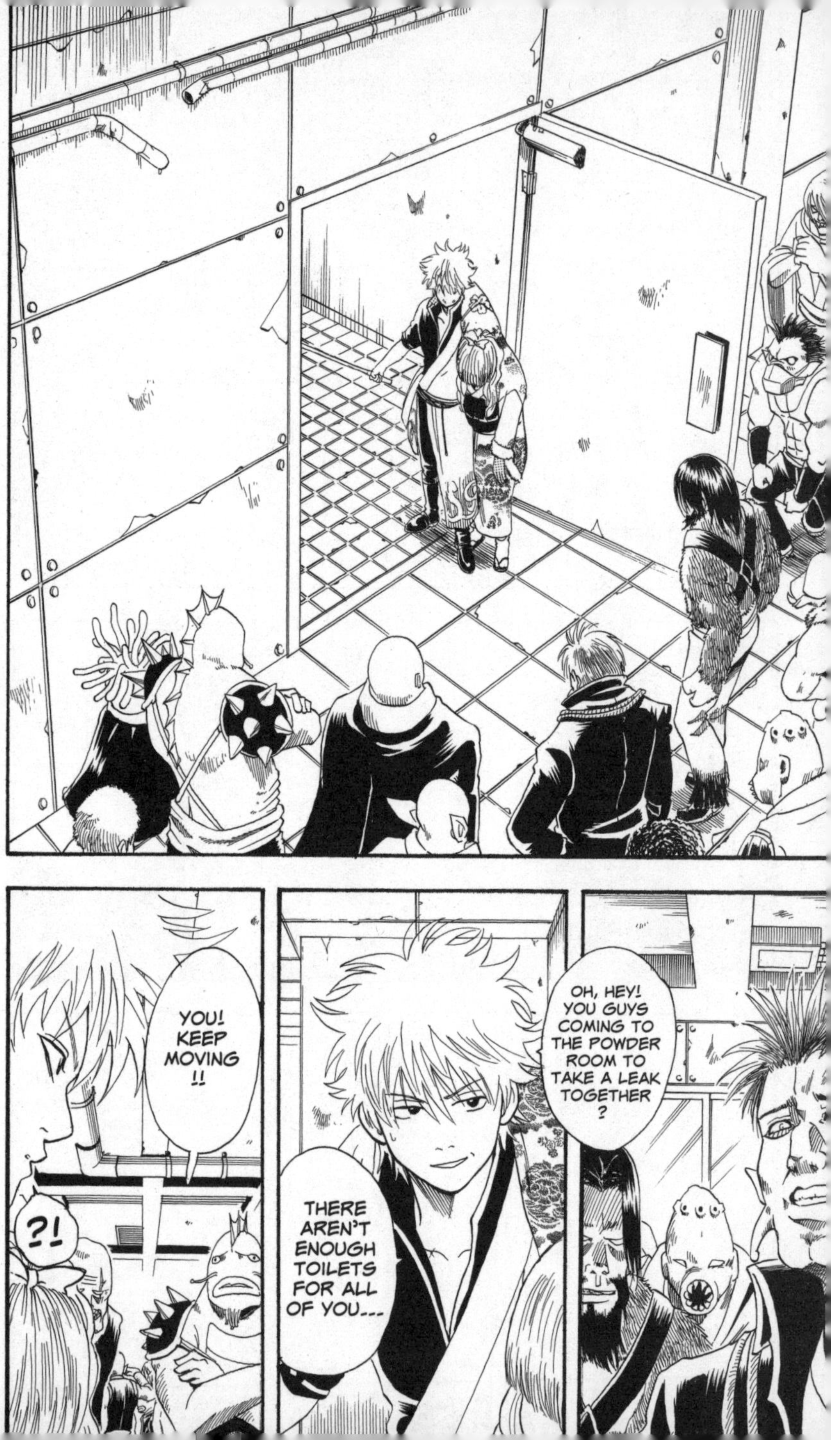
OH, HEY! YOU GUYS COMING TO THE POWDER ROOM TO TAKE A LEAK TOGETHER?
THERE AREN'T ENOUGH TOILETS FOR ALL OF YOU...
YOU! KEEP MOVING!!
?!

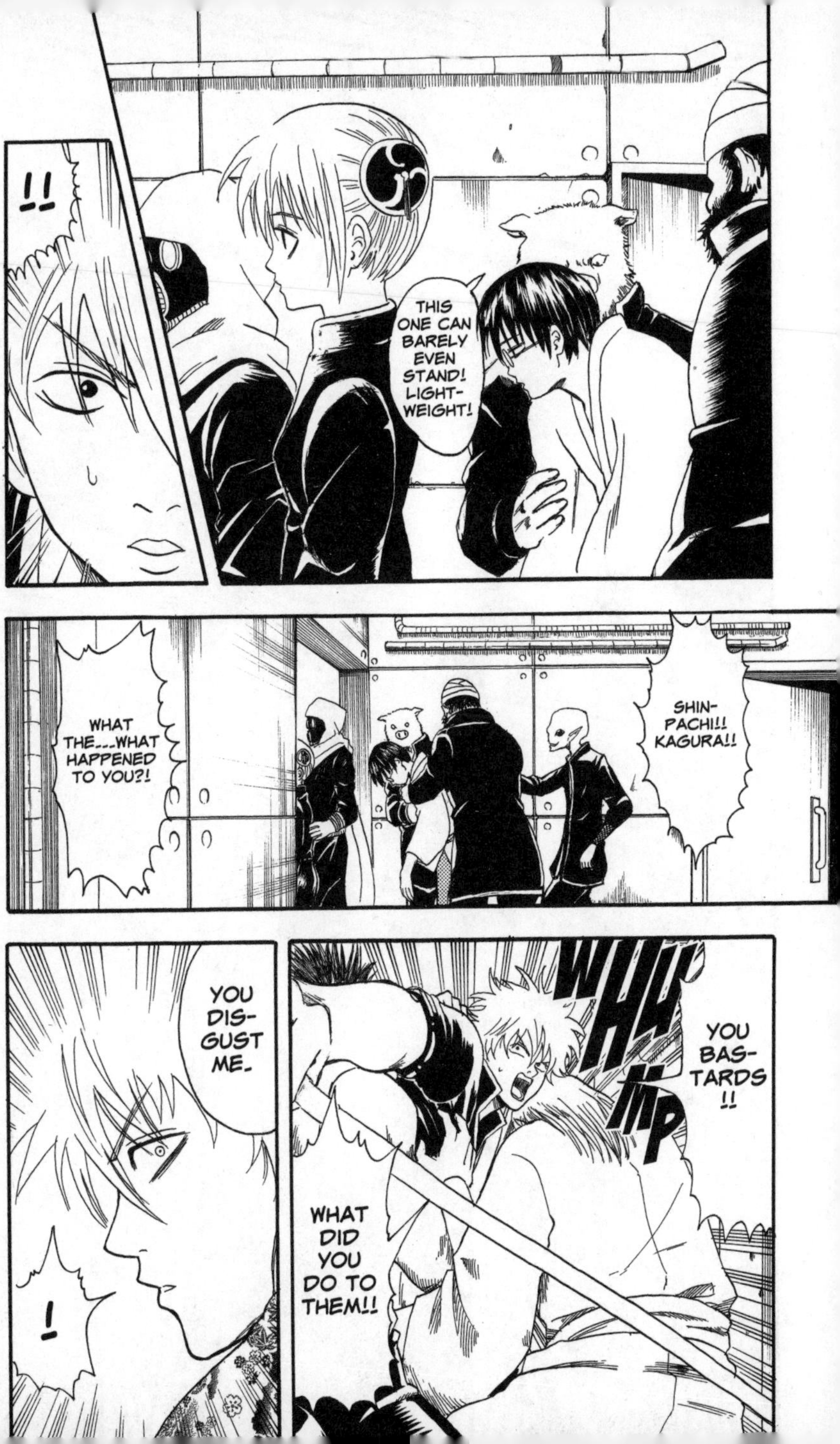
THIS ONE CAN BARELY EVEN STAND! LIGHT-WEIGHT!
!!
SHIN-PACHI!! KAGURA!!
WHAT THE...WHAT HAPPENED TO YOU?!
YOU BAS-TARDS!!
WHAT DID YOU DO TO THEM!!
YOU DIS-GUST ME.
!

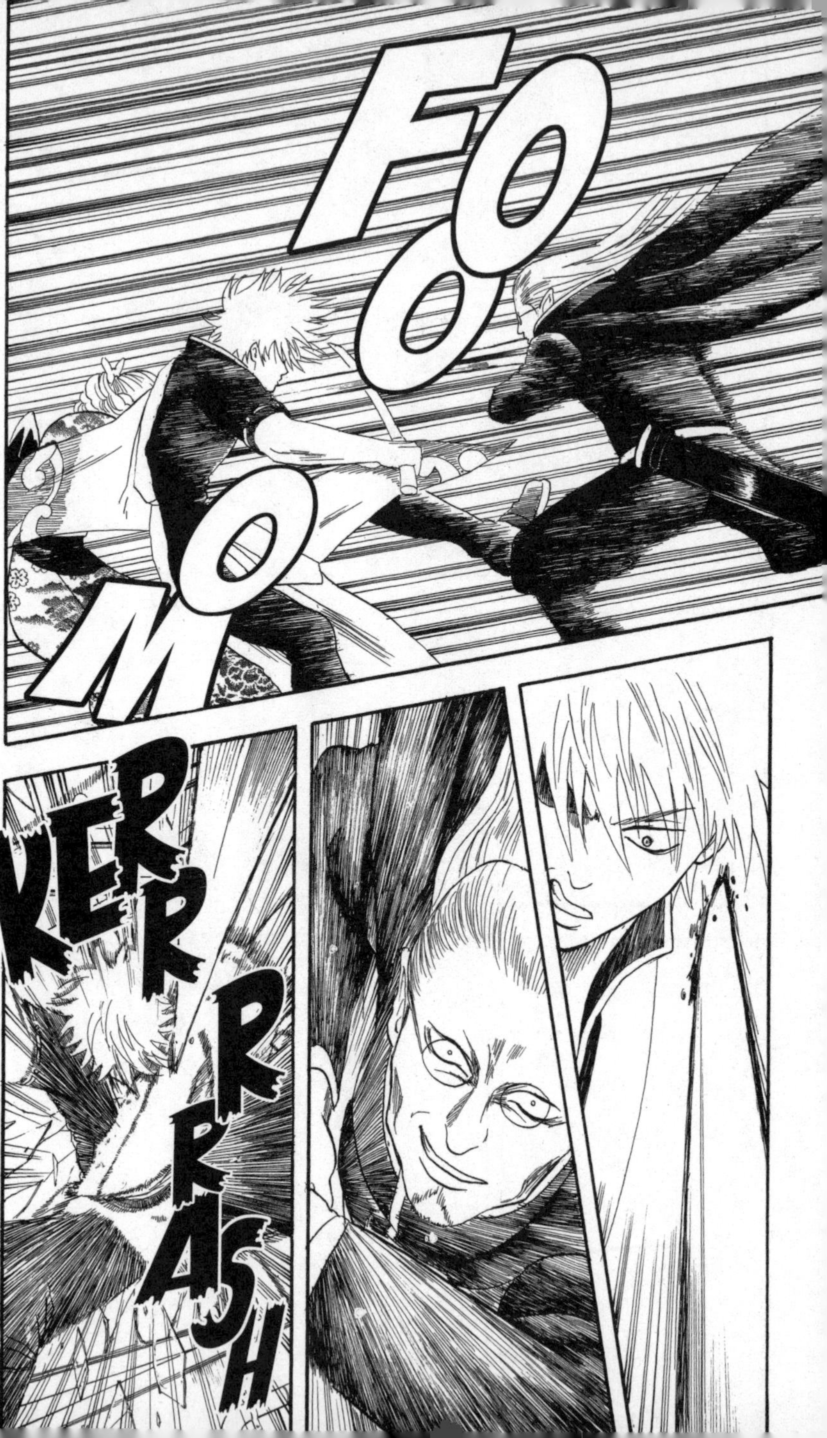
FOOOM
KERRRRASH

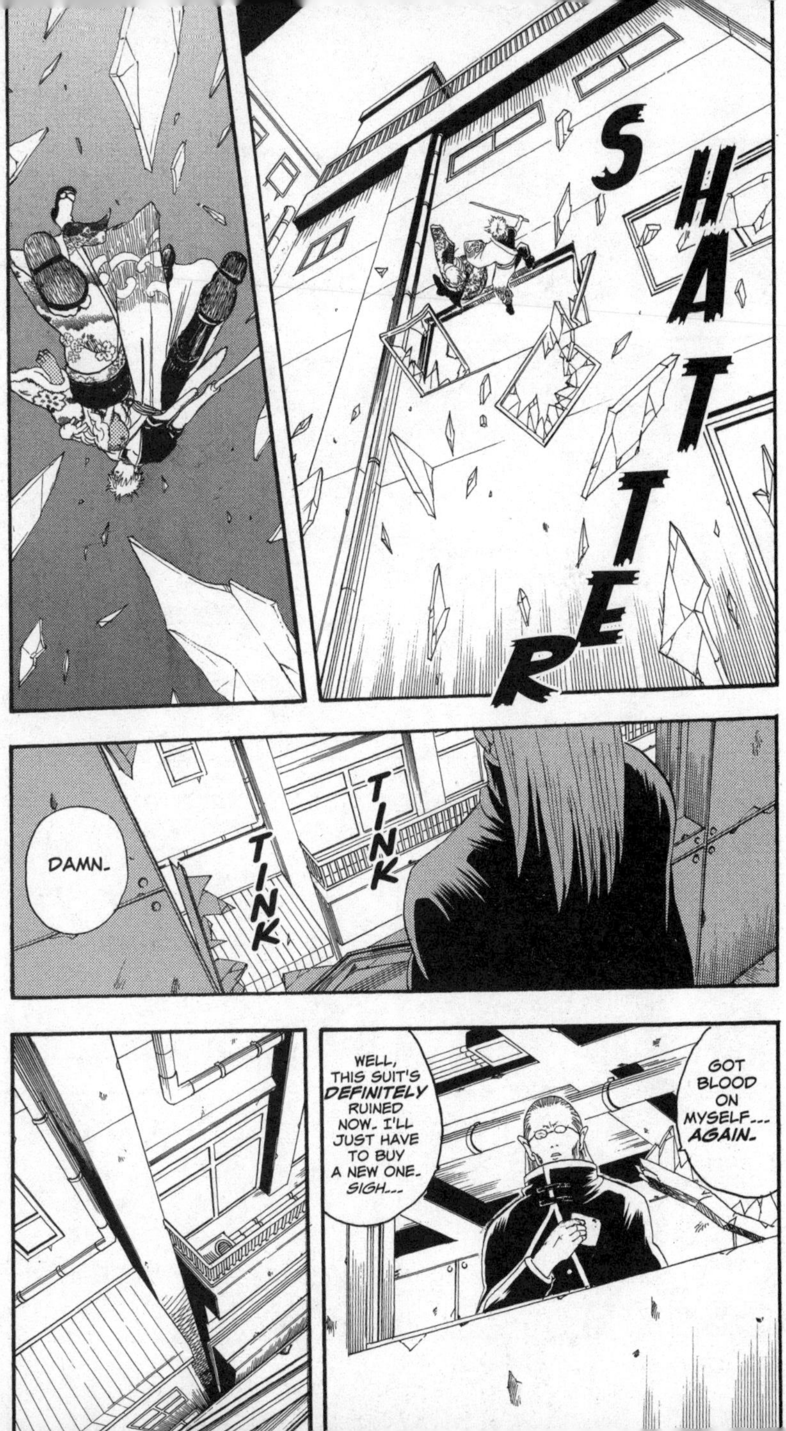
SHATTER
TINK TINK
DAMN.
GOT BLOOD ON MYSELF... AGAIN.
WELL, THIS SUIT'S DEFINITELY RUINED NOW. I'LL JUST HAVE TO BUY A NEW ONE. SIGH...

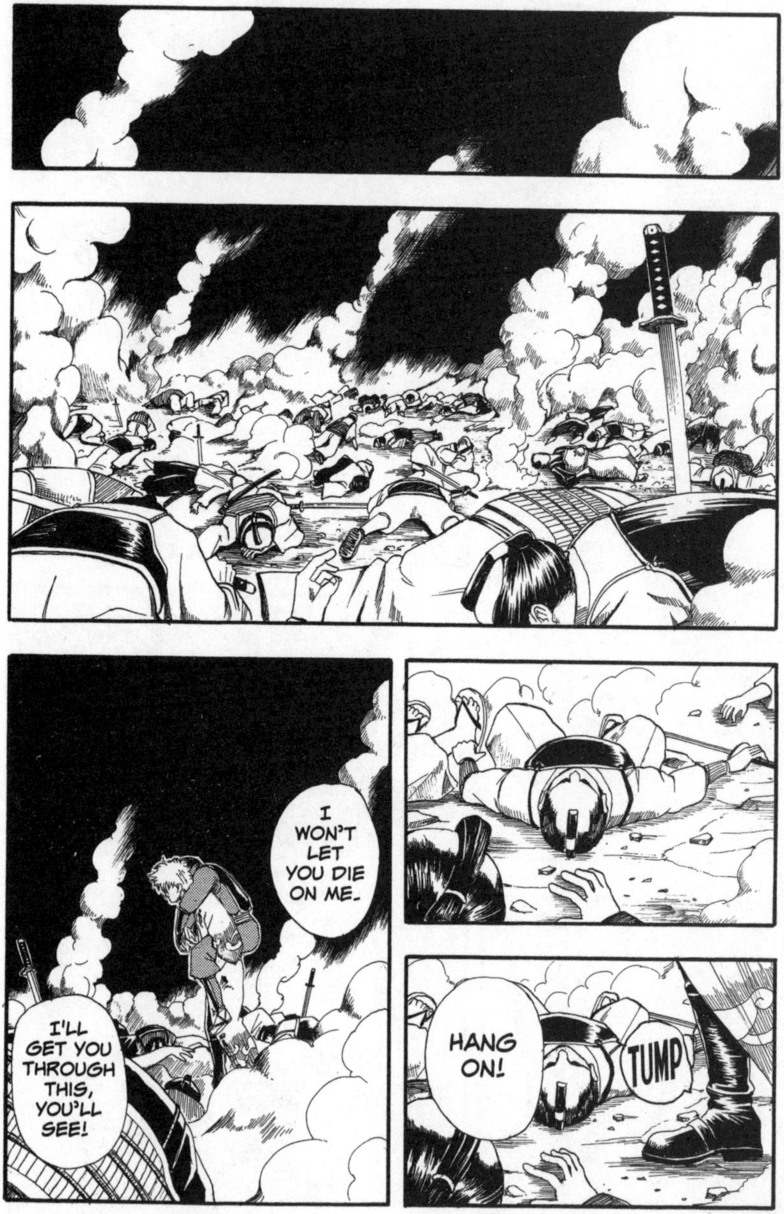
TUMP
HANG ON!
I WON'T LET YOU DIE ON ME...
I'LL GET YOU THROUGH THIS, YOU'LL SEE!

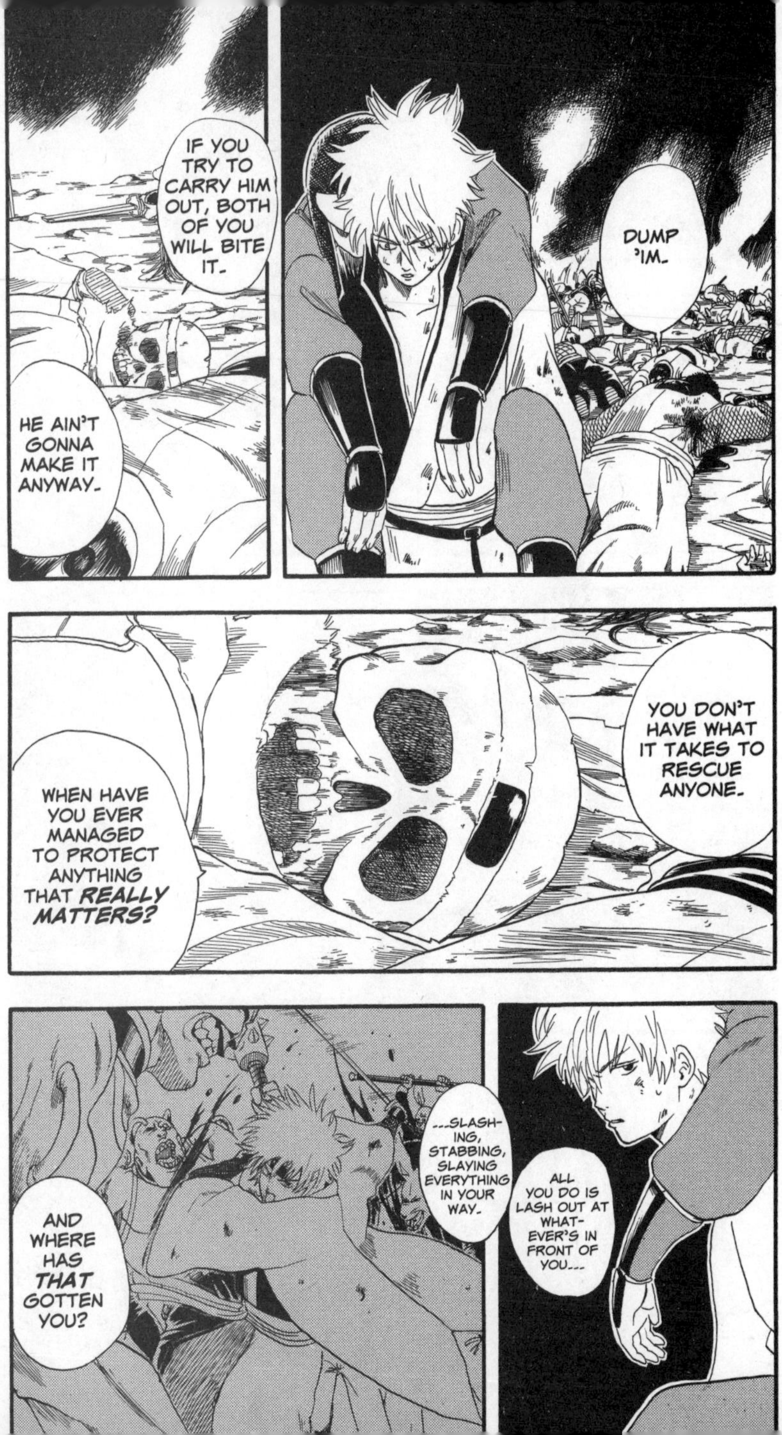
DUMP 'IM.
IF YOU TRY TO CARRY HIM OUT, BOTH OF YOU WILL BITE IT.
HE AIN'T GONNA MAKE IT ANYWAY.
YOU DON'T HAVE WHAT IT TAKES TO RESCUE ANYONE.
WHEN HAVE YOU EVER MANAGED TO PROTECT ANYTHING THAT *REALLY MATTERS?*
ALL YOU DO IS LASH OUT AT WHAT-EVER'S IN FRONT OF YOU...
...SLASH-ING, STABBING, SLAYING EVERYTHING IN YOUR WAY.
AND WHERE HAS *THAT* GOTTEN YOU?

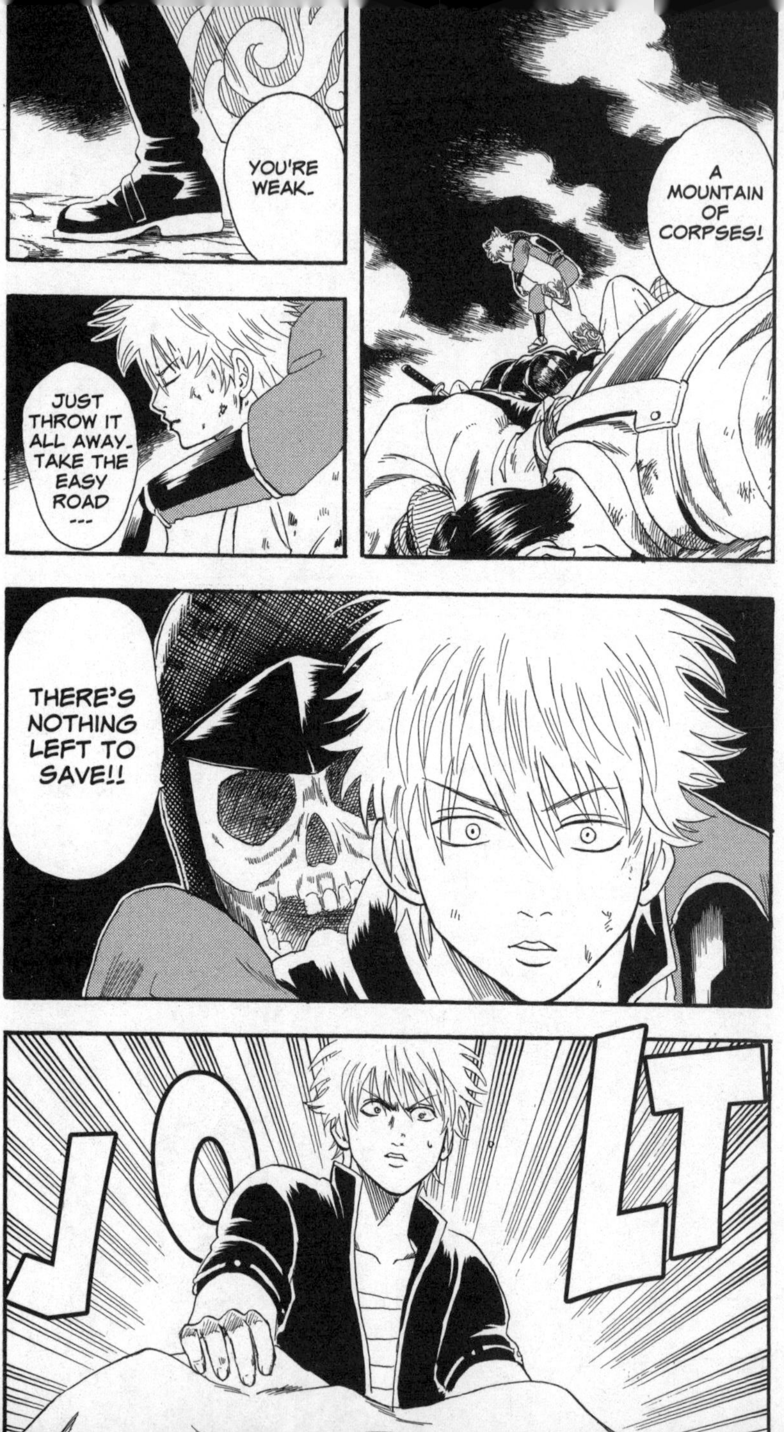
A MOUNTAIN OF CORPSES!
YOU'RE WEAK...
JUST THROW IT ALL AWAY... TAKE THE EASY ROAD ...
THERE'S NOTHING LEFT TO SAVE!!
JOLT

READ THIS WAY

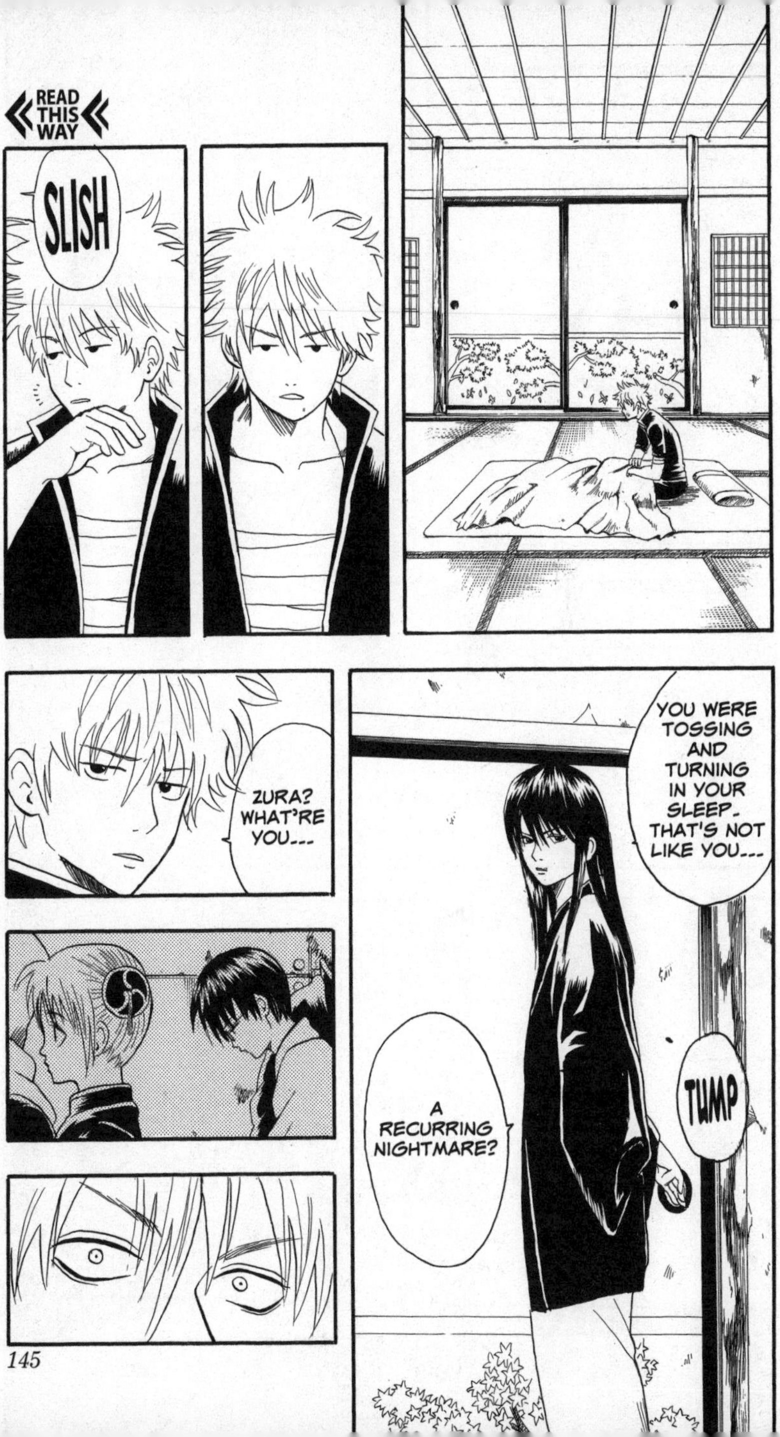
SLISH
YOU WERE TOSSING AND TURNING IN YOUR SLEEP. THAT'S NOT LIKE YOU...
TUMP
A RECURRING NIGHTMARE?
ZURA? WHAT'RE YOU...

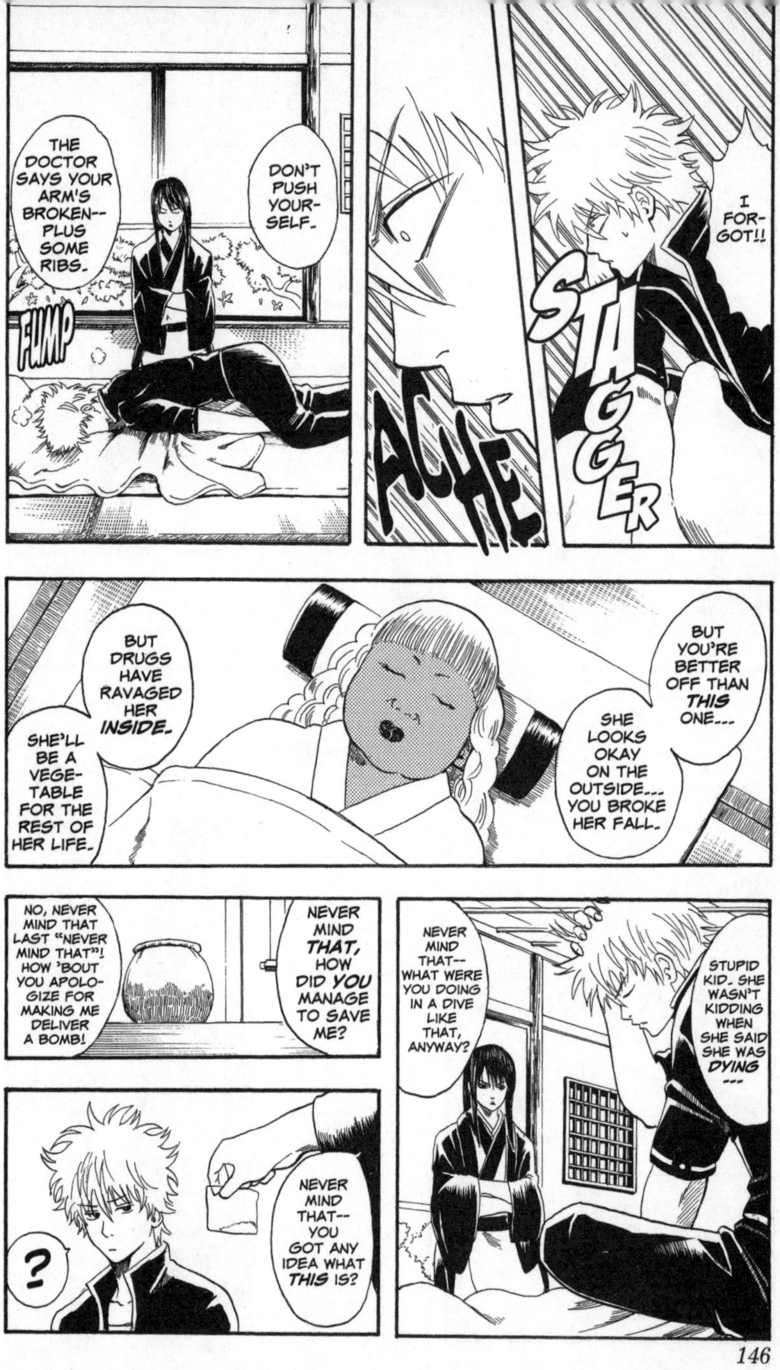
I FORGOT!!
STAGGER
ACHE
DON'T PUSH YOURSELF.
THE DOCTOR SAYS YOUR ARM'S BROKEN-- PLUS SOME RIBS.
FUMP
BUT YOU'RE BETTER OFF THAN THIS ONE...
SHE LOOKS OKAY ON THE OUTSIDE... YOU BROKE HER FALL.
BUT DRUGS HAVE RAVAGED HER INSIDE.
SHE'LL BE A VEGETABLE FOR THE REST OF HER LIFE.
STUPID KID. SHE WASN'T KIDDING WHEN SHE SAID SHE WAS DYING...
NEVER MIND THAT-- WHAT WERE YOU DOING IN A DIVE LIKE THAT, ANYWAY?
NEVER MIND THAT, HOW DID YOU MANAGE TO SAVE ME?
NO, NEVER MIND THAT LAST "NEVER MIND THAT"! HOW 'BOUT YOU APOLOGIZE FOR MAKING ME DELIVER A BOMB!
NEVER MIND THAT-- YOU GOT ANY IDEA WHAT THIS IS?
?

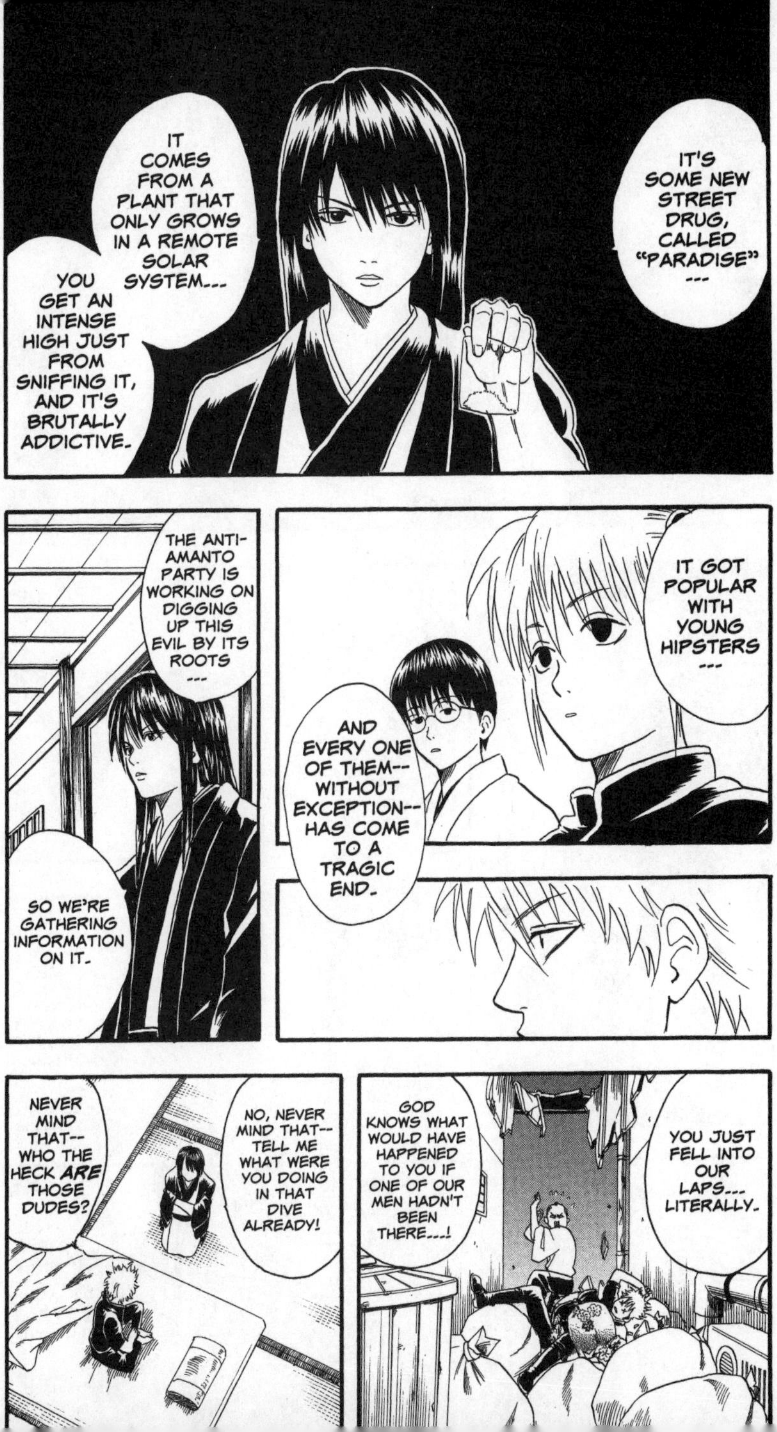
IT'S SOME NEW STREET DRUG, CALLED "PARADISE"---
IT COMES FROM A PLANT THAT ONLY GROWS IN A REMOTE SOLAR SYSTEM...
YOU GET AN INTENSE HIGH JUST FROM SNIFFING IT, AND IT'S BRUTALLY ADDICTIVE.
IT GOT POPULAR WITH YOUNG HIPSTERS---
AND EVERY ONE OF THEM--WITHOUT EXCEPTION--HAS COME TO A TRAGIC END.
THE ANTI-AMANTO PARTY IS WORKING ON DIGGING UP THIS EVIL BY ITS ROOTS---
SO WE'RE GATHERING INFORMATION ON IT.
YOU JUST FELL INTO OUR LAPS... LITERALLY.
GOD KNOWS WHAT WOULD HAVE HAPPENED TO YOU IF ONE OF OUR MEN HADN'T BEEN THERE...!
NO, NEVER MIND THAT--TELL ME WHAT WERE YOU DOING IN THAT DIVE ALREADY!
NEVER MIND THAT--WHO THE HECK *ARE* THOSE DUDES?

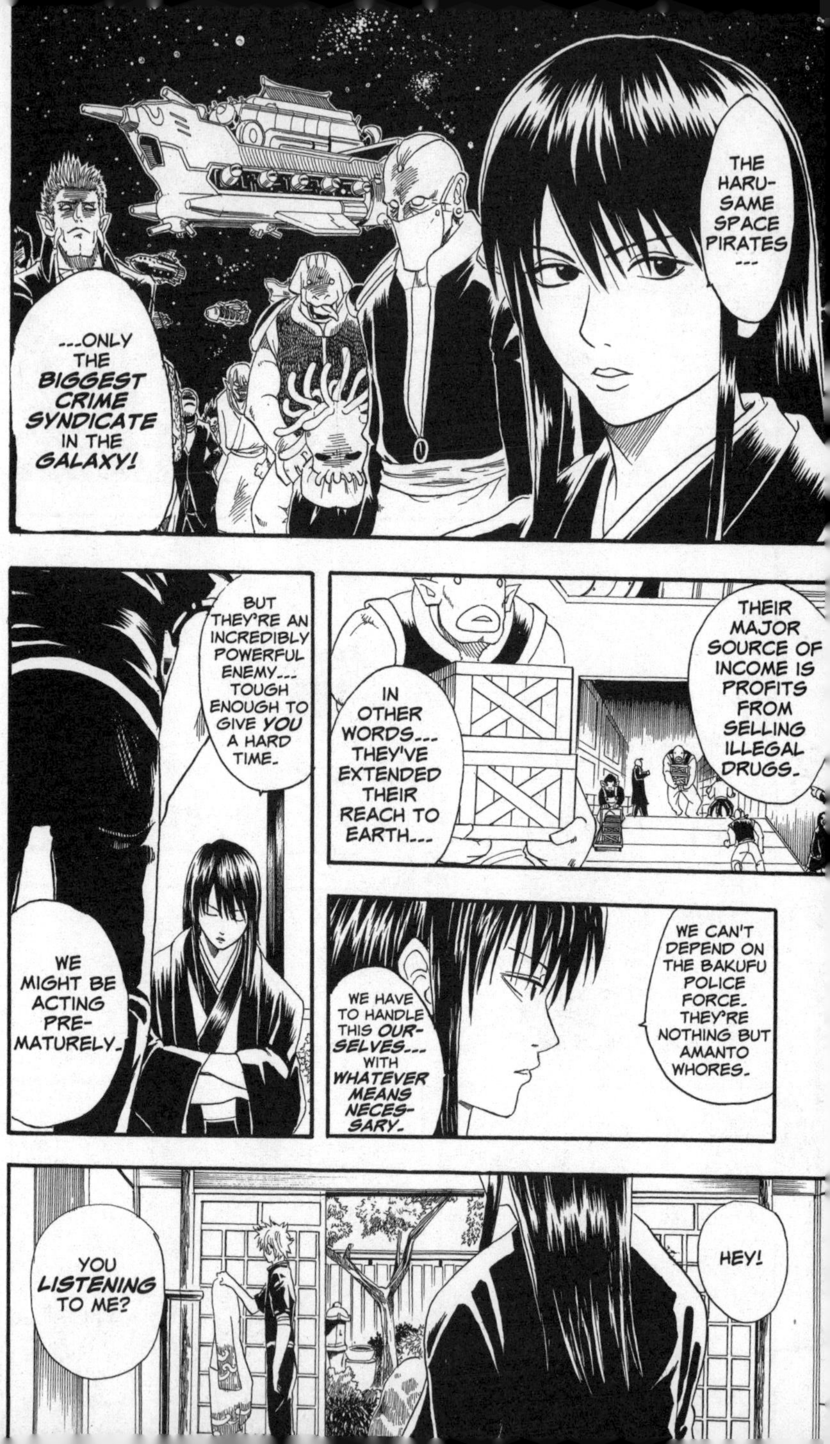
THE HARUSAME SPACE PIRATES---
---ONLY THE BIGGEST CRIME SYNDICATE IN THE GALAXY!
THEIR MAJOR SOURCE OF INCOME IS PROFITS FROM SELLING ILLEGAL DRUGS.
IN OTHER WORDS... THEY'VE EXTENDED THEIR REACH TO EARTH...
WE CAN'T DEPEND ON THE BAKUFU POLICE FORCE. THEY'RE NOTHING BUT AMANTO WHORES.
WE HAVE TO HANDLE THIS OURSELVES... WITH WHATEVER MEANS NECESSARY.
BUT THEY'RE AN INCREDIBLY POWERFUL ENEMY... TOUGH ENOUGH TO GIVE YOU A HARD TIME.
WE MIGHT BE ACTING PREMATURELY.
HEY!
YOU LISTENING TO ME?

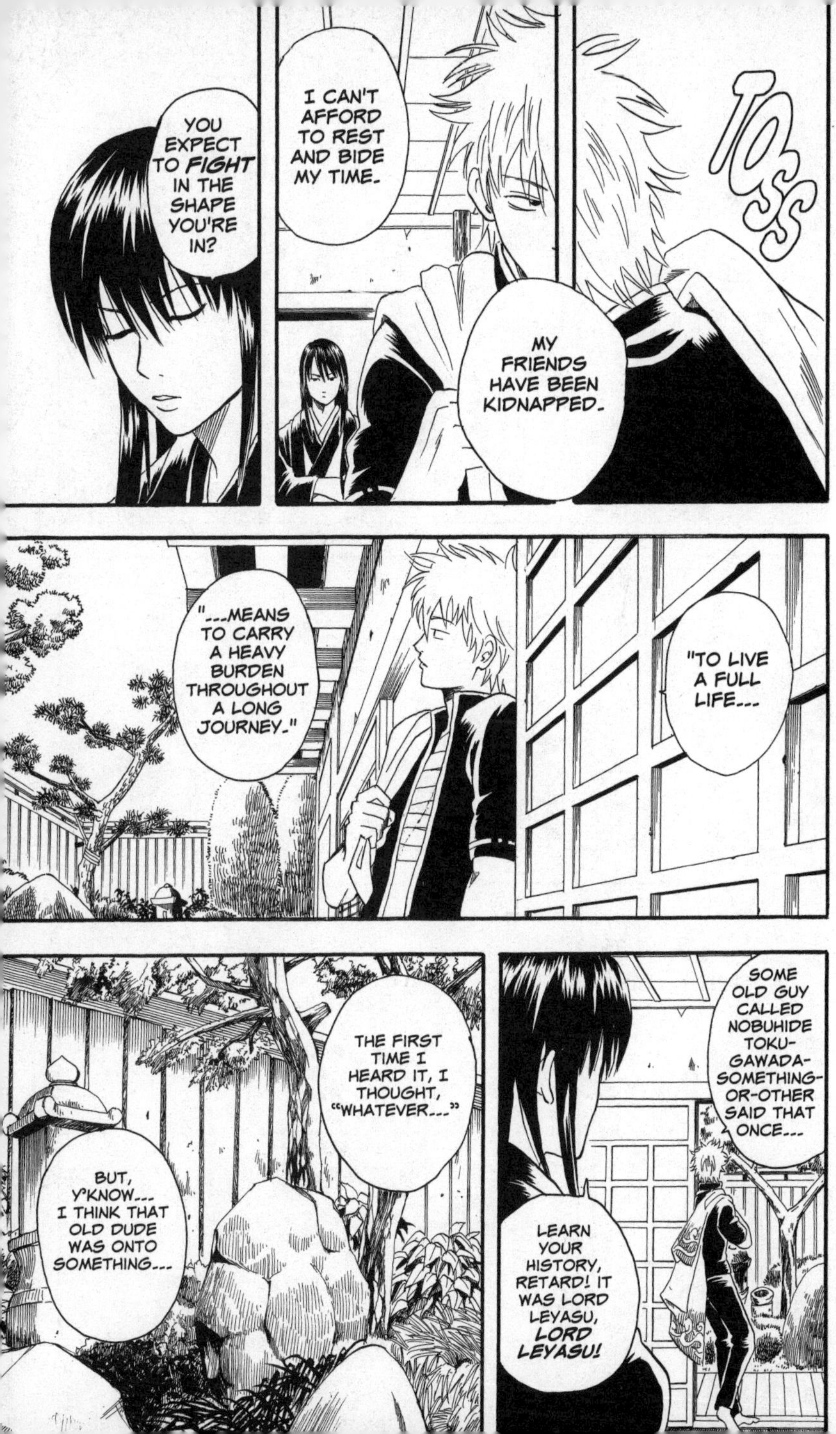
TOSS
MY FRIENDS HAVE BEEN KIDNAPPED.
I CAN'T AFFORD TO REST AND BIDE MY TIME.
YOU EXPECT TO *FIGHT* IN THE SHAPE YOU'RE IN?
"TO LIVE A FULL LIFE...
"...MEANS TO CARRY A HEAVY BURDEN THROUGHOUT A LONG JOURNEY."
SOME OLD GUY CALLED NOBUHIDE TOKU-GAWADA-SOMETHING-OR-OTHER SAID THAT ONCE...
LEARN YOUR HISTORY, RETARD! IT WAS LORD LEYASU, *LORD LEYASU!*
THE FIRST TIME I HEARD IT, I THOUGHT, "WHATEVER..."
BUT, Y'KNOW... I THINK THAT OLD DUDE WAS ONTO SOMETHING...

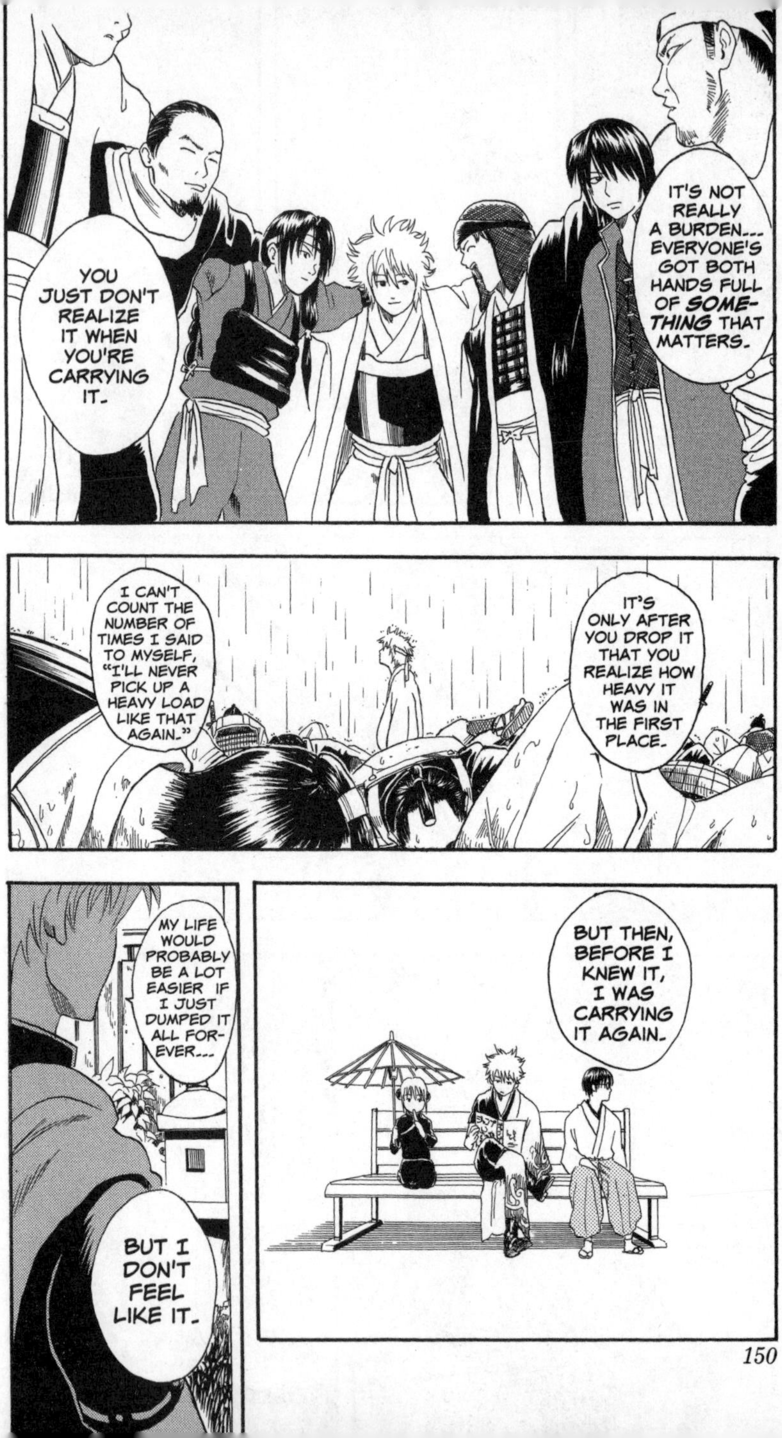
IT'S NOT REALLY A BURDEN... EVERYONE'S GOT BOTH HANDS FULL OF *SOMETHING* THAT MATTERS.
YOU JUST DON'T REALIZE IT WHEN YOU'RE CARRYING IT.
IT'S ONLY AFTER YOU DROP IT THAT YOU REALIZE HOW HEAVY IT WAS IN THE FIRST PLACE.
I CAN'T COUNT THE NUMBER OF TIMES I SAID TO MYSELF, "I'LL NEVER PICK UP A HEAVY LOAD LIKE THAT AGAIN."
BUT THEN, BEFORE I KNEW IT, I WAS CARRYING IT AGAIN.
MY LIFE WOULD PROBABLY BE A LOT EASIER IF I JUST DUMPED IT ALL FOREVER...
BUT I DON'T FEEL LIKE IT.

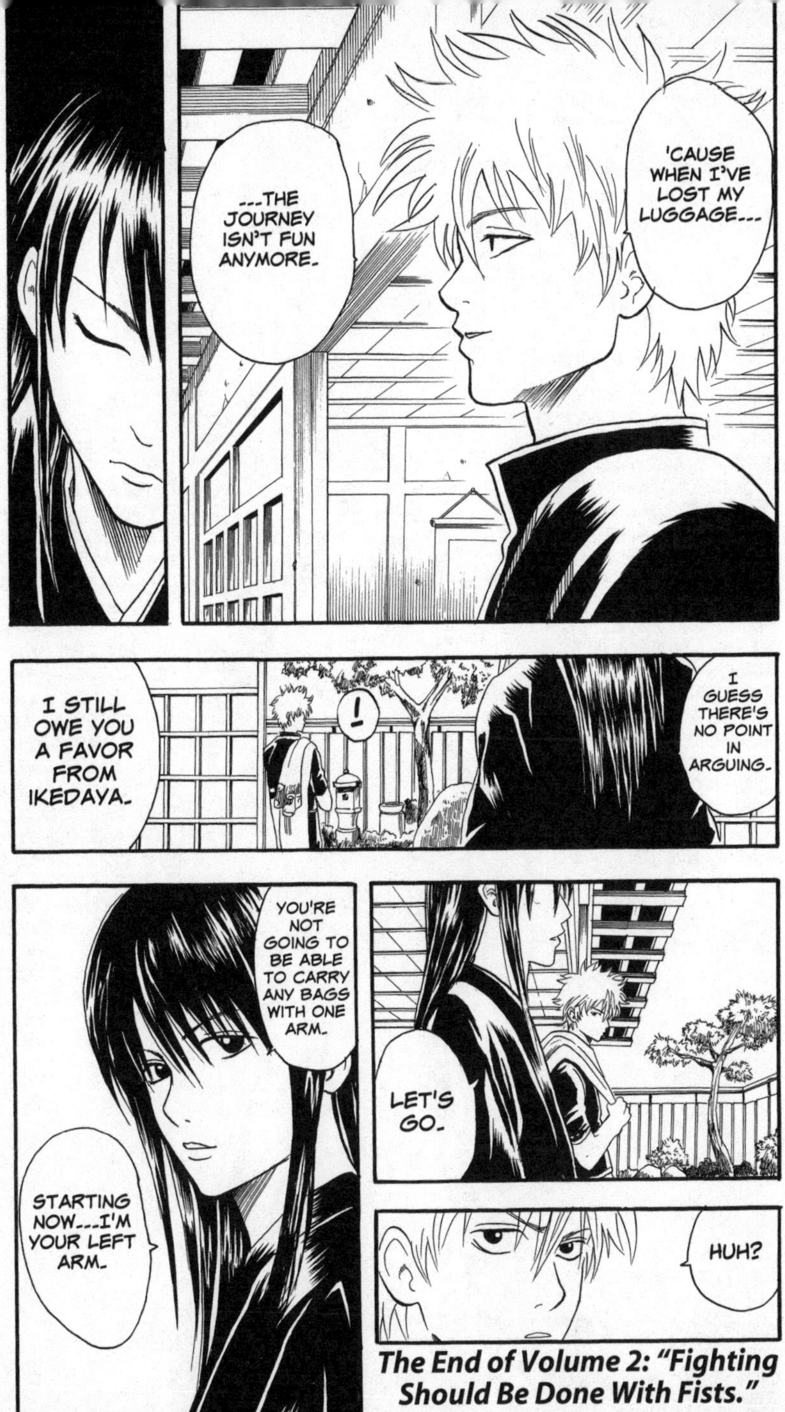
'CAUSE WHEN I'VE LOST MY LUGGAGE...
...THE JOURNEY ISN'T FUN ANYMORE.
I GUESS THERE'S NO POINT IN ARGUING.
!
I STILL OWE YOU A FAVOR FROM IKEDAYA.
LET'S GO.
HUH?
YOU'RE NOT GOING TO BE ABLE TO CARRY ANY BAGS WITH ONE ARM.
STARTING NOW...I'M YOUR LEFT ARM.

The End of Volume 2: "Fighting Should Be Done With Fists."

SHIROKURO*

THIS IS THE LAST STAND-ALONE MANGA FROM MY EARLY DAYS. IT SAVED MY CAREER AFTER A STINKER CALLED *DOJO BATTALION SAMURAIDA* GOT CHUCKED IN THE TRASH BY THE EDITORIAL DEPARTMENT. SUDDENLY, THIS STORY GOT OKAYED FOR PUBLICATION AND I WAS TOLD, "FINISH IT IN TWO WEEKS. AFTERWARDS, WE'LL HAVE YOU COME IN AND APOLOGIZE ON YOUR HANDS AND KNEES TO OUR CHIEF EDITOR." THAT'S WHEN I REALIZED, "AH, SHUEISHA IS YAKUZA."

SINCE I WAS TOLD TO KEEP IN MIND THAT THIS STORY MIGHT BE SERIALIZED, I HAD ALL THESE BIG IDEAS ABOUT TOMIKO GOING TO HIGH SCHOOL WITH YAMA AND HAVING ALL KINDS OF GHOST EXORCISM ADVENTURES--I AGONIZED OVER IT. BUT THEN MY EDITOR STARTED TALKING ABOUT THE SHINSENGUMI, AND MY DREAMS OF THIS BECOMING A SERIES ENDED UP IN THE TRASH. I'D LOVE IT IF EVERYONE WOULD DAYDREAM ABOUT THIS COMIC AND AGONIZE OVER ALL KINDS OF FUTURE STORYLINES, TOO. CATCH YOU LATER!

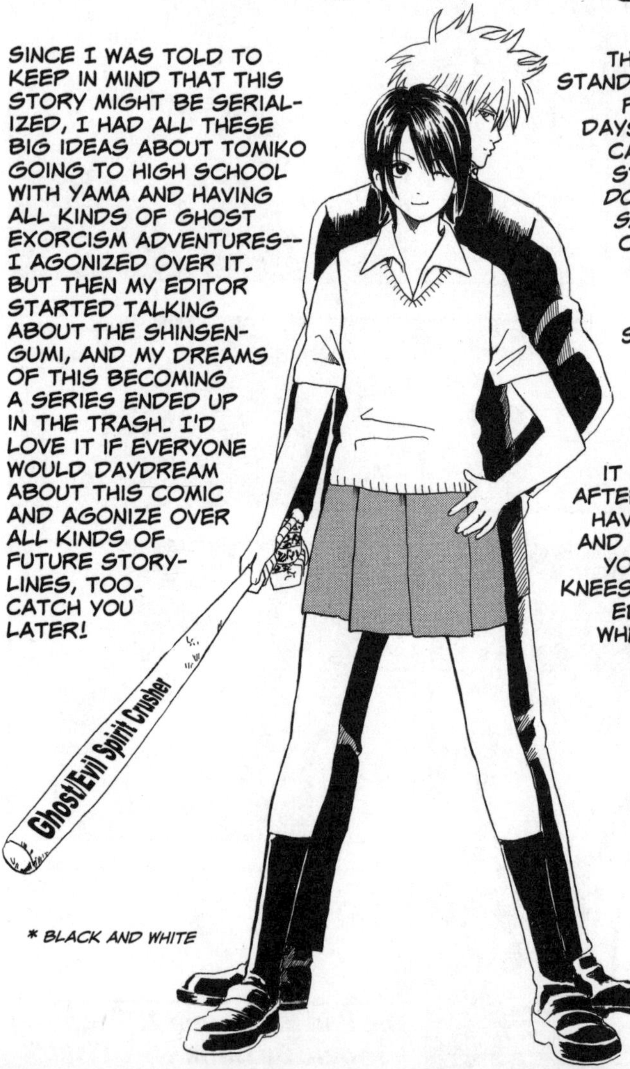
Ghost/Evil Spirit Crusher

* *BLACK AND WHITE*

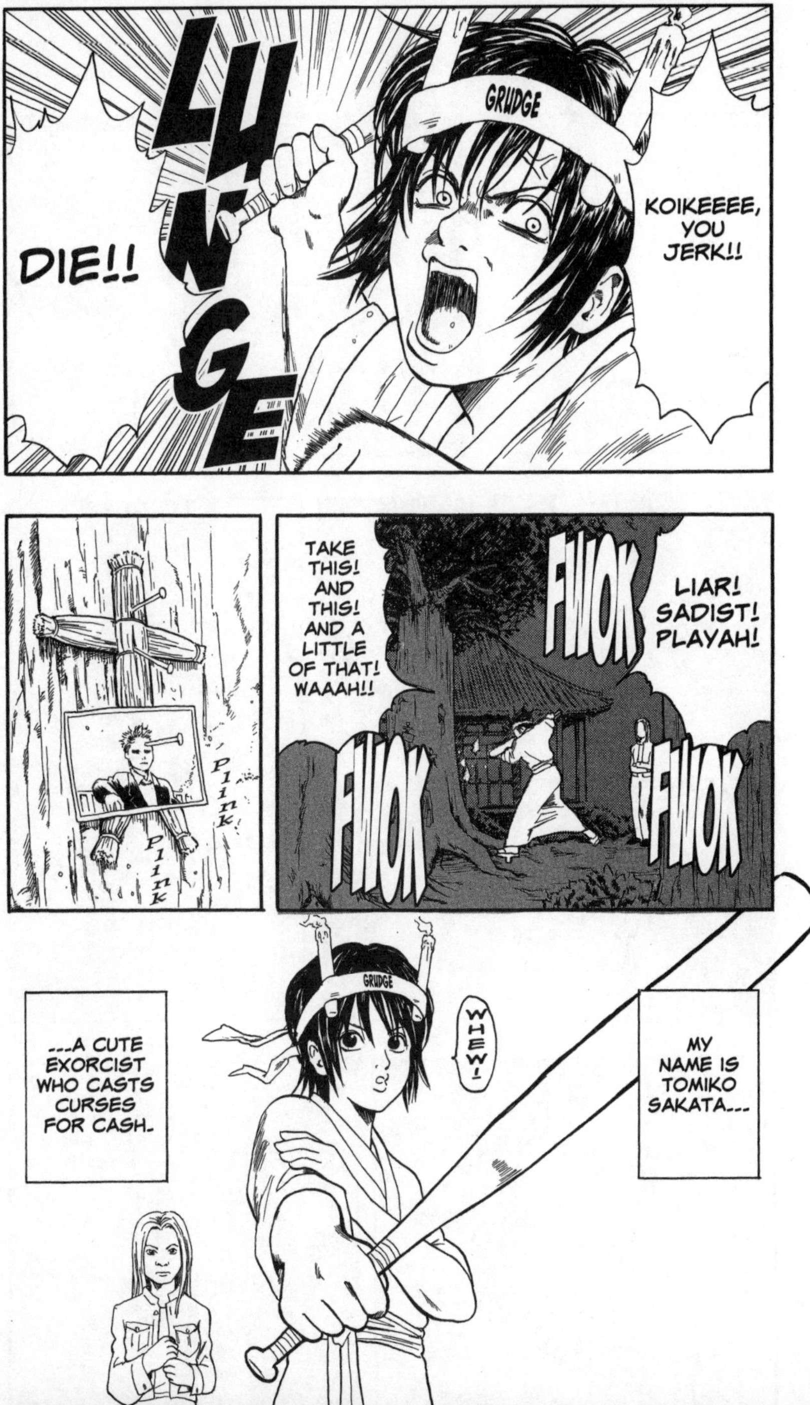
KOIKEEEE, YOU JERK!!
GRUDGE
LUNGE
DIE!!
LIAR! SADIST! PLAYAH!
FWOK
TAKE THIS! AND THIS! AND A LITTLE OF THAT! WAAAH!!
FWOK
FWOK
Plink
Plink
MY NAME IS TOMIKO SAKATA...
WHEW!
GRUDGE
...A CUTE EXORCIST WHO CASTS CURSES FOR CASH.

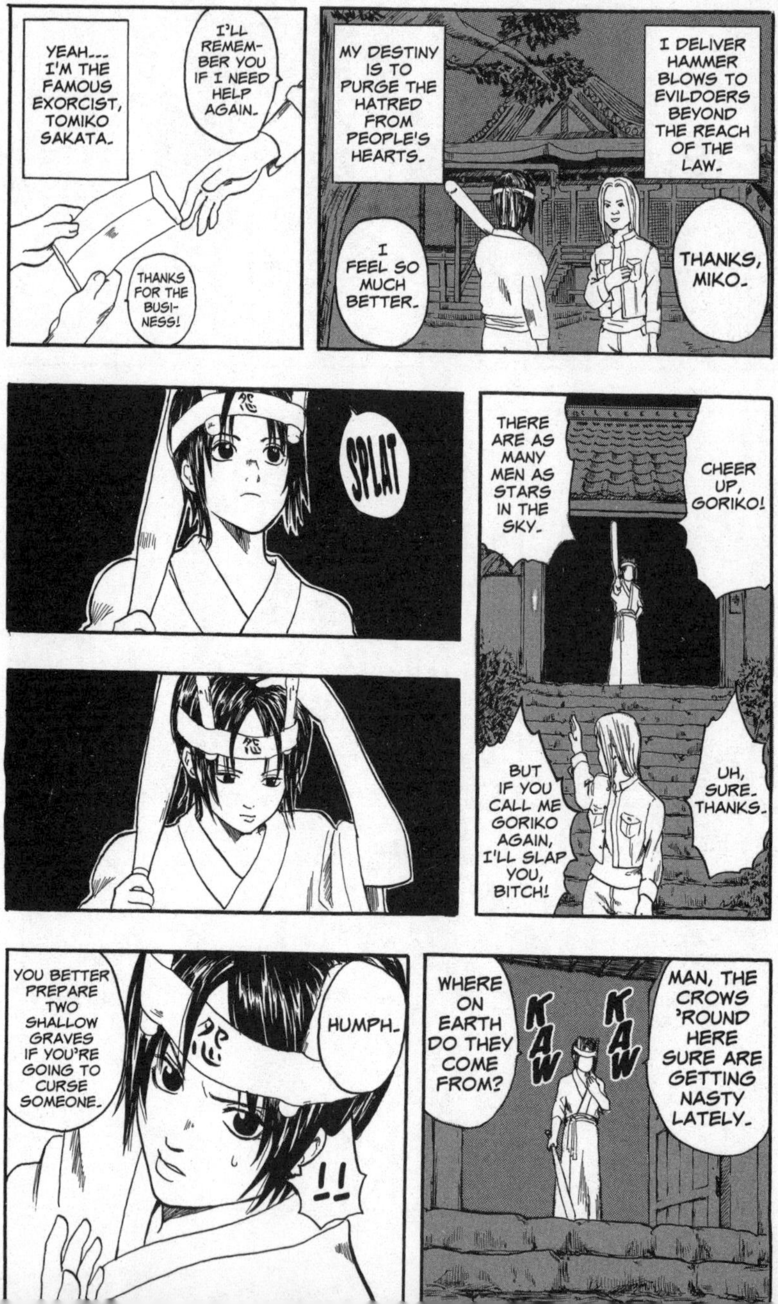
I DELIVER HAMMER BLOWS TO EVILDOERS BEYOND THE REACH OF THE LAW.
MY DESTINY IS TO PURGE THE HATRED FROM PEOPLE'S HEARTS.
THANKS, MIKO.
I FEEL SO MUCH BETTER.
I'LL REMEMBER YOU IF I NEED HELP AGAIN.
YEAH... I'M THE FAMOUS EXORCIST, TOMIKO SAKATA.
THANKS FOR THE BUSINESS!
CHEER UP, GORIKO!
THERE ARE AS MANY MEN AS STARS IN THE SKY.
UH, SURE. THANKS.
BUT IF YOU CALL ME GORIKO AGAIN, I'LL SLAP YOU, BITCH!
SPLAT
MAN, THE CROWS 'ROUND HERE SURE ARE GETTING NASTY LATELY.
KAW
KAW
WHERE ON EARTH DO THEY COME FROM?
HUMPH.
YOU BETTER PREPARE TWO SHALLOW GRAVES IF YOU'RE GOING TO CURSE SOMEONE.
!!

READ THIS WAY

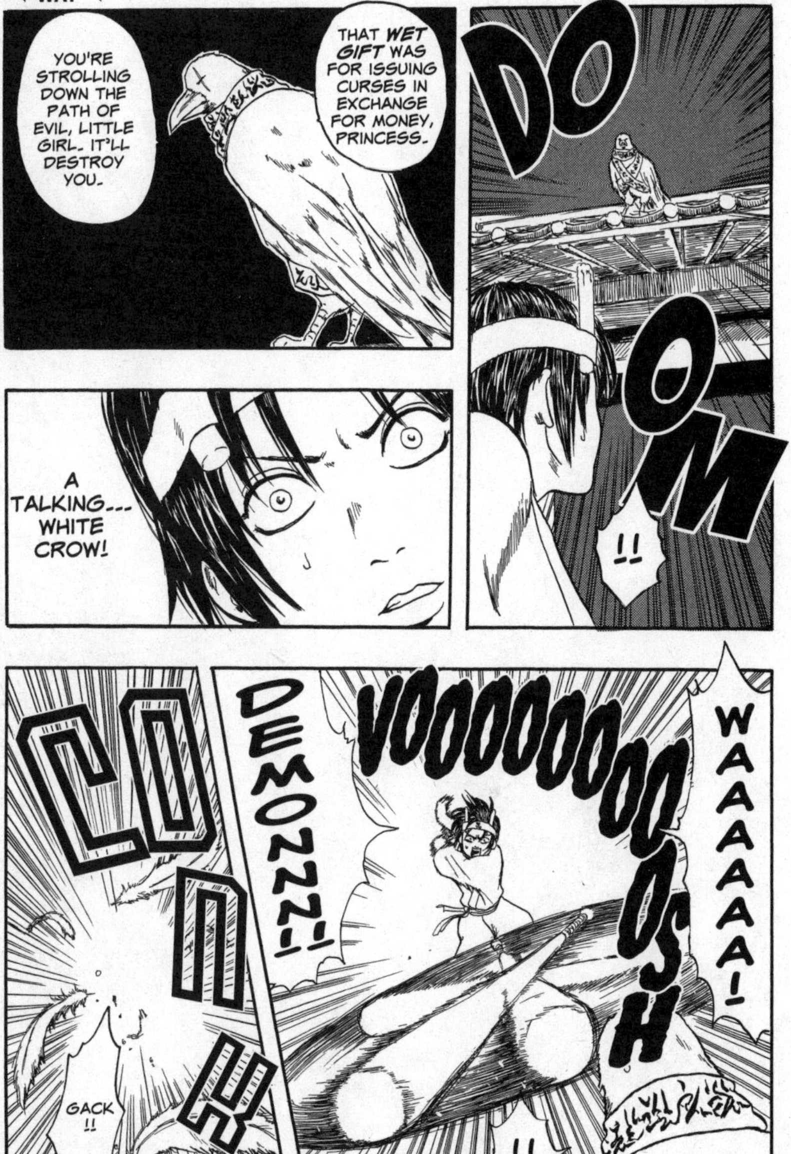

DOOM
!!
THAT WET GIFT WAS FOR ISSUING CURSES IN EXCHANGE FOR MONEY, PRINCESS.
YOU'RE STROLLING DOWN THE PATH OF EVIL, LITTLE GIRL. IT'LL DESTROY YOU.
A TALKING... WHITE CROW!
WAAAAAAI!
VOOOOOOOOOOOSH
DEMONNN!!
!!
CONK
GACK !!

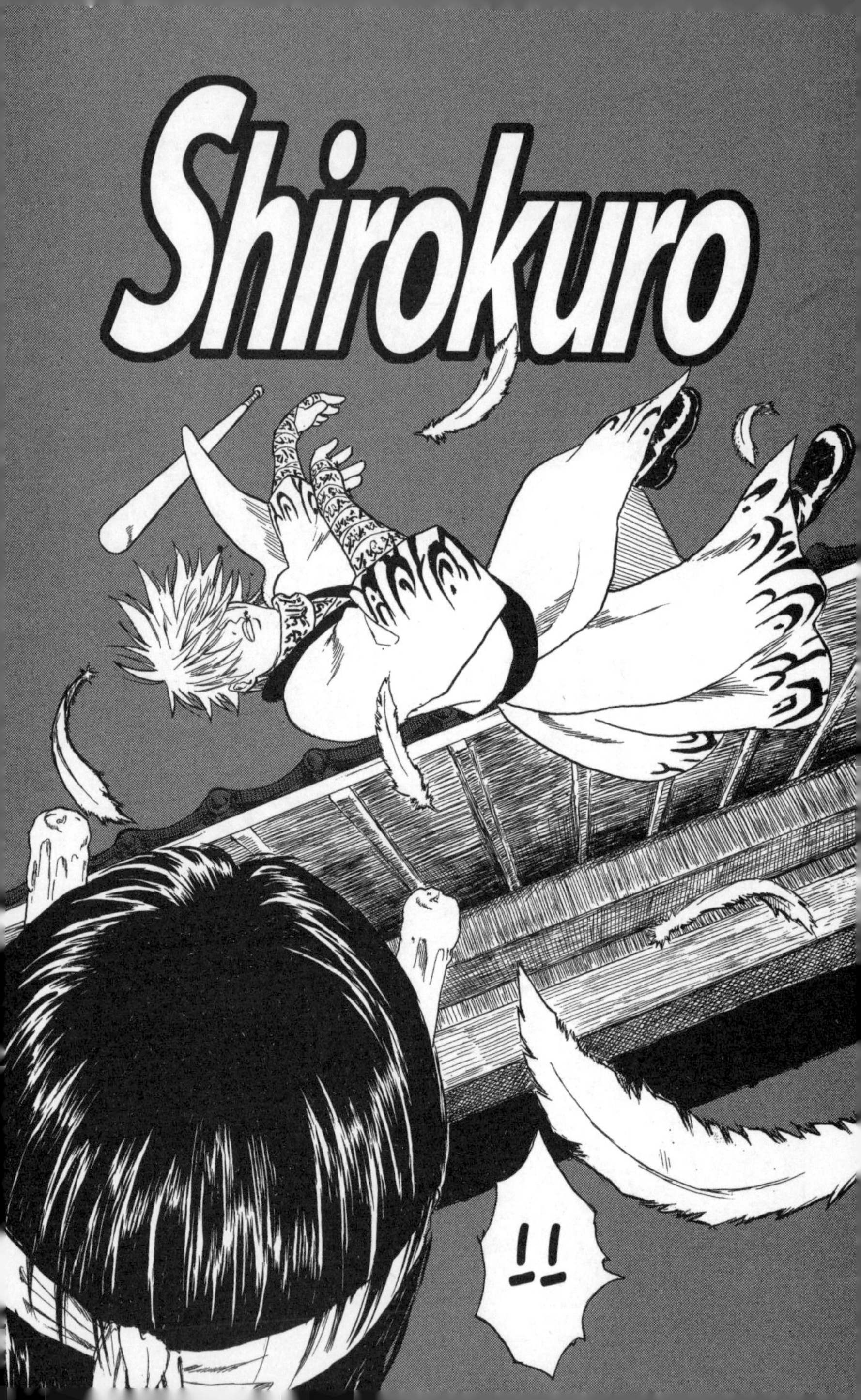
Shirokuro
!!

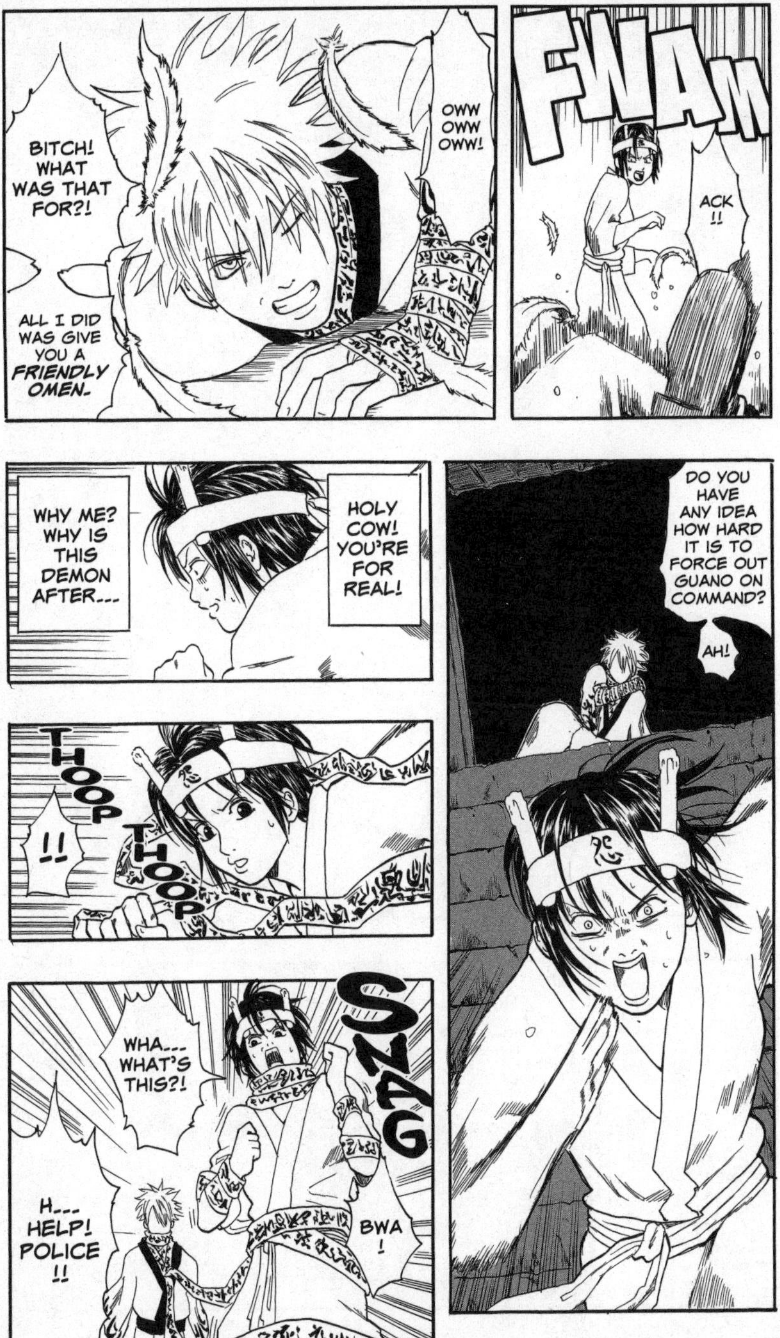
FWAM
ACK!!
OWW OWW OWW!
BITCH! WHAT WAS THAT FOR?!
ALL I DID WAS GIVE YOU A *FRIENDLY* *OMEN*.
DO YOU HAVE ANY IDEA HOW HARD IT IS TO FORCE OUT GUANO ON COMMAND?
AH!
HOLY COW! YOU'RE FOR REAL!
WHY ME? WHY IS THIS DEMON AFTER...
THOOP
THOOP
!!
SNAG
WHA... WHAT'S THIS?!
BWA!
H... HELP! POLICE!!

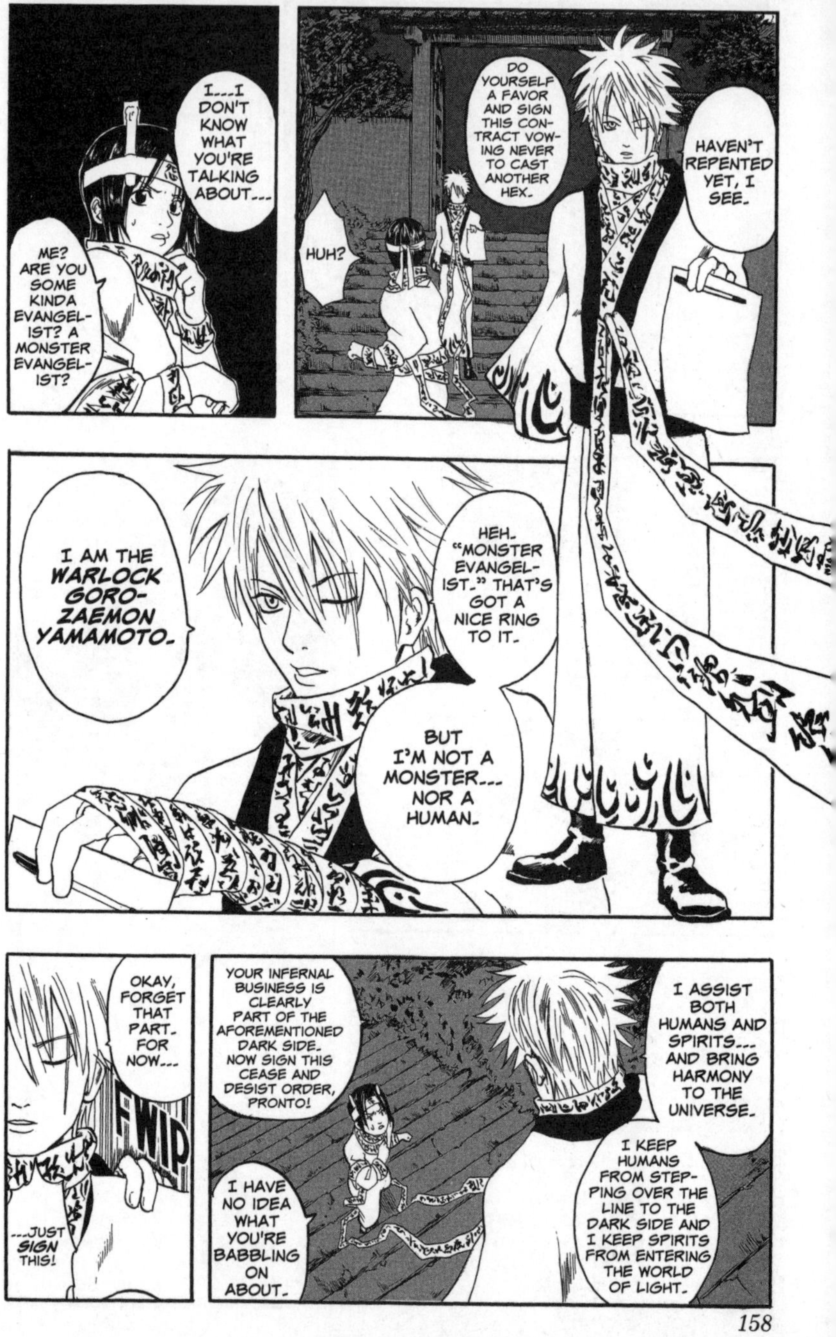
HAVEN'T REPENTED YET, I SEE.
DO YOURSELF A FAVOR AND SIGN THIS CONTRACT VOWING NEVER TO CAST ANOTHER HEX.
HUH?
I...I DON'T KNOW WHAT YOU'RE TALKING ABOUT...
ME? ARE YOU SOME KINDA EVANGELIST? A MONSTER EVANGELIST?
HEH. "MONSTER EVANGELIST." THAT'S GOT A NICE RING TO IT.
BUT I'M NOT A MONSTER... NOR A HUMAN.
I AM THE *WARLOCK GORO-ZAEMON YAMAMOTO.*
I ASSIST BOTH HUMANS AND SPIRITS... AND BRING HARMONY TO THE UNIVERSE.
I KEEP HUMANS FROM STEPPING OVER THE LINE TO THE DARK SIDE AND I KEEP SPIRITS FROM ENTERING THE WORLD OF LIGHT.
I HAVE NO IDEA WHAT YOU'RE BABBLING ON ABOUT.
YOUR INFERNAL BUSINESS IS CLEARLY PART OF THE AFOREMENTIONED DARK SIDE. NOW SIGN THIS CEASE AND DESIST ORDER, PRONTO!
OKAY, FORGET THAT PART. FOR NOW...
FWIP
...JUST *SIGN* THIS!

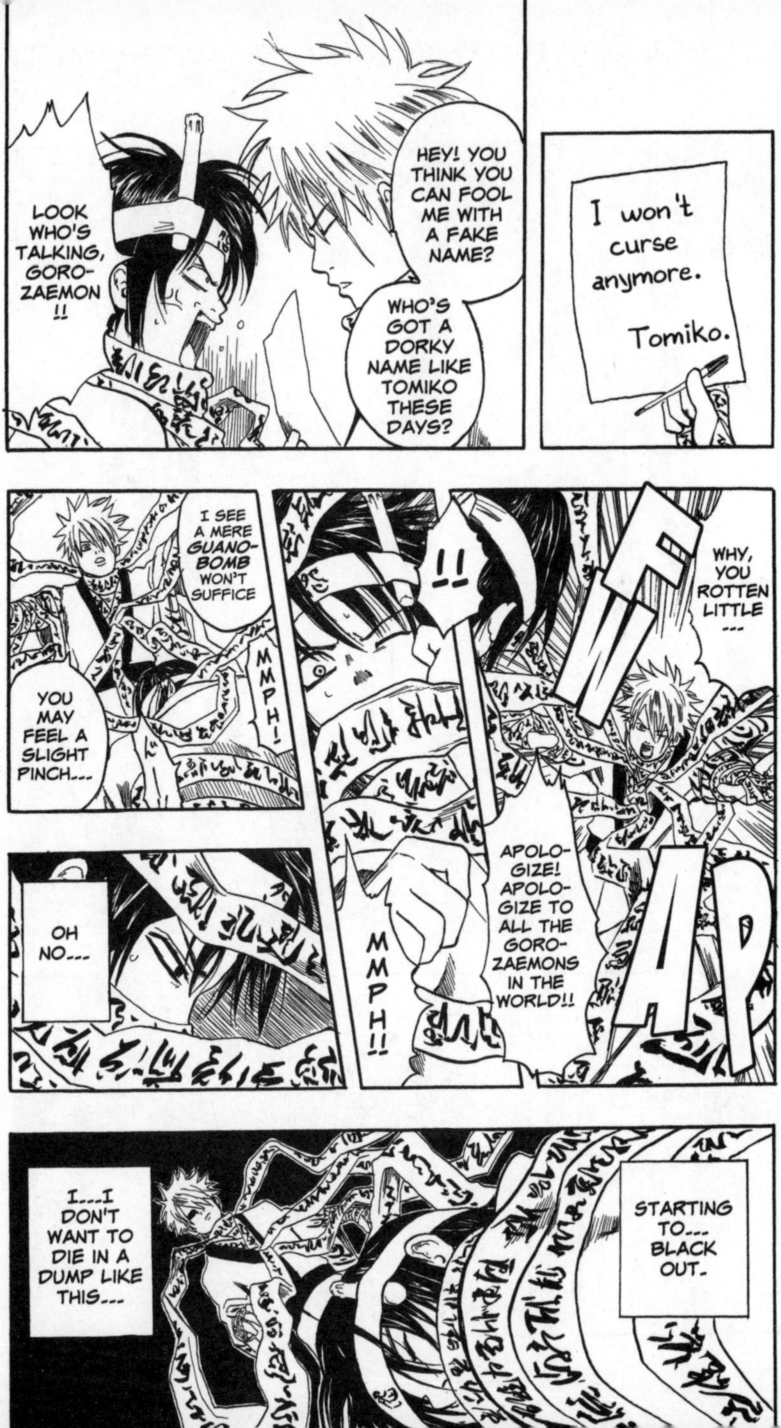
I won't curse anymore.
Tomiko.
HEY! YOU THINK YOU CAN FOOL ME WITH A FAKE NAME?
WHO'S GOT A DORKY NAME LIKE TOMIKO THESE DAYS?
LOOK WHO'S TALKING, GORO-ZAEMON!!
WHY, YOU ROTTEN LITTLE ---
APOLOGIZE! APOLOGIZE TO ALL THE GORO-ZAEMONS IN THE WORLD!!
MMPH!!
I SEE A MERE GUANO-BOMB WON'T SUFFICE
MMPH!
YOU MAY FEEL A SLIGHT PINCH...
OH NO...
STARTING TO... BLACK OUT.
I... I DON'T WANT TO DIE IN A DUMP LIKE THIS...

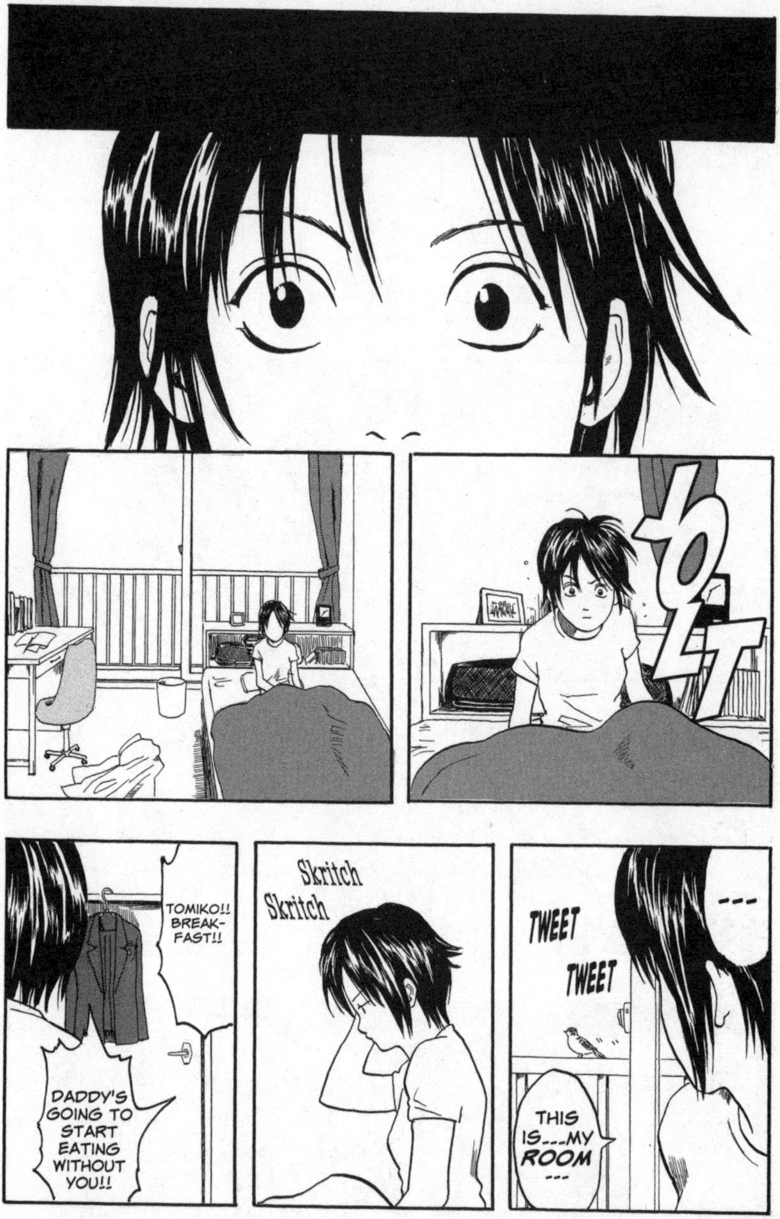
YOLT
...
TWEET
TWEET
THIS IS...MY ROOM...
Skritch
Skritch
TOMIKO!! BREAK-FAST!!
DADDY'S GOING TO START EATING WITHOUT YOU!!

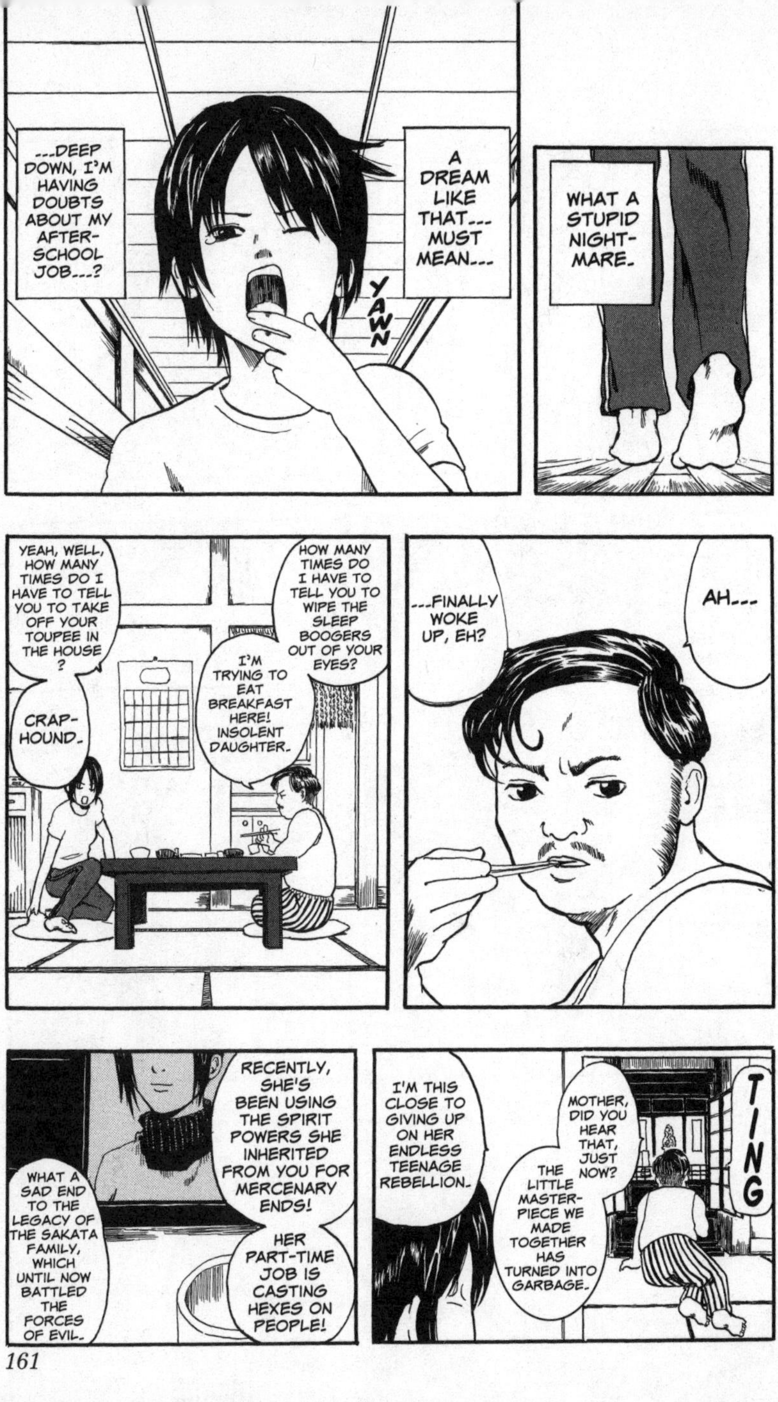
WHAT A STUPID NIGHT-MARE.
A DREAM LIKE THAT... MUST MEAN...
...DEEP DOWN, I'M HAVING DOUBTS ABOUT MY AFTER-SCHOOL JOB...?
YAWN
AH...
...FINALLY WOKE UP, EH?
HOW MANY TIMES DO I HAVE TO TELL YOU TO WIPE THE SLEEP BOOGERS OUT OF YOUR EYES?
I'M TRYING TO EAT BREAKFAST HERE! INSOLENT DAUGHTER.
YEAH, WELL, HOW MANY TIMES DO I HAVE TO TELL YOU TO TAKE OFF YOUR TOUPEE IN THE HOUSE?
CRAP-HOUND.
TING
MOTHER, DID YOU HEAR THAT, JUST NOW?
THE LITTLE MASTER-PIECE WE MADE TOGETHER HAS TURNED INTO GARBAGE.
I'M THIS CLOSE TO GIVING UP ON HER ENDLESS TEENAGE REBELLION.
RECENTLY, SHE'S BEEN USING THE SPIRIT POWERS SHE INHERITED FROM YOU FOR MERCENARY ENDS!
HER PART-TIME JOB IS CASTING HEXES ON PEOPLE!
WHAT A SAD END TO THE LEGACY OF THE SAKATA FAMILY, WHICH UNTIL NOW BATTLED THE FORCES OF EVIL.

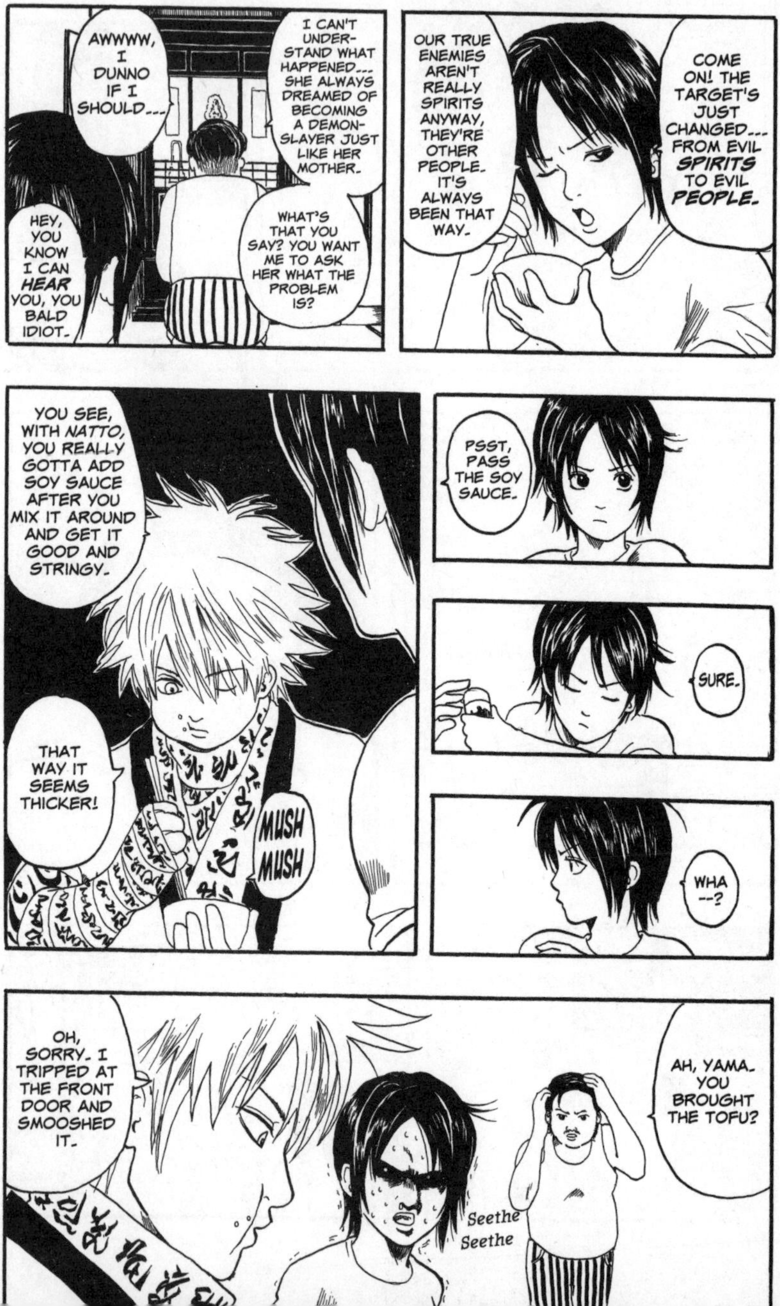
COME ON! THE TARGET'S JUST CHANGED... FROM EVIL *SPIRITS* TO EVIL *PEOPLE*.
OUR TRUE ENEMIES AREN'T REALLY SPIRITS ANYWAY, THEY'RE OTHER PEOPLE. IT'S ALWAYS BEEN THAT WAY.
I CAN'T UNDER-STAND WHAT HAPPENED... SHE ALWAYS DREAMED OF BECOMING A DEMON-SLAYER JUST LIKE HER MOTHER.
AWWWW, I DUNNO IF I SHOULD...
WHAT'S THAT YOU SAY? YOU WANT ME TO ASK HER WHAT THE PROBLEM IS?
HEY, YOU KNOW I CAN *HEAR* YOU, YOU BALD IDIOT.
PSST, PASS THE SOY SAUCE.
SURE.
WHA --?
YOU SEE, WITH *NATTO*, YOU REALLY GOTTA ADD SOY SAUCE AFTER YOU MIX IT AROUND AND GET IT GOOD AND STRINGY.
MUSH MUSH
THAT WAY IT SEEMS THICKER!
AH, YAMA. YOU BROUGHT THE TOFU?
Seethe Seethe
OH, SORRY. I TRIPPED AT THE FRONT DOOR AND SMOOSHED IT.

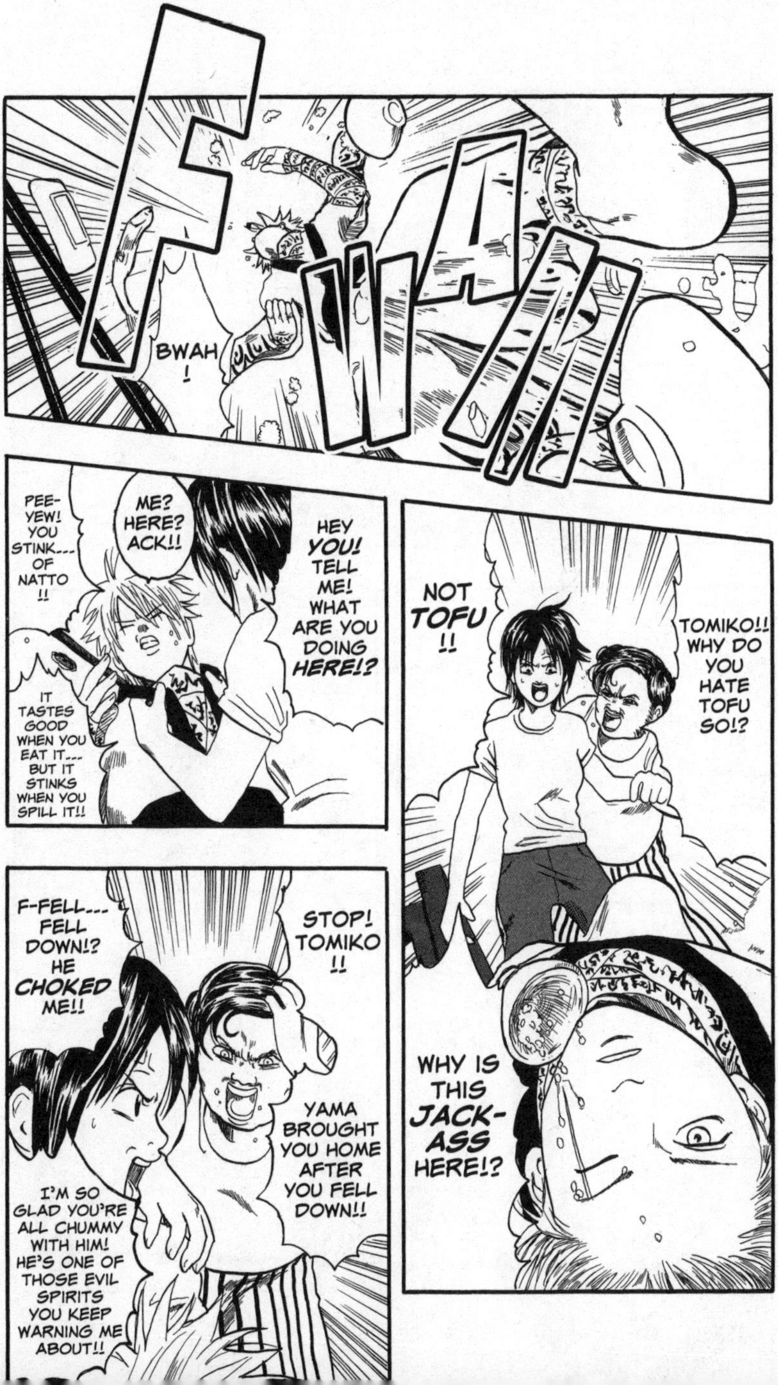
FWAM
BWAH!
TOMIKO!! WHY DO YOU HATE TOFU SO!?
NOT TOFU!!
WHY IS THIS JACKASS HERE!?
HEY YOU! TELL ME! WHAT ARE YOU DOING HERE!?
ME? HERE? ACK!!
PEE-YEW! YOU STINK... OF NATTO!!
IT TASTES GOOD WHEN YOU EAT IT... BUT IT STINKS WHEN YOU SPILL IT!!
STOP! TOMIKO!!
F-FELL... FELL DOWN!? HE CHOKED ME!!
YAMA BROUGHT YOU HOME AFTER YOU FELL DOWN!!
I'M SO GLAD YOU'RE ALL CHUMMY WITH HIM! HE'S ONE OF THOSE EVIL SPIRITS YOU KEEP WARNING ME ABOUT!!

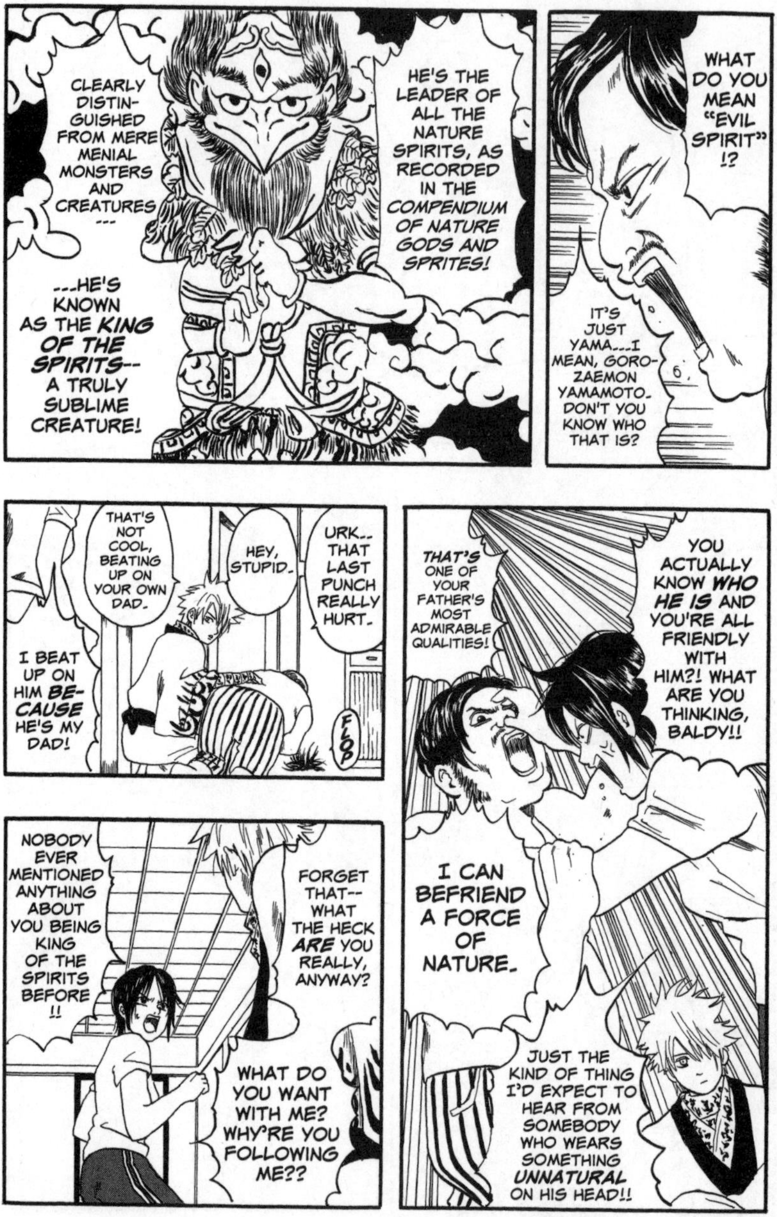
WHAT DO YOU MEAN "EVIL SPIRIT" !?
IT'S JUST YAMA... I MEAN, GOROZAEMON YAMAMOTO. DON'T YOU KNOW WHO THAT IS?
HE'S THE LEADER OF ALL THE NATURE SPIRITS, AS RECORDED IN THE *COMPENDIUM OF NATURE GODS AND SPRITES!*
CLEARLY DISTINGUISHED FROM MERE MENIAL MONSTERS AND CREATURES...
...HE'S KNOWN AS THE ***KING OF THE SPIRITS***-- A TRULY SUBLIME CREATURE!
YOU ACTUALLY KNOW ***WHO HE IS*** AND YOU'RE ALL FRIENDLY WITH HIM?! WHAT ARE YOU THINKING, BALDY!!
THAT'S ONE OF YOUR FATHER'S MOST ADMIRABLE QUALITIES!
I CAN BEFRIEND A FORCE OF NATURE.
JUST THE KIND OF THING I'D EXPECT TO HEAR FROM SOMEBODY WHO WEARS SOMETHING ***UNNATURAL*** ON HIS HEAD!!
URK.. THAT LAST PUNCH REALLY HURT.
HEY, STUPID.
THAT'S NOT COOL, BEATING UP ON YOUR OWN DAD.
I BEAT UP ON HIM ***BECAUSE*** HE'S MY DAD!
FLOP
FORGET THAT-- WHAT THE HECK ***ARE*** YOU REALLY, ANYWAY?
NOBODY EVER MENTIONED ANYTHING ABOUT YOU BEING KING OF THE SPIRITS BEFORE !!
WHAT DO YOU WANT WITH ME? WHY'RE YOU FOLLOWING ME??

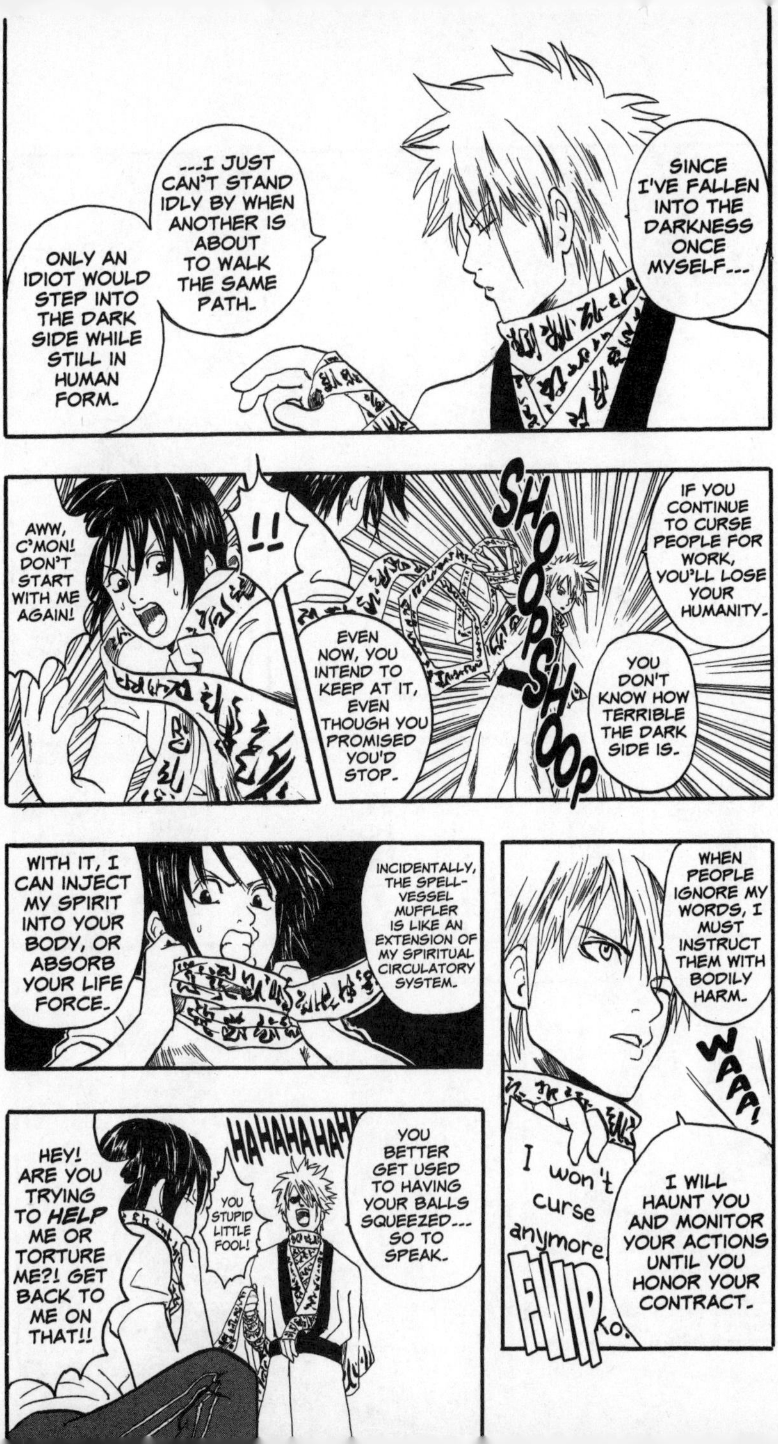
SINCE I'VE FALLEN INTO THE DARKNESS ONCE MYSELF...
...I JUST CAN'T STAND IDLY BY WHEN ANOTHER IS ABOUT TO WALK THE SAME PATH.
ONLY AN IDIOT WOULD STEP INTO THE DARK SIDE WHILE STILL IN HUMAN FORM.
IF YOU CONTINUE TO CURSE PEOPLE FOR WORK, YOU'LL LOSE YOUR HUMANITY.
SHOOPSHOOP
YOU DON'T KNOW HOW TERRIBLE THE DARK SIDE IS.
EVEN NOW, YOU INTEND TO KEEP AT IT, EVEN THOUGH YOU PROMISED YOU'D STOP.
!!
AWW, C'MON! DON'T START WITH ME AGAIN!
WHEN PEOPLE IGNORE MY WORDS, I MUST INSTRUCT THEM WITH BODILY HARM.
WAAA!
I WILL HAUNT YOU AND MONITOR YOUR ACTIONS UNTIL YOU HONOR YOUR CONTRACT.
I won't curse anymore
FWIP
ko.
INCIDENTALLY, THE SPELL-VESSEL MUFFLER IS LIKE AN EXTENSION OF MY SPIRITUAL CIRCULATORY SYSTEM.
WITH IT, I CAN INJECT MY SPIRIT INTO YOUR BODY, OR ABSORB YOUR LIFE FORCE.
YOU BETTER GET USED TO HAVING YOUR BALLS SQUEEZED... SO TO SPEAK.
HAHAHAHAHA
YOU STUPID LITTLE FOOL!
HEY! ARE YOU TRYING TO *HELP* ME OR TORTURE ME?! GET BACK TO ME ON THAT!!

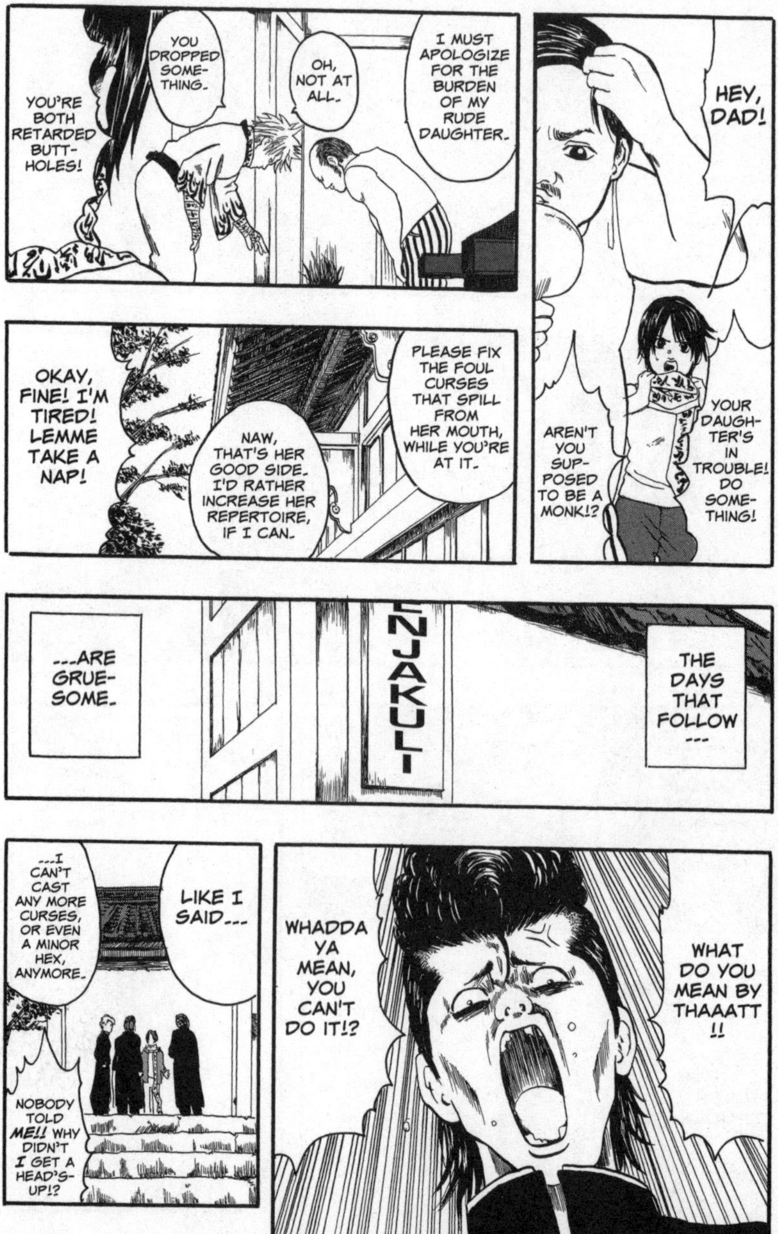
HEY, DAD!
YOUR DAUGHTER'S IN TROUBLE! DO SOMETHING!
AREN'T YOU SUPPOSED TO BE A MONK!?
I MUST APOLOGIZE FOR THE BURDEN OF MY RUDE DAUGHTER.
OH, NOT AT ALL.
YOU DROPPED SOMETHING.
YOU'RE BOTH RETARDED BUTTHOLES!
PLEASE FIX THE FOUL CURSES THAT SPILL FROM HER MOUTH, WHILE YOU'RE AT IT.
NAW, THAT'S HER GOOD SIDE. I'D RATHER INCREASE HER REPERTOIRE, IF I CAN.
OKAY, FINE! I'M TIRED! LEMME TAKE A NAP!
THE DAYS THAT FOLLOW...
NJAKUJI
...ARE GRUESOME.
WHAT DO YOU MEAN BY THAAATT!!
WHADDA YA MEAN, YOU CAN'T DO IT!?
LIKE I SAID...
...I CAN'T CAST ANY MORE CURSES, OR EVEN A MINOR HEX, ANYMORE.
NOBODY TOLD *ME!!* WHY DIDN'T *I* GET A HEAD'S-UP!?

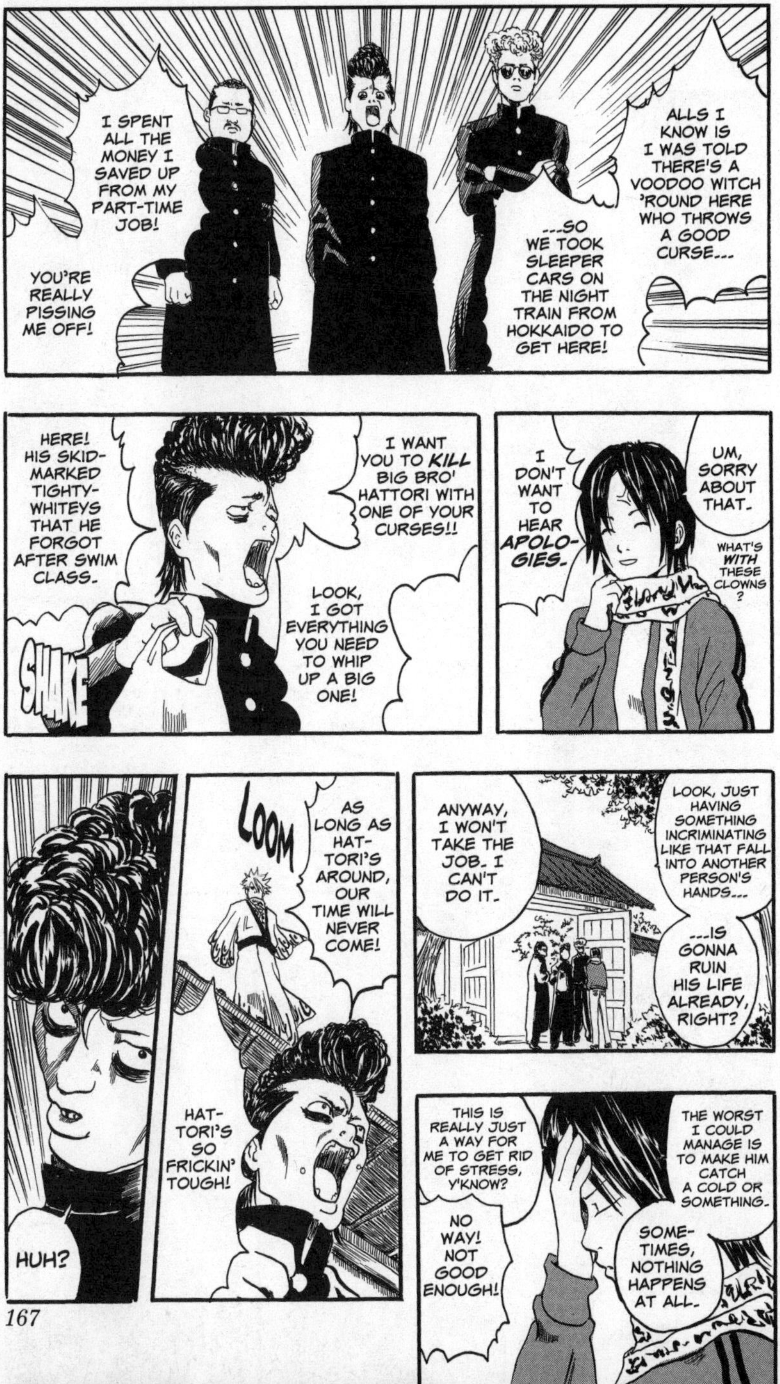
ALLS I KNOW IS I WAS TOLD THERE'S A VOODOO WITCH 'ROUND HERE WHO THROWS A GOOD CURSE...
...SO WE TOOK SLEEPER CARS ON THE NIGHT TRAIN FROM HOKKAIDO TO GET HERE!
I SPENT ALL THE MONEY I SAVED UP FROM MY PART-TIME JOB!
YOU'RE REALLY PISSING ME OFF!
UM, SORRY ABOUT THAT.
WHAT'S *WITH* THESE CLOWNS?
I DON'T WANT TO HEAR **APOLOGIES.**
I WANT YOU TO ***KILL*** BIG BRO' HATTORI WITH ONE OF YOUR CURSES!!
HERE! HIS SKID-MARKED TIGHTY-WHITEYS THAT HE FORGOT AFTER SWIM CLASS.
LOOK, I GOT EVERYTHING YOU NEED TO WHIP UP A BIG ONE!
SHAKE
LOOK, JUST HAVING SOMETHING INCRIMINATING LIKE THAT FALL INTO ANOTHER PERSON'S HANDS...
...IS GONNA RUIN HIS LIFE ALREADY, RIGHT?
ANYWAY, I WON'T TAKE THE JOB. I CAN'T DO IT.
THE WORST I COULD MANAGE IS TO MAKE HIM CATCH A COLD OR SOMETHING.
THIS IS REALLY JUST A WAY FOR ME TO GET RID OF STRESS, Y'KNOW?
SOME-TIMES, NOTHING HAPPENS AT ALL.
NO WAY! NOT GOOD ENOUGH!
AS LONG AS HAT-TORI'S AROUND, OUR TIME WILL NEVER COME!
LOOM
HAT-TORI'S SO FRICKIN' TOUGH!
HUH?

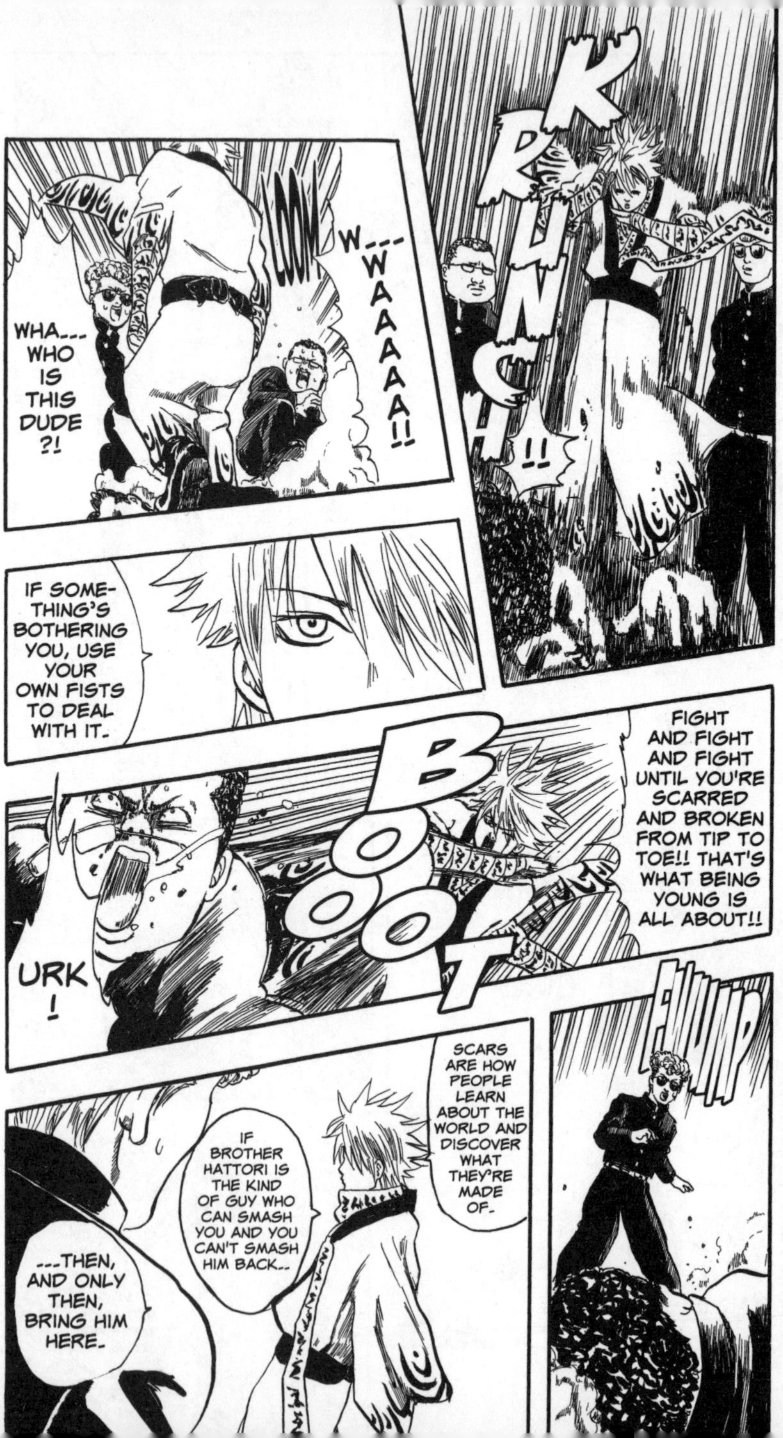
KRUNCH!!
LOOM
W... WAAAAA!!
WHA... WHO IS THIS DUDE?!
IF SOMETHING'S BOTHERING YOU, USE YOUR OWN FISTS TO DEAL WITH IT.
FIGHT AND FIGHT AND FIGHT UNTIL YOU'RE SCARRED AND BROKEN FROM TIP TO TOE!! THAT'S WHAT BEING YOUNG IS ALL ABOUT!!
BOOOT
URK!
THUMP
SCARS ARE HOW PEOPLE LEARN ABOUT THE WORLD AND DISCOVER WHAT THEY'RE MADE OF.
IF BROTHER HATTORI IS THE KIND OF GUY WHO CAN SMASH YOU AND YOU CAN'T SMASH HIM BACK...
...THEN, AND ONLY THEN, BRING HIM HERE.

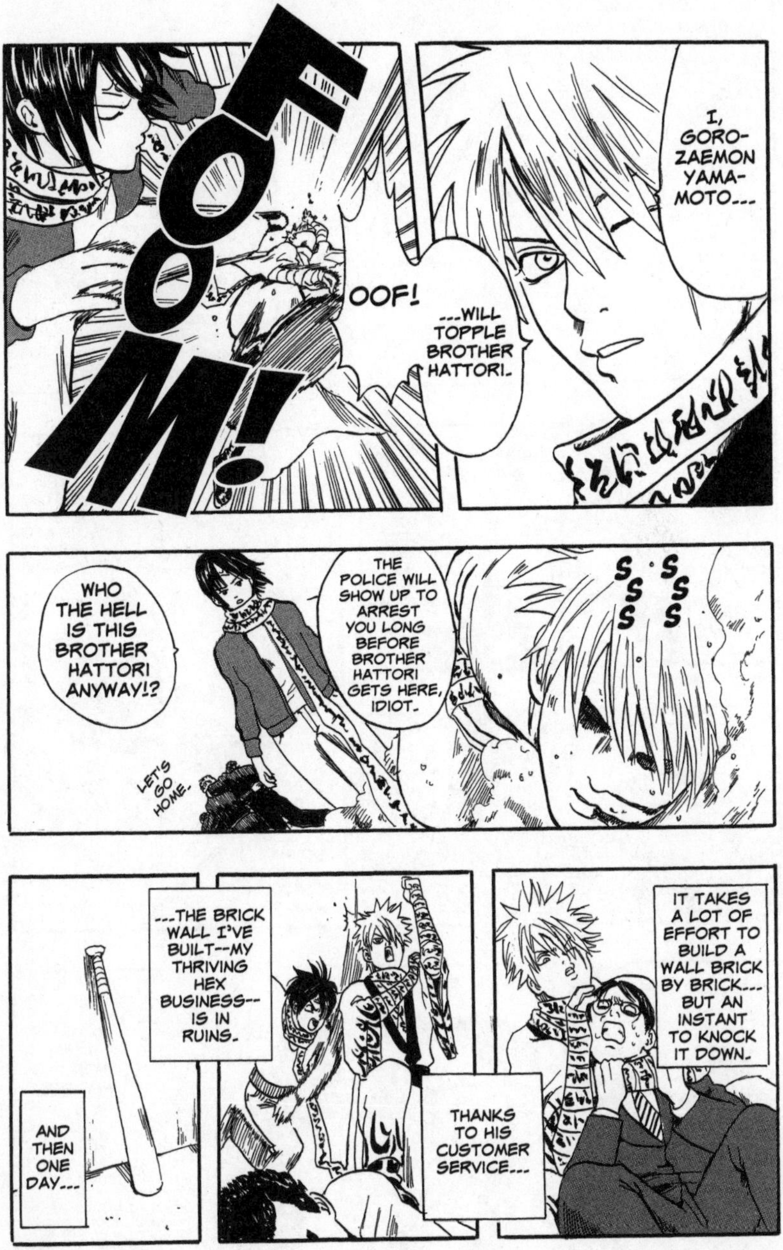
I, GORO-ZAEMON YAMA-MOTO...
...WILL TOPPLE BROTHER HATTORI.
OOF!
FOOM!
SSS SSS
THE POLICE WILL SHOW UP TO ARREST YOU LONG BEFORE BROTHER HATTORI GETS HERE, IDIOT.
WHO THE HELL IS THIS BROTHER HATTORI ANYWAY!?
LET'S GO HOME.
IT TAKES A LOT OF EFFORT TO BUILD A WALL BRICK BY BRICK... BUT AN INSTANT TO KNOCK IT DOWN.
THANKS TO HIS CUSTOMER SERVICE...
...THE BRICK WALL I'VE BUILT--MY THRIVING HEX BUSINESS--IS IN RUINS.
AND THEN ONE DAY...

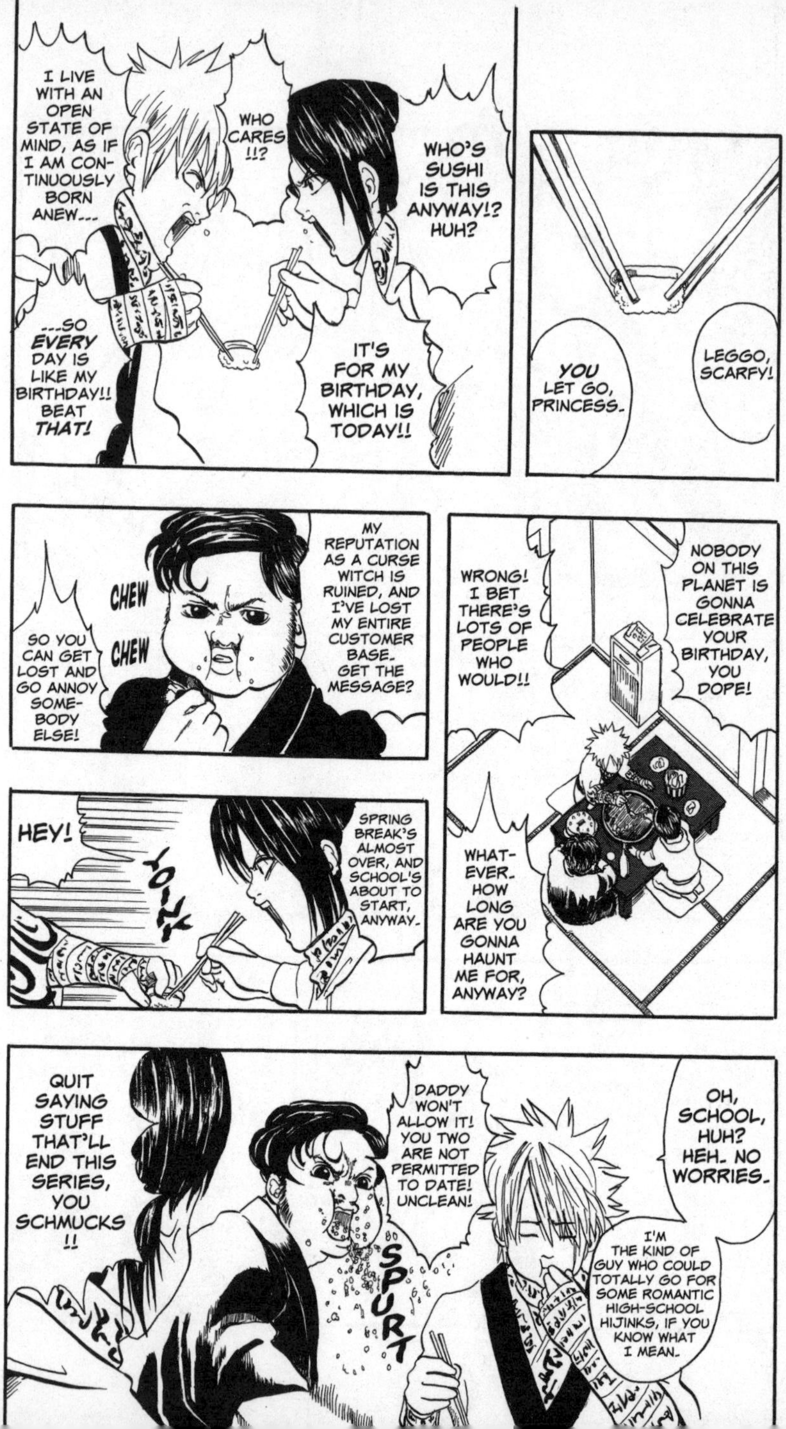
LEGGO, SCARFY!
YOU LET GO, PRINCESS.
WHO'S SUSHI IS THIS ANYWAY!? HUH?
IT'S FOR MY BIRTHDAY, WHICH IS TODAY!!
WHO CARES!!?
I LIVE WITH AN OPEN STATE OF MIND, AS IF I AM CONTINUOUSLY BORN ANEW...
...SO EVERY DAY IS LIKE MY BIRTHDAY!! BEAT THAT!
NOBODY ON THIS PLANET IS GONNA CELEBRATE YOUR BIRTHDAY, YOU DOPE!
WRONG! I BET THERE'S LOTS OF PEOPLE WHO WOULD!!
WHAT-EVER. HOW LONG ARE YOU GONNA HAUNT ME FOR, ANYWAY?
MY REPUTATION AS A CURSE WITCH IS RUINED, AND I'VE LOST MY ENTIRE CUSTOMER BASE. GET THE MESSAGE?
CHEW
CHEW
SO YOU CAN GET LOST AND GO ANNOY SOMEBODY ELSE!
SPRING BREAK'S ALMOST OVER, AND SCHOOL'S ABOUT TO START, ANYWAY.
YO-INK
HEY!
OH, SCHOOL, HUH? HEH. NO WORRIES.
I'M THE KIND OF GUY WHO COULD TOTALLY GO FOR SOME ROMANTIC HIGH-SCHOOL HIJINKS, IF YOU KNOW WHAT I MEAN.
DADDY WON'T ALLOW IT! YOU TWO ARE NOT PERMITTED TO DATE! UNCLEAN!
SPURT
QUIT SAYING STUFF THAT'LL END THIS SERIES, YOU SCHMUCKS!!

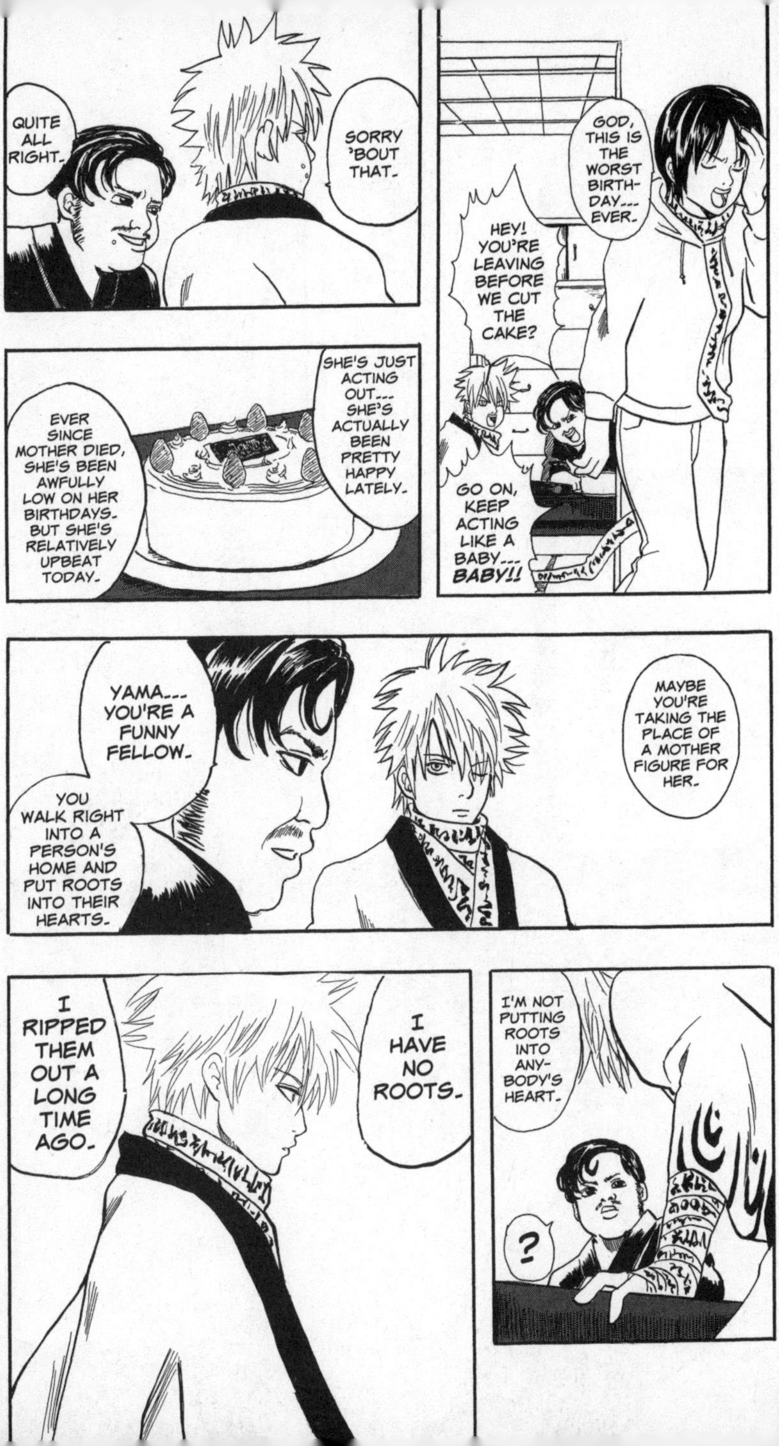
GOD, THIS IS THE WORST BIRTHDAY... EVER.
HEY! YOU'RE LEAVING BEFORE WE CUT THE CAKE?
GO ON, KEEP ACTING LIKE A BABY... *BABY!!*
SORRY 'BOUT THAT.
QUITE ALL RIGHT.
SHE'S JUST ACTING OUT... SHE'S ACTUALLY BEEN PRETTY HAPPY LATELY.
EVER SINCE MOTHER DIED, SHE'S BEEN AWFULLY LOW ON HER BIRTHDAYS. BUT SHE'S RELATIVELY UPBEAT TODAY.
MAYBE YOU'RE TAKING THE PLACE OF A MOTHER FIGURE FOR HER.
YAMA... YOU'RE A FUNNY FELLOW.
YOU WALK RIGHT INTO A PERSON'S HOME AND PUT ROOTS INTO THEIR HEARTS.
I'M NOT PUTTING ROOTS INTO ANYBODY'S HEART.
?
I HAVE NO ROOTS.
I RIPPED THEM OUT A LONG TIME AGO.

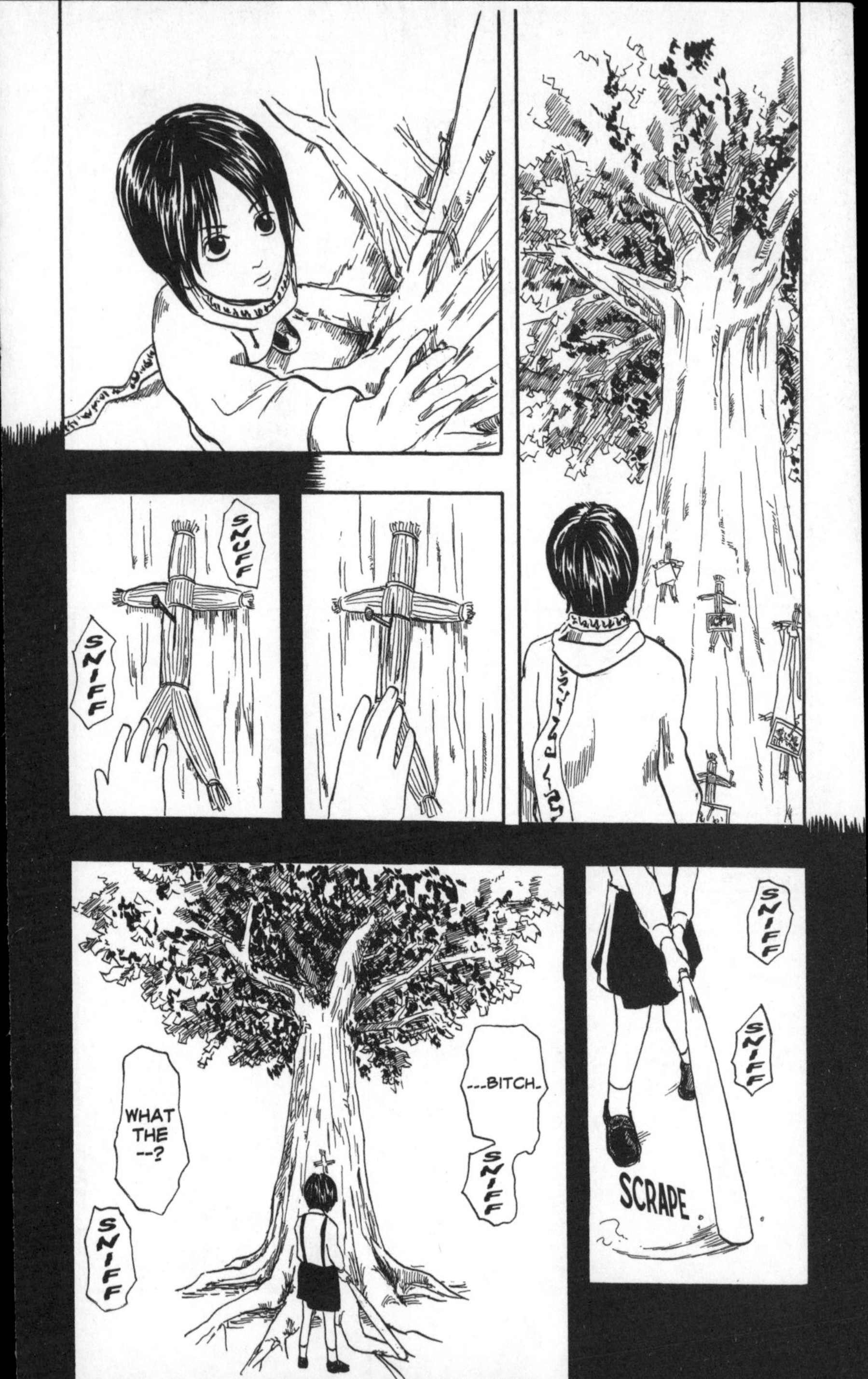
SNUFF
SNIFF
SNIFF
SNIFF
SCRAPE
---BITCH.
SNIFF
WHAT THE --?
SNIFF

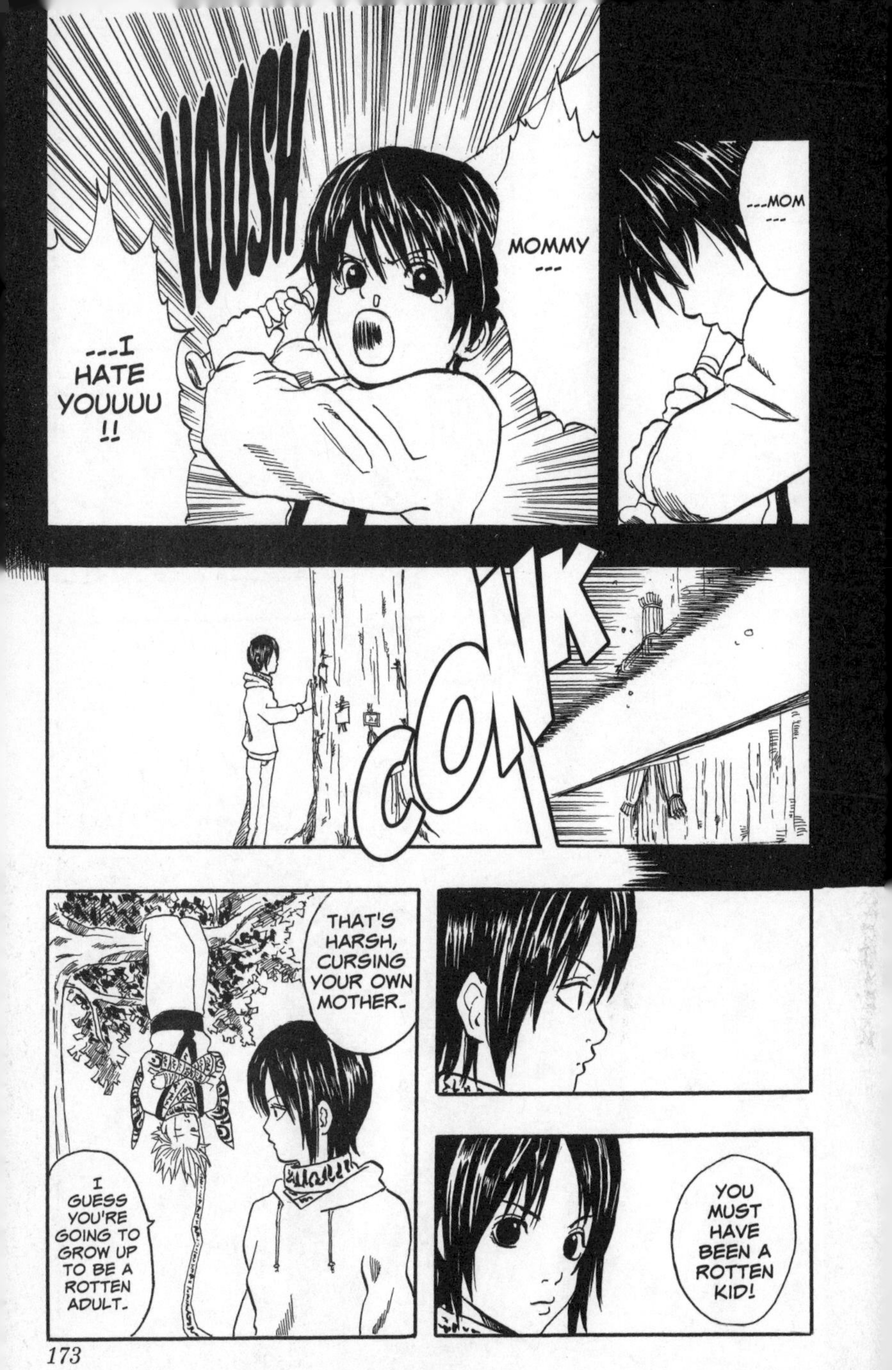
---MOM ---
MOMMY ---
VOOSH
---I HATE YOUUUU !!
CONK
YOU MUST HAVE BEEN A ROTTEN KID!
THAT'S HARSH, CURSING YOUR OWN MOTHER.
I GUESS YOU'RE GOING TO GROW UP TO BE A ROTTEN ADULT.

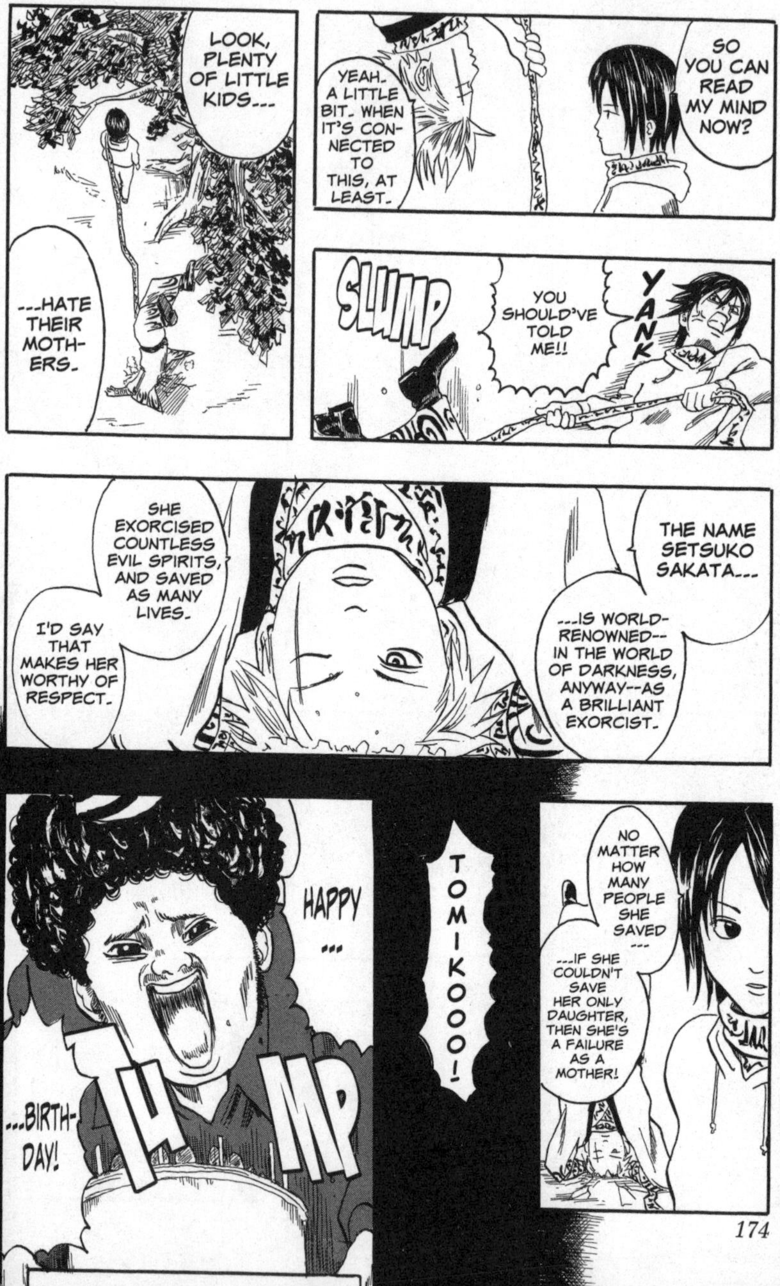
SO YOU CAN READ MY MIND NOW?
YEAH. A LITTLE BIT. WHEN IT'S CONNECTED TO THIS, AT LEAST.
YANK
YOU SHOULD'VE TOLD ME!!
SLUMP
LOOK, PLENTY OF LITTLE KIDS...
...HATE THEIR MOTHERS.
THE NAME SETSUKO SAKATA...
...IS WORLD-RENOWNED--IN THE WORLD OF DARKNESS, ANYWAY--AS A BRILLIANT EXORCIST.
SHE EXORCISED COUNTLESS EVIL SPIRITS, AND SAVED AS MANY LIVES.
I'D SAY THAT MAKES HER WORTHY OF RESPECT.
NO MATTER HOW MANY PEOPLE SHE SAVED...
...IF SHE COULDN'T SAVE HER ONLY DAUGHTER, THEN SHE'S A FAILURE AS A MOTHER!
TOMIKOOO!
HAPPY...
...BIRTH-DAY!
THUMP

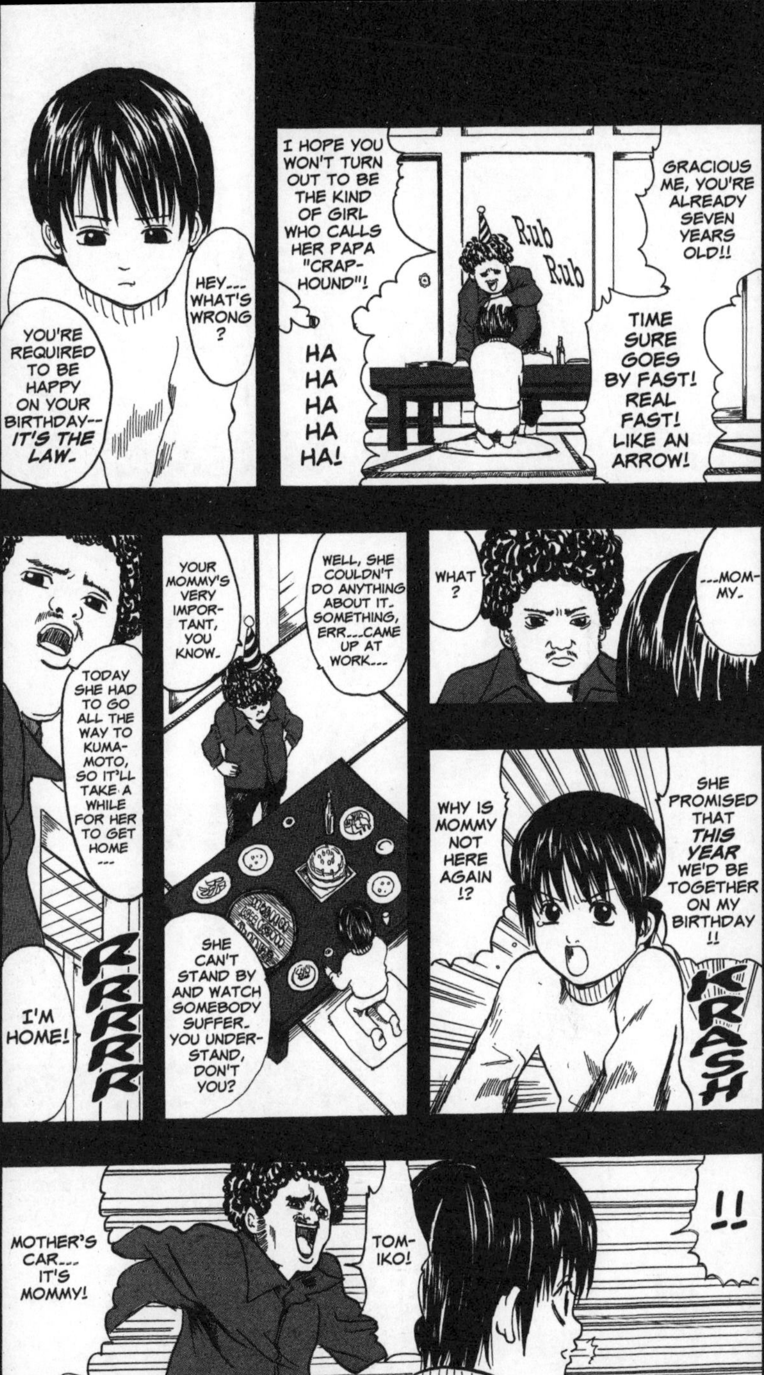
GRACIOUS ME, YOU'RE ALREADY SEVEN YEARS OLD!!
Rub Rub
TIME SURE GOES BY FAST! REAL FAST! LIKE AN ARROW!
I HOPE YOU WON'T TURN OUT TO BE THE KIND OF GIRL WHO CALLS HER PAPA "CRAP-HOUND"!
HA HA HA HA HA!
HEY... WHAT'S WRONG?
YOU'RE REQUIRED TO BE HAPPY ON YOUR BIRTHDAY--*IT'S THE LAW.*
...MOMMY.
WHAT?
SHE PROMISED THAT *THIS YEAR* WE'D BE TOGETHER ON MY BIRTHDAY!!
WHY IS MOMMY NOT HERE AGAIN!?
KRASH
WELL, SHE COULDN'T DO ANYTHING ABOUT IT. SOMETHING, ERR...CAME UP AT WORK...
YOUR MOMMY'S VERY IMPOR-TANT, YOU KNOW.
SHE CAN'T STAND BY AND WATCH SOMEBODY SUFFER. YOU UNDER-STAND, DON'T YOU?
TODAY SHE HAD TO GO ALL THE WAY TO KUMA-MOTO, SO IT'LL TAKE A WHILE FOR HER TO GET HOME...
RRRRR
I'M HOME!
!!
TOM-IKO!
MOTHER'S CAR... IT'S MOMMY!

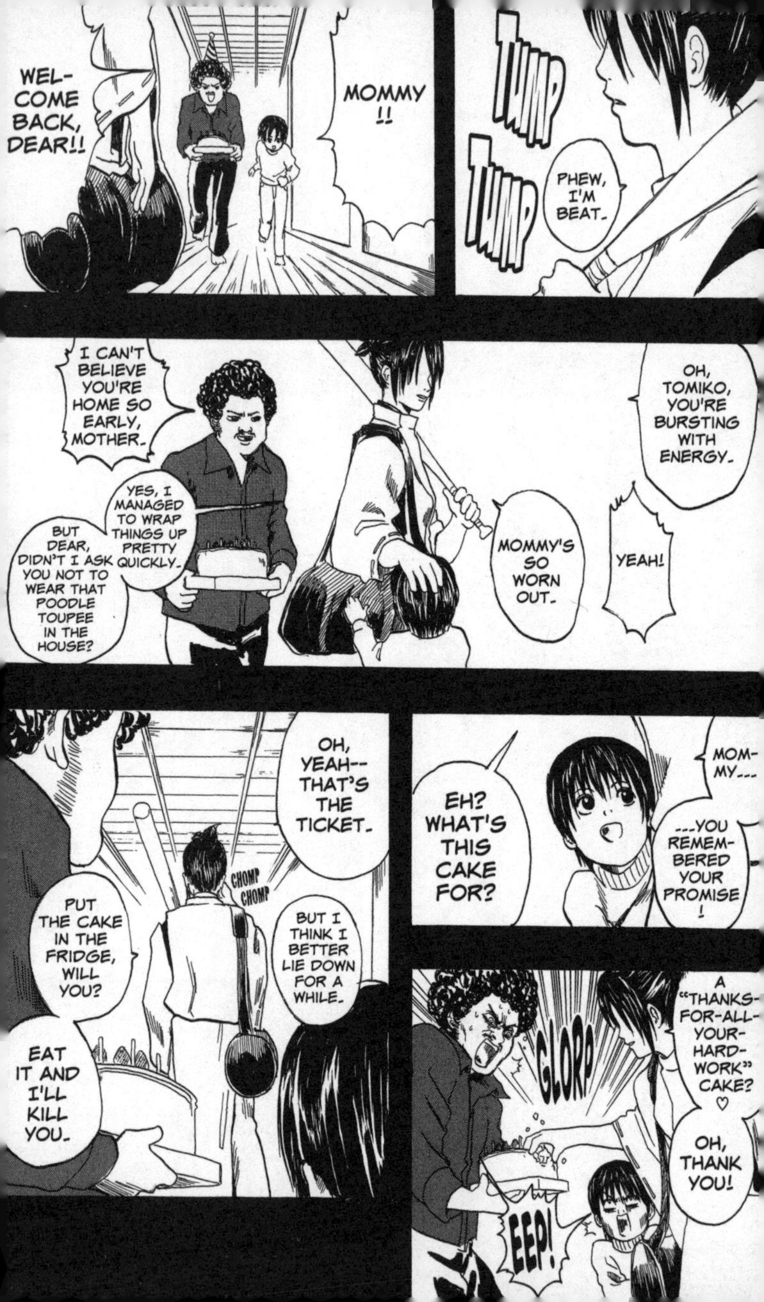
THUMP
THUMP
PHEW, I'M BEAT.
MOMMY!!
WEL-COME BACK, DEAR!!
OH, TOMIKO, YOU'RE BURSTING WITH ENERGY.
YEAH!
MOMMY'S SO WORN OUT.
I CAN'T BELIEVE YOU'RE HOME SO EARLY, MOTHER.
YES, I MANAGED TO WRAP THINGS UP PRETTY QUICKLY.
BUT DEAR, DIDN'T I ASK YOU NOT TO WEAR THAT POODLE TOUPEE IN THE HOUSE?
MOM-MY...
...YOU REMEM-BERED YOUR PROMISE!
EH? WHAT'S THIS CAKE FOR?
A "THANKS-FOR-ALL-YOUR-HARD-WORK" CAKE? ♡
GLORP
OH, THANK YOU!
EEP!
OH, YEAH-- THAT'S THE TICKET.
CHOMP
CHOMP
BUT I THINK I BETTER LIE DOWN FOR A WHILE.
PUT THE CAKE IN THE FRIDGE, WILL YOU?
EAT IT AND I'LL KILL YOU.

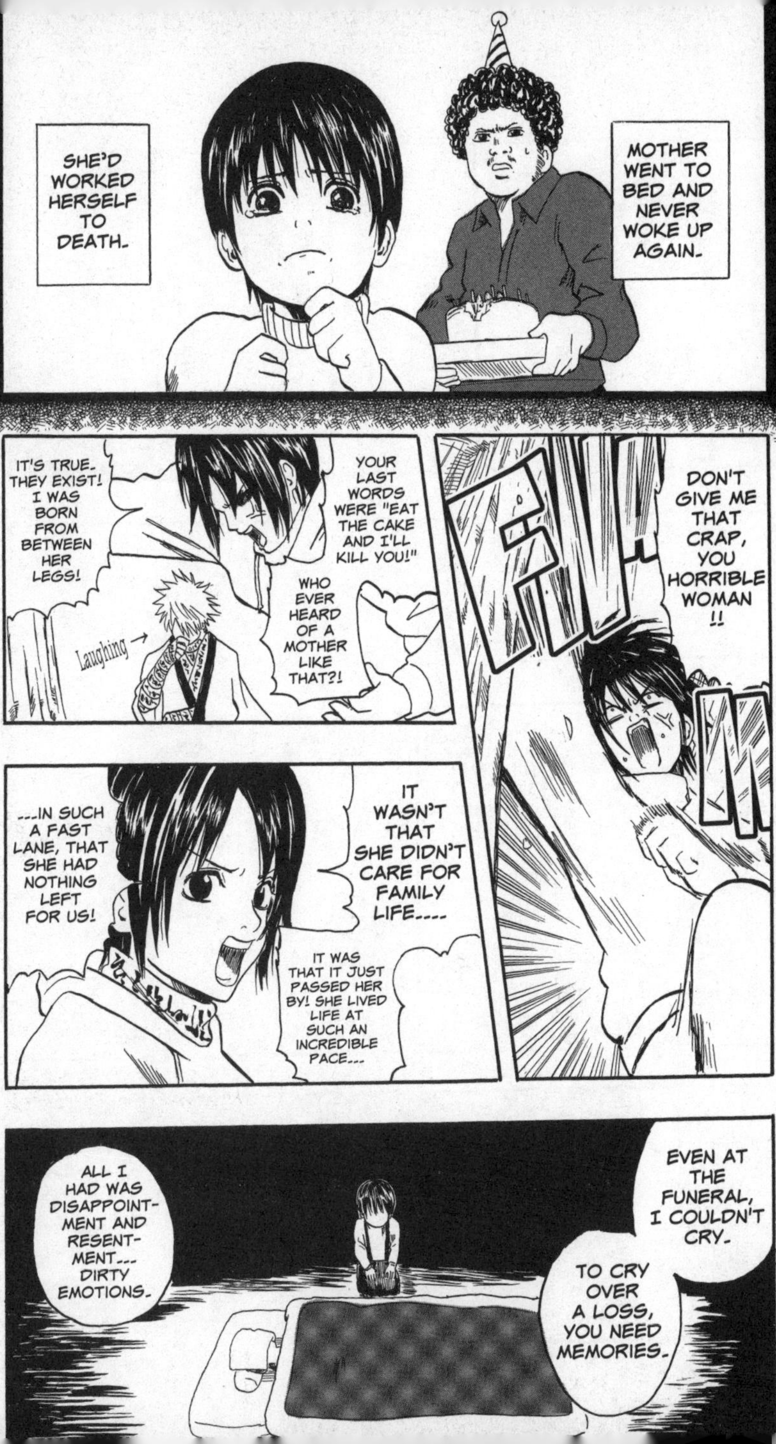
MOTHER WENT TO BED AND NEVER WOKE UP AGAIN.
SHE'D WORKED HERSELF TO DEATH.
DON'T GIVE ME THAT CRAP, YOU HORRIBLE WOMAN!!
YOUR LAST WORDS WERE "EAT THE CAKE AND I'LL KILL YOU!"
WHO EVER HEARD OF A MOTHER LIKE THAT?!
IT'S TRUE. THEY EXIST! I WAS BORN FROM BETWEEN HER LEGS!
Laughing →
IT WASN'T THAT SHE DIDN'T CARE FOR FAMILY LIFE....
IT WAS THAT IT JUST PASSED HER BY! SHE LIVED LIFE AT SUCH AN INCREDIBLE PACE...
...IN SUCH A FAST LANE, THAT SHE HAD NOTHING LEFT FOR US!
EVEN AT THE FUNERAL, I COULDN'T CRY.
TO CRY OVER A LOSS, YOU NEED MEMORIES.
ALL I HAD WAS DISAPPOINTMENT AND RESENTMENT... DIRTY EMOTIONS.

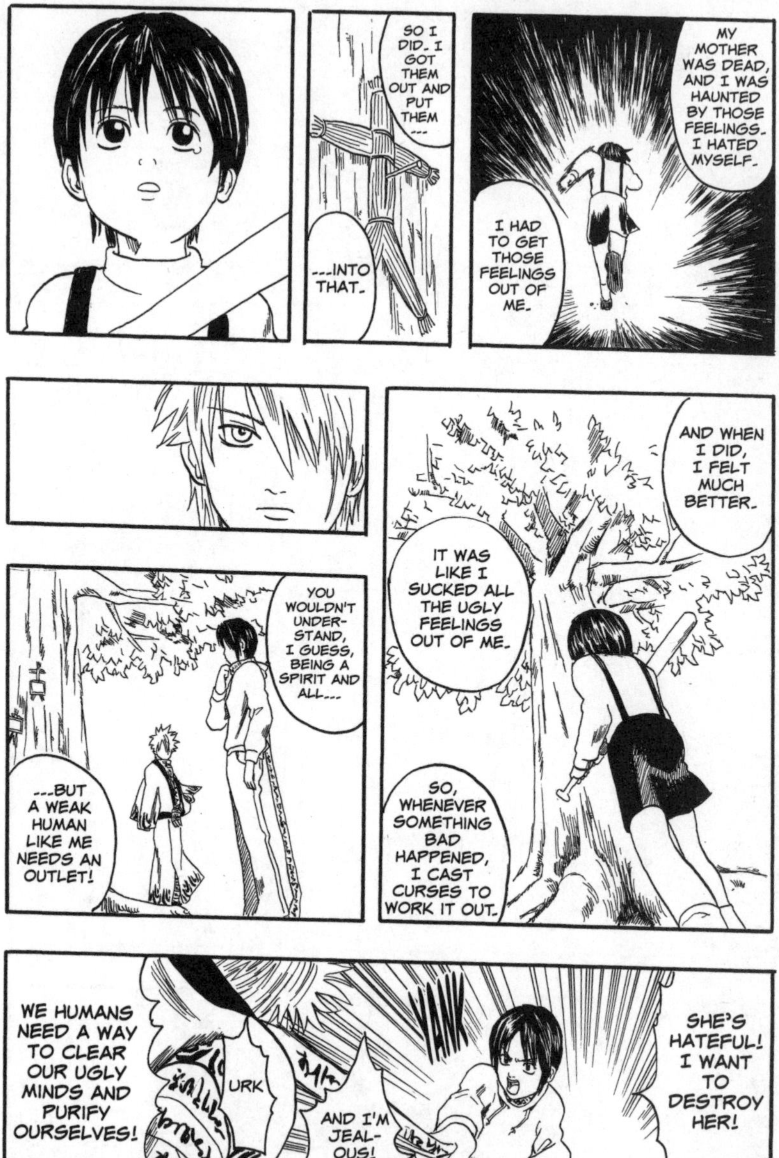
MY MOTHER WAS DEAD, AND I WAS HAUNTED BY THOSE FEELINGS. I HATED MYSELF.
I HAD TO GET THOSE FEELINGS OUT OF ME.
SO I DID. I GOT THEM OUT AND PUT THEM...
...INTO THAT.
AND WHEN I DID, I FELT MUCH BETTER.
IT WAS LIKE I SUCKED ALL THE UGLY FEELINGS OUT OF ME.
SO, WHENEVER SOMETHING BAD HAPPENED, I CAST CURSES TO WORK IT OUT.
YOU WOULDN'T UNDER-STAND, I GUESS, BEING A SPIRIT AND ALL...
...BUT A WEAK HUMAN LIKE ME NEEDS AN OUTLET!
SHE'S HATEFUL! I WANT TO DESTROY HER!
YANK
AND I'M JEAL-OUS! I ENVY HER!
URK
WE HUMANS NEED A WAY TO CLEAR OUR UGLY MINDS AND PURIFY OURSELVES!

READ THIS WAY

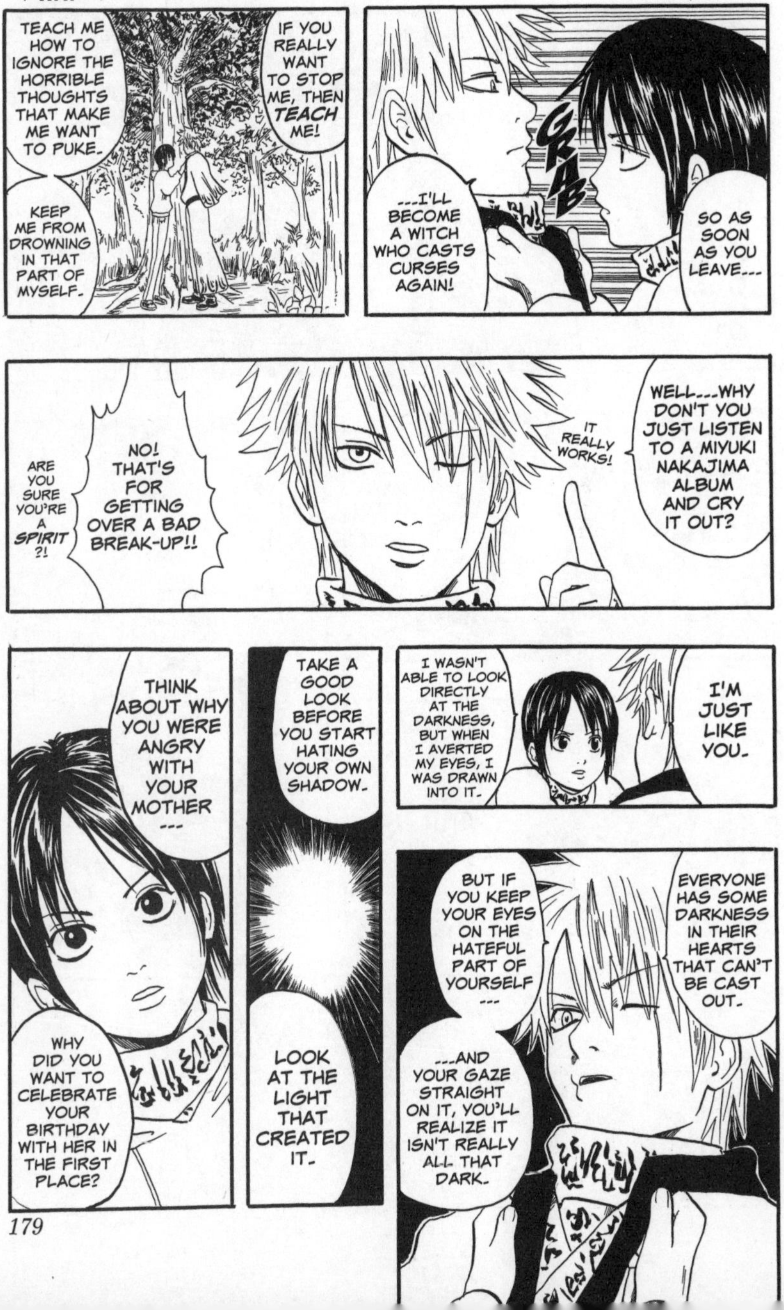

SO AS SOON AS YOU LEAVE...
GRAB
...I'LL BECOME A WITCH WHO CASTS CURSES AGAIN!
IF YOU REALLY WANT TO STOP ME, THEN *TEACH* ME!
TEACH ME HOW TO IGNORE THE HORRIBLE THOUGHTS THAT MAKE ME WANT TO PUKE.
KEEP ME FROM DROWNING IN THAT PART OF MYSELF.
WELL...WHY DON'T YOU JUST LISTEN TO A MIYUKI NAKAJIMA ALBUM AND CRY IT OUT?
IT REALLY WORKS!
NO! THAT'S FOR GETTING OVER A BAD BREAK-UP!!
ARE YOU SURE YOU'RE A *SPIRIT*?!
I'M JUST LIKE YOU.
I WASN'T ABLE TO LOOK DIRECTLY AT THE DARKNESS, BUT WHEN I AVERTED MY EYES, I WAS DRAWN INTO IT.
EVERYONE HAS SOME DARKNESS IN THEIR HEARTS THAT CAN'T BE CAST OUT.
BUT IF YOU KEEP YOUR EYES ON THE HATEFUL PART OF YOURSELF ...
...AND YOUR GAZE STRAIGHT ON IT, YOU'LL REALIZE IT ISN'T REALLY ALL THAT DARK.
TAKE A GOOD LOOK BEFORE YOU START HATING YOUR OWN SHADOW.
LOOK AT THE LIGHT THAT CREATED IT.
THINK ABOUT WHY YOU WERE ANGRY WITH YOUR MOTHER ...
WHY DID YOU WANT TO CELEBRATE YOUR BIRTHDAY WITH HER IN THE FIRST PLACE?

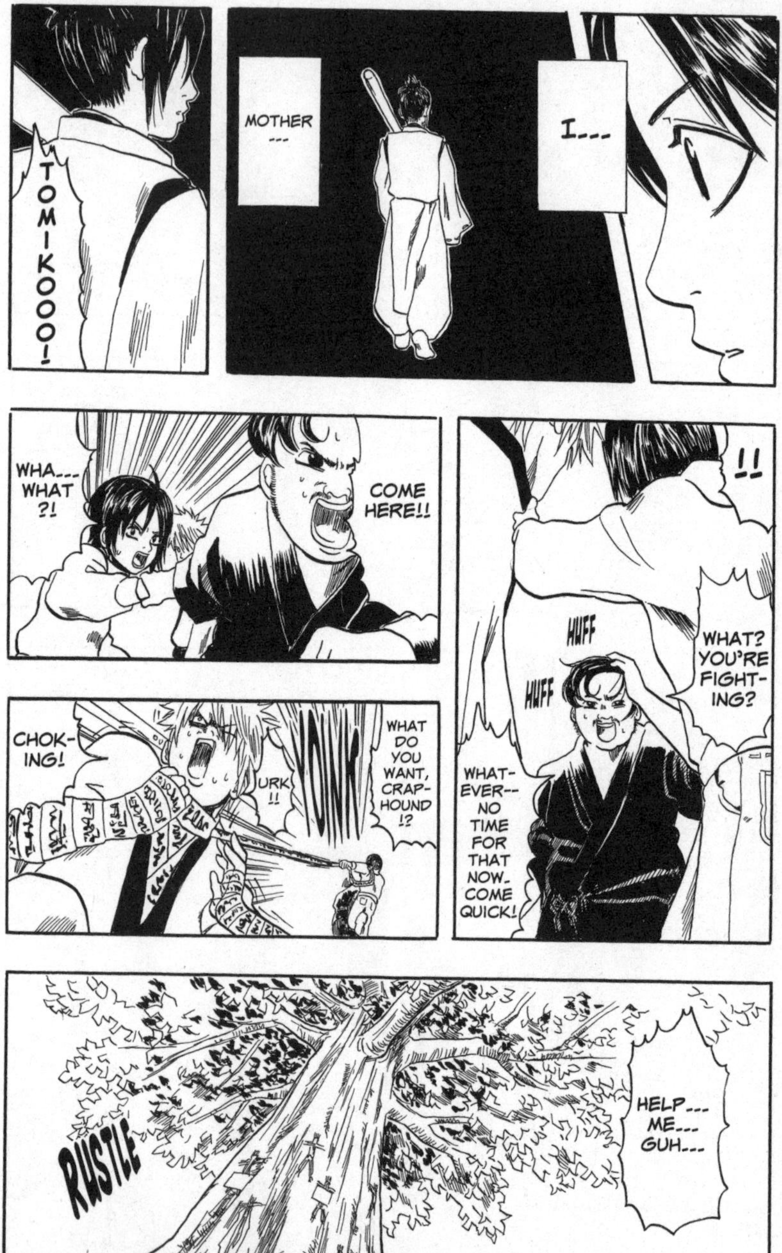
I...
MOTHER...
TOMIKOOOO!
!!
WHAT? YOU'RE FIGHTING?
HUFF
HUFF
WHATEVER-- NO TIME FOR THAT NOW. COME QUICK!
COME HERE!!
WHA... WHAT?!
WHAT DO YOU WANT, CRAPHOUND!?
YOINK
URK!!
CHOKING!
HELP... ME... GUH...
RUSTLE

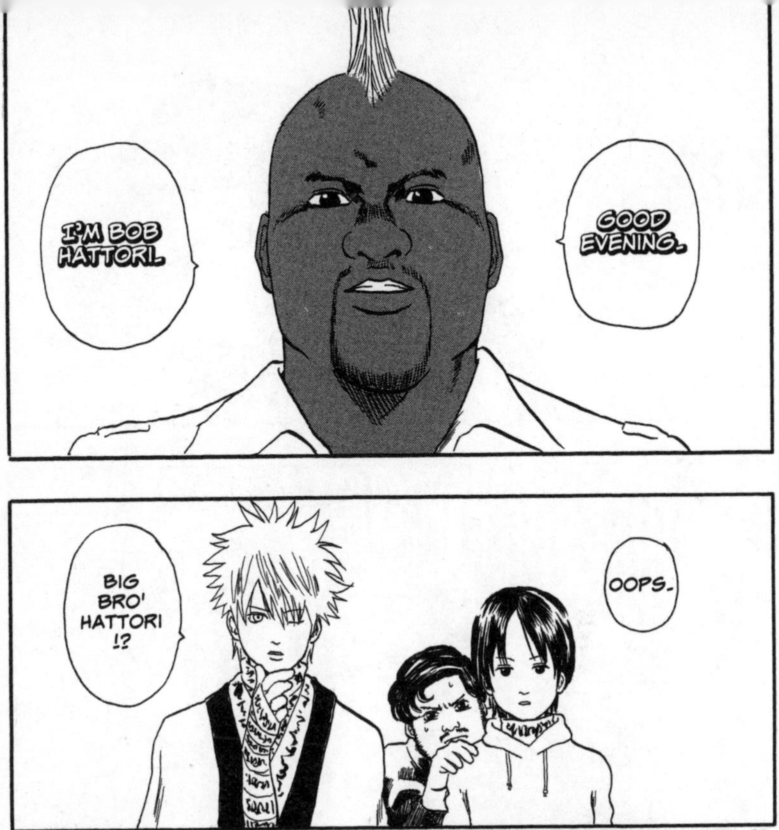
GOOD EVENING.
I'M BOB HATTORI.
OOPS.
BIG BRO' HATTORI !?

1 CHIHARU MATSUYAMA , A VERY POPULAR HOKKAIDO POP SINGER/SONGWRITER--ED.
2 JINGISUKAN OR GENGHIS KHAN. ALSO A TYPE OF MUTTON BARBEQUE POPULAR IN HOKKAIDO.--ED.

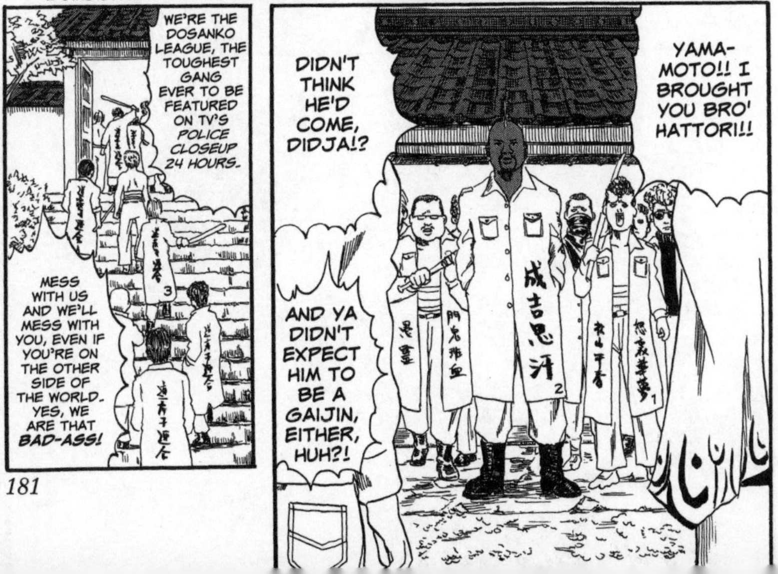
YAMA-MOTO!! I BROUGHT YOU BRO' HATTORI!!
DIDN'T THINK HE'D COME, DIDJA!?
AND YA DIDN'T EXPECT HIM TO BE A GAIJIN, EITHER, HUH?!
WE'RE THE DOSANKO LEAGUE, THE TOUGHEST GANG EVER TO BE FEATURED ON TV'S *POLICE CLOSEUP 24 HOURS*.
MESS WITH US AND WE'LL MESS WITH YOU, EVEN IF YOU'RE ON THE OTHER SIDE OF THE WORLD. YES, WE ARE THAT *BAD-ASS!*

3 MONCHICHI. A FRANCHISE OF MONKEY-LIKE DOLLS AND CHARACTERS. ALSO MR. SORACHI'S NAME FOR HIS *GIN TAMA* EDITOR.--ED.

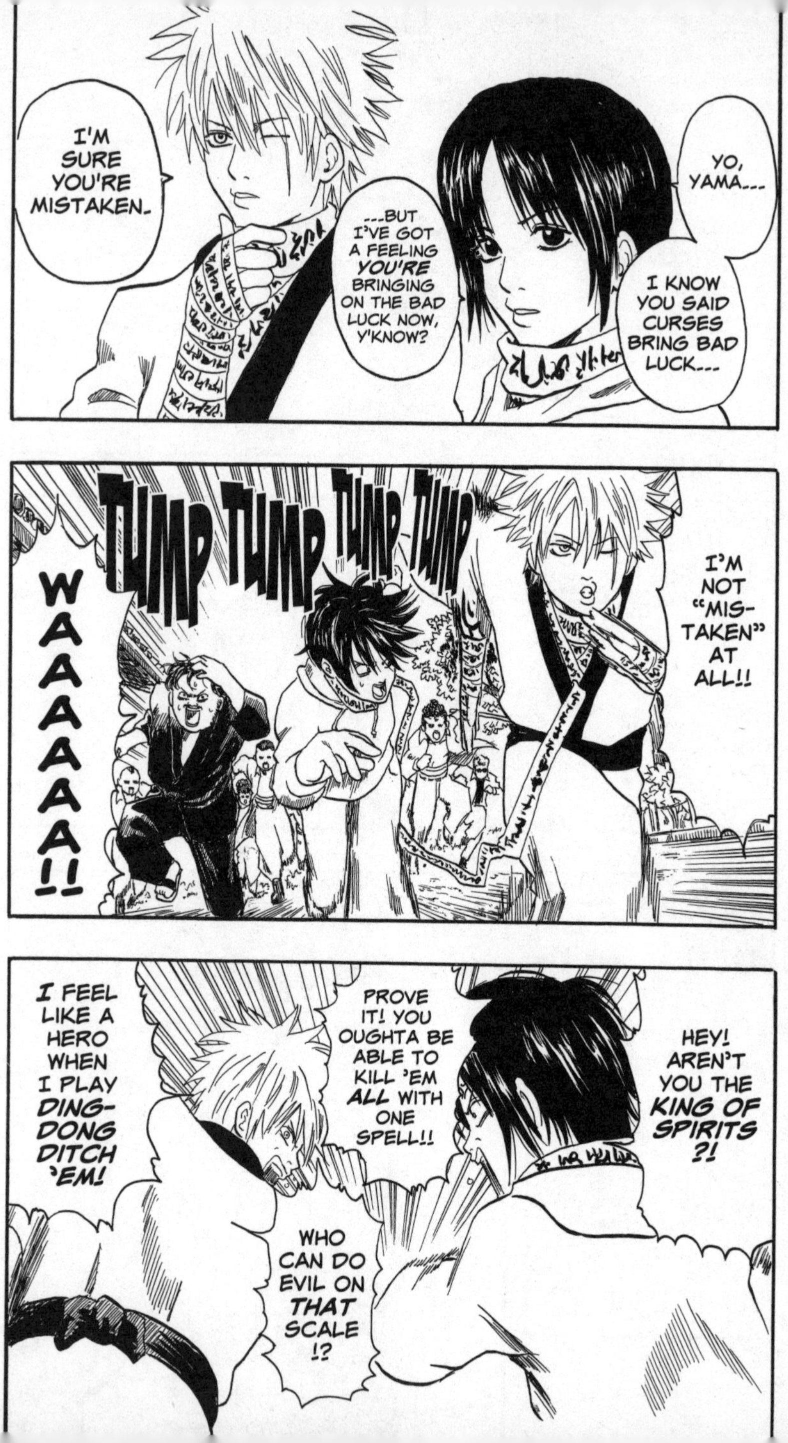
YO, YAMA...
I KNOW YOU SAID CURSES BRING BAD LUCK...
...BUT I'VE GOT A FEELING YOU'RE BRINGING ON THE BAD LUCK NOW, Y'KNOW?
I'M SURE YOU'RE MISTAKEN.
I'M NOT "MIS-TAKEN" AT ALL!!
TUMP TUMP TUMP TUMP
WAAAAAAA!!
HEY! AREN'T YOU THE KING OF SPIRITS?!
PROVE IT! YOU OUGHTA BE ABLE TO KILL 'EM ALL WITH ONE SPELL!!
I FEEL LIKE A HERO WHEN I PLAY DING-DONG DITCH 'EM!
WHO CAN DO EVIL ON THAT SCALE!?

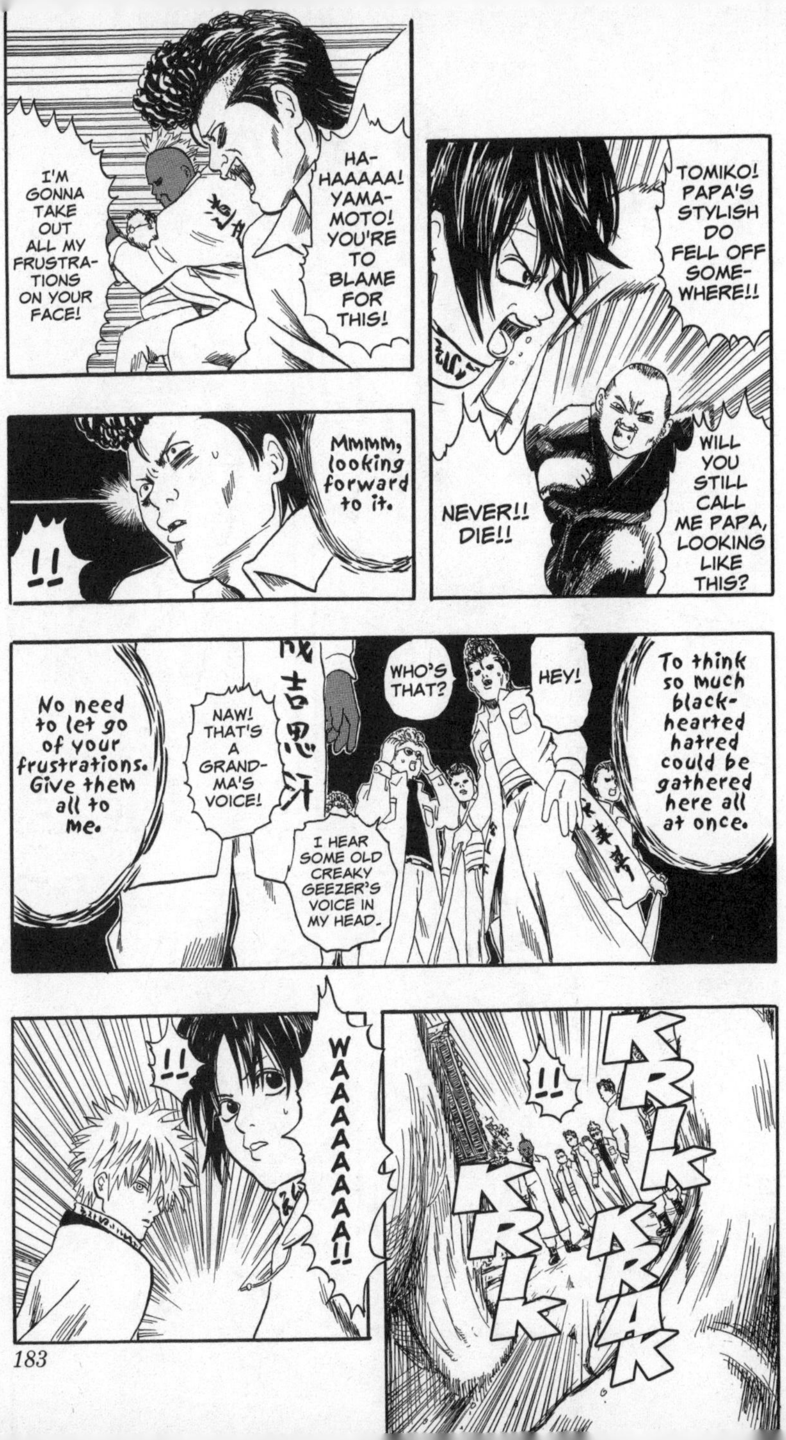
TOMIKO! PAPA'S STYLISH DO FELL OFF SOMEWHERE!!
WILL YOU STILL CALL ME PAPA, LOOKING LIKE THIS?
NEVER!! DIE!!
HA-HAAAAAA! YAMAMOTO! YOU'RE TO BLAME FOR THIS!
I'M GONNA TAKE OUT ALL MY FRUSTRATIONS ON YOUR FACE!
Mmmm, looking forward to it.
!!
To think so much black-hearted hatred could be gathered here all at once.
HEY!
WHO'S THAT?
NAW! THAT'S A GRANDMA'S VOICE!
I HEAR SOME OLD CREAKY GEEZER'S VOICE IN MY HEAD.
No need to let go of your frustrations. Give them all to me.
!!
KRIK
KRAK
KRIK
WAAAAAAAAAA!!
!!

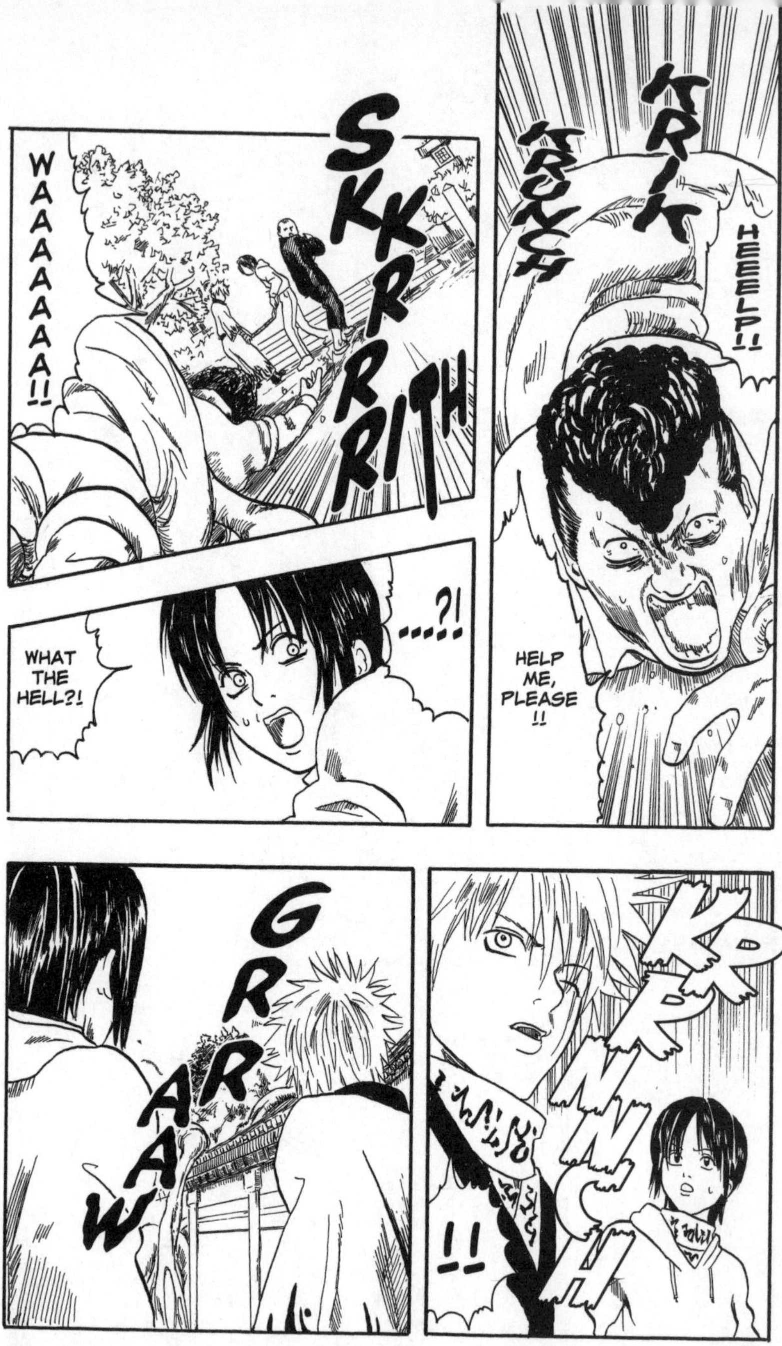
KRIK
KRUNCH
HEEELP!!
HELP ME, PLEASE!!
SKKRRRRITH
WAAAAAAA!!
...?!
WHAT THE HELL?!
KRRNNCH
!!
GRRAAW

READ THIS WAY

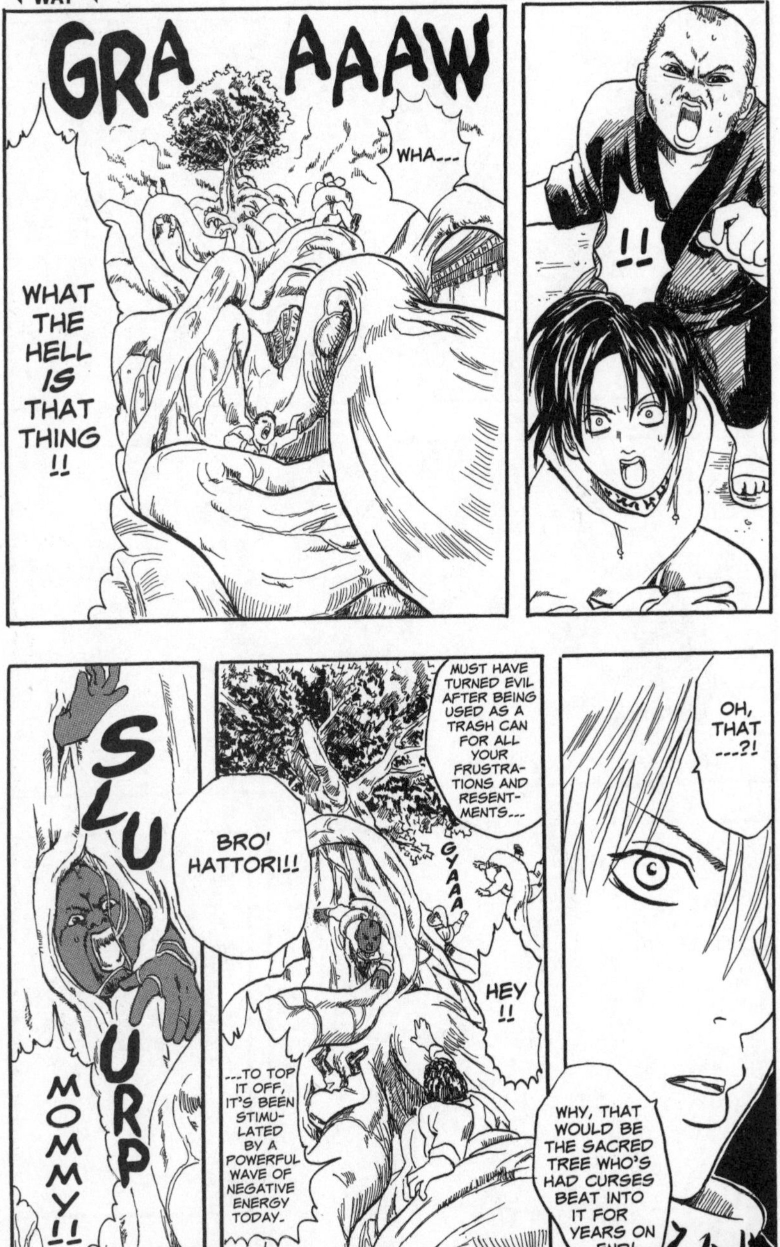
!!
GRA AAAW
WHA...
WHAT THE HELL IS THAT THING!!
OH, THAT...?!
WHY, THAT WOULD BE THE SACRED TREE WHO'S HAD CURSES BEAT INTO IT FOR YEARS ON END!
MUST HAVE TURNED EVIL AFTER BEING USED AS A TRASH CAN FOR ALL YOUR FRUSTRATIONS AND RESENTMENTS...
GYAAAA
BRO' HATTORI!!
HEY!!
...TO TOP IT OFF, IT'S BEEN STIMULATED BY A POWERFUL WAVE OF NEGATIVE ENERGY TODAY.
SLURP
MOMMY!!

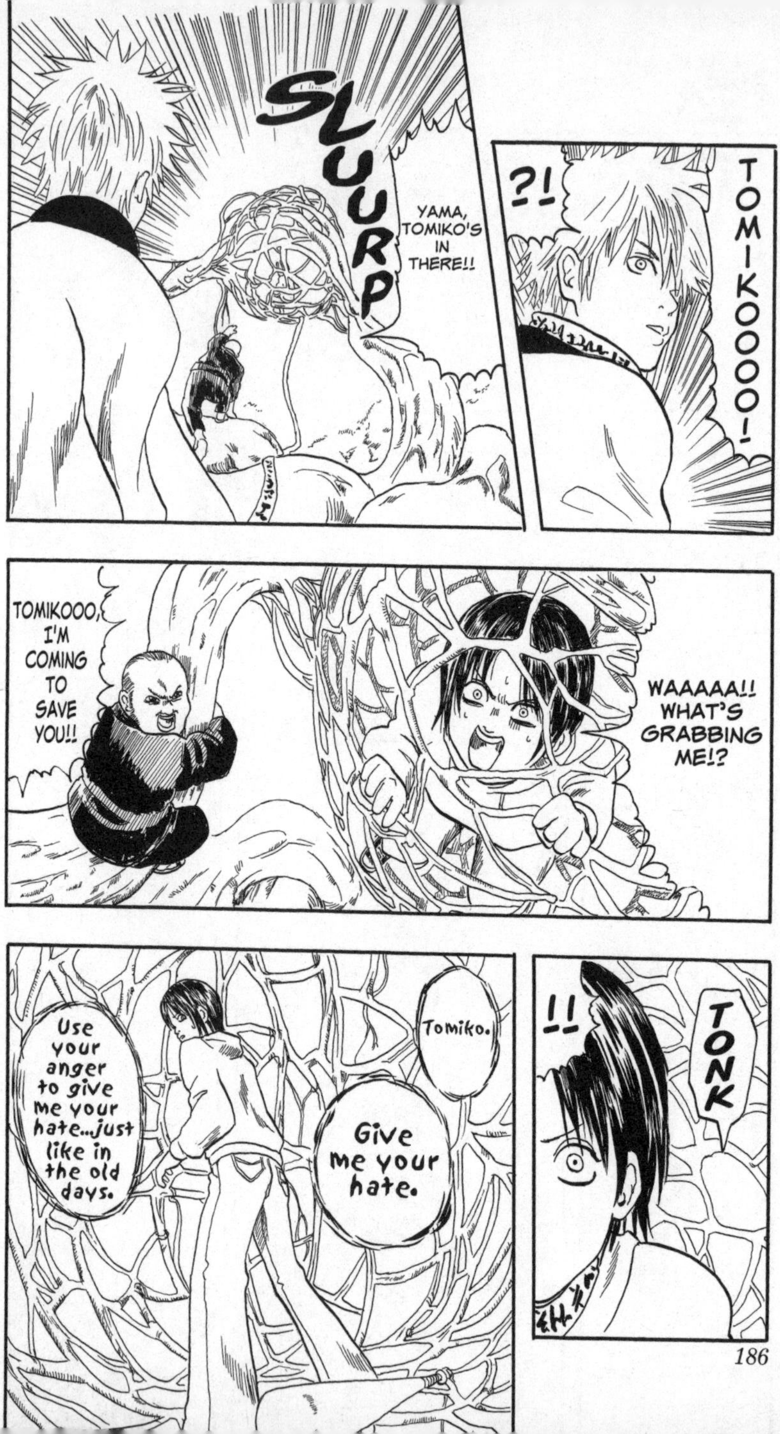
TOMIKOOOOO!
?!
SLUURP
YAMA, TOMIKO'S IN THERE!!
WAAAAA!! WHAT'S GRABBING ME!?
TOMIKOOO, I'M COMING TO SAVE YOU!!
TONK
!!
Tomiko.
Give me your hate.
Use your anger to give me your hate...just like in the old days.

READ THIS WAY

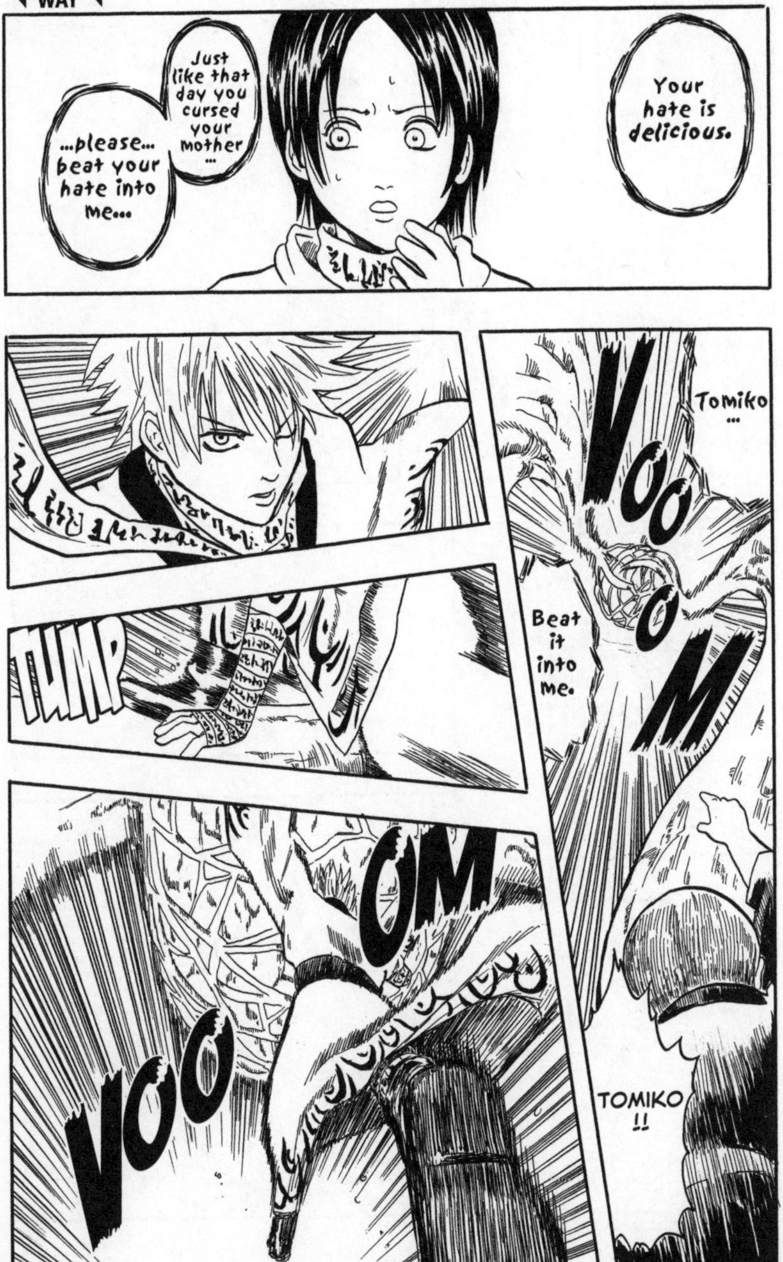
Your hate is delicious.
Just like that day you cursed your mother...
...please... beat your hate into me...
Tomiko...
VOOOM
Beat it into me.
TOMIKO!!
THUMP
VOOOM

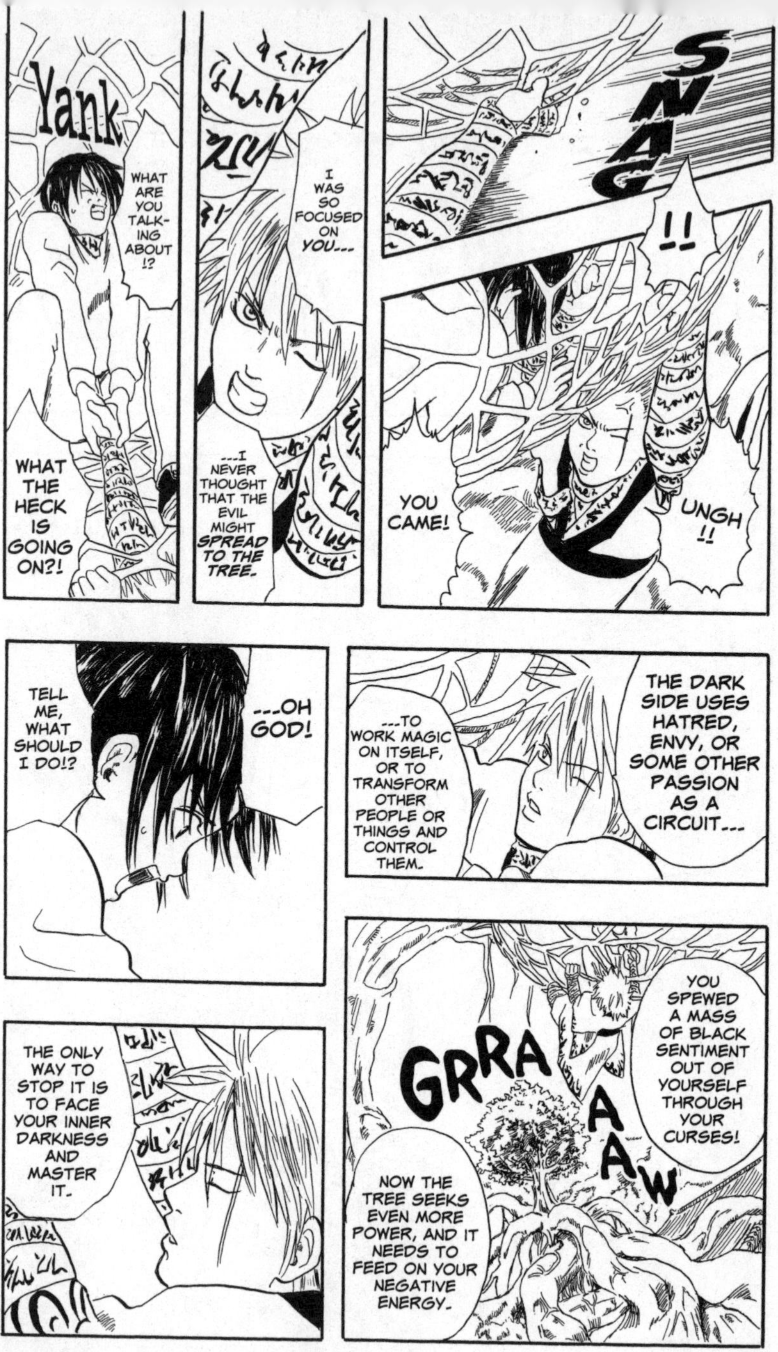

SNAG
!!
UNGH!!
YOU CAME!
I WAS SO FOCUSED ON YOU...
...I NEVER THOUGHT THAT THE EVIL MIGHT SPREAD TO THE TREE.
Yank
WHAT ARE YOU TALKING ABOUT!?
WHAT THE HECK IS GOING ON?!
THE DARK SIDE USES HATRED, ENVY, OR SOME OTHER PASSION AS A CIRCUIT...
...TO WORK MAGIC ON ITSELF, OR TO TRANSFORM OTHER PEOPLE OR THINGS AND CONTROL THEM.
...OH GOD!
TELL ME, WHAT SHOULD I DO!?
YOU SPEWED A MASS OF BLACK SENTIMENT OUT OF YOURSELF THROUGH YOUR CURSES!
GRRAAAW
NOW THE TREE SEEKS EVEN MORE POWER, AND IT NEEDS TO FEED ON YOUR NEGATIVE ENERGY.
THE ONLY WAY TO STOP IT IS TO FACE YOUR INNER DARKNESS AND MASTER IT.

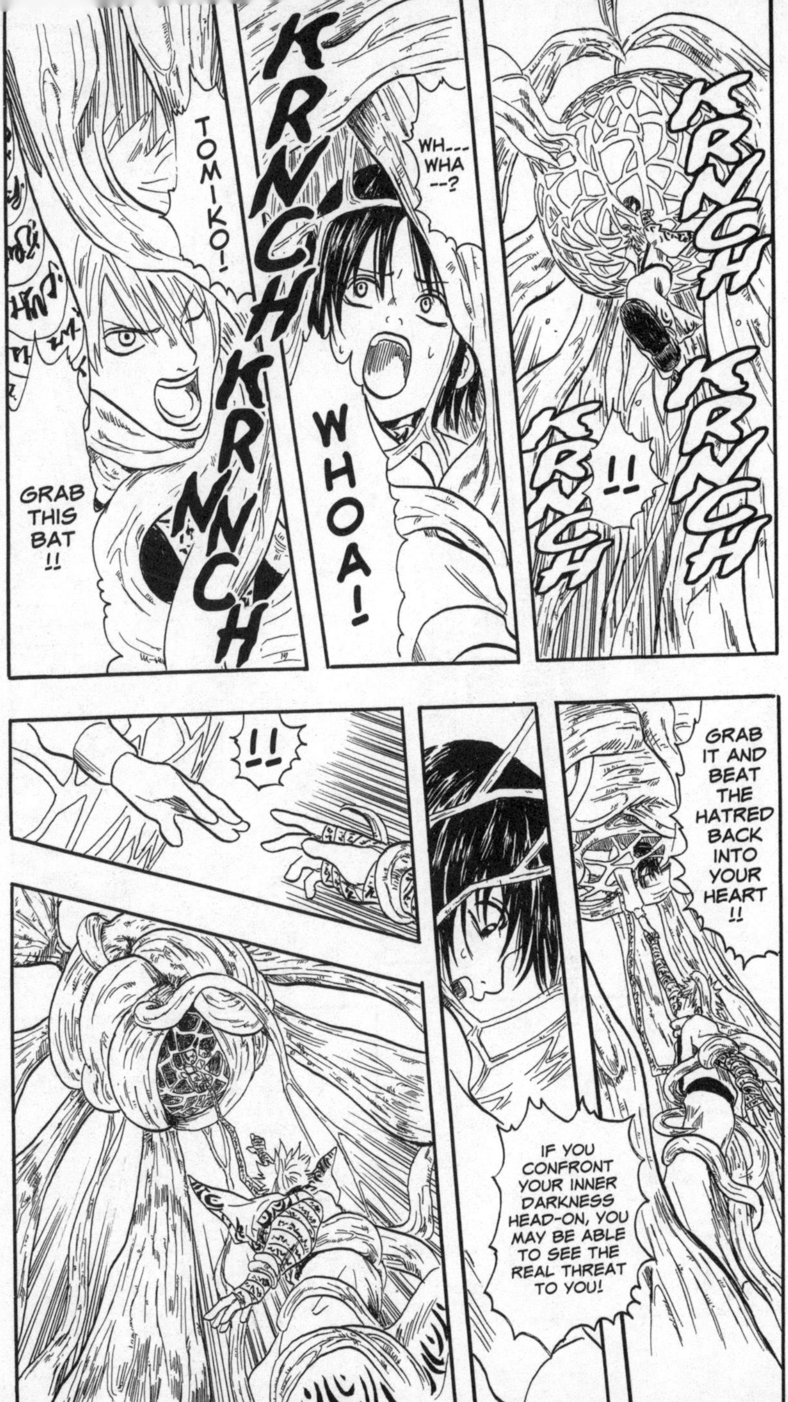
KRNCH
KRNCH
KRNCH
!!
KRNCH
WH--- WHA --?
WHOA!
TOMIKO!
KRNNCH
GRAB THIS BAT !!
GRAB IT AND BEAT THE HATRED BACK INTO YOUR HEART !!
IF YOU CONFRONT YOUR INNER DARKNESS HEAD-ON, YOU MAY BE ABLE TO SEE THE REAL THREAT TO YOU!
!!

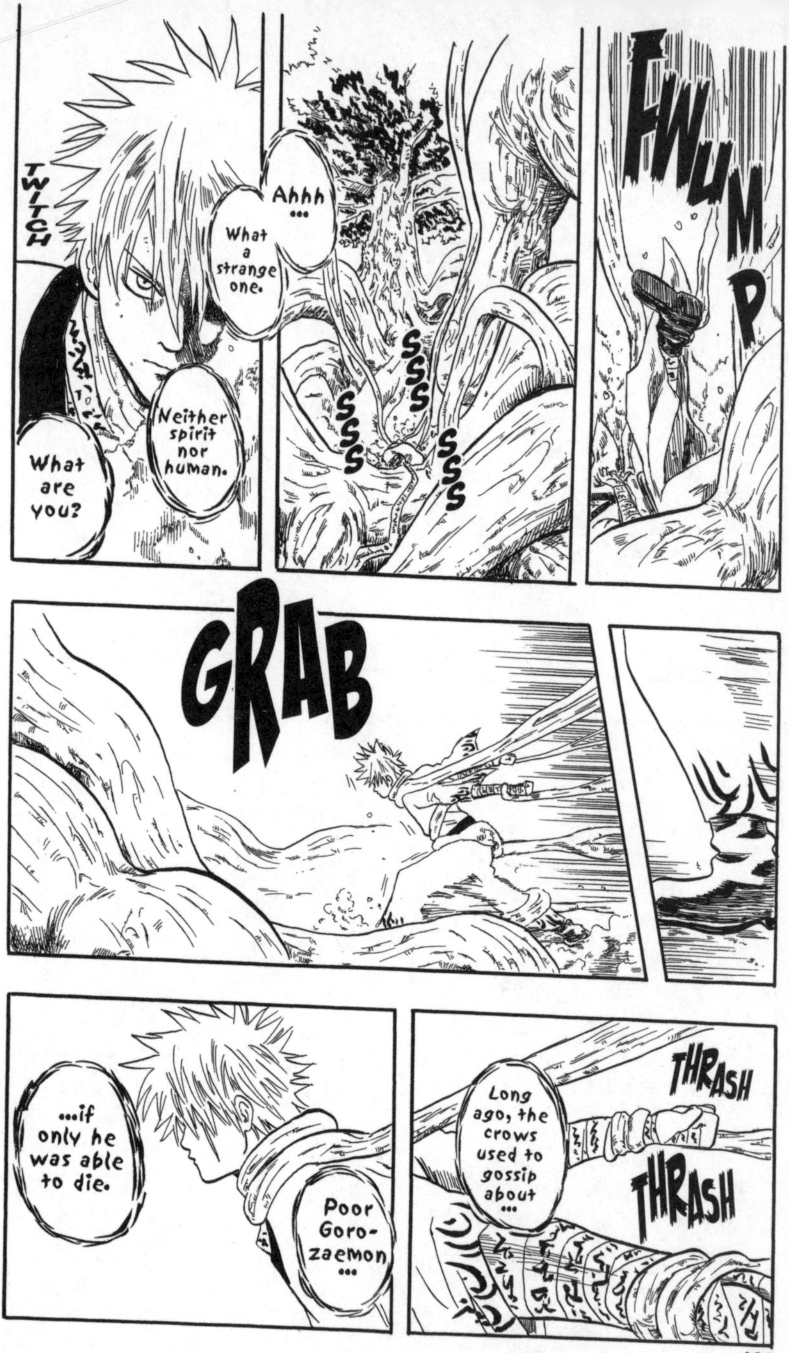
FWUMP
Ahhh...
What a strange one.
SSS
SSS
SSS
TWITCH
Neither spirit nor human.
What are you?
GRAB
THRASH
THRASH
Long ago, the crows used to gossip about...
Poor Gorozaemon...
...if only he was able to die.

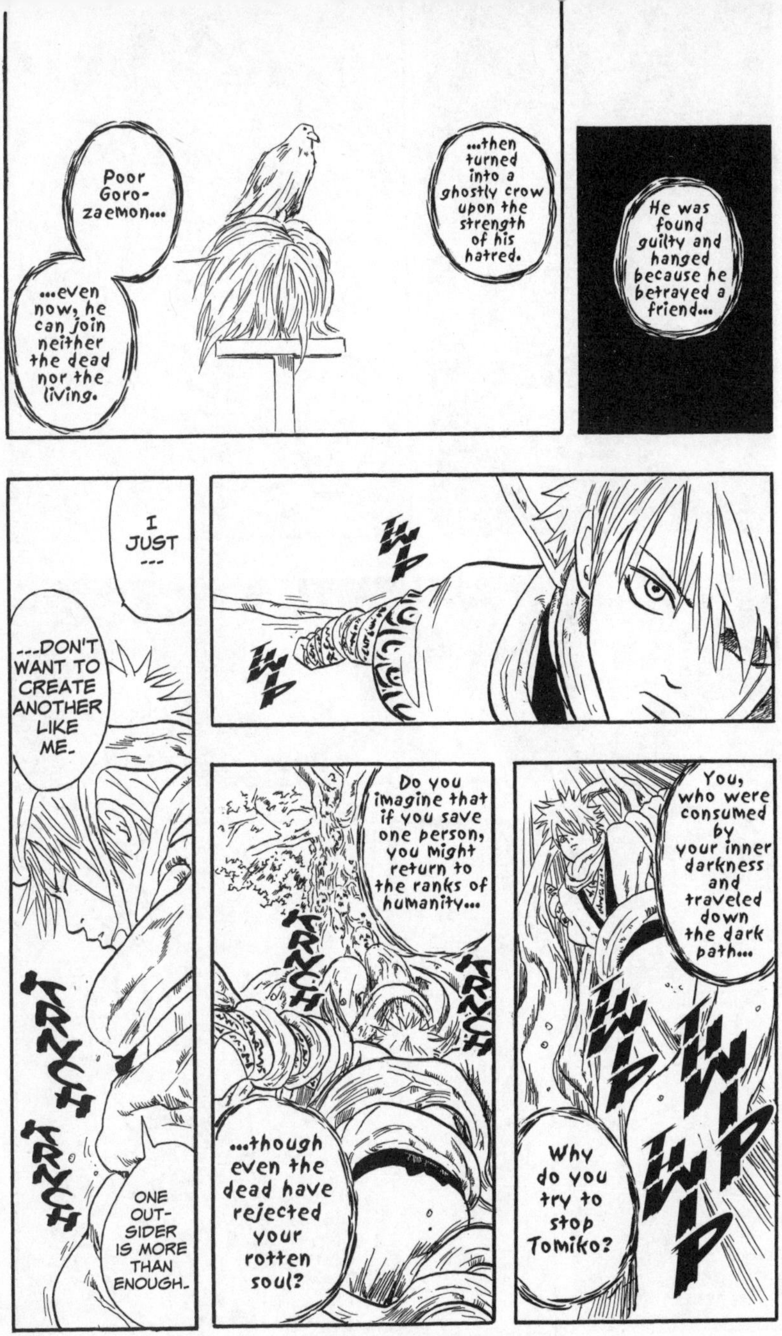
He was found guilty and hanged because he betrayed a friend...
...then turned into a ghostly crow upon the strength of his hatred.
Poor Goro-zaemon...
...even now, he can join neither the dead nor the living.
WIP
WIP
You, who were consumed by your inner darkness and traveled down the dark path...
WIP WIP
WIP WIP
Why do you try to stop Tomiko?
Do you imagine that if you save one person, you might return to the ranks of humanity...
KRNCH
KRNCH
...though even the dead have rejected your rotten soul?
I JUST ---
---DON'T WANT TO CREATE ANOTHER LIKE ME.
KRNCH
KRNCH
ONE OUT-SIDER IS MORE THAN ENOUGH.

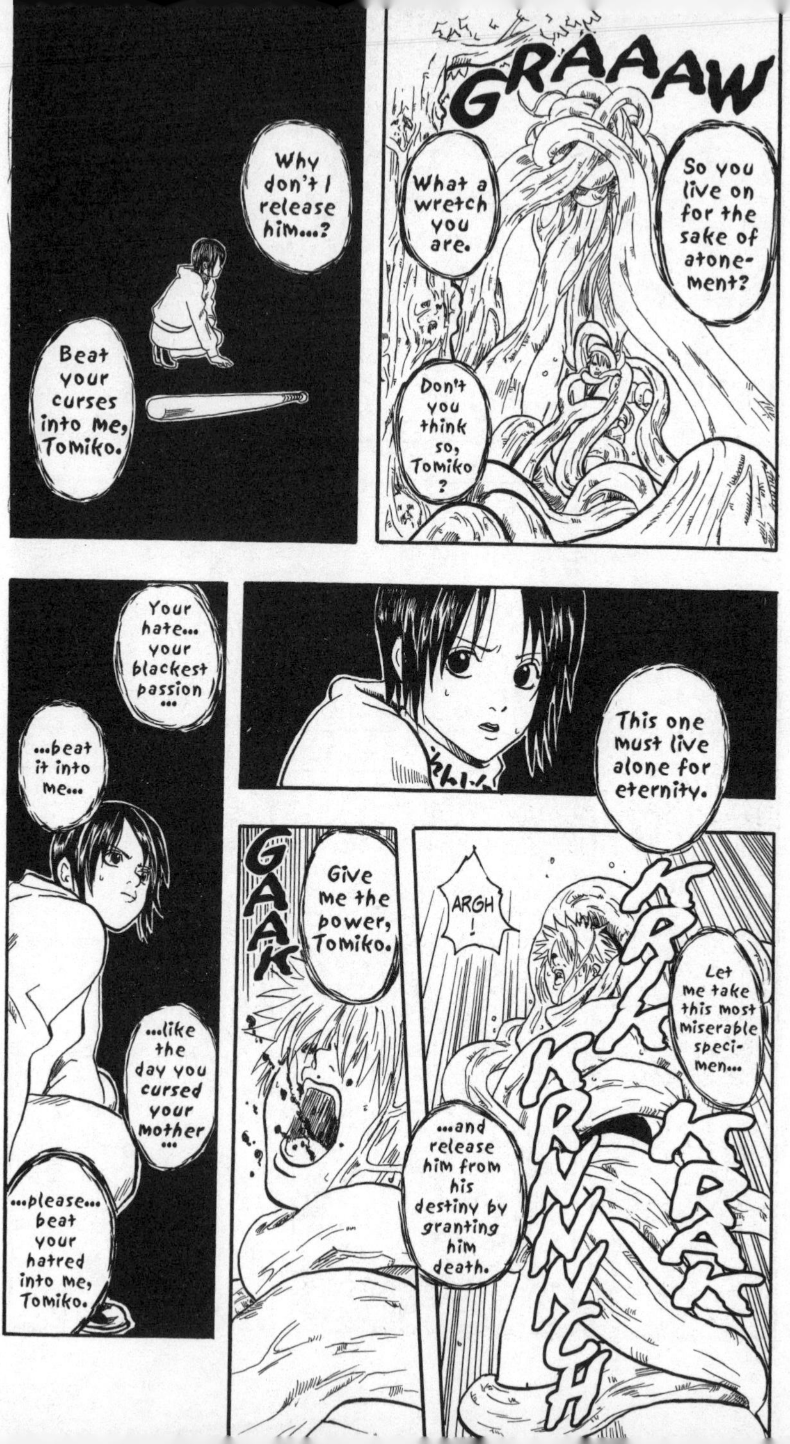
GRAAAW
So you live on for the sake of atonement?
What a wretch you are.
Don't you think so, Tomiko?
Why don't I release him...?
Beat your curses into me, Tomiko.
This one must live alone for eternity.
ARGH!
KRAK KRAK
Let me take this most miserable specimen...
...and release him from his destiny by granting him death.
KRUNNNCH
GAAK
Give me the power, Tomiko.
Your hate... your blackest passion...
...beat it into me...
...like the day you cursed your mother...
...please... beat your hatred into me, Tomiko.

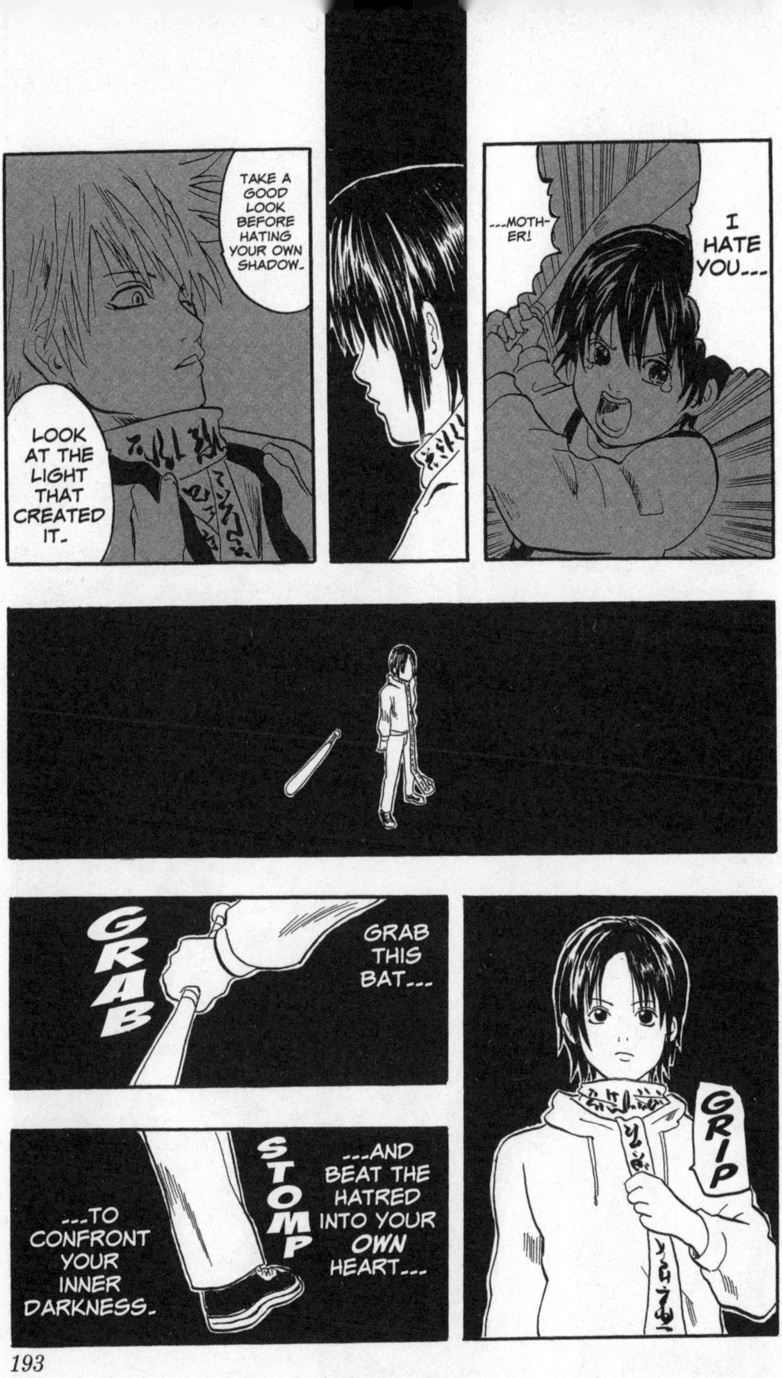
I HATE YOU...
...MOTHER!
TAKE A GOOD LOOK BEFORE HATING YOUR OWN SHADOW.
LOOK AT THE LIGHT THAT CREATED IT.
GRIP
GRAB THIS BAT...
GRAB
...AND BEAT THE HATRED INTO YOUR OWN HEART...
STOMP
...TO CONFRONT YOUR INNER DARKNESS.

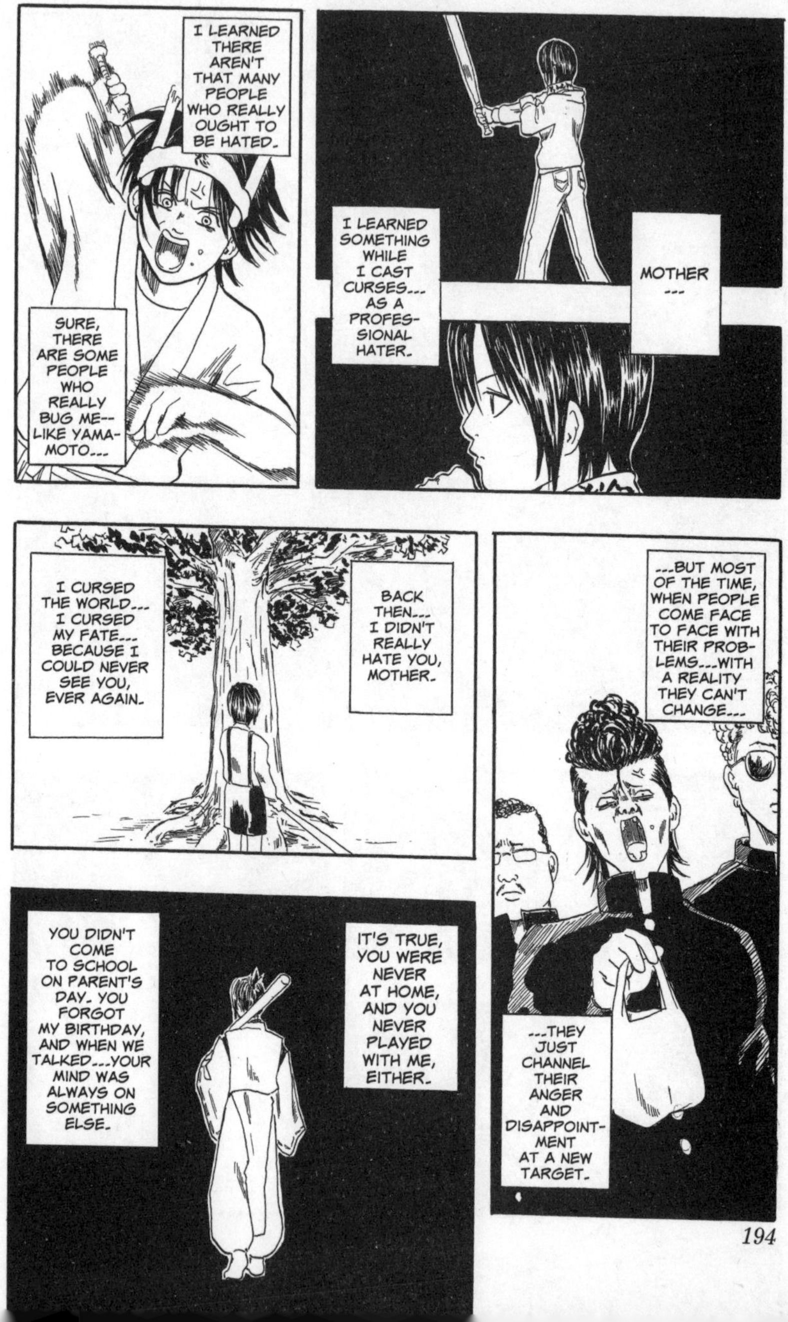
I LEARNED SOMETHING WHILE I CAST CURSES... AS A PROFESSIONAL HATER.
MOTHER...
I LEARNED THERE AREN'T THAT MANY PEOPLE WHO REALLY OUGHT TO BE HATED.
SURE, THERE ARE SOME PEOPLE WHO REALLY BUG ME--LIKE YAMAMOTO...
...BUT MOST OF THE TIME, WHEN PEOPLE COME FACE TO FACE WITH THEIR PROBLEMS...WITH A REALITY THEY CAN'T CHANGE...
...THEY JUST CHANNEL THEIR ANGER AND DISAPPOINTMENT AT A NEW TARGET.
BACK THEN... I DIDN'T REALLY HATE YOU, MOTHER.
I CURSED THE WORLD... I CURSED MY FATE... BECAUSE I COULD NEVER SEE YOU, EVER AGAIN.
IT'S TRUE, YOU WERE NEVER AT HOME, AND YOU NEVER PLAYED WITH ME, EITHER.
YOU DIDN'T COME TO SCHOOL ON PARENT'S DAY. YOU FORGOT MY BIRTHDAY, AND WHEN WE TALKED...YOUR MIND WAS ALWAYS ON SOMETHING ELSE.

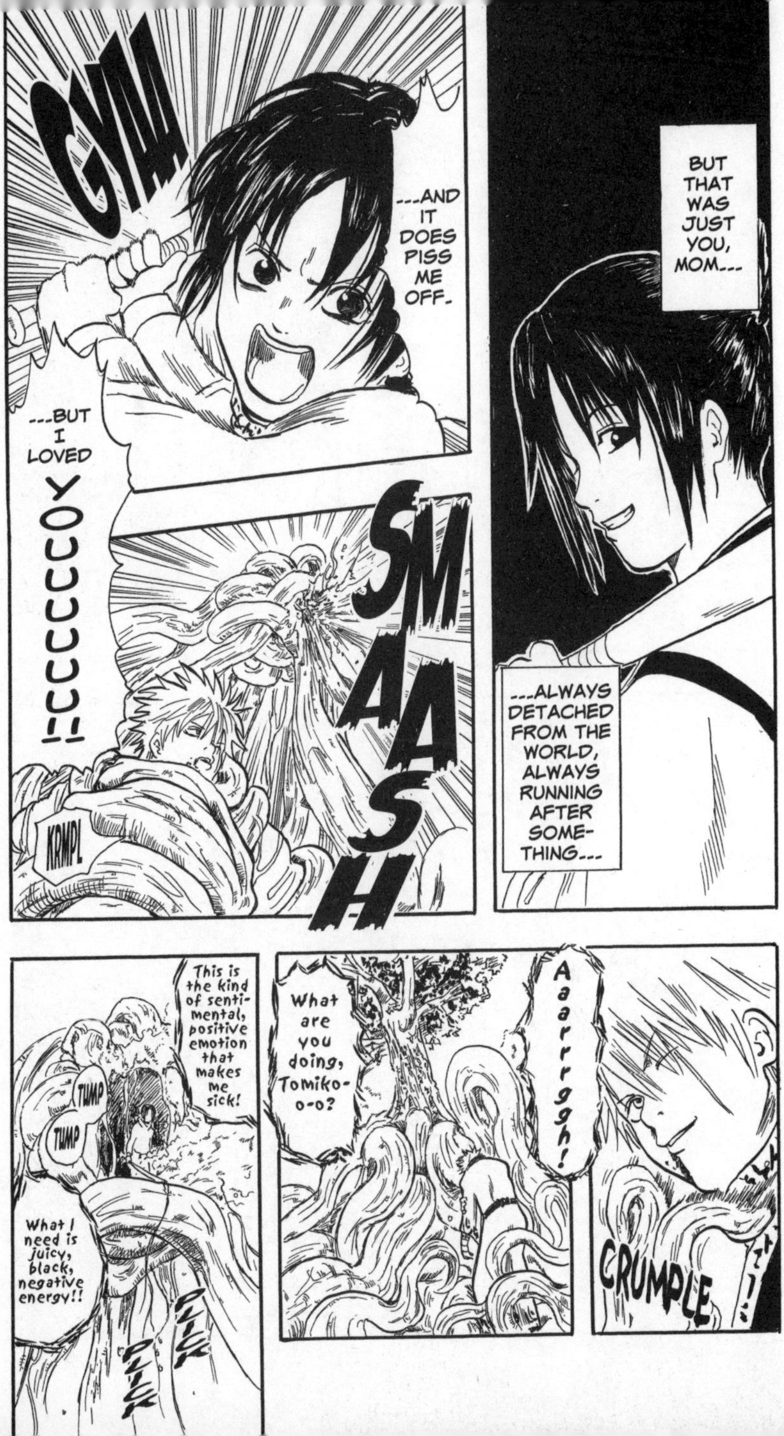
BUT THAT WAS JUST YOU, MOM...
...ALWAYS DETACHED FROM THE WORLD, ALWAYS RUNNING AFTER SOME-THING...
GYAA
...AND IT DOES PISS ME OFF.
...BUT I LOVED YOUUUUUUUU!!
SMAASH
KRMPL
Aaarrrggh!
CRUMPLE
What are you doing, Tomiko-o-o?
This is the kind of senti-mental, positive emotion that makes me sick!
THUMP
THUMP
What I need is juicy, black, negative energy!!
PLICK
PLICK

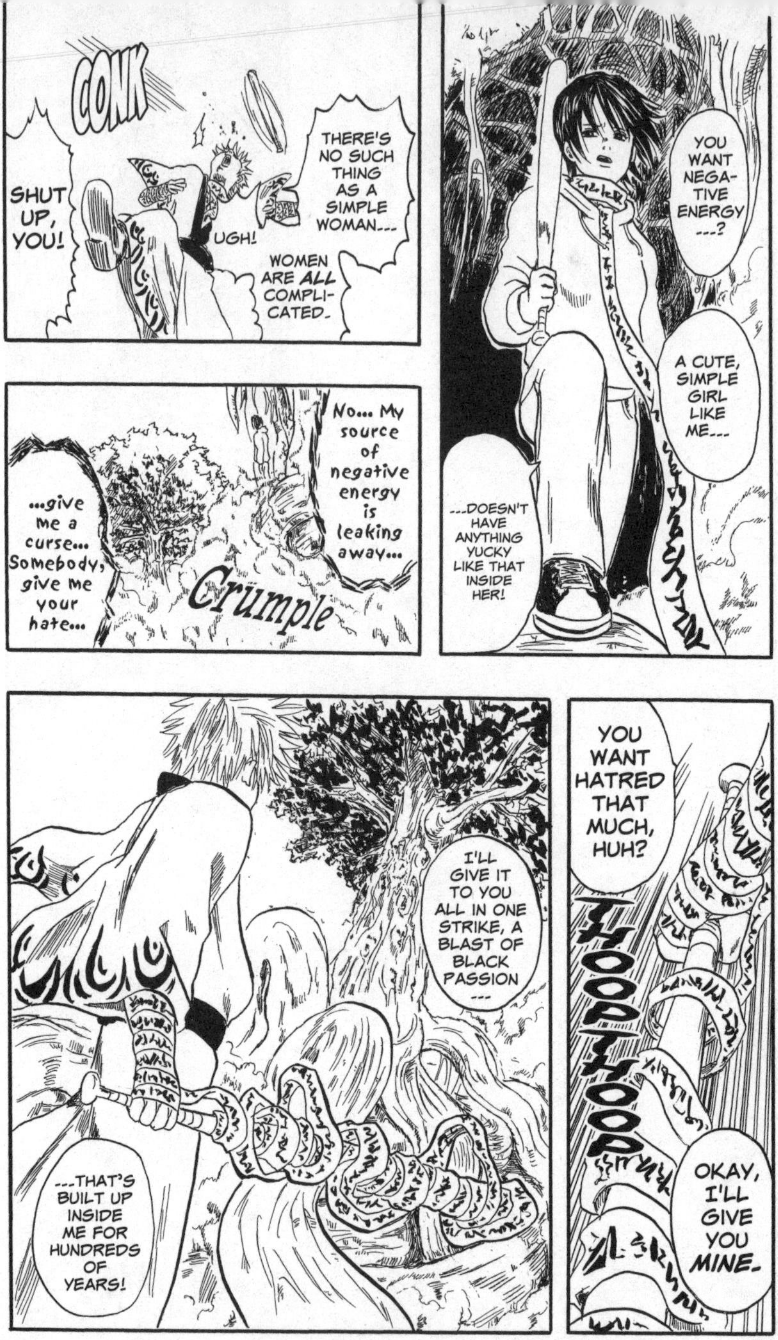
YOU WANT NEGATIVE ENERGY...?
A CUTE, SIMPLE GIRL LIKE ME...
...DOESN'T HAVE ANYTHING YUCKY LIKE THAT INSIDE HER!
THERE'S NO SUCH THING AS A SIMPLE WOMAN...
WOMEN ARE ***ALL*** COMPLICATED.
CONK
SHUT UP, YOU!
UGH!
No... My source of negative energy is leaking away...
...give me a curse... Somebody, give me your hate...
Crumple
YOU WANT HATRED THAT MUCH, HUH?
WHOOPWHOOP
OKAY, I'LL GIVE YOU ***MINE.***
I'LL GIVE IT TO YOU ALL IN ONE STRIKE, A BLAST OF BLACK PASSION...
...THAT'S BUILT UP INSIDE ME FOR HUNDREDS OF YEARS!

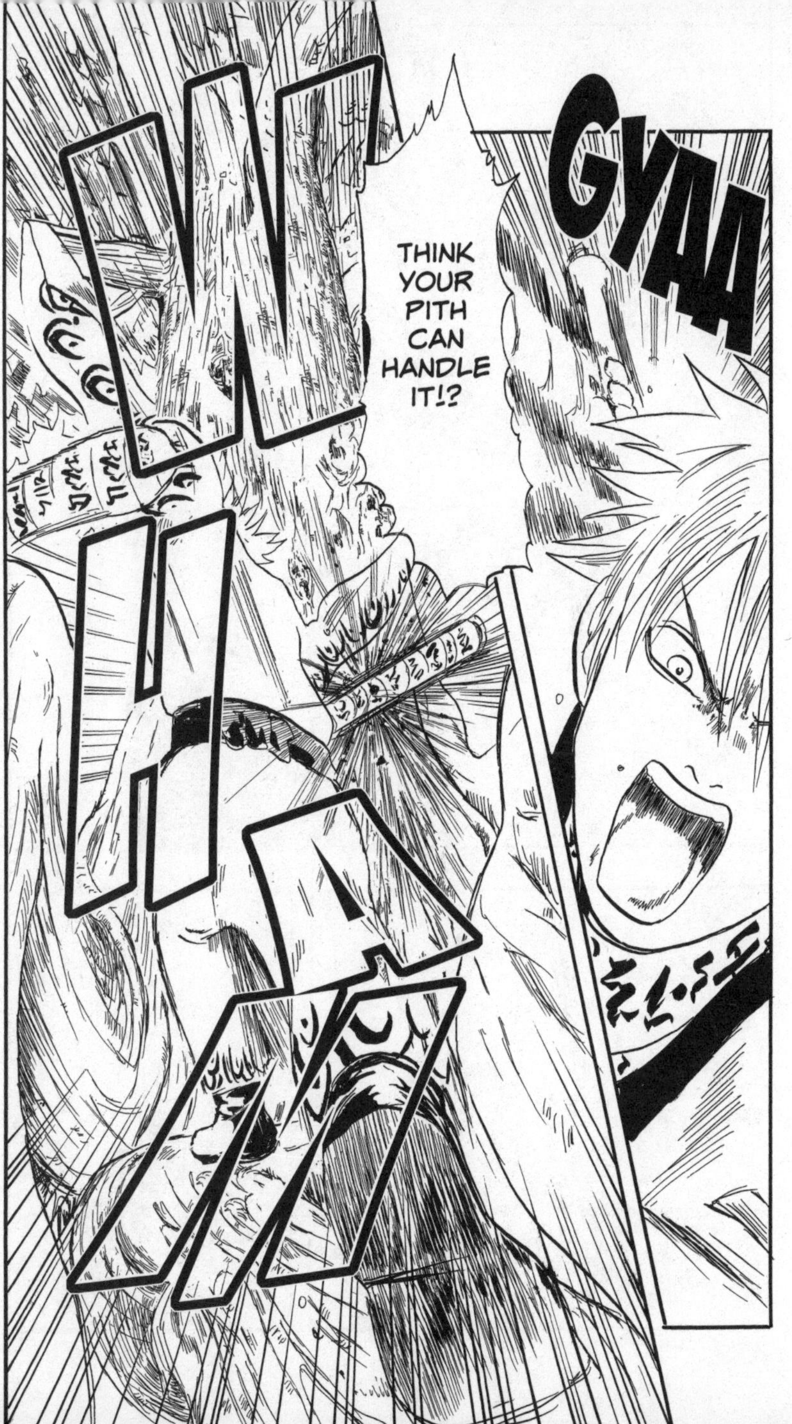
GYAA
THINK YOUR PITH CAN HANDLE IT!?
WHAM

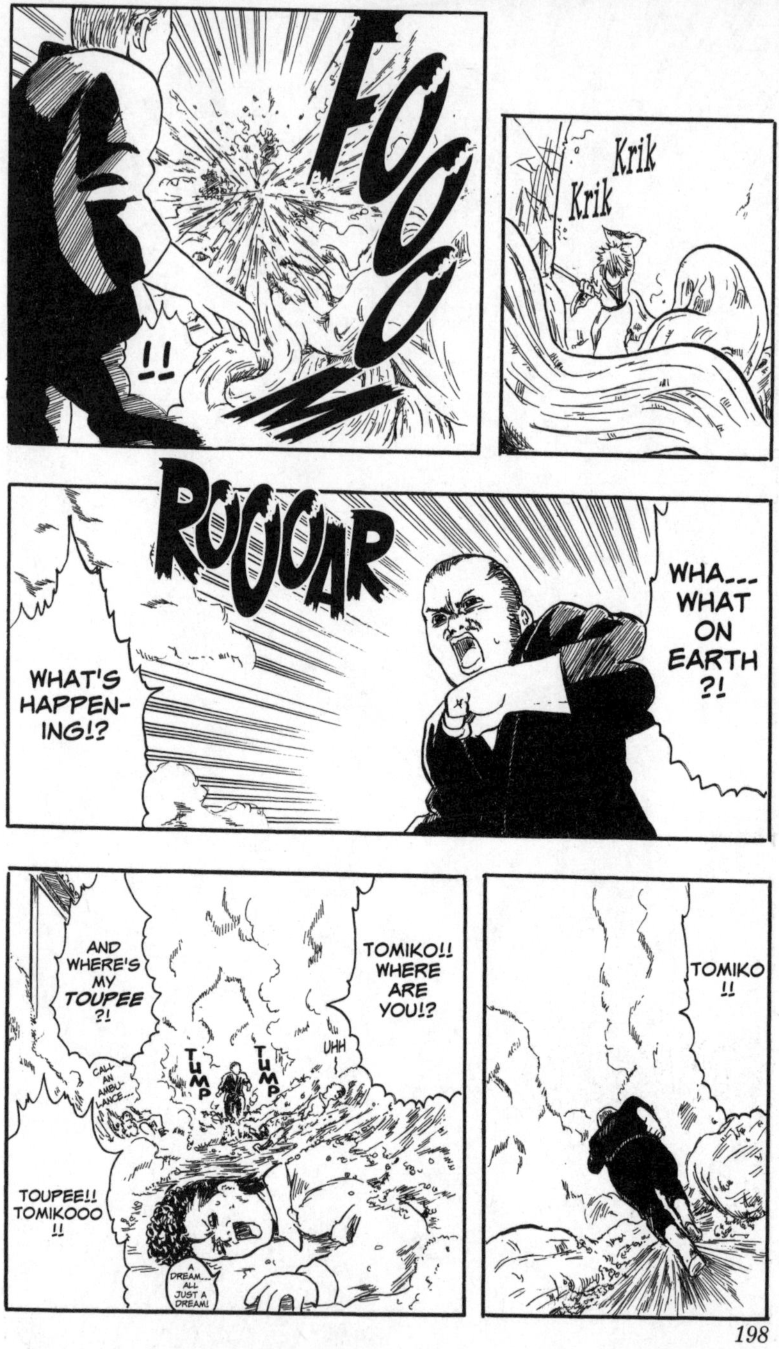
Krik
Krik
FOOOM
!!
ROOOAR
WHA... WHAT ON EARTH ?!
WHAT'S HAPPEN-ING!?
TOMIKO !!
TOMIKO!! WHERE ARE YOU!?
UHH
TUMP
TUMP
AND WHERE'S MY TOUPEE ?!
CALL AN AMBU-LANCE...
TOUPEE!! TOMIKOOO !!
A DREAM... ALL JUST A DREAM!

READ THIS WAY

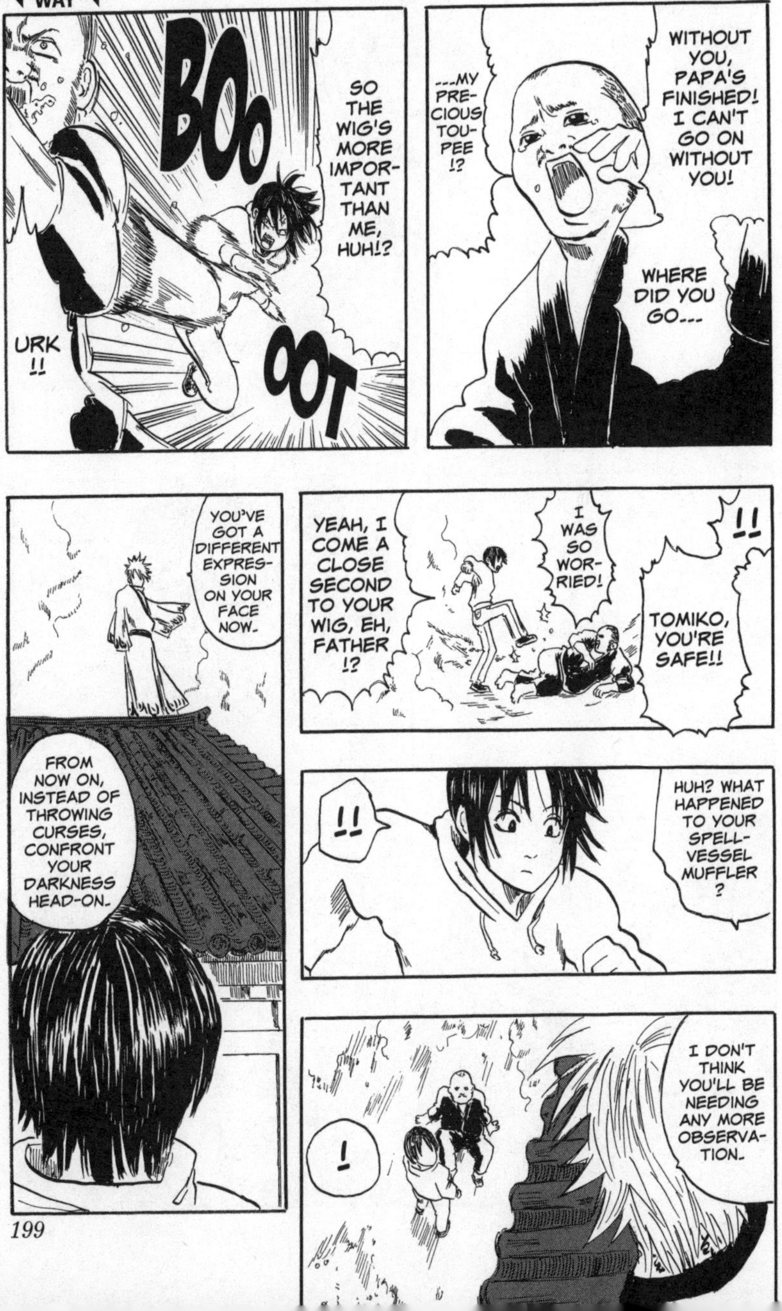
WITHOUT YOU, PAPA'S FINISHED! I CAN'T GO ON WITHOUT YOU!
---MY PRECIOUS TOUPEE !?
WHERE DID YOU GO...
SO THE WIG'S MORE IMPORTANT THAN ME, HUH!?
BOOOOT
URK !!
!!
TOMIKO, YOU'RE SAFE!!
I WAS SO WORRIED!
YEAH, I COME A CLOSE SECOND TO YOUR WIG, EH, FATHER !?
HUH? WHAT HAPPENED TO YOUR SPELL-VESSEL MUFFLER ?
!!
I DON'T THINK YOU'LL BE NEEDING ANY MORE OBSERVATION.
!
YOU'VE GOT A DIFFERENT EXPRESSION ON YOUR FACE NOW.
FROM NOW ON, INSTEAD OF THROWING CURSES, CONFRONT YOUR DARKNESS HEAD-ON.

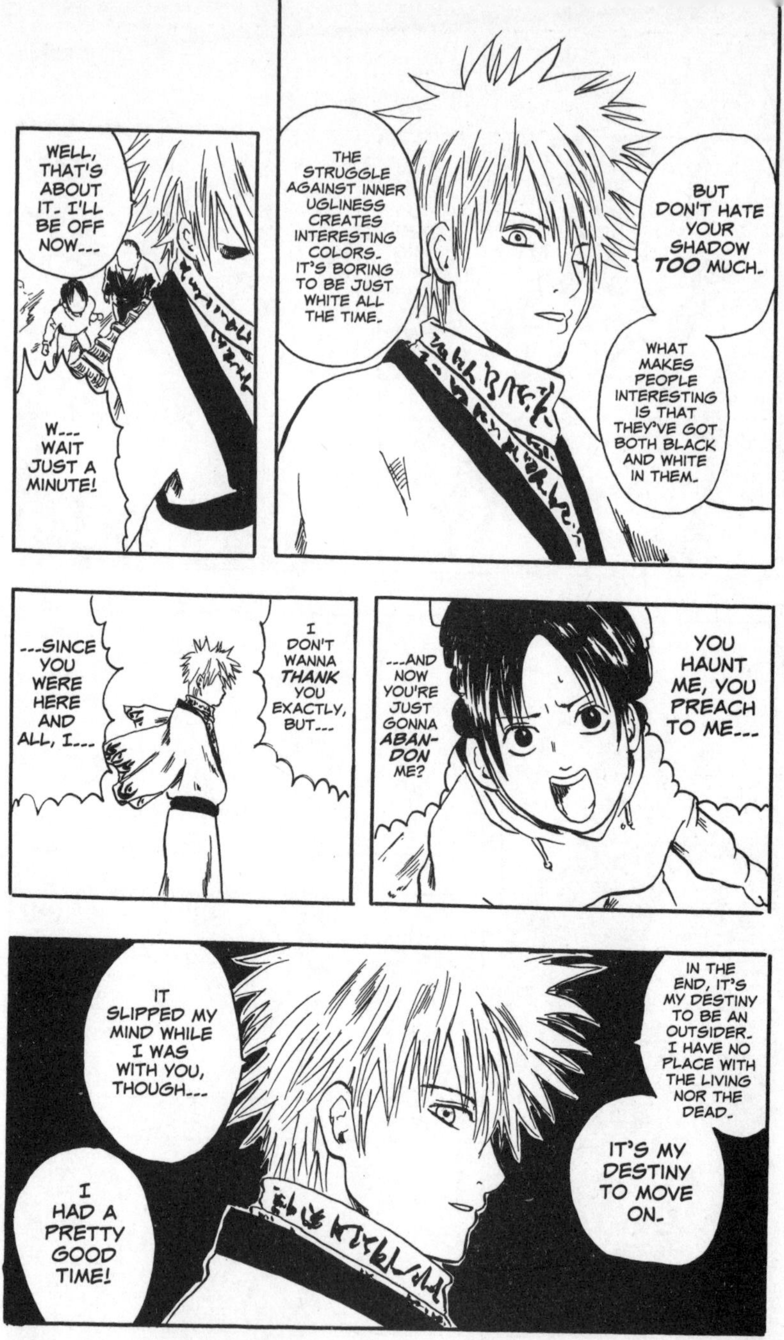
BUT DON'T HATE YOUR SHADOW TOO MUCH.
WHAT MAKES PEOPLE INTERESTING IS THAT THEY'VE GOT BOTH BLACK AND WHITE IN THEM.
THE STRUGGLE AGAINST INNER UGLINESS CREATES INTERESTING COLORS. IT'S BORING TO BE JUST WHITE ALL THE TIME.
WELL, THAT'S ABOUT IT. I'LL BE OFF NOW...
W... WAIT JUST A MINUTE!
YOU HAUNT ME, YOU PREACH TO ME...
...AND NOW YOU'RE JUST GONNA ABANDON ME?
I DON'T WANNA THANK YOU EXACTLY, BUT...
...SINCE YOU WERE HERE AND ALL, I...
IN THE END, IT'S MY DESTINY TO BE AN OUTSIDER. I HAVE NO PLACE WITH THE LIVING NOR THE DEAD.
IT'S MY DESTINY TO MOVE ON.
IT SLIPPED MY MIND WHILE I WAS WITH YOU, THOUGH...
I HAD A PRETTY GOOD TIME!

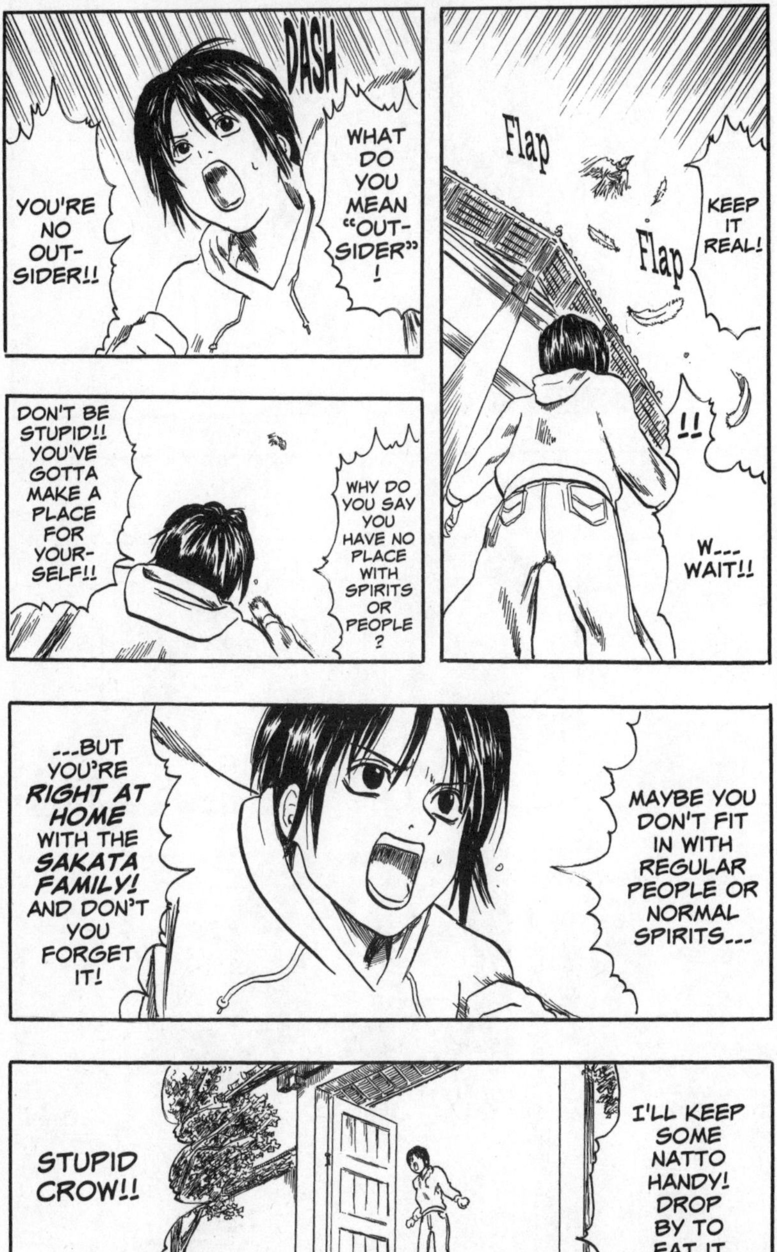
Flap
Flap
KEEP IT REAL!
!!
W... WAIT!!
DASH
WHAT DO YOU MEAN "OUTSIDER"!
YOU'RE NO OUTSIDER!!
WHY DO YOU SAY YOU HAVE NO PLACE WITH SPIRITS OR PEOPLE?
DON'T BE STUPID!! YOU'VE GOTTA MAKE A PLACE FOR YOURSELF!!
MAYBE YOU DON'T FIT IN WITH REGULAR PEOPLE OR NORMAL SPIRITS...
...BUT YOU'RE RIGHT AT HOME WITH THE SAKATA FAMILY! AND DON'T YOU FORGET IT!
I'LL KEEP SOME NATTO HANDY! DROP BY TO EAT IT ANYTIME!
STUPID CROW!!

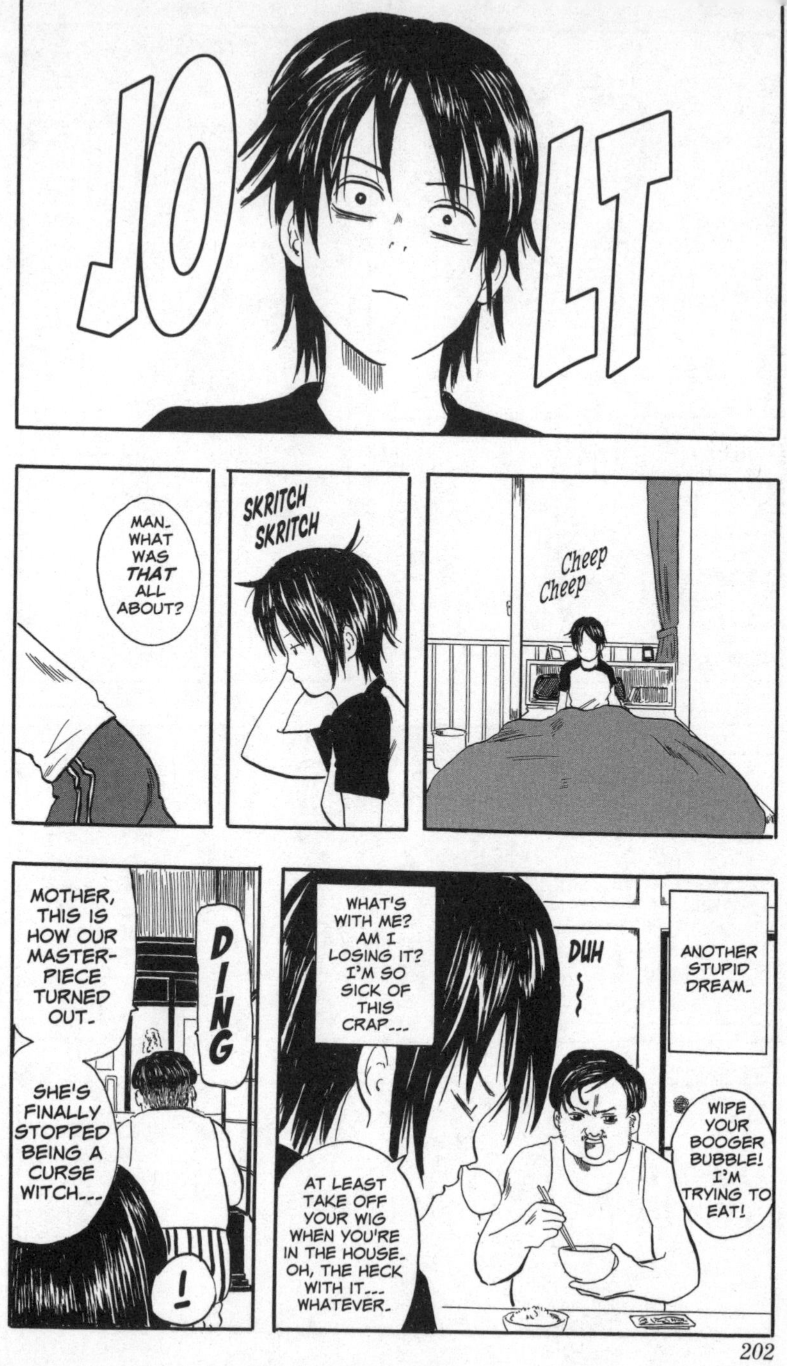
JOLT
Cheep Cheep
SKRITCH SKRITCH
MAN... WHAT WAS *THAT* ALL ABOUT?
ANOTHER STUPID DREAM...
WHAT'S WITH ME? AM I LOSING IT? I'M SO SICK OF THIS CRAP...
DUH
WIPE YOUR BOOGER BUBBLE! I'M TRYING TO EAT!
AT LEAST TAKE OFF YOUR WIG WHEN YOU'RE IN THE HOUSE. OH, THE HECK WITH IT... WHATEVER.
DING
MOTHER, THIS IS HOW OUR MASTER-PIECE TURNED OUT.
SHE'S FINALLY STOPPED BEING A CURSE WITCH...
!

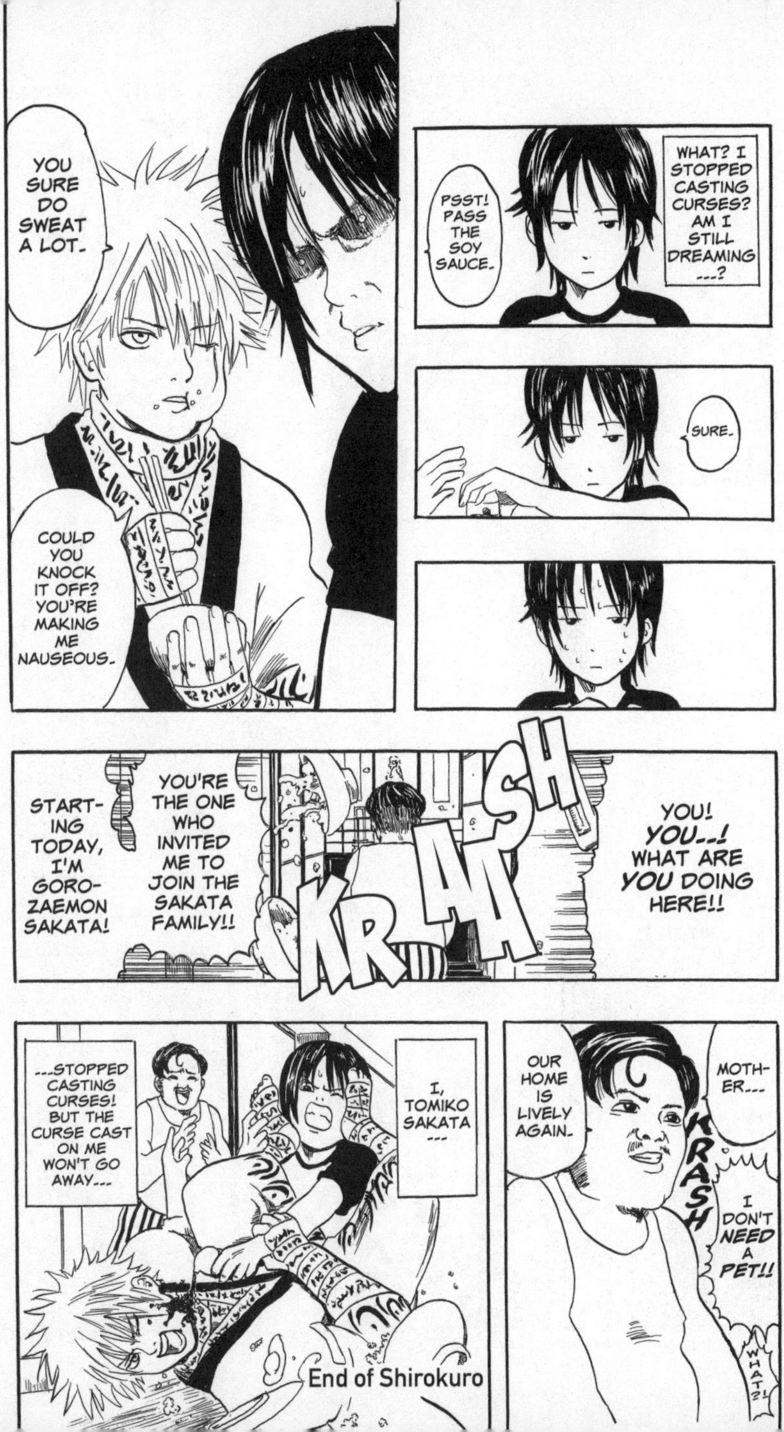
WHAT? I STOPPED CASTING CURSES? AM I STILL DREAMING...?
PSST! PASS THE SOY SAUCE.
SURE.
YOU SURE DO SWEAT A LOT.
COULD YOU KNOCK IT OFF? YOU'RE MAKING ME NAUSEOUS.
YOU! YOU...! WHAT ARE YOU DOING HERE!!
KRASH
YOU'RE THE ONE WHO INVITED ME TO JOIN THE SAKATA FAMILY!!
STARTING TODAY, I'M GOROZAEMON SAKATA!
MOTHER...
OUR HOME IS LIVELY AGAIN.
KRASH
I DON'T NEED A PET!!
WHAT?!
I, TOMIKO SAKATA...
...STOPPED CASTING CURSES! BUT THE CURSE CAST ON ME WON'T GO AWAY...
End of Shirokuro

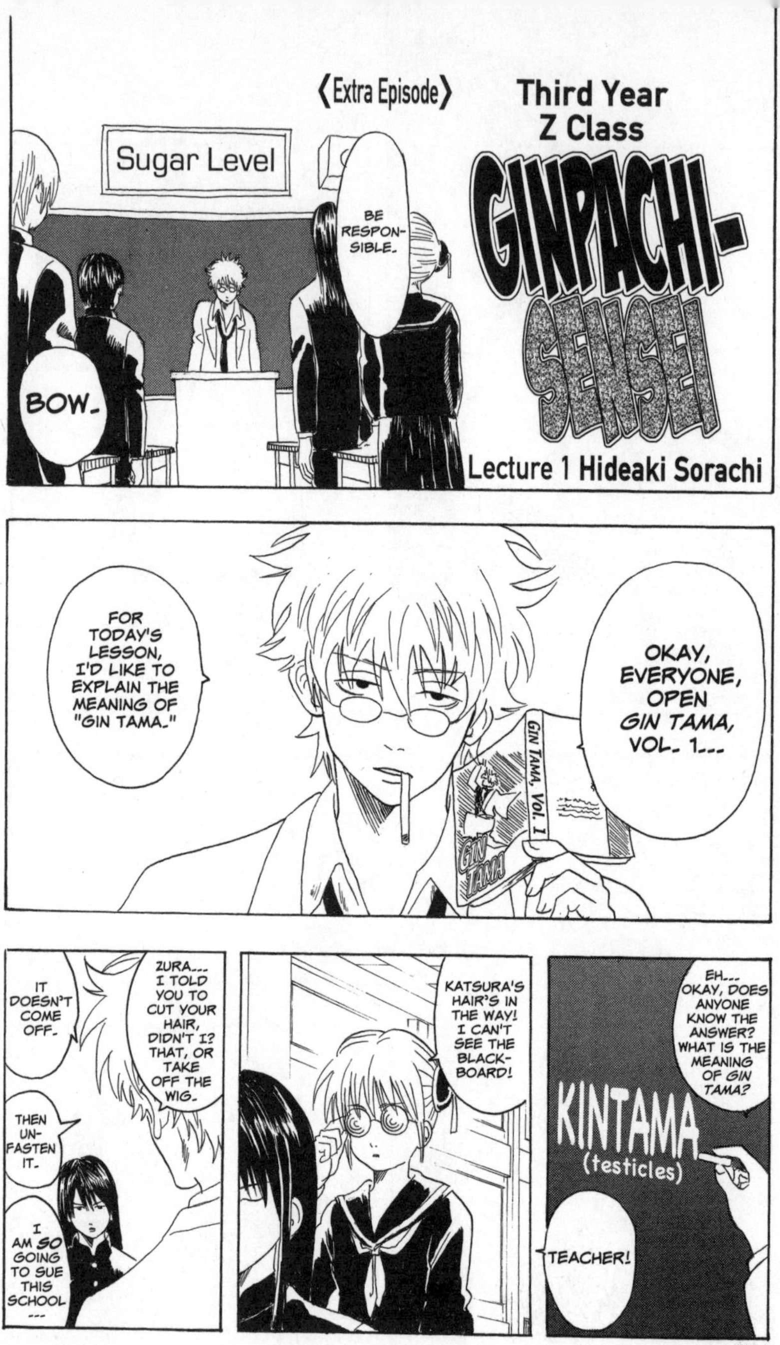

《Extra Episode》
Third Year Z Class
GINPACHI-SENSEI
Lecture 1 Hideaki Sorachi
Sugar Level
BE RESPONSIBLE.
BOW.
OKAY, EVERYONE, OPEN GIN TAMA, VOL. 1...
GIN TAMA, VOL. 1
FOR TODAY'S LESSON, I'D LIKE TO EXPLAIN THE MEANING OF "GIN TAMA."
EH... OKAY, DOES ANYONE KNOW THE ANSWER? WHAT IS THE MEANING OF GIN TAMA?
KINTAMA
(testicles)
TEACHER!
KATSURA'S HAIR'S IN THE WAY! I CAN'T SEE THE BLACKBOARD!
ZURA... I TOLD YOU TO CUT YOUR HAIR, DIDN'T I? THAT, OR TAKE OFF THE WIG.
IT DOESN'T COME OFF.
THEN UNFASTEN IT.
I AM SO GOING TO SUE THIS SCHOOL...

READ THIS WAY

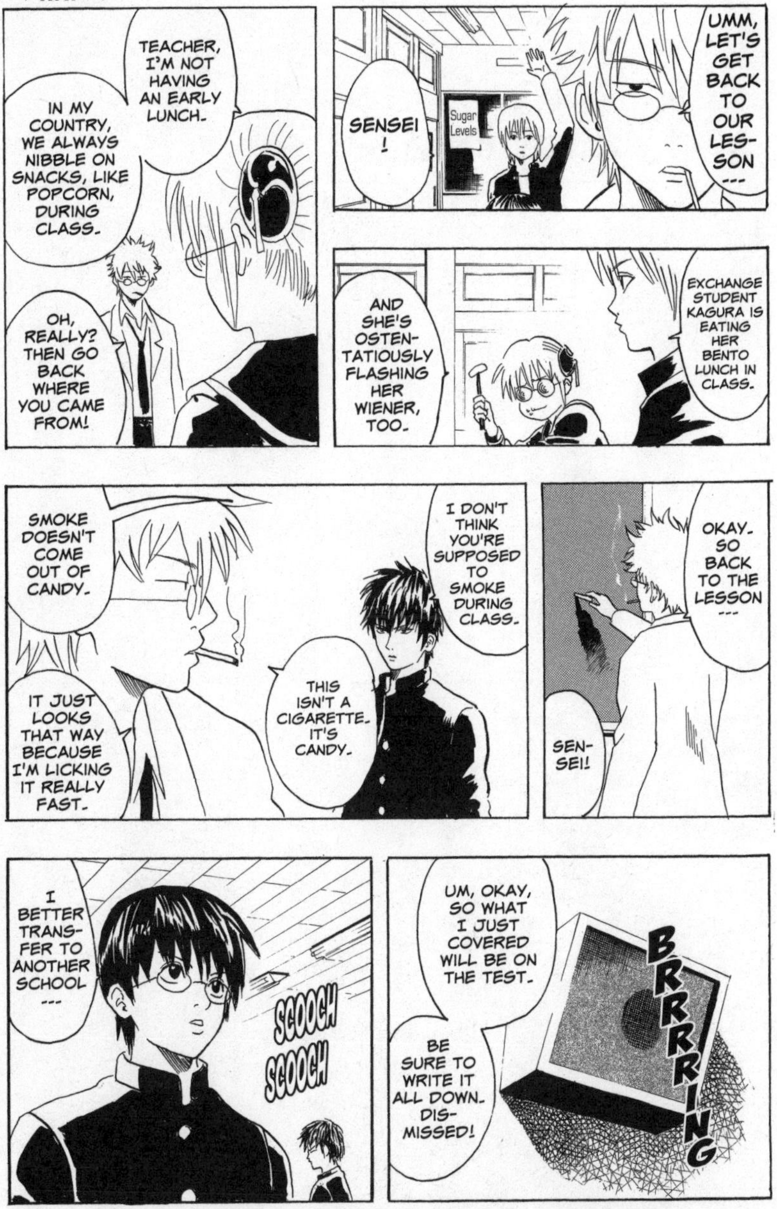
UMM, LET'S GET BACK TO OUR LES-SON ---
SENSEI!
Sugar Levels
EXCHANGE STUDENT KAGURA IS EATING HER BENTO LUNCH IN CLASS.
AND SHE'S OSTEN-TATIOUSLY FLASHING HER WIENER, TOO.
TEACHER, I'M NOT HAVING AN EARLY LUNCH.
IN MY COUNTRY, WE ALWAYS NIBBLE ON SNACKS, LIKE POPCORN, DURING CLASS.
OH, REALLY? THEN GO BACK WHERE YOU CAME FROM!
OKAY. SO BACK TO THE LESSON ---
SEN-SEI!
I DON'T THINK YOU'RE SUPPOSED TO SMOKE DURING CLASS.
THIS ISN'T A CIGARETTE. IT'S CANDY.
SMOKE DOESN'T COME OUT OF CANDY.
IT JUST LOOKS THAT WAY BECAUSE I'M LICKING IT REALLY FAST.
UM, OKAY, SO WHAT I JUST COVERED WILL BE ON THE TEST.
BE SURE TO WRITE IT ALL DOWN. DIS-MISSED!
BRRRRING
I BETTER TRANS-FER TO ANOTHER SCHOOL ---
SCOOCH SCOOCH

End of Third Year Z Class with Ginpachi Sensei

Next Volume Preview

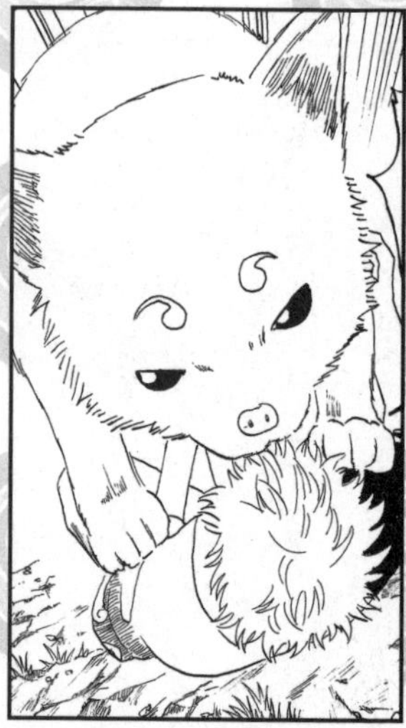

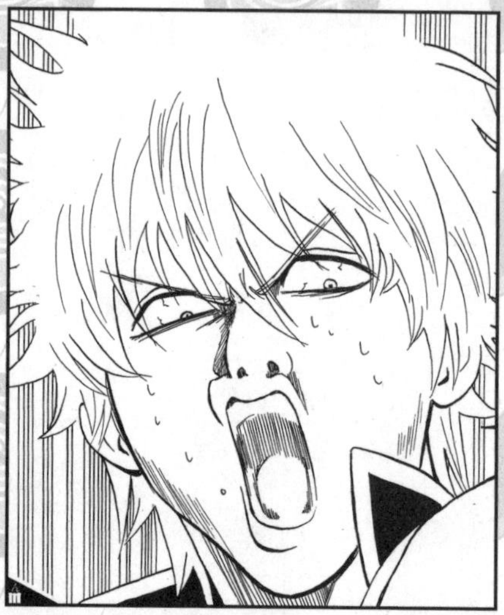

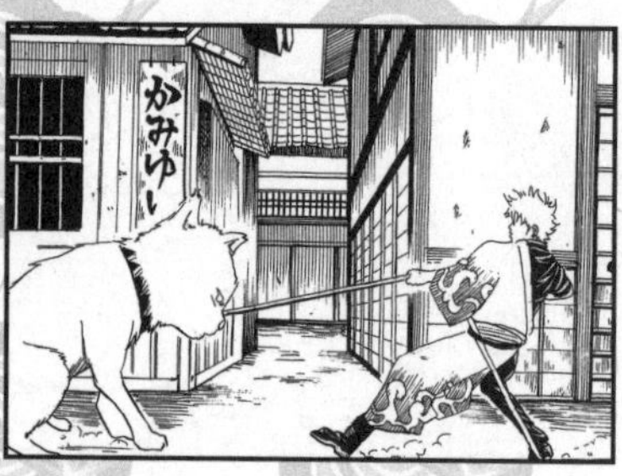
かみゆい

Gin's "to do" list for this volume:

1. Pick a fight with those Shinsengumi losers
2. Throw out my old SHONEN JUMP magazines
3. Save Shinpachi and Kagara AGAIN
4. Take Kagura's so-called dog for a walk
5. Protect the environment

AVAILABLE NOW

Claymore

Story and Art by
NORIHIRO YAGI

TO SAVE HUMANITY, MUST CLARE SACRIFICE HER OWN?

In a world where monsters called Yoma prey on humans
and live among them in disguise, humanity's only hope
is a new breed of warrior known as Claymores. Half
human, half monster, these silver-eyed slayers possess
supernatural strength, but are condemned to fight their
savage impulses or lose their humanity completely.

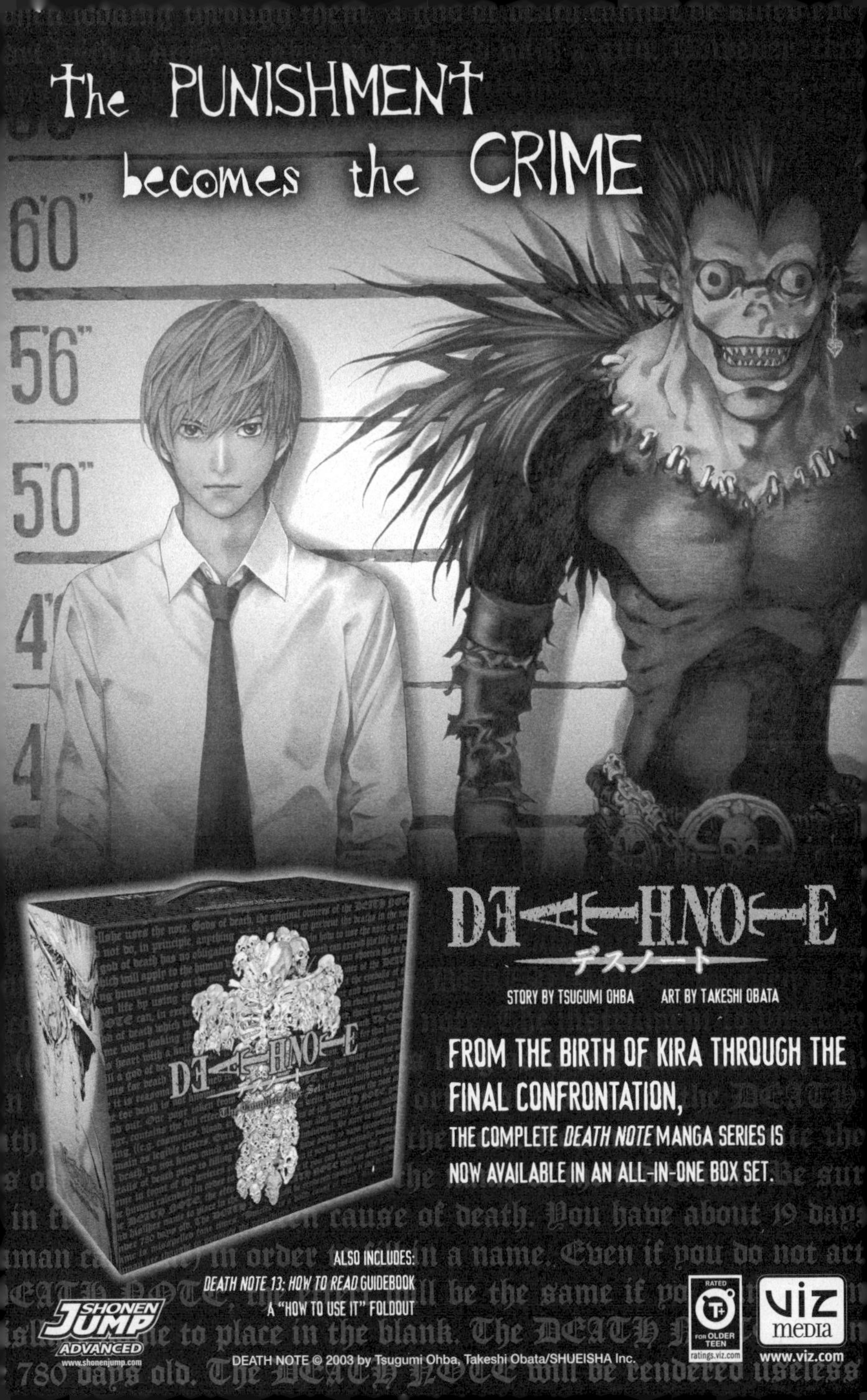
The PUNISHMENT becomes the CRIME
DEATH NOTE
デスノート
STORY BY TSUGUMI OHBA ART BY TAKESHI OBATA
FROM THE BIRTH OF KIRA THROUGH THE FINAL CONFRONTATION,
THE COMPLETE *DEATH NOTE* MANGA SERIES IS NOW AVAILABLE IN AN ALL-IN-ONE BOX SET.
ALSO INCLUDES:
DEATH NOTE 13: HOW TO READ GUIDEBOOK
A "HOW TO USE IT" FOLDOUT
SHONEN JUMP ADVANCED
www.shonenjump.com
DEATH NOTE © 2003 by Tsugumi Ohba, Takeshi Obata/SHUEISHA Inc.
RATED T+ FOR OLDER TEEN
ratings.viz.com
viz media
www.viz.com

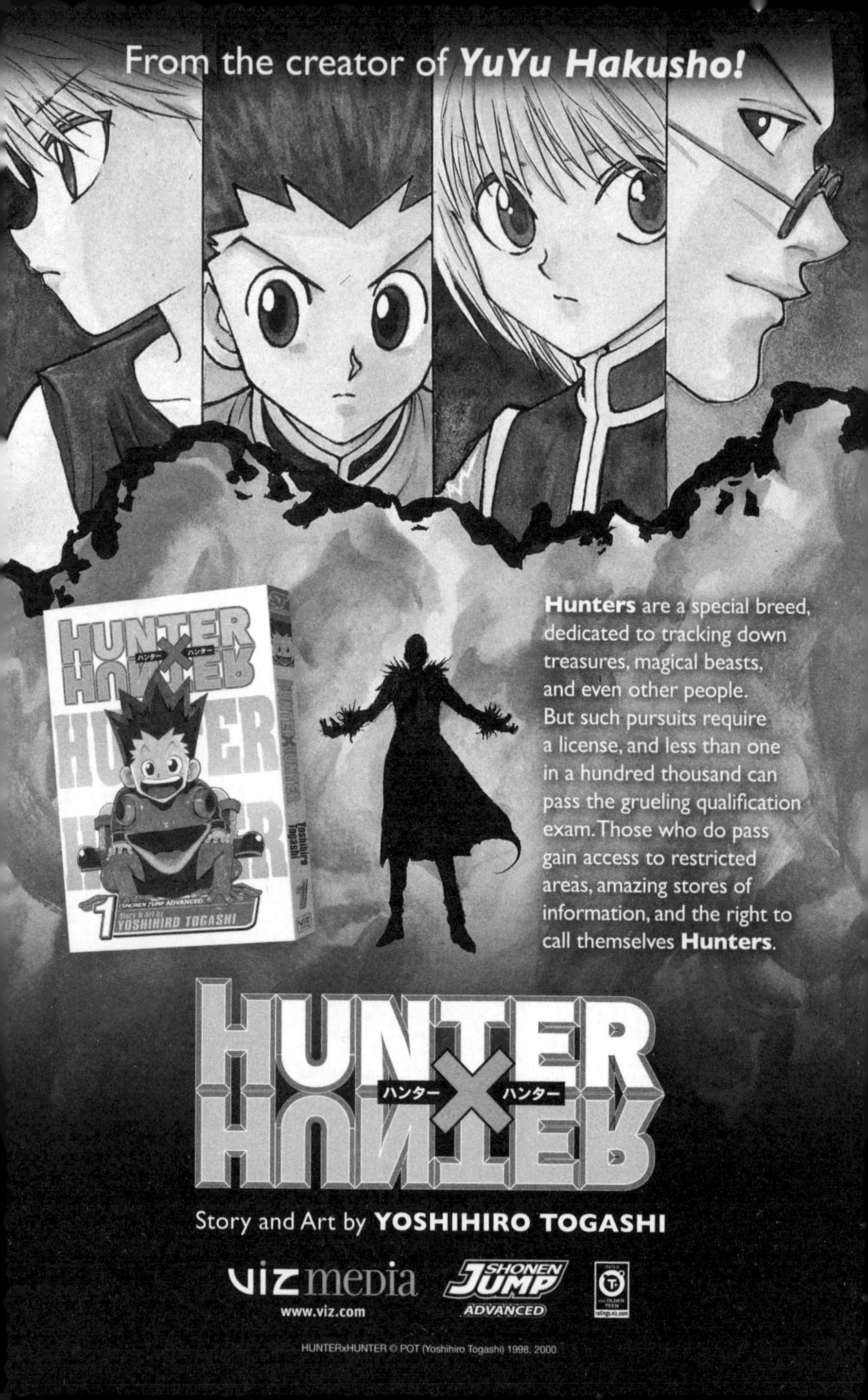
From the creator of *YuYu Hakusho!*
HUNTER × HUNTER
ハンター ハンター
1
SHONEN JUMP ADVANCED
Story & Art by
YOSHIHIRO TOGASHI
Hunters are a special breed, dedicated to tracking down treasures, magical beasts, and even other people. But such pursuits require a license, and less than one in a hundred thousand can pass the grueling qualification exam. Those who do pass gain access to restricted areas, amazing stores of information, and the right to call themselves **Hunters**.
HUNTER × HUNTER
ハンター ハンター
Story and Art by **YOSHIHIRO TOGASHI**
viz media
www.viz.com
SHONEN JUMP ADVANCED
RATED T+ OLDER TEEN ratings.viz.com
HUNTERxHUNTER © POT (Yoshihiro Togashi) 1998, 2000

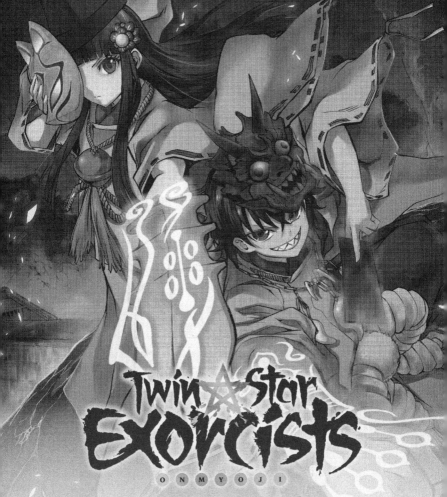